Technology and Mental Health

I0130915

Technology and Mental Health provides mental health clinicians with expert, practical, clinical advice on the questions and considerations associated with the adoption of mental health technology tools in the computer age.

Increasingly, clinicians want to use technology to provide clients with support through smartphones and mobile applications or to reach clients in remote or rural areas. However, using these tools in practice raises many practical and ethical questions. The book explains current technological developments in therapy, including mobile apps, telemental health, and virtual reality programs. Each chapter gives real-world guidance on adopting and using technology interventions, and the book spans a wide range of client populations. Providers are introduced to the evidence supporting various technology-based interventions and areas for future development. Combining theory, research, and case studies, this practical guide teaches clinicians how to integrate technology into therapeutic interventions with clients.

Greg M. Reger, PhD, is a clinical psychologist and associate professor in the Department of Psychiatry and Behavioral Sciences at the University of Washington School of Medicine, Seattle, WA, USA.

Clinical Topics in Psychology and Psychiatry

Series Editor: Bret A. Moore, PsyD

Boulder Crest Retreat, Virginia, USA

Much of the available information relevant to mental health clinicians is buried in large and disjointed academic textbooks and expensive and obscure scientific journals. Consequently, it can be challenging for the clinician and student to access the most useful information related to practice. **Clinical Topics in Psychology and Psychiatry** includes authored and edited books that identify and distill the most relevant information for practitioners and presents the material in an easily accessible format that appeals to the psychology and psychiatry student, intern or resident, early career psychologist or psychiatrist, and the busy clinician.

For more information about this series, please visit: www.routledge.com/ Clinical-Topics-in-Psychology-and-Psychiatry/book-series/TFSE00310

Technology and Mental Health

A Clinician's Guide to Improving Outcomes

Edited by Greg M. Reger

R Routledge
Taylor & Francis Group

NEW YORK AND LONDON

First published 2021
by Routledge
52 Vanderbilt Avenue, New York, NY 10017

and by Routledge
2 Park Square, Milton Park, Abingdon, Oxon, OX14 4RN

Routledge is an imprint of the Taylor & Francis Group, an informa business

Library of Congress Cataloging-in-Publication Data
A catalog record for this book has been requested

ISBN: 978-1-138-35392-3 (hbk)
ISBN: 978-1-138-35394-7 (pbk)
ISBN: 978-0-429-02053-7 (ebk)

Typeset in Bembo
by Apex CoVantage, LLC

This book is dedicated to our many courageous clients and patients who have helped us learn how to best use technology in mental health practice. Personally, I also dedicate this work to my lovely wife, Darlene, and my two great kids, Katie and Will, who encourage all my projects and sacrifice family time so that I might pursue them.

Contents

Figures

Tables

Contributors

Christina Armstrong Connected Health Branch, Defense Health Agency, Tacoma, WA, United States.

Sean M. Barnes Rocky Mountain Mental Illness, Research, Education and Clinical Center (MIRECC) for Suicide Prevention, Rocky Mountain Regional VAMC, Aurora, CO, United States; Department of Psychiatry, University of Colorado Anschutz School of Medicine, Aurora, CO, United States.

Jeffrey E. Barnett Department of Psychology, Loyola University Maryland, Baltimore, Maryland, United States.

Kelly Blasko Connected Health Branch, Defense Health Agency, Tacoma, WA, United States.

Robert Boland is Associate Professor of Psychiatry, Department of Psychiatry at Brigham and Women's Hospital, Boston, Massachusetts, United States.

Lisa A. Brenner Departments of Psychiatry, Physical Medicine & Rehabilitation and Neurology, Rocky Mountain Mental Illness, Research, Education and Clinical Center (MIRECC) for Suicide Prevention, Rocky Mountain Regional VAMC, Aurora, CO, United States; Departments of Psychiatry, Physical Medicine & Rehabilitation and Neurology, University of Colorado Anschutz School of Medicine, Aurora, CO, United States.

Millard D. Brown Tripler Army Medical Center, Honolulu, Hawaii, United States.

Mark S. Burton is Assistant Professor, Emory University School of Medicine, Atlanta, GA, United States.

Jamie T. Carreno-Davidson U.S. Army Research Institute of Environmental Medicine, Natick, MA, United States.

Renée Cavanagh Connected Health Branch, Defense Health Agency, Tacoma, WA, United States.

Kelly R. Chrestman Center for Deployment Psychology, Uniformed Services University of the Health Sciences, Bethesda, MD, United States.

Robert Ciulla Connected Health Branch, Defense Health Agency, Tacoma, WA, United States.

Patrick L. Dulin Department of Psychology, University of Alaska Anchorage, Anchorage, AK, United States.

Jenna Ermold Center for Deployment Psychology, Uniformed Services University of the Health Sciences, Bethesda, MD, United States.

Ellen E. Fitzsimmons-Craft Department of Psychiatry, Washington University School of Medicine, St. Louis, MO, United States.

Laurel A. Gaeddert Rocky Mountain Mental Illness, Research, Education and Clinical Center (MIRECC) for Suicide Prevention, Rocky Mountain Regional VAMC, Aurora, CO, United States.

Jessica R. Goodnight Postdoctoral Fellow, Anxiety and Trauma Clinic of Atlanta, Atlanta, GA, United States.

Noah Hammer Entrepreneur, Founder of Stoak.

Ellen Herbst Department of Psychiatry and Behavioral Sciences, University of California, San Francisco (UCSF), San Francisco, CA, United States; Mental Health Service, San Francisco Veterans Affairs (VA) Health Care System (SFVAHCS), San Francisco, CA, United States.

Ryan Holliday Rocky Mountain Mental Illness, Research, Education and Clinical Center (MIRECC) for Suicide Prevention, Rocky Mountain Regional VAMC, Aurora, CO, United States; Department of Psychiatry, University of Colorado Anschutz School of Medicine, Aurora, CO, United States.

Kevin M. Holloway Center for Deployment Psychology, Uniformed Services University of the Health Sciences, Bethesda, MD, United States.

Tim Hoyt Connected Health Branch, Defense Health Agency, Tacoma, WA, United States.

Michael Hsu Psychiatry Resident, Department of Psychiatry at Brigham and Women's Hospital, Boston, Massachusetts, United States.

Christine L. Jackson Rocky Mountain Mental Illness, Research, Education and Clinical Center (MIRECC) for Suicide Prevention, Rocky Mountain Regional VAMC, Aurora, CO, United States.

Diane K. King Center for Behavioral Health Research and Services, Institute of Social and Economic Research, University of Alaska Anchorage, Anchorage, AK, United States.

Julie Kinn Connected Health Branch, Defense Health Agency, Tacoma, WA, United States.

Eric Kuhn National Center for PTSD, Dissemination & Training Division, Department of Veterans Affairs Palo Alto Healthcare System, Palo Alto, CA, United States; Department of Psychiatry and Behavioral Sciences, Stanford University School of Medicine, Stanford, CA, United States.

Jessica Lipschitz Instructor in Psychiatry, Department of Psychiatry at Brigham and Women's Hospital, Boston, Massachusetts, United States.

Anayansi Lombardero Department of Psychology, University of Alaska Anchorage, Anchorage, AK, United States.

David D. Luxton Department of Psychiatry and Behavioral Sciences at the University of Washington School of Medicine, Seattle, WA, United States.

Pearl McGee-Vincent National Center for PTSD, Dissemination & Training Division, Department of Veterans Affairs Palo Alto Healthcare System, Palo Alto, CA, United States.

Robyn Mertz Department of Psychology, University of Alaska Anchorage, Anchorage, AK, United States.

Logan Micheel Connected Health Branch, Defense Health Agency, Tacoma, WA, United States.

Matt Mishkind Johnson Depression Center, University of Colorado School of Medicine, Anschutz Medical Campus, Aurora, CO, United States.

Sarra Nazem Rocky Mountain Mental Illness, Research, Education and Clinical Center (MIRECC) for Suicide Prevention, Rocky Mountain Regional VAMC, Aurora, CO, United States; Departments of Psychiatry and Physical Medicine and Rehabilitation, University of Colorado Anschutz School of Medicine, Aurora, CO, United States.

James Phillips Geriatric Research, Education, and Clinical Center (GRECC) and Mental Illness Research, Education, and Clinical Center, VA Puget Sound Health Care System, Seattle, WA, United States; Department of Psychiatry and Behavioral Sciences, University of Washington, Seattle, WA, United States.

Greg M. Reger Department of Psychiatry and Behavioral Sciences, University of Washington School of Medicine, Seattle, WA, United States; VA Puget Sound Healthcare System, Tacoma/Seattle, WA, United States; Washington State Army National Guard, Camp Murray, WA, United States.

Elsa Rojas-Ashe Department of Psychiatry and Behavioral Sciences, Stanford University School of Medicine, Stanford, CA, United States.

Barbara O. Rothbaum Professor, Emory University School of Medicine, Atlanta, GA, United States.

Shiri Sadeh-Sharvit Department of Psychiatry and Behavioral Sciences, Stanford University School of Medicine, Stanford, CA, United States, Center for m2Health, Palo Alto University, Palo Alto, CA, United States, Baruch Ivcher School of Psychology, Interdisciplinary Center, Herzliya, Israel.

Sarah Schwenk Johnson Depression Center, University of Colorado School of Medicine, Anschutz Medical Campus, Aurora, CO, United States.

Andrew M. Sherrill Assistant Professor, Emory University School of Medicine, Atlanta, GA, United States.

Brittany Shoemaker In private practice with Realize Wellness, LLC. She was employed by the Steven A. Cohen Military Family Clinic at the University of Colorado Anschutz Medical Campus when the chapter was written.

Andrew Shutes-David Geriatric Research, Education, and Clinical Center (GRECC) and Mental Illness Research, Education, and Clinical Center, VA Puget Sound Health Care System, Seattle, WA, United States; Department of Psychiatry and Behavioral Sciences, University of Washington, Seattle, WA, United States.

C. Barr Taylor Department of Psychiatry and Behavioral Sciences, Stanford University School of Medicine, Stanford, CA, United States, Center for m2Health, Palo Alto University, Palo Alto, CA, United States.

Naira Topocco Internet, Health and Clinical Psychology Research Group, Department of Behavioral Sciences and Learning, Linkoping University, Sweden.

John Torous Director of Digital Psychiatry Division, Department of Psychiatry at Beth Israel Deaconess Medical Center, Boston, Massachusetts, United States.

Janice Tsoh Department of Psychiatry and Behavioral Sciences, University of California, San Francisco (UCSF), San Francisco, CA, United States.

Debby W. Tsuang Geriatric Research, Education, and Clinical Center (GRECC) and Mental Illness Research, Education, and Clinical Center, VA Puget Sound Health Care System, Seattle, WA, United States; Department of Psychiatry and Behavioral Sciences, University of Washington, Seattle, WA, United States.

Denise E. Wilfley Department of Psychiatry, Washington University School of Medicine, St. Louis, MO, United States.

Series Editor's Foreword

Technology and Mental Health: A Clinician's Guide to Improving Outcomes is the latest volume in one of Routledge's most popular series, Clinical Topics in Psychology and Psychiatry (CTPP). The overarching goal of CTPP is to provide mental health practitioners with practical information on psychological and psychopharmacological topics. Each volume is comprehensive but easy to digest and integrate into day-to-day clinical practice. It is multidisciplinary, covering topics relevant to the fields of psychology and psychiatry, and it appeals to the student, novice, and senior clinician. Books chosen for the series are authored or edited by national and international experts in their respective areas, and contributors are also highly respected clinicians. The current volume exemplifies the intent, scope, and aims of the CTPP series.

Technological advances in the delivery of mental health services have grown considerably over the past decade. This should not be surprising, considering the relatively recent proliferation of smartphones, innovations in computer hardware and software, and technological advancements in the broader health care system. In fact, even before clinicians and behavioral health organizations began to intentionally incorporate technology into their practice, consumers were connecting through a variety of mobile applications and computer learning platforms for the purpose of reducing distress and increasing overall psychological well-being. In this instance, the field decided to "catch-up" with the consumer.

In concert with advances in technological applications within the areas of mental health and wellness, the ever-growing focus on patient-centered care has resulted in more informed, engaged, and directive consumers of mental health services. Indeed, the days of the passive patient taking directives from the health care provider are gone. Many consumers of health care services in general, and mental health services specifically, play an integral part in the selection of interventions and clinical outcomes. As a means to support this engagement, mental health providers should develop an awareness of the myriad technological tools—self-directed or collaboratively used in session—that can enhance their practice. The current volume provides the mental health provider practical and clinically driven knowledge on the adoption and implementation of cutting-edge applications, techniques, systems, and programs focused on integrating technology into a comprehensive plan of care.

In *Technology and Mental Health: A Clinician's Guide to Improving Outcomes*, Dr. Greg M. Reger provides a superb review of the most important aspects of technology and mental health care. He brings together some of the country's top experts in psychology and psychiatry, technology, and translational science. The volume includes a discussion of the potential advantages of each technology as well as its limitations. Chapter authors provide practical advice regarding technical intervention adoption and utilization as well as ethical issues related to the use of technology in clinical practice. Future innovations not yet fully developed or implemented are also covered.

I am convinced that *Technology and Mental Health: A Clinician's Guide to Improving Outcomes* will become one of the lead textbooks in training future clinicians in the effective integration of technology within their practice. It will also function as an excellent review for academicians and researchers on this important and fast-growing area of clinical investigation.

Bret A. Moore, PsyD, ABPP
Series Editor
Clinical Topics in Psychology and Psychiatry

1 Enabling Behavioral Health Measurement-Based Care With Technology

Millard D. Brown and Jamie T. Carreno-Davidson

The behavioral health (BH) field has long been challenged by changing definitions of mental disorders, imprecise descriptions of mental phenomena, a wide variety of treatment modalities, and a broad range of training levels of BH providers. These challenges have made it difficult to consider measuring outcomes in BH treatment efforts in community settings. However, an ever-deepening body of literature has demonstrated the value of many therapeutic modalities while also finding ubiquitous common therapy factors that correlate highly with positive outcomes (Lambert & Barley, 2001). The accelerating pace and rapidly falling costs of technology now bring an unprecedented opportunity to rapidly improve the quality of BH care delivery in all communities and potentially open up new funding opportunities for BH programs by utilizing technology to implement measurement-based care (MBC) practices.

The impact of MBC on improving treatment effectiveness and efficiency is growing. Research teams led by Drs. Trivedi, Miller, and Lambert have shown how MBC practices can markedly increase the probability of response to treatment efforts (see discussion later in the chapter). One of the best-designed studies to look at MBC using medication in a depressed sample showed marked improvements in response and remission rates (Guo et al., 2015). Brickman et al. have shown that structured outcome feedback to clinicians also improves outcomes in youth (2011). However, not all research in this area has shown improvement, and more work is needed to determine key MBC implementation elements to ensure improved outcomes (Hansson, Rundberg, Österling, Öjehagen, & Berglund, 2013; Knaup, Koesters, Schoefer, Becker, & Puschner, 2009).

U.S. Army experience with a large MBC practice implementation—The U.S. Army medical leadership began planning to rebuild its BH system in 2008, as the traditional system was straining under the weight of five years of war. Over the next five years, a BH Service Line was created standardizing funding, structure, and implementation of 12 core program efforts across 50+ Army hospitals and clinics. One of the key initiatives involved building an MBC process that would support real-time care delivery and feed aggregated data to leadership to inform program effectiveness. The MBC system we built is called the Behavioral Health Data Portal (BHDP). With the support of senior Army medical leadership, the Army behavioral health team built the BHDP based on lessons learned from prior prototypes and started program implementation in 2012. Within six months, 30+ bases started using the BHDP. Within 12 months, all 50+ hospitals and clinics had started using BHDP in their BH clinics with over 30,000 questionnaires completed monthly. By 2014, we had collected questionnaires of standard clinical data and clinical measures from over 600,000 appointments. As of late 2019, we have over 5.6 million questionnaires in the BHDP, and the system is now used in BH clinics across the Army, Navy, and Air Force.

Army BH leadership uses aggregated BHDP data to monitor outcome tracking across all 50+ BH clinics for key illnesses like depressive-, anxiety-, and trauma-related disorders. The Army BH Service Line can now review what treatment actions and courses of care are most beneficial to our patients, thus further informing the ongoing development of our system of care. This capability is a key component to building a robust data-informed learning organization spanning local clinics and hospitals and up to senior Army medicine leadership. We will be detailing many lessons learned from our efforts in building and fielding an MBC program across the Army in the rest of this chapter as a means of encouraging other health systems to implement MBC practices.

We will first explore the evidence for MBC in BH care delivery. We will then discuss how technology use is critical to maximizing the full potential of MBC efforts. Using our lessons learned from real-world MBC implementation efforts over the past ten years, we will detail core implementation principles that are necessary to consider for successful MBC implementation efforts. Finally, we will explore common concerns about MBC, highlight emerging technologies, and finish with a review of how MBC can be the key link to accessing larger funding streams needed to transform how BH care is delivered.

Throughout this chapter, we will use the term MBC utilized by Dr. Scott and colleagues to refer to a procedure that can be broadly defined as the use of systematic data collection to monitor client progress and directly inform care decisions (Scott & Lewis, 2015). The data collected during the initial interview is used as an aid in developing a more complete diagnostic picture that includes supporting initial diagnostic specificity and establishing a clinical severity baseline. Additional measurements are utilized on a regular basis throughout an episode of care to monitor real-time progress toward treatment goals, to inform whether treatment efforts need to be adjusted, and to determine when treatment is successful.

Why Should We Use MBC?

Diagnostic support and increased accuracy—A fully implemented MBC system has the ability to markedly improve the consistency and quality of diagnoses within a clinical setting. Historically, diagnostic inter-rater agreement between clinicians has been as low as 45% when standardized tools have not been used (Basco et al., 2000). This lack of diagnostic precision may lead to increased diagnostic errors of commission and omission that will subsequently impact the efficacy of any treatment efforts and threaten the crucial establishment of a strong therapeutic alliance. Unrecognized comorbid disorders can easily derail the best treatment efforts. When providers attempt to collect interview data, they are often unaware of how the phrasing, cadence, and tone utilized can affect the patient's responses and thus potentially affect the accuracy and completeness of their data collection. Further, provider nonverbal behaviors can also impact their interview data collection. Despite a provider's best effort, a patient's fear of shame can also cause relevant sensitive data to not be shared in interviews. This is likely why some research has shown more accurate data collection from computer questioning rather than from providers (Carr, Ghosh, & Ancill, 1983). The implementation of standardized questions and data collection can improve inter-rater agreement rates toward 75–80% (Miller, 2001).

Tracking treatment progress—Over the last 20 years, several research groups have shown that tracking clinical outcomes with clinical scales on a frequent basis can significantly improve the probability of treatment response. For example, Dr. Lambert's group tested how OQ-45 utilization impacted clinical outcomes. Over several studies, his team varied whether OQ-45 results were shown in real-time to no one, only the therapist, or to the therapist and the patient. Their results show that sharing weekly OQ-45 results to the therapist improves outcomes over usual care, but showing data to the therapist and the patient improves outcomes nearly 300% more often than usual care (Shimokawa, Lambert, & Smart, 2010). Dr. Miller created the Outcome Rating Scale (ORS) to improve the feasibility of outcome tracking within outpatient clinics. His team showed similar results with the three-question ORS as found in Dr. Lambert's previous work (Miller, Duncan, Brown, Sparks, & Claud, 2003). In the Army, system-wide outcome results for depression and PTSD improved by over 25% during the first several years of implementation of BHDP even though most of the leadership's efforts were focused on MBC implementation and other system structural changes and little attention was paid to altering the provider–patient interaction. These combined findings suggest that a key ingredient may be simply implementing an MBC process that tracks progress throughout a course of treatment with real-time data available to providers and patients that informs treatment decisions.

Patient-centered goal setting—Regardless of therapy modality chosen for treatment, several common therapeutic factors have been shown to correlate with positive outcomes. A sampling of these factors include the following: a patient and a provider sharing an understanding of the patient's problem; a shared understanding of the therapeutic procedures to be utilized; a strong therapeutic alliance; and a sense of hopefulness about the future (Imel &

Wampold, 2008). MBC can facilitate the establishment of shared goals, improve objectivity in tracking progress toward those goals, and determining when goals have been achieved. A patient may be more likely to engage with goal setting when it is based on symptoms and functional status data he or she has provided. MBC can also help track whether a patient is on track for a positive recovery, thus allowing for a quicker modification of treatment efforts when a patient is shown to likely not be on a recovery track. Henkel and colleagues (2009) demonstrated that early treatment response of at least 20% to an antidepressant predicts improved response and remission at later time points. More recent findings show that lack of response to medication after two weeks predicts a 93% chance of no remission at 12 weeks, suggesting that early treatment change is important (Hicks et al., 2019). Without MBC, the ability to determine initial response is very difficult. Thus, routine MBC is needed to consistently detect change (or the lack thereof) in real-world clinical settings to allow full use of research findings like those described earlier. Finally, many patients continue with care longer than is necessary, thus increasing the costs of care and limiting access to care for those not able to find available treatment. MBC data can help providers determine when the patient has improved enough to consider initiating the termination process.

Improve patient engagement and psychological mindedness—Reviewing measures during each treatment session provides nuanced benefits to the patient. In-session review of completed measures shows respect for the time and effort patients have spent completing such instruments and allows patients to highlight current concerns. It also serves to reinforce the importance and utility of this task. Routinely reviewing items from clinical measures with patients teaches them psychological mindedness about their current struggles and can help organize patient experiences into coherent and understandable phenomena. Using the metrics to support a change or sustainment of the current treatment plan provides transparency in joint decision making. The MBC in-session review process further strengthens collaboration and therapeutic alliance between the provider and the patient.

MBC allows for actionable feedback in support of building learning organizations— Over the past 20 years, efforts to improve health care delivery quality have led to many health system efforts to develop learning organizations and highly reliable processes (Pronovost et al., 2006; Senge, 1990; Till, Amin, & McKimm., 2016). Real-time clinical data can be de-identified and aggregated at higher levels to inform the ongoing performance of a clinic, identify areas of program strength and weakness, and serve to identify areas of potential gaps in care. Learning organizations and high reliability efforts require ongoing systemic outcome data feeds in order to be successful. Meaningful feedback is the lifeblood of a well-functioning learning organization. Only with this data can we move beyond process outcomes and secondary indicators of treatment effectiveness and move toward truly useful quality improvement efforts by looking at actual clinical outcomes. Well-executed

MBC programs can simultaneously provide this data for providers at the point of care and for leaders throughout all levels of an organization.

Why Is Technology Needed to Perform MBC?

MBC has been implemented by many BH providers using paper-based measures, and in fact, continues to be paper-based in many settings. The feasibility and simplicity of using paper is hard to match. Paper-based standard forms and clinical scales can be very valuable in collecting real-time feedback reflecting current thoughts and feelings about the session. However, the use of technology can open up many other opportunities for the amount and type of data collected, the timing of data collection, methods of data presentation to providers, and use of aggregated data to inform clinic and health system program evaluation. The proliferation of mobile computing and touch screen technology has made the use of technology ubiquitous across most age groups, thus decreasing previous hardware and usability issues. The use of technology to adopt MBC can improve the consistency of care processes, minimize friction points in patient and clinician experiences, help build routine practices in data collection, allow for real-time data analysis and display, and allow for aggregation of data for program analyses, as follows:

Consistent process of care—MBC technology use allows opportunities for data collection across multiple time points within an episode of care that can include time points between appointments. Clinics can monitor data collection needs electronically and can minimize the hassle of lost paperwork, filing of papers, transcribing data to databases, or scanning papers into an electronic health record (EHR). Screening and periodic outcome tracking via paper in clinic settings do not allow for automation and are subject to many types of errors. Without technology, clinics will likely have a difficult time determining which measures to provide a patient and when the measures should be administered to each patient. This critical issue can result in the abandonment of MBC practices or lead a team to just measure the beginning and end of care, but not at intervals throughout an episode of care. Consequently, the ability of MBC practices to inform real-time clinical decision making during the course of treatment can be quickly lost. This is a critical issue, as the most likely ingredient for MBC to improve overall outcomes is the real-time feedback to providers informing treatment decision making. Setting consistent MBC timing processes help providers focus on reviewing and analyzing data rather than scheduling data collection. When building the BHDP, we addressed this issue by developing a standard intake questionnaire across the Army. We ensured stakeholders from across the country were involved in building the questionnaire in order to maximize the consensus base when launching BHDP. We built in default clinical measure frequency settings for measures to standardize baseline data collection. Providers can override these frequencies when clinically indicated.

The BHDP tracks frequency settings for each patient, allowing for an auto-mated data collection process that does not depend on any person to decide which measures are given on the day of the appointment. These types of functions are critical to the success of MBC implementation.

Periodic data collection throughout treatment also helps remind the patient to review his or her current status compared to previous levels of functioning. This type of work can help reinforce the teaching of psycho-logical mindedness, reinforce hopefulness about the future, and improve self-management through the structure of routine tracking of key symp-toms and functionality. In our work with MBC tools, we have found that showing patients graphing of clinical measures help patients respond more accurately to MBC data collection over time and build a therapeutic alli-ance. At times, patients will report subjective lack of improvement despite clinical scores decreasing. We use these moments to check whether a patient is tracking actual improvement leading to a possible increase in hopeful-ness about recovery. Other times, patients may not report clinical measure improvement despite improvement in our clinical observations. In these cases, we can discuss the incongruity and sometimes find that patients are doing better with coping with symptoms and with overall function, even if symptom severity has not decreased. When symptom improvement is not occurring, we can review the most problematic issues to reset the treatment plan to meet the most current needs.

Minimizing friction points in patient and clinician experiences—Many providers worry that MBC implementation will affect their patient sessions. A paper MBC process involves human scoring of scales, management of paper usage by providers, translation of data into an EHR, and potential transport of the form to providers. These challenges are expensive to manage and are a fre-quent cause of MBC implementation failures. The use of a web-based data collection system allows for the collection of data before a treatment session, automated scoring of measures, graphing visualizations, and presentation of data in an easily reviewable manner for a busy provider. Real-time data viewing by providers is critical, as it allows providers to utilize the data at the point of care for treatment planning decisions. Avoiding the cost of staff data collection, hand-scoring of scales, and translation into medical records can often lead to an affordable web-based MBC system. Recent procedure coding changes also allow for billing for clinical measure execution that can offset MBC system costs (CPT code 96127).

Technology use allows us to build visualization tools for clinicians that cannot be achieved with a paper-based process. We can build color-coded schemes for quick reviews of hot spot areas of concern. We can mark areas of pathology vs. normal to give visual markers of severity of deviation from baseline. We can also design systems to highlight high-value data while also giving access to complete datasets, when desired, by providers. Finally, we can build in clinical decision support tools with smart algorithms that are not possible with paper-based processes. For example, some MBC systems are able to show expected recovery paths and when a patient may be deviating off of these paths. This allows providers to see when patients may be stalling in their recovery efforts and allow for earlier adjustments to treatment plans. All of these tools increase the usability and acceptability of MBC technology by providers.

Build routine data collection—As our team built an MBC process, a key design principle was to use technology to help routine things happen routinely and free up time to let humans do human things. We determined which questions should be asked and answered in routine ways at intake or follow-up sessions. These elements were put into the web-based data collection system. Provider questions that were more open-ended, nuanced, or required contextual understanding were left to providers to collect in their interviews. As providers learned to trust the routine data collection process, more time became available for the providers to pursue patient-specific unique questions that are key to understanding the patient's story and to establishing an initial therapeutic alliance. Although not discretely tested, many providers confirmed to us that routine web-based data collection has led to more time for understanding the patient's unique story and building an initial therapeutic alliance—a critical predictor of a positive clinical outcome.

Real-time data analysis and display—Technology allows many benefits beyond automatic collection and scoring of data. It allows for real-time display of data and for many options of presenting data in an easily understandable way—a critical issue in behavioral health care as we have many different types of providers. For example, in the Army, we needed to find a way to quickly communicate scores for nearly 2,000 providers who may not have often used clinical measures in the past. A web-based MBC process allowed us to color code different measure severity levels, graph treatment progress over time, and present different time scales of data based on provider need. This allowed us to train providers to quickly scan and synthesize large amounts of information for use in their treatment sessions. On initial intakes, providers can quickly see hot spots with clinical measures with more severe symptoms. Providers can then prioritize questioning in clinical domains most likely to yield important information. We also utilized the BHDP to set vocabulary standards for identifying key risk level definitions and encouraged the use of those standards in their data interpretation and documentation of risk concerns across care teams. This shared vocabulary reinforcement is critical in large care teams communicating elements of treatment planning and risk concern.

Aggregation of Data to Drive Clinic/Hospital/System Quality Improvement and Innovation—Finally, technology allows data collected for real-time care to be tracked in aggregate at clinic, hospital, and health care system levels. This ability is critical to help determine whether various program efforts are driving improved quality and outcomes desired. There are many clinical phenomena that happen too infrequently at a provider level to have any statistical power to show whether certain decisions truly impact clinical outcomes. In these situations, providers will also not be able to detect within their own practices how some actions will affect outcomes. However, when such events are aggregated across a hospital or health system, we gain the ability to see what actions may be impacting outcomes. This feedback is critical to help a learning organization efficiently drive optimal quality improvement efforts.

Learning health systems are always looking for innovation to help drive quality improvement. Standardizing data collection can actually improve innovation efforts. One of the largest barriers to innovation is the proper data collection to show the value of such innovation. Technology-enabled MBC programs help ensure that the data collection process is already embedded in clinical practices. Therefore, teams can focus on program innovation instead of how to measure its effectiveness.

What Are the Key Technology-Based MBC Implementation Principles?

There are numerous stakeholders, from care delivery teams at the ground level to hospital and health system leaders to insurance payers. It is difficult to align incentives to ensure the maximal probability of success for an MBC implementation effort. Organizations can increase the probability of successfully implementing an MBC technology solution by following these seven key implementation principles"

1. High-level leadership support is imperative. When building an MBC implementation plan, a team will have several challenges to overcome that require consistent and enthusiastic leadership support. First, resources need to be dedicated at a level that supports not only the purchase of technology but also the training and support services needed for implementation and sustainment. Leadership needs to actively engage with accountability and incentive measures at the provider, clinic, and hospital levels. When implementing BHDP, we traveled to nearly every base to talk to providers in person about why MBC is important. We incentivized local leaders to engage by paying a small bonus to clinics for every questionnaire not just started, but completed. In later years, we built other metrics with MBC data to shift to a value-based payment model for a proportion of clinic budgets. All of this required persistent senior Army medical leadership support to communicate to hospital leaders the importance of this effort and to reinforce accountability efforts. Similar leadership engagement is critical to any MBC implementation effort.

2. Maximize feasibility and minimize the impact on patient–provider interaction time. A strong therapeutic alliance is one of the most important predictors of psychotherapy outcomes. Any MBC plan must respect the patient–provider interaction time involved in executing the MBC process. If it does not, then the therapeutic alliance can be adversely affected. Also, patients and providers will not utilize the MBC process if it is not clear to them how MBC supports current treatment. In our BHDP efforts, we made explicit design decisions to keep the MBC administrative processes out of the provider–patient appointment window as much as possible. This is a key reason why we chose patient-rated measures instead of clinician-rated measures. The three most important elements of an MBC process that impact patient–provider interaction time are the time needed for data collection, the ease of provider visualization and analysis, and the seamlessness of the MBC plan integration with clinical documentation processes. Any MBC plan must address these critical issues, and plan development must keep the patient–provider engagement as the central focus. For example, one of our provider's favorite parts of BHDP was an effort to pre-populate patient note templates with patient-entered data that helped improve the completeness of medical record notes with less provider documentation time, thus leading to more time available for engaging patients.

MBC plan designers also need to anticipate that many requests will be received to add data elements. Therefore, teams will need to have a transparent adjudication process in place to rapidly and coherently address these requests. Without tight control of the amount of data collected, the level of feasibility can plummet and risk implementation failure due to patients complaining of too much data collection and providers frustrated by sorting through too much information.

3. Ensure relevant and safe data collection. Due to the nature of the MBC data collection process, the data collected must be relevant to the core stakeholders—patients and providers. If these stakeholders cannot see the value of the data collected to their real-time mission, then stakeholder buy-in will be impaired. For our system, we ensured all patient-entered data was viewable by the provider and relevant to diagnostic assessment or ongoing treatment planning. For the few data elements asked of providers, we ensured those data points entered were minimized and used for functions that made their clinical work easier to execute. For example, when providers entered diagnoses and treatment modality choices for a patient in the BHDP, the system would automatically update default frequency settings for clinical scale data collection. The timing of data collection may drive which questions can be asked. Data collected immediately before an appointment have few limitations for safety concerns since a provider will be reviewing the data immediately after data collection. When data is collected between or after appointments, then implementation teams need to put safeguards in place if suicidal ideation or other safety-related questions will be asked.

4. Usability and feasibility must be maximized throughout the MBC design process. The MBC process must be highly feasible for patients and providers. For patients, the hardware used for data collection must be easy to manipulate. Tablet-like devices are useful if most questions are of the multiple-choice type. However, virtual keyboards are harder to use vs. physical ones when free text responses are expected. The patient authentication process in the software needs to be highly accurate but not overly cumbersome for patients with a large variance in comfort with technology. For providers, the data visualization process must be well thought out to allow for quick viewing of the most relevant data while allowing providers to drill down in specific areas for more clarity. Individual question items need to be quickly viewable and scannable for high-value information. For example, we developed a flag for each item that indicated a response that is important for a provider not to miss. These items can include risk items (i.e., harm to self or others) but also include other important items (i.e., pregnancy status, financial issues, or serious sleep issues). We then created a "hot sheet" of all critical responses of import that a provider can scan in less than 30 seconds to ensure critical data is not missed.

5. Have clear data use plans at all system levels early in the MBC design phase. MBC teams need to think through how data will be used at all health system levels throughout the building, implementation, and sustainment phases. Data use plans will be informed by structural, process, and clinical outcomes utilized during implementation. For example, we tracked how many surveys were started and then completed. The gap between these two data points informed us of business process issues within a clinic. Tracking the time spent by a patient on each question taught us to remove nearly all free text response questions and leave those for the clinical interview. Aggregated data can be utilized to inform program evaluation efforts. Therefore, prior to finalizing MBC planning, careful thought must be given as to what outcome and other types of data are needed to build coherent program evaluation metrics. Finally, data analysis teams should be built early in the implementation process to help initially build key process indicators and then shift to helping clinics fully utilize the data to inform quality improvement efforts. Without dedicated data analysis team support, health system learning and quality improvement efforts are severely compromised.

6. Ensure the data collection strategy meets key stakeholder needs. The most basic assessment standards require the use of psychometrically valid measures of mental disorder symptoms and symptom clusters. The Diagnostic and Statistical Manual of Mental Disorders (DSM-V, American Psychiatric Association, 2013) delineates categories of disorders along with their respective diagnostic criteria. It does not, however, claim to be exhaustive in capturing the full range of psychopathology, nor does it discount the importance of understanding the severity or valence of each individual symptom. Furthermore, other outcomes besides symptom intensity are often of interest to patients and providers, such as patient satisfaction or functional impairment. Therefore, a holistic assessment strategy is recommended encompassing measures of symptom counts, severity, and frequency along with functional impairment and general indicators of well-being. Finding the right balance between comprehensive data collection and execution feasibility can be challenging.

It is important for general outpatient clinics to carefully weigh the importance of a fully comprehensive assessment and the potential patient burden of an exhaustive diagnostic battery. There are several approaches to obtaining this balance. First, short screening measures (PHQ-2, GAD-2, AUDIT-C) with reasonable diagnostic specificity can help to narrow the clinical interview with little impact from data collection efforts. Alternatively, outpatient clinics may choose to focus initial assessments on disorders and symptom clusters that have the highest base rates in an attempt to capture similar baseline information across the largest group of patients. Collecting the same limited set of information from a large segment of consumers can serve to monitor the severity of clientele and overall effectiveness of a clinic over time.

For specialty settings, developing context-specific initial screenings and baseline metrics is somewhat more straightforward. Validated measures of symptoms central to a clinic (i.e., symptoms of PTSD in a PTSD-focused program) are essential to understanding symptom severity at initial presentation, symptom change through treatment, and disorder remission. This information provides both individual data points (for each patient) and program level information on population severity and program efficacy that can be utilized to drive meaningful quality improvement efforts.

In addition to disorder-specific measurements of symptoms, the measurement of transdiagnostic maladaptive behaviors adds to treatment planning and progress monitoring. Suicidal thoughts and self-injurious behavior are the most important transdiagnostic variables to continuously monitor. Specific measures of suicide thoughts and behaviors are readily available for use and have been adopted by large health systems throughout the world (The Columbia Lighthouse Project, 2016). Providers sometimes fear that asking patients about thoughts of suicide may put the idea in their mind. Apprehensions of producing or eliciting suicidal thoughts or behaviors as a result of regular assessment of self-injurious thoughts or actions is not supported by the current body of literature. Conversely, the regular assessment of such thoughts and behaviors serves multiple functions, including opening the opportunity for the patient to disclose information about these serious thoughts or actions, allowing the provider to assess for immediate risk factors, and providing feedback on treatment progress.

Other problem-based assessments are often overlooked in systematic measurement. A specific measurement of occupational, social, and interpersonal functioning provides standardized information on how patients interact with the world around them. Measures of anger and sleep disturbance may also provide important information about general functioning (Carreno & Wilk, 2016). The bidirectional relationship of these variables with psychopathology provides both additional information about BH problems and additional avenues for intervention.

A growing body of literature supports the inclusion of assessments of nutritional habits (Lai et al., 2013) and exercise in behavioral health (Chekroud et al., 2018). The assessment of nutritional patterns and activity levels may provide supplemental information at intake to aid in initial clinical conceptualization and treatment planning. Improvement of baseline wellness and health promotion activities could serve as a complementary measure of progress throughout treatment.

The use of psychometrically sound data collection instruments is of central importance when deciding on the totality of your initial and follow-on assessments. This includes giving primary consideration to assessment tools considered to be the "gold standard" for the measurement of particular diagnostic categories. These instruments must also have the ability to adequately detect clinically meaningful change over time.

In the Army, we combined several of these approaches. We utilized short screeners with automated decision-making algorithms to determine whether to present the full clinical measure. For example, we used the PHQ-2, and the gated scores of three or higher to automatically present the rest of the PHQ-9 to the patient. We did similar gating for the GAD-2 to the GAD-7 for general anxiety, PC-PTSD to the PCL for PTSD, and the AUDIT-C to the full AUDIT for alcohol concerns. We also used the C-SSRS suicide ideation subscale to screen for safety issues. We used a general distress scale (BASIS-24) to have a consistent measure of distress across diagnoses that can be tracked across an episode of care.

7. *The timing of data collection needs to be designed consistent with clinical business practices.* The outcomes domains that are chosen to be tracked and whether patient- or provider-reported measures are chosen will dictate data collection timing strategies in an MBC system. Clinics may consider collecting data before an upcoming appointment, during an appointment, or between appointments. Collecting data before an appointment allows for the least disruption to the clinical encounter. If data is not collected proximally to a clinical encounter, then safety-related questions may be limited due to concern about provider liability. However, if proper legal safeguards are put in place, collecting safety-related data between appointments can potentially save lives. Pre-appointment data collection also impairs the ability to collect timely therapeutic alliance data. The main benefits of data collection proximal to appointments include the ability to collect therapeutic alliance data, to clarify patient questions on data collection, and to respond to any acute concerns. Tracking data across multiple points of time between appointments provides an opportunity to elicit symptom variability over time and reinforce psychological mindedness learning for patients in their natural environment. The omnipresence of smartphones and other mobile technology allows for an exploration of how this type of data collection can impact treatment.

What Are the Concerns and Challenges About MBC That Must Be Addressed?

There are several concerns with MBC implementation that need to be addressed. In general, providers will need training on how to collect data, review the data efficiently, and incorporate findings in their clinical assessments and ongoing treatment efforts. Providers will find there is a balance in not ignoring the data but also not over-focusing on data review at the expense of patient engagement. Some examples of the most common concerns follow.

Patient self-reported data is not validated and may be under/over-reported. Patient self-reported data, like all patient-reported data, is not validated until a provider reviews the relevancy of the report. However, this can be minimized with structured clinical measures and other clear questioning. The STAR*D trials utilized both clinician-rated and patient-reported measures that demonstrated nearly identical results (Warden, Rush, Trivedi, Fava, & Wisniewski, 2007). Providers do need to consider both under- and over-reporting, especially on the initial evaluation and in certain patient subgroups. We have found that once providers explain the purpose of MBC data collection, patients generally report data more accurately.

Clinical measure scores will force providers to make a diagnosis or treatment decision. We are not aware of any clinical practice guideline or standard of care that mandates specific diagnoses based on a self-reported clinical measure. The clinical interview will always take precedence over any measure results. When a clinical measure is inconsistent with a provider's assessment, a provider can seek to integrate, explore, and interpret the divergent sources of data and document the discrepancy and the assessment results.

Providers don't have time to look at this data. Teams that design and implement MBC practices need to plan well on how to sequence data collection and provider data viewing. Great care needs to be taken to ensure the maximal usability of provider dashboards for timely review of data. The use of color and prioritizing which data is displayed on front pages can help clinicians rapidly review the most relevant data often in less than 1–2 minutes.

Patients do not have time to complete questionnaires. MBC implementation does require thoughtful planning for data collection. In the Army, patients were only able to complete web-based forms in the clinic. Several strategies were developed to maximize opportunities for patient data collection. Some clinics designed appointment slips describing arrival time as earlier than the appointment time. Other clinics scheduled appointments to start earlier than the provider appointment time to allow automated reminder systems to support timely patient arrival. We also streamlined data collection over time to minimize the time needed to collect data.

MBC data will be used to discipline or fire providers. Leaders need to make transparent decisions as to how data will be used to evaluate providers. We chose not to show provider-level data to clinics to ensure data was not misused. Issues like case-mix differences, team-based care, and adequate sampling of data need to be addressed before any provider-level analysis can even begin.

MBC data increases provider malpractice risk. MBC practice can likely lower malpractice risk with standardized data collection. Collecting screening data on core diagnoses and safety domains while regularly monitoring treatment progress likely decreases the chance of bad outcomes. The key malpractice risk point is when an MBC plan collects data that a provider does not review to inform clinical decision making. The most obvious example would be a clinician ignoring organizational policy and not reviewing a critical item indicating an acute risk that is subsequently followed by a bad patient outcome.

Some patients are too ill to accurately report data. There will be clinical situations where collecting standardized data is not possible due to limitations in the patient's ability to engage meaningfully in the MBC process. We typically ask our providers to simply wait and collect MBC data when the patient is more stable.

Current Technology Options and Future Opportunities for MBC Utilization

As of early 2019, we are not aware of any of the largest electronic medical record (EMR) system companies supporting robust automated BH measurement-based care practices as described in this chapter. Most behavioral health-specific EMRs do not have such capability either. However, there are several offerings available for supporting MBC implementation efforts. Some examples are:

1. www.oqmeasure.com—Dr. Michael Lambert and his team utilize the OQ-45 and other OQ measures in this platform. They have developed the OQ-Analyst capability based on their research to help predict when patients are not on track for treatment success to help identify earlier those who may need a change in their treatment plan. (Shimokawa et al., 2010)
2. www.myoutcomes.com—Dr. Scott Miller developed the Outcome Rating Scale (ORS) and Session Rating Scale (SRS) as simplified and feasible measures to use in MBC efforts. His team has also built analytic, prediction, and tracking tools to support real-time clinical care efforts

called PCOMS—Patient-Centered Outcomes Management System. (Campbell & Hemsley, 2009; Miller et al., 2003)

3. www.betteroutcomesnow.com—Dr. Duncan and colleagues use a similar version of PCOMS to help clinics and agencies implement MBC practices. This system supports real-time feedback to providers and other aggregate reporting. (Reese, Norsworthy, & Rowlands, 2009)

4. www.mirah.com—The M3 scale is a validated 27-item measure that screens for depressive, anxiety, PTSD and bipolar disorders, and was built for primary care but can also be used as a single multi-condition measure in specialty clinics The M3 measure has been built into a web-based tool along with other common outcome measures. (Gaynes et al., 2010)

Widespread MBC adoption within BH service delivery has the potential to rapidly drive improvements in care practices. A few key areas are described next.

MBC Data Can Feed Future Predictive Modeling Efforts to Inform Precision Medicine Efforts

Predictive modeling efforts are starting to be used in the BH field to look at finding risk for low-frequency events (Kessler et al., 2015). However, their robustness and utility are not well known yet, especially since many of them were not developed with access to MBC data. Other examples of predictive modeling may be more immediately useful. For example, Chekroud et al. (2016) have shown that machine learning technology can use data from baseline MBC efforts and data typically discovered at an initial assessment to predict which type of patient will be more likely to improve with certain medication choices. These findings were then successfully tested on an out-of-sample set of data, with similar results. This type of work may lead to improved medication choice decisions without resorting to expensive genomic testing.

Computer Adaptive Testing (CAT) May Lead to More Feasible MBC Systems

Computer adaptive testing is a process where the choice of each standard question asked depends on the answers to previous questions to help rule in or out specific diagnoses. Instead of presenting the PHQ-9 questions for depression screening, a CAT system can increase the accuracy of depression detection with fewer questions. The NIH PROMIS (Reeve et al., 2007) effort is one example of this work. One challenge for ongoing monitoring is that each data collection may not ask the same questions, thus impair the ability of a provider and patient to track specific symptom questions.

Regardless, CAT may become very helpful in addressing core feasibility issues in MBC implementation.

MBC Enables Opportunities With Value-Based Payment Models and New Funding Sources

Health insurers are developing value-based funding models and testing several types of risk-sharing and incentive structures in order to manage BH care costs. As value-based health care payment methods become more prevalent, increasing pressure will mount on BH providers to show positive clinical outcomes. Not only will effectiveness need to be tracked but efficiency in clinical efforts will also be rewarded. Tracking clinical outcomes using MBC can help health systems align the appropriate level of care to the severity of illness, potentially allowing for more efficient care delivery. MBC practices can reduce costs by informing when patients are ready for termination earlier in the course of usual care. There is an increasing recognition that effective BH treatment can decrease overall health care costs across a health system (Melek et al., 2018). The potential savings in overall health care utilization can be significant and serve as an additional funding source through the sharing of such savings with BH programs. Without well-established MBC practices in place, BH providers will not be able to demand higher payment rates for services, and leaders will not be well positioned to seek increased funding for BH initiatives.

In conclusion, the confluence of the expanding evidence of the effectiveness of MBC with the ubiquitous spread of technology now allows us an opportunity to rapidly improve the effectiveness, efficiency, and overall quality of BH care. The scarcity of BH resources compared to the population need demands that we find ways to use our limited resources more effectively. Access to improved funding streams will only be available if we embrace MBC throughout all areas of BH practice. Training programs for all types of BH providers need to incorporate MBC practices into their programs to ensure our future providers are fully ready for this future.

References

American Psychiatric Publishing (2013). *Diagnostic and statistical manual of mental disorders: DSM-5*. Washington, DC: Author.

Basco, M. R., Bostic, J. Q., Davies, D., Rush, A. J., Witte, B., Hendrickse, W., & Barnett, V. (2000). Methods to improve diagnostic accuracy in a community mental health setting. *American Journal of Psychiatry, 157*(10), 1599–1605.

Bickman, L., Kelley, S. D., Breda, C., de Andrade, A. R., & Riemer, M. (2011). Effects of routine feedback to clinicians on mental health outcomes of youths: Results of a randomized trial. *Psychiatric Services, 62*(12), 1423–1429.

Campbell, A., & Hemsley, S. (2009). Outcome rating scale and session rating scale in psychological practice: Clinical utility of ultra-brief measures. *Clinical Psychologist, 13*(1), 1–9.

Carr, A. C., Ghosh, A., & Ancill, R. J. (1983). Can a computer take a psychiatric history? *Psychological Medicine*, *13*(1), 151–158.

Carreno, J. T., & Wilk, J. E. (2016). Sleep, agitation, and irritation: Proxies for functional impairment among service members seeking mental health treatment. *Military Behavioral Health*, *4*(2), 108–114.

Chekroud, A. M., Zotti, R. J., Shehzad, Z., Gueorguieva, R., Johnson, M. K., Trivedi, M. H., . . . Corlett, P. R. (2016). Cross-trial prediction of treatment outcome in depression: A machine learning approach. *The Lancet Psychiatry*, *3*(3), 243–250.

Chekroud, S. R., Gueorguieva, R., Zheutlin, A. B., Paulus, M., Krumholz, H. M., Krystal, J. H., & Chekroud, A. M. (2018). Association between physical exercise and mental health in 1.2 million individuals in the USA between 2011 and 2015: A cross-sectional study. *The Lancet Psychiatry*, *5*(9), 739–746.

The Columbia Lighthouse Project (2016). Retrieved from http://cssrs.columbia.edu/the-columbia-scale-c-ssrs/evidence/

Gaynes, B. N., Deveaugh-Geiss, J., Weir, S., Gu, H., Macpherson, C., Schulberg, H. C., . . . Rubinow, D. R. (2010). Feasibility and diagnostic validity of the M-3 checklist: A brief, self-rated screen for depressive, bipolar, anxiety, and post-traumatic stress disorders in primary care. *The Annals of Family Medicine*, *8*(2), 160–169. doi:10.1370/afm.1092

Guo, T., Xiang, Y. T., Xiao, L., Hu, C. Q., Chiu, H. F., Ungvari, G. S., . . . Feng, Y. (2015). Measurement-based care versus standard care for major depression: A randomized controlled trial with blind raters. *American Journal of Psychiatry*, *172*(10), 1004–1013.

Hansson, H., Rundberg, J., Österling, A., Öjehagen, A., & Berglund, M. (2013). Intervention with feedback using outcome questionnaire 45 (OQ-45) in a Swedish psychiatric outpatient population: A randomized controlled trial. *Nordic Journal of Psychiatry*, *67*, 274–281.

Henkel, V., Seemüller, F., Obermeier, M., Adli, M., Bauer, M., Mundt, C., . . . Zeiler, J. (2009). Does early improvement triggered by antidepressants predict response/remission?—Analysis of data from a naturalistic study on a large sample of inpatients with major depression. *Journal of Affective Disorders*, *115*(3), 439–449.

Hicks, P. B., Sevilimedu, V., Johnson, G. R., Tal, I., Chen, P., Davis, L. L., . . . Zisook, S. (2019). Predictability of nonremitting depression after first 2 weeks of antidepressant treatment: A VAST-D trial report. *Psychiatric Research and Clinical Practice*, appi-prcp.

Imel, Z. E., & Wampold, B. E. (2008). The importance of treatment and the science of common factors in psychotherapy. *Handbook of Counseling Psychology*, *4*, 249–266.

Kessler, R. C., Warner, C. H., Ivany, C., Petukhova, M. V., Rose, S., Bromet, E. J., . . . Army STARRS Collaborators (2015). Predicting suicides after psychiatric hospitalization in US Army soldiers: the Army Study To Assess Risk and rEsilience in Servicemembers (Army STARRS). JAMA psychiatry, *72*(1), 49–57. https://doi.org/10.1001/jamapsychiatry.2014.1754

Knaup, C., Koesters, M., Schoefer, D., Becker, T., & Puschner, B. (2009). Effect of feedback of treatment outcome in specialist mental healthcare: Meta analysis. *The British Journal of Psychiatry*, *195*(1), 15–22.

Lai, J. S., Hiles, S., Bisquera, A., Hure, A. J., Mcevoy, M., & Attia, J. (2013). A systematic review and meta-analysis of dietary patterns and depression in community-dwelling adults. *The American Journal of Clinical Nutrition*, *99*(1), 181–197. doi:10.3945/ajcn.113.069880

Lambert, M. J., & Barley, D. E. (2001). Research summary on the therapeutic relationship and psychotherapy outcome. *Psychotherapy: Theory, Research, Practice, Training, 38*(4), 357.

Melek, S. P., Norris, D. T., Paulus, J., Matthews, K., Weaver, A., & Davenport, S. (2018). *Potential economic impact of integrated medical-behavioral healthcare: Updated projections for 2017.* Seattle, WA: Milliman Research Report.

Miller, P. R. (2001). Inpatient diagnostic assessments: 2. Interrater reliability and outcomes of structured vs. unstructured interviews. *Psychiatry Research, 105*(3), 265–271.

Miller, S. D., Duncan, B. L., Brown, J., Sparks, J. A., & Claud, D. A. (2003). The outcome rating scale: A preliminary study of the reliability, validity, and feasibility of a brief visual analog measure. *Journal of Brief Therapy, 2*(2), 91–100.

Pronovost, P. J., Berenholtz, S. M., Goeschel, C. A., Needham, D. M., Sexton, J. B., Thompson, D. A., . . . Hunt, E. (2006). Creating high reliability in health care organizations. *Health Services Research, 41*(4p2), 1599–1617.

Reese, R. J., Norsworthy, L. A., & Rowlands, S. R. (2009). Does a continuous feedback system improve psychotherapy outcome? *Psychotherapy: Theory, Research, Practice, Training, 46*(4), 418.

Reeve, B. B., Hays, R. D., Bjorner, J. B., Cook, K. F., Crane, P. K., Teresi, J. A., . . . Cella, D. (2007). Psychometric evaluation and calibration of health-related quality of life item banks. *Medical Care, 45*(Suppl. 1). doi:10.1097/01.mlr.0000250483.85507.04

Senge, P. (1990). *The fifth discipline: The art and practice of the learning organisation.* London: Doubleday and Century Business.

Scott, K., & Lewis, C. C. (2015). Using measurement-based care to enhance any treatment. *Cognitive and Behavioral Practice, 22*(1), 49–59.

Shimokawa, K., Lambert, M. J., & Smart, D. W. (2010). Enhancing treatment outcome of patients at risk of treatment failure: Meta-analytic and mega-analytic review of a psychotherapy quality assurance system. *Journal of Consulting and Clinical Psychology, 78*(3), 298.

Till, A., Amin, M., & McKimm, J. (2016). Leadership in learning organizations: A strategy for improvement. *British Journal of Hospital Medicine, 77*(11), 620–623.

Warden, D., Rush, A. J., Trivedi, M. H., Fava, M., & Wisniewski, S. R. (2007). The STAR★ D Project results: A comprehensive review of findings. *Current Psychiatry Reports, 9*(6), 449–459.

2 Practical Guidance on Reaching Remote Patients Through Telemental Health

Matt Mishkind, Sarah Schwenk, and Brittany Shoemaker

Introduction

Telemental Health (TMH), which is the use of technology to provide mental health care at a geographic or temporal distance, is a rapidly growing mode of service delivery that offers viable solutions to problems associated with growing mental health need, provider shortages, and patient obstacles, especially as related to geography, mobility, and stigma to care access (Bashshur, Shannon, Bashshur, & Yellowlees, 2015; Hilty et al., 2013; Hubley, Schneck, Thomas, & Shore, 2016). TMH has increased in acceptance and utilization, as it has the capacity to make a significant and positive impact on mental health delivery systems by its ability to not only increase access to care but also to more effectively tailor mental health services to individual or community-based health care needs (Adams et al., 2018). This includes the promotion of a stepped care approach by providing health care beneficiaries with a range of increasingly specialized and intensive services that may include accessing mobile applications, web-based services, and other computer-assisted services for some concerns (Wright, Mishkind, Eells, & Chan, 2019). For other concerns, TMH provides for a direct person-to-person connection with a mental health provider and thus helps to mitigate a variety of care access and disparity challenges. This service flexibility has increased, as many of the technologies and peripherals used to deliver services today are ubiquitous to consumers because they encounter them in other commercial uses and applications.

Historical Perspective

Given the rate of technological advancement over the past 20 years, there is a common misconception that the use of technology to deliver health care services is a new concept, when on the contrary, using the technology of the day to deliver health information has a robust history (Mishkind, Waugh, & Hubley, 2018). Some evidence suggests that information about bubonic plague was spread across Europe using heliographs and bonfires, the same communications used to spread information about war and famine (Zundel,

1996). Telegraph was used to order medical supplies and even transmit casualty lists during the American Civil War (Zundel, 1996), suggesting one of the first examples of synchronous (or near synchronous) telehealth. Alexander Graham Bell patented the telephone in 1876, long-distance telephone links appeared in the 1880s, and we now have a nationwide 9–1–1 system and the ability to send and receive text messages with health care information from everyday smartphones.

The National Aeronautics and Space Administration (NASA) helped pioneer telemedicine applications to monitor astronaut health for the manned space program (Cermack, 2006). The 1950s also saw an expansion in the use of closed-circuit television, with one of the first medical uses demonstrated in Nebraska in 1964, and in 1967 a television-based telemedicine system was developed linking the medical station at Boston's Logan Airport with Massachusetts General Hospital. While these, and many other initial programs, demonstrated the potential of technology, they were not sustainable due to the technological limitations and administrative maintenance costs. It may be argued that not until home computing and telecommunications technologies such as the internet became ubiquitous that telehealth really started to expand.

Telemental health as we currently know it has roots in providing mental health care from one institution (e.g., hospital or university) to another using costly and, at times, unreliable synchronous two-way, audio and video connections (Shore, 2015). While some health care advances originate from individual clinicians, the necessary infrastructure of early TMH programs required the resources of large institutions to be effective. Fortunately, TMH has expanded rapidly over the past two decades, concurrently with revolutions in technology and devices such as smartphones and telecommunications – including the internet and overall changes in the health care landscape focused on improving care and access while reducing costs.

Efficacy Evidence

While history is important, administrators and clinicians alike view an understanding of the current evidence-base as critical to making initial decisions about engaging the use of technology to deliver mental health services. This chapter is not designed to be an exhaustive review of the literature; however, an overview is important to set the context and rationale for engaging in the development and delivery of TMH care. Overall, the body of telemental health literature points to the conclusion that use of two-way audio and visual technologies to deliver mental health treatment is no less effective than in-person care delivery for a broad range of mental health concerns (Mishkind et al., 2018). Hilty and colleagues (2013) conducted a review of 70 articles and determined that TMH care was as effective as in-person care for depression, post-traumatic stress disorder, and substance use. Hubley et al. (2016) reviewed seven studies comparing telepsychiatry to in-person psychiatric care and found equivalent outcomes in six studies. Fletcher and colleagues (2018) conducted a review of in-home TMH care and found that all ten evaluated randomized controlled trials (RCTs) for depression (5), PTSD (4), Substance Abuse (1), and Obsessive-Compulsive Disorder (1) reported significant clinical improvements. Four of five RCTs showed non-inferiority of TMH to in-person care. They further identified that TMH care overall was less expensive than traditional in-person care when patients were able to use their own devices. Finally, a 2018 review of 14 randomized controlled studies comparing in-person and TMH treatment for depression showed that most studies reported inconclusive or no statistical difference in clinical outcomes (Berryhill et al., 2018).

Chapter Overview

Despite the robust history of technology-based care, evidence showing that TMH is efficacious as a standard of care, and patient satisfaction ratings comparable to in-person treatment (Jenkins-Guarnieri, Pruitt, Luxton, & Johnson, 2015), the promise of TMH remains to be met with the expected broad-based implementation success. A large part of the implementation failure is due to the limited practical references that provide clinicians with how-to guidance using real-world examples and solutions. This chapter is designed to help fill implementation gaps by providing practical guidance on the use of technology in mental health practice. There will be a focus on more traditional telemental health (i.e., synchronous audio and visual services); however, many strategies will generalize across technologies and services. Topics will include administrative factors such as conducting a needs assessment, developing policies and procedures, marketing services, and training; clinical factors include establishing rapport and therapeutic alliance, HIPAA compliance, verification of location, setting boundary standards with patients, and managing safety within the context of the environment.

Administrative Factors, Guidelines, and Training— Preparing for Telemental Health

Delivering effective TMH services should begin well before the first session is scheduled to prevent program planning failures that too often begin with finding a use for technology rather than using technology to meet a need. Other planning issues include not understanding patient populations and the willingness or capacity of staff to deliver new services. Finally, technology evolves much faster than policy, and programs can fail when they do not fit within existing regulatory environments.

Case Example

Program Tell E. Mental Health was designed to deliver outpatient TMH services in a remote rural community. A community-based program had demonstrated success using local resources to provide face-to-face mental health services. Due to its success, the program developers were given an opportunity to expand services to a neighboring community with the understanding that expansion would require partnering with a larger health care organization to utilize TMH services, thus creating the Tell E. Mental Health initiative. The program developers made assumptions about the need for services and successfully contracted for TMH providers and support staff based on these assumptions. Unfortunately, the assumptions about service need were not supported in practice. The developers also neglected to account for regulatory and operational constraints, and the service was shut down after several months.

Conducting a Needs Assessment

Planning should begin with a needs assessment, as recommended by a recent joint guideline between the American Telemedicine Association and American Psychiatric Association (ATA-APA; Shore et al., 2018). The overall goal of a needs assessment is to understand the intent of the program—who will be served, who will provide the services, with what technology, in what location(s), and with what expected outcomes. The final product should be a "Program Overview Statement," which is a straightforward purpose statement about the problem to be solved that serves as a guiding point for the program and future decisions. Begin by thinking about the population to be served and what services to provide (e.g., synchronous therapy, computer-assisted treatments, augmented care with mobile apps). It is important to differentiate patient need from patient willingness to engage to ensure that not only is there a need to be served but that patients will access services that are offered. Next, make certain that there is a willingness and ability among staff to deliver technology-based care. Research indicates that patients are initially more accepting of receiving TMH services than providers are of delivering them (Brooks, Turvey, & Augusterfer, 2013). For some providers there are additional concerns about how best to engage patients and most effectively use technologies to enhance care and maintain patient–provider relationships (Kramer, Kinn, & Mishkind, 2015).

Match Technology to Program Needs

The services to be provided and the needs of your program should drive the technology. The lure of new, interesting technology may create pressure to plan the technology before appropriately understanding the use cases for it. A technology plan should begin with an evaluation of needs identified in the previous steps with additional focus on the functions needed by the patient and provider. The goal is to match the technology to what is needed to deliver your planned services to your planned patient population as effectively and efficiently as possible. Inquire within your organization about existing technology and agreements (e.g., Business Associate Agreement or BAA) before looking to external vendors and remember that the best technology is the technology that best fits your needs.

Understand Your Operational Space and Regulatory Requirements

Using technology to deliver mental health care affords opportunities to provide services in varied operational spaces, including clinically supervised (e.g., outpatient mental health clinic) and clinically unsupervised (e.g., patient home) settings. Where the patient is located (the originating site) rather than where the provider is located (the distant site) is where care is typically said to be delivered, and much of the innovation in technology-based care comes from understanding how to utilize different spaces given regulatory constraints. Understanding your operational space is critical because state laws and state licensing authorities often have different regulations for clinically supervised and unsupervised settings and plans for providing services in one jurisdiction will not immediately equate to a similar plan in another location. An effective way to understand your operational space is to evaluate the step-by-step needs of your program to determine where care can be delivered appropriately, and then work through what is likely to be a typical clinical visit beginning before the encounter and continuing through to referrals and other next steps.

Licensure, credentialing and privileging, and malpractice insurance are often seen as the primary regulatory barriers to implementing TMH services (Kramer et al., 2015). While important, there are other less referenced regulations that are equally important to address for a successful program. For example, you will need to comply with the Ryan Haight Act Online Pharmacy Consumer Protection Act (federal law that amended the Controlled Substances Act) if you plan to prescribe controlled substances (Mackey, Kalyanam, Katsuki, & Lanckriet, 2017). Or, if you are a HIPAA-covered entity you will likely need a business associate agreement (BAA) with your technology vendor to ensure security of protected health information (PHI).

Develop Policies, Procedures, and Protocols

The needs assessment should provide the information and details necessary to develop local policies, procedures, and protocols. The next step is focused on filling in gaps and developing standard processes and documents that support the patient, the referring provider, the remote clinic staff, and the local staff. Many professional associations including the American Telemedicine

Association (ATA) and the American Psychiatric Association (APA) have written guidelines that should be referenced to assist with document development (Myers et al., 2017; Shore et al., 2014; Shore et al., 2018; Turvey et al., 2013). Incorporating additional requirements into already existing documents is recommended to assist implementation; be mindful to not unnecessarily replicate existing procedures. Translating these documents into approved clinical protocols can be done once a commitment is made to implement a program and procedures have been tested in practice.

> *Recommendation*: Develop policies that promote decision making at the provider and patient level rather than unnecessarily limiting the provision of services. For example, one large program developed local policies that limited telehealth to clinically supervised settings for both patients and providers. Rather than connect from other settings, patients were required to travel to a traditional clinic or hospital setting only to connect to another traditional clinic setting. State laws and provider licensing boards did not require that care originate from clinical settings, and it was a local policy that limited accessibility. The policy focused on the setting rather than promoting flexibility at the service level, and patients were ultimately reluctant to access available TMH services.

Develop a Business Plan

Reimbursement is often cited as a significant barrier to telemental health program implementation, and despite many states having passed some form of telehealth parity law, it can be difficult to sustain services based entirely on clinical reimbursements. Developing a business plan that understands costs, revenues, and return-on-investment is a critical step that is often omitted but is necessary for sustainability of the program. The next step is a marketing plan that includes communication to leaders of the community, patients, health care providers, and other health care organizations. Developing relationships with major local employers and highlighting how the TMH service can assist their employees is a method for reaching captive audiences. Another effective strategy is to develop a referral partnership with other health care disciplines such as local primary care clinics that may be struggling with addressing mental health needs of patients. Finally, develop community training programs that highlight an area of expertise (e.g., youth anxiety) and to promote the services you offer. Marketing helps develop hybrid-partnership models that include grants, contracts, and direct reimbursements that may help offset gaps from a single source of revenue:

- *Grants.* Grants are often useful to help initiate programs and obtain up-front funding for technology and personnel. Grants rarely provide sustainment funding.

- *Contracts.* Contracting with a partner organization in need of services can be an effective way to sustain operations. This can be accomplished as a direct contract hire or a full-time equivalent buyout to provide specialty services.
- *Partnering with the Payer.* It is becoming more common for providers to directly partner with payers to fulfill a need or even local mandates for access to care.

Evaluate Training Needs

Many concerns about initiating technology-based services may be due to limited training opportunities for providers to better engage with and understand the functional delivery of services. One study found that about half of providers using TMH felt properly trained to deliver services (Jameson, Farmer, Head, Fortney, & Teal, 2011). As a result, training and education tends to be a focal point when implementing a new service. Fortunately, there is evidence to suggest that when given information about the utility of technology-based services, and provided opportunities to engage service delivery, provider reluctance can be reduced. To develop standardized training and improve the quality of TMH care, Maheu and colleagues (2018) developed seven TMH competencies domains, each with three levels of expertise (novice, proficient, and authority). The seven domains are: (1) Clinical evaluation and care, (2) Virtual environment and telepresence, (3) Technology, (4) Legal and regulatory issues, (5) Evidence-base and ethical practice, (6) Mobile health technologies including applications (apps), and (7) Telepractice development. Mishkind, Boyd, Kramer, Ayers, and Miller (2013) suggested five best practices for training sessions with the goal of providing comprehensive training across all roles and responsibilities; these practices can also be used to develop the seven competencies. The overarching theme is that interactive training in the form of live, simulated clinical and technical scenarios is an invaluable training method. The American Psychiatric Association (APA) maintains a telepsychiatry toolkit developed by the APA Workgroup on Telepsychiatry (www.psychiatry.org/psychia trists/practice/telepsychiatry/toolkit). A relatively new and useful feature is a series of videos representing TMH scenarios (e.g., safety, boundary setting) that can be used to supplement other training initiatives. Table 2.1 provides an overview of the best practices.

Develop an Evaluation Plan

The success of a TMH program can extend far beyond the initially proposed goals, and it can be rewarding to think about changes to the overall health care system. For example, improving access to mental health services has been shown to lead to reductions in hospital visits and other clinical

Table 2.1 Best Practices for TMH Training Sessions

One:	Identify topics best trained in a live setting and those best learned through didactic modalities such as background, history, and evidence-base of TMH.
Two:	Focus on live, interactive sessions to gain experience with technology, developing rapport, and implementing operating procedures prior to initiating TMH care.
Three:	Use lessons learned to develop real-life scenarios.
Four:	Incorporate activities into daily learning sessions such as hosting meetings using synchronous audio-visual communications rather than audio-only calls.
Five:	Tailor training to staff roles, but ensure all stakeholders have the same base competencies and knowledge sets.

outcomes (Godleski, Darkins, & Peters, 2012). While it may be inviting to think about system impact goals, regulations change, populations shift, new technologies are developed, and the costs associated with various aspects of a program go up and down, and it is more realistic to focus on an evaluation plan that can be directed and executed with local impact. By vigilantly monitoring the different aspects of a program, you can see trends before they happen and modify programs before it is necessary. Treat new initiatives as pilots you know will require modifications. Learn from evaluations, capture quantitative and qualitative data, and adjust as necessary.

Clinical Preparation—Promoting Access and Reducing No-Show Rates

Telemental health services are most effective when patients show up for visits and truly understand the TMH process. The use of TMH has been shown to reduce no-show rates to as low as 2% when patient homes are used as originating sites. This reduction does not happen automatically and requires preparation, planning, and patient engagement to be most effective. Prior to initiating a first session it is useful to consider the familiarity that patients have, or don't have, with technology-based services and technology in general. Other recommendations include developing a brief informational pamphlet or introductory video, explaining the benefits and procedures of TMH services, and conducting short test sessions to familiarize patients with the technology and procedures.

Case Example

The Tele Show Up Program is based out of an outpatient mental health clinic serving a state with a high percentage of rural residents. The clinic overall has maintained relatively low no-show and cancellation rates but struggled with ongoing access for, and no-show rates with, patients in more remote locations. The clinic evaluated its telemental health services and noted that while many patients initially expressed an understanding of TMH, many did not show up for initial sessions. The clinic team spoke to patients about this and discovered that many were confused about their role in the process, how to use the technology, and expectations about maintaining a private setting especially for in-home TMH. The Tele Show Up Program was developed to better familiarize patients by conducting test calls prior to the initial session to give patients the opportunity to use the technology, ask questions, ensure reliable connectivity, and identify a proper location for care. The number of patients opting for TMH sessions increased by over 100% and no-show rates fell significantly to under 10% for all TMH sessions.

Patient Selection

There are no absolute contraindications to patients being assessed or treated using TMH, and the primary exclusion to its use is a patient denying the service when offered. There may be times when a provider may decide that TMH is not the best choice for a specific condition or treatment plan or determines that the patient is not a suitable candidate. Therefore, the use of TMH with any individual patient should be at the discretion of the provider, with patient agreement. Telemental health services delivered to a clinically unsupervised setting (e.g., patient home) requires that the patient take a more active and cooperative role in the treatment process, and as a result may require additional considerations for whether TMH is appropriate. In many clinically unsupervised settings, patients will need to set up and maintain the videoconferencing system (likely a personal computing device), establish appropriate clinical space, and cooperate for effective safety management. The consent process may need to be modified to focus more on session management such that the patient is aware that services may be discontinued if they can no longer be served at a clinically unsupervised TMH location. Other factors to consider when determining appropriateness of care in clinically unsupervised settings include:

- Patient's cognitive capacity, history regarding cooperativeness with treatment professionals, personality and history of disruptive behavior, current and past difficulties with substance abuse, and history of violence or self-injurious behavior.
- Geographic distance to the nearest emergency medical facility, efficacy of patient's support system, and current medical status.
- Lack of a private and/or safe environment to receive services.
- Limited bandwidth such that audio and/or visual connections are not seamless.

Patient Education

Patients may state up front that they are aware of TMH and understand the process. However, do not assume a patient's level of understanding and consistently make plans to educate patients on the benefits of TMH and the process to initiate and receive services. As noted previously in the chapter, training all staff up to a specific competency level helps to ensure that anyone can properly explain TMH and the process to patients. Providing marketing and informational materials and links to resources such as the National Consortium of Telehealth Resource Centers (www.telehealthre sourcecenter.org/) is helpful. It is now cheap and relatively easy to develop short one to three-minute videos to demonstrate the TMH process. Potential videos include an overview of TMH from an actual provider, a mock session between a patient and provider, and next steps, including scheduling of future sessions.

> *Recommendation*: Conduct at least one test session with each patient prior to initiating any services. The test session should last no more than 10 minutes and can be completed by an assistant or other staff. The purpose of the session is to test connectivity, answer questions, and orient patients to the technology. It can also be used to evaluate the appropriateness of the patient location and to have an initial view of the location to use for verification in later sessions. Remind patients of the need to have a secure and private location and that TMH sessions should be treated with the same standards as in-person sessions. Keep the clinical setting free of clutter and remember to also represent the space as a professional, clinical environment.

Consent, Documentation, and Billing

There are additional logistical issues to consider prior to engaging in TMH services. The clinician and/or the agency need to have a clear plan for obtaining consent from patients to use telehealth as a specific entity and must have a plan also for documenting this consent within the chart or medical record. This documentation should include both the consent acknowledged and the location of both the clinician and the patient in accordance with state statues and limitations which may exist regarding TMH. Determine whether written consent and other documents will be sent electronically through encrypted email and safe systems such as those built into electronic health records, or through other means such as traditional mail or hand delivered if an initial session is conducted in person. The agency should have a plan in place for payment and insurance verification, if necessary, prior to seeing a patient through this modality. This should include verifying that insurance providers will reimburse for and that malpractice coverage will extend to the service.

Clinical Practice—Providing Competent and Ethical Care

Telemental health has been employed in numerous settings, with various patient populations, and is a viable care alternative for a range of mental health concerns. Research and practice have been supported by and informed several practice guidelines to help administrators and clinicians provide TMH services. The American Telemedicine Association (ATA) published its first of now seven TMH-specific guidelines in 2009, with other associations, such as the American Psychological Association (APA) and the American Counseling Association (ACA) publishing their own guidelines as well. The American Psychiatric Association (APA) and ATA published a joint guideline, "Best Practices in Videoconferencing-Based Telemental Health," in 2018 (Shore et al., 2018). These guidelines are critical to setting standards for the ethical delivery of TMH services. The next section of this chapter is intended to build upon those guidelines to focus further on developing practical, clinical competence.

Case Example

A TMH training was conducted for a clinical organization, and a subset of the clinicians were skeptical about the evidence-base and the ability to develop a therapeutic alliance. The evidence-base was presented during the initial session of the training, and most clinicians accepted the evidence as presented; however, a couple of the clinicians remained skeptical about TMH therapeutic alliance as the training progressed to simulated clinical sessions. However, one of the more skeptical clinicians noted during the training debrief that after just a few minutes of the mock TMH session she no longer noticed the technology and was able to focus on her session partner and remarked that the practice session changed her impression of technology-based care.

Establishing Rapport/Therapeutic Alliance

One of the most significant concerns providers have about delivering TMH services is a fear that therapeutic alliance will not be established, resulting in less than adequate treatment outcomes (Richards, Simpson, Bastiampillai, Pietrabissa, & Castelnuovo, 2018). Fortunately, there are strategies to facilitate the therapeutic alliance and research and anecdotal evidence to suggest that therapeutic alliance with TMH is as good as that developed in traditional face-to-face settings (Hernandez-Tejada, Zoller, Ruggiero, Kazley, & Acierno, 2014). It is not uncommon for providers, and patients, to note how quickly one is able to focus on the clinical encounter rather than the technology or other assumed distractions. Therapeutic alliance forms the base for most successful treatments and the following section provides advice about the patient–provider relationship across the treatment spectrum. It is interesting to note that patients tend to report higher levels of alliance than providers (Hubley et al., 2016; Richards et al., 2018; Simpson & Reid, 2014). The reason for this may be as simple as clinicians are trained to focus on the therapeutic alliance and are therefore more aware of nuances (Lopez, Schwenk, Schneck, Griffin, & Mishkind, 2019). Clinicians should take heart knowing that despite their own concerns, patients view the relationship positively, and clinical outcomes do not suffer.

Developing the therapeutic alliance should begin before the first session, as noted previously in the chapter. A study with parolees utilizing telemental health demonstrated that technological difficulties/failures such as poor connection, bad camera angles, and more, can impact a patient's perception of clinician expertise and ability (Farabee, Calhoun, & Veliz, 2016). If these concerns arise, it is meaningful to have a plan for what to do if the connection is lost or another technological failure occurs. This should include a good direct number (not mobile) for the patient (or staff member, if the patient is office-based) who is managing the technology on the patient end.

In an initial session, and periodically afterwards, it is valuable for clinicians to remind themselves of the differences that exist between face-to-face sessions and telemental health sessions. Be acutely aware that nonverbal cues are key to therapeutic alliance, yet with the addition of a camera, one has to more directly address this issue. Many cameras are placed at the top of the computer screen and looking directly at the patient in the screen may appear as if you are looking down. To maintain eye contact, look directly into the camera regularly, even if the video image of the patient is in a different location. If you have a computer arrangement that requires you to regularly look away from the camera, inform the patient of what you are doing, "I want you to know that when I'm looking to the left, I'm looking at my other screen where your chart is located." For a more anxious patient, you may wish to move the camera around your office space, to help them orient and feel comfortable as to the confidentiality and privacy conferred by your space.

Case Example

Mrs. Y is a 35-year-old female who was being treated for depression and anxiety via weekly outpatient telehealth sessions. She connected into her third session on time, though appeared to be located in the family room of her home, rather than in her home office where she had been located for her two previous telehealth sessions. The provider also noticed the sounds of small children in the background and that Mrs. Y appeared to be distracted by something in her close physical vicinity. Provider immediately inquired about Mrs. Y's current physical surroundings, and specifically, about what was demanding her attention. Mrs. Y then informed the provider that she was unable to secure childcare arrangements for her two small children (five years old and eight months old), suggesting that she would be able to care for her children and attend the telehealth session simultaneously. Provider reminded Mrs. Y that, as they had discussed in their initial meeting, attending therapy via telehealth platform is not a solution for one's inability to make childcare arrangements, and that her children need to be supervised by an appropriate guardian (based on her specific state's legal requirements) for the entire duration of each of her telehealth sessions. Mrs. Y was further informed that, for this reason, this session would need to be rescheduled for a time when childcare arrangements can be made.

Safety Within Context of the Clinical Setting Clinical

Telemental health session standards occur within the context of the environment mutually agreed upon between patient and clinician. This includes locations with well-established safety protocols, as well as those requiring additional competence to manage. Given that the context may change, be aware of the impact of TMH on perceptions of control over the clinical interaction. A common argument against expanding the range of TMH settings is that there is limited control over the encounter compared to traditional in-person sessions. However, this argument does not represent the real amount of control a provider has both in session and the significant amount of time outside of sessions when there may not be any patient–provider contact. It also doesn't recognize that for some patients a TMH encounter may be the only direct connection available with a provider. Gros and colleagues (2011) provided one of the first reports of the use of telehealth services to identify suicidality in a patient and intervene with a safety plan using a series of enhanced telecommunications. The authors suggest that the telehealth equipment provided three benefits during the emergency: (1) A secondary route of communication for the provider, allowing for external safety planning to occur simultaneously, (2) Constant visual observation for ongoing assessment of distress, and (3) Observation of other potentially self-harming behaviors. The use of TMH in this situation was instrumental to, rather than inhibiting of, patient safety management.

> *Recommendation*: Emergency services such as 9–1–1 calls are local, and it is critical to have patient location, and local emergency service numbers, at the patient's location, prior to any TMH session. All safety planning protocols should be written out in a standard operating procedure and discussed with patients. Discuss the importance of location consistency with patients and be aware of the impact of location on emergency management protocols, including location of emergency resources and emergency contacts. Consider the use of a "Patient Support Person" (PSP) in clinically unsupervised locations, and as clinically indicated. A PSP is a family member, friend, or community member selected by the patient who could be called upon for support in the case of an emergency.

Establishing Guidelines and Standards

Although the hypothetical patient Mrs. Y in the Case Example presented earlier was willing to proceed with her session, the provider determined that the value of this session would likely have been moderated by the distractions caused by her children. Moreover, there are various ethical concerns about allowing a child to be present during their parent's therapy session. This case serves as a reminder that maintaining clinical standards is a mutual role and that the provider ultimately has the responsibility to determine if a session should continue. Therefore, in addition to orienting yourself to technology and the impact of this on alliance, it is also valuable to set mutually agreed upon expectations with the patient prior to a session, including expectations for interruptions such as an expectation to put cell phones away and to minimize the presence of non-necessary individuals. Patients may require education around appropriate attire and space, especially as it relates to privacy for both themselves and the clinical process. Although TMH allows for access to care in alternative locations other than a traditional office setting, there is a need to define those spaces where this is not appropriate. Patients must be in a location that is safe, is private, and has adequate bandwidth connectivity to maintain audio and visual connections throughout the session. Actual locations should be an agreement between the patient and provider. For example, a table at a local coffee shop is not a suitable location, but many providers will consider a patient's personal automobile in the parking lot of the coffee shop to meet location criteria. Additionally, enforce a no-driving policy for the patient to ensure safety and adequate attention to the work being completed. Table 2.2 provides an

Table 2.2 Establishing Alliance and Setting Expectations

Prepare for the Initial Visit:	Develop a clear plan for consent, payments, verifying insurance, and safety planning, and discuss with patients—conduct a test session
Acknowledge the Awkward:	Have open conversations about how TMH services differ from traditional in-person care and work together to overcome any challenges
Set Expectations:	Clearly discuss expectations about maintaining professional environments and encounters—proper attire, location management, privacy, interruptions
Be Engaging:	Be mindful of nonverbal cues, look into the camera, and acknowledge when you may need to look away from the patient
Plan for Technology:	Have a plan for what to do if a connection is lost or there are other technical failures—always have a way to connect that is not bandwidth- or mobile-dependent (e.g., a land-line telephone)

overview of steps to take for establishing the therapeutic alliance and setting expectations (Lopez et al., 2019).

Case Example

Mr. X is a 37-year-old male Operation Iraqi Freedom veteran who was being seen for outpatient mental health services via telehealth. He was consistent in his attendance of a structured, 12-week evidence-based treatment protocol. When Mr. X connected into his fifth session of the protocol, the provider noticed that, instead of his typical background of an NFL team poster on his home office wall, Mr. X's background was now a brick wall. Provider could also hear the ambient noise of a crowd at his location. Provider queried Mr. X about his location, and he informed her that he had an unexpected opportunity to fly to see his favorite NFL team, and that he was presently located at a restaurant outside the stadium. Provider reminded Mr. X that his telehealth sessions should be treated as if they are in-person, with the same level of privacy and focused attention.

Location Verification

The patient in the earlier case was further informed that engaging in a therapy session in a public place, or at any location in which the session can be witnessed by another individual, might lead him to censor himself in various ways or become distracted during the session, which would diminish the effectiveness of the session. The provider also commended the patient for his dedication to his treatment but noted that the session could not commence and would need to be rescheduled. This case example is a good representation of how the use of telehealth can increase access and compliance but still requires verification of the client's location at the beginning of each session. It also deals with consistent boundary setting to protect the privacy and integrity of the session. Location verification is especially important for determining if care is provided across state lines or requires updates to the safety plan. While a patient may not understand jurisdictional requirements, providers must be acutely aware of any licensure and malpractice risks if patients are not in their stated location. Remember that safety planning also requires that providers have the correct phone numbers and other contact information for the specific patient location.

> *Recommendation*: Verify patient location at the beginning of each session. This can be as easy as noting wall art or other aspects of a room during previous sessions and saying something such as "I see the poster

of your NFL team, looks like you are in your home office again." If you do not recognize the location or otherwise doubt where the patient is located, seek verification. If you do not feel able to verify, then it is appropriate to reschedule the session. Always remember to document that you verified the location.

Complying With HIPAA Regulations

A necessary consideration when providing a service via a telehealth platform is compliance with HIPAA standards and guidelines. The Health Insurance Portability and Accountability Act (HIPAA) establishes specific requirements about the protection and secure transmission of protected health information (PHI), including electronic forms for such information (ePHI). Standards for patient privacy and confidentiality that must be upheld when providing a service in person must also be upheld when providing TMH services. Complying with HIPAA via TMH is not an impossible task, but it does have added complexity given that data is being transmitted electronically, and there may be less physical control of documents. The following are recommendations for maintaining compliance with HIPAA regulations:

- Ensure any printed documents are received in a secure location and picked up immediately.
- Use a secure network with encrypted videoconferencing software.
- Encrypt hard drives and all emails and other electronic document transfers with patient data.
- Password-protect your computer (as well as any other devices used to provide services) and change your password regularly (at least twice per year).
- Use a firewall.

Conclusion

The use of TMH services continues to expand, with patients and providers alike benefiting from improved access to efficacious mental health care. Patients have traditionally been more willing to engage with technology-based care, and although several guidelines exist, many providers have expressed reluctance to engage in TMH care because of a lack of training and practical guidance. This chapter was designed to help fill the gaps between guidance and practical tips for implementation. It is admittedly not an exhaustive list of recommendations, as technologies advance, regulations evolve, and patient and provider comfort levels with risk and safety management change. Many of the tips in this chapter will generalize across technologies and situations, and it is our hope that the information provided moves individuals from skeptic to novice or from novice to authority. Table 2.3 provides an overview checklist for conducting TMH sessions.

Table 2.3 Telemental Health Sessions Checklist

- Assess for and work out any technical issues—screen view, sound, microphone, etc.
- Share provider's location—inform client of provider's state licensure and importance of provider being licensed in state where patient is located.
- Verify client's location and specific address.
  o Is client in a private location?
- If not, problem-solve for them finding and using a private location for their sessions and/or keeping their current location private.
  o Is the client in a safe location?
- Are there weapons in their immediate vicinity? If so, inform them that all weapons (e.g., guns, knives, etc.) must be removed from the room where therapy will be occurring (via teleconferencing) and locked up, if possible.
- Inform client that the contact information for their local first responders will be on hand throughout each of their telehealth appointments and that they may be contacted if the client is ever deemed to be in imminent danger (of either mental health or physical health risks), or to be an imminent danger to someone else.
- Determine if support person is warranted and/or prudent.
  o If so, collect the name, likely location, and direct phone number of the person identified, as well as his/her relationship to the client. Obtain an appropriate Release of Information to contact this person, should it be necessary.
- Inform client of limitations to confidentiality. Inform client that the same confidentiality limitations that would apply in person.
- Instruct client of procedures if connections drop.
- Review other important guidelines for attendance of telehealth appointments:
  o Appropriate dress
  o Appropriate behavior
  o Minimizing distractions
  o Telehealth sessions should be treated the same as in-person sessions
  o Verify that the client can't be heard by those around them, thus minimizing the likelihood that they feel the need to censor themselves.
  o Establish the rule that doing therapy via telehealth platform should not be used as a substitute for childcare.

References

Adams, S. M., Rice, M. J., Jones, S. L., Herzog, E., Mackenzie, L. J., & Oleck, L. G. (2018). TeleMental health: Standards, reimbursement, and interstate practice. *Journal of the American Psychiatric Nurses Association, 24*(4), 295–305.

Bashshur, R. L., Shannon, G. W., Bashshur, N., & Yellowlees, P. M. (2015). The empirical evidence for telemedicine interventions in mental disorders. *Journal of Telemedicine and E-Health, 22*(2), 87–113.

Berryhill, M. B., Culmer, N., Williams, N., Halli-Tierney, A., Betancourt, A., Roberts, H., & King, M. (2018). Videoconferencing psychotherapy and depression: A systematic review. *Telemedicine and e-Health,*

Brooks, E., Turvey, C., & Augusterfer, E. F. (2013). Provider barriers to telemental health: Obstacles overcome, obstacles remaining. *Telemedicine and e-Health, 19*(6), 433–437.

Cermack, M. (2006). Monitoring and telemedieince support in remote environments and in human space flight. *British Journal of Anaesthesia, 97*(1), 107–114.

Farabee, D., Calhoun, S., & Veliz, R. (2016). An experimental comparison of telepsychiatry and convention psychiatry for parolees. *Psychiatric Services, 67*, 5.

Fletcher, T. L., Hogan, J. B., Keegan, F., Davis, M. L., Wassef, M., Day, S., & Lindsay, J. A. (2018). Recent advances in delivering mental health treatment via video to home. *Current Psychiatry Reports, 20*, 56–64.

Godleski, L., Darkins, A., & Peters, J. (2012). Outcomes of 98,609 U.S. department of veterans affairs patients enrolled in telemental health services, 2006–2010. *Psychiatric Services, 2012, 63*(4), 383–385.

Gros, D. F., Veronee, K., Strachan, M., Ruggiero, K. J., & Acierno, R. (2011). Managing suicidality in home-based telehealth. *Journal of Telemedicine and Telecare, 17*, 332–335.

Hernandez-Tejada, M. A., Zoller, J. S., Ruggiero, K. J., Kazley, A. S., & Acierno, R. (2014). Early treatment withdrawal from evidence-based psychotherapy for PTSD: Telemedicine and in-person parameters. *International Journal of Psychiatry in Medicine, 48*(1), 22–55.

Hilty, D. M., Ferrer, D. C., Parish, M. B., Johnston, B., Callahan, E. J., & Yellowlees, P. M. (2013). The effectiveness of telemental health: A 2013 Review. *Telemedicine and e-Health, 19*(6), 444–454.

Hubley, S., Schneck, C., Thomas, M., & Shore, J. (2016). Review of key telepsychiatry outcomes. *World Journal of Psychiatry, 6*(2), 269–282.

Jameson, J. P., Farmer, M. S., Head, K. J., Fortney, J., & Teal, C. R. (2011). VA community mental health service providers' utilization of and attitudes toward telemental healthcare: The gatekeeper's perspective. *Journal of Rural Health, 27*, 425–432.

Jenkins-Guarnieri, M. A., Pruitt, L. D., Luxton, D. D., & Johnson, K. (2015). Patient perceptions of telemental health: Systematic review of direct comparisons to in-person psychotherapeutic treatments. *Telemedicine and e-Health, 21*(8), 652–660.

Kramer, G. M., Kinn, J. T., & Mishkind, M. C. (2015). Legal, regulatory, and risk management issues in the use of technology to deliver mental health care. *Cognitive and Behavioral Practice, 22*, 258–268.

Lopez, A., Schwenk, S., Schneck, C. D., Griffin, R. J., & Mishkind, M. C. (2019). Technology-based mental health treatment and the impact on the therapeutic alliance. *Current Psychiatry Reports, 21*, 76–82.

Mackey, T. K., Kalyanam, J., Katsuki, T., & Lanckriet, G. (2017). Twitter-based detection of illegal online sale of prescription opioid. *American Journal of Public Health, 107*(12), 1910–1915.

Mishkind, M. C., Boyd, A., Kramer, G. M., Ayers, T., & Miller, P. A. (2013). Evaluating the benefits of a live, simulation-based telebehavioral health training for a deploying army reserve unit. *Military Medicine, 187*(12), 1322–1327.

Mishkind, M. C., Waugh, M., & Hubley, S. (2018). Telepsychiatry and health technologies: A guide for mental health professionals. In P. Yellowlees & J. H. Shore (Eds.), *Evidence base for use of videoconferencing and other technologies in mental health care*. Arlington, VA: American Psychiatric Association Publishing.

Myers, K., Nelson, E. L., Rabinowitz, T., Hilty, D., Baker, D., Barnwell, S. S., . . . Bernard, J. (2017). American telemedicine association practice guidelines for telemental health with children and adolescents. *Telemedicine and e-Health, 23*(10), 779–804.

Richards, P., Simpson, S., Bastiampillai, T., Pietrabissa, G., & Castelnuovo, G. (2018). The impact of technology on therapeutic alliance and engagement in psychotherapy: The therapist's perspective. *Clinical Psychologist, 22*(2), 171–181.

Shore, J. H. (2015). The evolution and history of telepsychiatry and its impact on psychiatric care: Current implications for psychiatrists and psychiatric organizations. *International Review of Psychiatry, 27*(6), 469–475.

Shore, J. H., Mishkind, M. C., Bernard, J., Doarn, C. R., Bell, I., Bhatla, R., . . . Vo, A. (2014). A lexicon of assessment and outcome measures for telemental health. *Telemedicine and e-Health, 23*(3), 282–292.

Shore, J. H., Yellowlees, P., Caudill, R., Johnston, B., Turvey, C., Mishkind, M., . . . Hilty, D. (2018). Best practices in videoconferencing-based telemental health. *Telemedicine and e-Health, 24*(11), 827–832.

Simpson, S. G., & Reid, C. L. (2014). Therapeutic alliance in videoconferencing psychotherapy: A review. *Australian Journal of Rural Health, 22*(6), 280–299.

Turvey, C., Coleman, M., Dennison, O., et al. (2013). ATA practice guidelines for video-based online mental health services. *Telemedicine and e-Health, 19*(9), 722–730.

Wright, J. H., Mishkind, M., Eells, T. D., & Chan, S. R. (2019). Computer-assisted cognitive-behavior therapy and mobile apps for depression and anxiety. *Current Psychiatry Reports, 21*, 62–70.

Zundel, K. M. (1996). Telemedicine: History, applications, and impact on librarianship. *Bulletin of the Medical Library Association, 84*(1), 71–79.

3 Internet–Based Mental Health Interventions

Evidence, Practical Considerations, and Future Directions

Kelly Blasko, Robert Ciulla, Renée Cavanagh, Julie Kinn, Christina Armstrong, Logan Micheel and Tim Hoyt

Using the Internet for Health Education

A growing number of people are using the internet to access information about medical care and to obtain information about diagnostics, treatment options, and self-care topics. With no more than a subscription to an internet service, a user interested in obtaining information about a medical condition has 24-hour access to an array of web-based information, guidance, and links to additional support. Recent or enduring symptoms either experienced personally or by a loved one can be checked quickly, privately, and usually at no cost. Other reasons for online health-seeking include a lack information about a particular condition, dissatisfaction with one-on-one interactions, or a desire to be an empowered health care consumer (Lee, Hoti, Hughes, & Emmerton, 2014). The availability of web-based medical content represents a move away from a "hierarchical, unidirectional, health operator-patient model" (Rossi, 2006, p. 10) to a focus on the patient, "a self-help movement proper, for which the Internet is the natural sphere of expression" (Rossi, 2006, p. 10). Writers have noted the disruptive combination of personal health records combined with social networks and the shift from a doctor-as-gatekeeper model to a more patient-centric model (Eysenbach, 2008). Immediate access to medical information is producing a "mental health literate" community of both patients and clinicians (Christensen & Griffiths, 2003). Online information can be delivered in a variety of formats, including both passive content (narrative text, videos, podcasts, and blogs) and active content (interactive modules, games, surveys, assessments, and guided navigation). With the greater aim toward consumer mental health literacy (Jorm, 2000), these web tools provide information to expand a user's knowledge, attitude, intended behaviors, and recognition of mental illness symptoms (Brijnath, Protheroe, Mahtani, & Antoniades, 2016). The stigma associated with mental illness may lead to avoiding or postponing treatment. Delaying needed services may result in worsening symptoms and, in tragic circumstances, patients dying by suicide (Han, Compton, Gfroerer, & McKeon, 2014). In instances where stigma is not a concern, the availability of providers may be lacking. One analysis found that the number of mental health providers met only 26 percent of the need (Henry J. Kaiser Family Foundation, 2018). Internet-based therapies can minimize the impact of provider unavailability, geographical distance from a professional, a lack of providers who are versed in a particular therapy, waiting lists for care, transportation difficulties, and lack of insurance (Rogers, Lemmen, Kramer, Mann, & Chopra, 2017). Other advantages include access to evidence-based treatments, enhanced learning insofar as a patient can return to a module, and providers' ability to monitor progress remotely (Andersson & Titov, 2014).

Health Information Online: Is It Accurate?

Although the potential to reach so many internet users with evidenced-based health information is considerable (Rogers et al., 2017), the emergence of internet-based medical information and the overwhelming number of public-facing sites raises concerns about the quality and the accuracy of the content. Whereas the flexibility of websites allows them to deliver most any type of intervention, the theoretical underpinning of a site's content and capabilities may be difficult to ascertain. For example, a repository of psychoeducational information found on a website may or may not have been curated by a subject matter expert or with the latest evidence-based materials (Bhochhibhoya, Hayes, Branscum, & Taylor, 2015). One study found that only 67.5% of all evaluated web sites had content that was rated "good" or better in quality (Grohol, Slimowicz, & Granda, 2014). The most common web sites in the study's searches were HelpGuide, PsychCentral, Mayo Clinic, Wikipedia, and WebMD. Further, the quality of the information was not uniform across disorders: higher-quality information was more evident for dysthymia, bipolar disorder, and schizophrenia, whereas lower-quality information was found for phobia, anxiety, and panic disorder. Clearly, a site's popularity is not enough to recommend it in a clinical setting (Christensen & Griffiths, 2003).

The Internet and Peer Support

To prompt compliance and facilitate peer support, websites integrate communication tools like email reminders and social forums. Pew found that 24% of adults obtained health-based information from others with the same health condition (Fox & Duggan, 2013). Knowing about others' experiences with medical illnesses can affect overall adjustment and how decisions are made, underscoring the particular value in peer-to-peer support available online (Ziebland & Wyke, 2012). Given the reach of this technology, internet-based treatments can also have a substantial role in population-health initiatives to help with early intervention following a large-scale traumatic event (Ennis, Sijercic, & Monson, 2018).

Internet-Based Interventions: The Evidence

Beyond information searches, nomenclature issues have arisen when discussing the use of the internet for treatment purposes. Internet-based interventions (IBIs) have been referred to as "digital therapy, internet interventions . . . computerized psychotherapy . . . web-based psychotherapy and online psychotherapy" (Andersson, Titov, Dear, Rozental, & Carlbring, 2019, p. 22). Another report cited several other terms: "e-therapy, cybertherapy, online therapy, e-mental health, computer-mediated interventions . . . web-based treatments" (Berger, 2017, p. 2). The American Psychological Association (APA) included the internet in its definition of "telecommunication technologies," as follows: "telephone, mobile devices, interactive videoconferencing, email, chat, text, and Internet (e.g., self-help websites, blogs, and social media)" (Joint Task Force for the Development of Telepsychology Guidelines for Psychologists, 2013, p. 792). This range in labels reflects the current status of health technologies and the need for a standardized lexicon—is it *telemedicine* or *telehealth* or *telemental health*? Berger (2017) defined an internet intervention as "any kind of psychological intervention in which mental health care professionals use the internet to provide mental health services" (p. 2). For this chapter's purpose, internet-based intervention involves "treatments that are mainly delivered via the internet with at least some therapeutic tasks delegated to the computer" (Andersson & Titov, 2014, p. 4).

Psychologically oriented internet interventions had their origin in evidence-based treatments, the large volume of guided self-help literature, and the development of computerized cognitive testing (Andersson, 2018). Several researchers have noted that cognitive-behavioral therapy is the most frequently used treatment method in internet-based programs for mental disorders (Hennemann, Farnsteiner, & Sander, 2018; Sander, Rausch, & Baumeister, 2016), although programs also exist for psychodynamic and acceptance and commitment therapy (ACT) (Andersson, 2018). Programs using internet-based cognitive-behavioral therapy (ICBT) tend to approximate actual face-to-face clinical encounters with respect to length and content (Carlbring, Andersson, Cuijpers, Riper, & Hedman-Lagerlöf, 2018). The ICBT platform contains assessment tools and content delivered via text, audio and video, homework, repeated symptom measures, and clinician interactions or automated support (Andersson et al., 2019). ICBT can deliver treatment anonymously, treat patients located in areas where there is a shortage of mental health providers, and complement face-to-face cognitive-behavioral therapy (Arnberg, Linton, Hultcrantz, Heintz, &

Jonsson, 2014; Baumeister, Reichler, Munzinger, & Lin, 2014; Erbe, Eichert, Riper, & Ebert, 2017; Olthuis et al., 2016).

ICBT has demonstrated consistently strong support for the treatment of psychiatric and somatic disorders (Andersson, Cuijpers, Carlbring, Riper, & Hedman, 2014; Andrews, Cuijpers, Craske, McEvoy, & Titov, 2010; Karyotaki et al., 2017; Vigerland et al., 2016). Using ICBT to treat anxiety disorders (e.g., panic, social anxiety, generalized anxiety disorder) is effective and comparable to face-to-face CBT (Andersson et al., 2014; Arnberg et al., 2014; Richards, Richardson, Timulak, & McElvaney, 2015; van Beugen, 2014). The impact of ICBT for eating disorders appears to be related to reducing specific symptoms, such as body dissatisfaction (Andersson et al., 2014) or binging and purging behaviors (Dölemeyer, Tietjen, Kersting, & Wagner, 2013), although findings from a meta-analysis by Loucas and colleagues (2014) did not support the use of IBI for eating disorder symptoms due to limited evidence.

In recent years, Mindfulness-Based Interventions (MBI), including Acceptance and Commitment Therapy (ACT), Mindfulness-Based Cognitive Therapy (MBCT), and Mindfulness-Based Stress Reduction (MBSR), have been integrated into IBIs. Internet-based MBI (IMBI) has demonstrated equivalency to face-to-face treatment for stress management, demonstrating comparable effect sizes to in-person MBSR and MBCT (Spijkerman, Pots, & Bohlmeijer, 2016). Additionally, IMBI has demonstrated significant reductions in depression and anxiety symptoms (Brown, Glendenning, Hoon, & John, 2016; Sevilla-Llewellyn-Jones, Santesteban-Echarri, Pryor, McGorry, & Alvarez-Jimenez, 2018; Spijkerman et al., 2016). Although IMBI has demonstrated improvements in anxiety and depression symptoms, more research is needed to determine whether treatment outcomes utilizing this methodology are equivalent to face-to-face MBI.

Unguided Internet–Based Interventions

Internet interventions are either entirely automated (i.e., without human support) or involve some level of human support guiding the intervention (Baumeister et al., 2014). At one end of the spectrum, unguided self-help may involve simple information-seeking or minimal guidance such as topic suggestions by a therapist who is familiar with (though has not necessarily created) the recommended site. During unguided use, a user visits a website that provides health information and peruses content about a topic of interest, such as nutrition or sleep hygiene, or arrives at the site wanting information about a specific symptom. A user may also be seeking information or clarification about medical terms or diagnoses following an appointment with a health professional. The intent is educational, and the target site is most likely one that provides aggregated content from a range of contributors that includes medical and behavioral literature. "Pure" (i.e., unguided) self-help sites have certain advantages: they reach users who are unwilling or not able to obtain direct care and may be less costly than assisted or guided interventions (Fleming et al., 2018).

Illustrative Case #1: For the past month, Jane has been feeling down, lacks energy, can't concentrate, and doesn't have much of an appetite. Having only a general idea of what depression is, Jane logs on to WebMD where she has gotten information previously about a medical problem. The site is easy to navigate, and Jane finds depression under Health A-Z and arrives at a page called Depression Health Center. This page provides information about depression (e.g., an overview, causes, treatments), offers video-based instruction, blogs, message boards, a how-much-do-you-know-about-depression quiz, various topic-related articles, and a depression assessment. *Jane is using the internet in an unguided fashion to learn about a mood problem.*

Another form of unguided use involves sites that are more *programmatic* in design. Such sites have a specific clinical (or perhaps transdiagnostic) purpose, steering the user through a series of modules that mirror treatment that can be obtained in real-world clinical settings. The intent of such programs surpasses basic education or bibliotherapy-type reading materials. Such programs are likely to include a range of content and multimedia presentations designed to produce a clinical outcome.

Illustrative Case #2: Jane is now more knowledgeable about her condition but reluctant to schedule an appointment with a provider. Through her search, she learns about a website that provides depression treatment in a series of modules, based on something called cognitive-behavior therapy (CBT). She enrolls in the course and works through the program, taking periodic assessments, completing homework assignments before accessing a new module, and learning various skills to help her with her moods. *Jane has participated in an unguided, modularized, internet-based intervention.*

Guided (Blended) Internet-Based Interventions

At the other end of the spectrum is internet-based psychotherapy involving more direct therapist input, such that internet content is augmented via email, text-based chat, and videoconferencing (Berger, 2017). Guided internet-based interventions (also referred to as blended interventions), tend to use elements of both face-to-face and an internet component (Erbe et al., 2017). The user logs in to a site, reviews materials sequentially or in modules, completes homework assignments included in the lessons, and takes periodic computerized questionnaires; a therapist is available to monitor progress (Andersson & Titov, 2014). Most studies describe a condition in which the clinician guides the patient through the internet program, offering feedback on homework and responses to questions (Andersson et al., 2019). Therapist-delivered interventions may occur in real time (i.e., synchronous, as in a live telephone call) or delayed (i.e., asynchronous such as an email), and may be used in combination over time with a particular patient (Andersson & Titov, 2014). Guided ICBT tends to show better results when compared with unguided ICBT (Andersson, 2018; Andersson et al., 2019). In a systematic review and meta-analysis, guided ICBT and face-to-face treatment showed equivalent effects (Andersson et al., 2014). An economic evaluation of internet-based treatment found that for depression, anxiety, alcohol use, and smoking cessation, guided interventions were more cost-effective when compared with face-to-face treatment-as-usual and unguided ICBT (Donker et al., 2015). Compared to stand-alone face-to-face care, blended treatments can save a clinician time and lessen dropout rates (Erbe et al., 2017). Such IBIs may also be valuable for aftercare or treatment maintenance (Erbe et al., 2017).

Illustrative Case #3: Jack's primary care physician has referred him to a psychologist for depression treatment. At the end of the initial evaluation, the psychologist refers Jack to a website that involves a series of skills-development modules. The psychologist instructs Jack to complete the first module and the homework assignment for that module before Jack's next appointment. The psychologist explains that the website will help Jack with learning about depression and will provide practice with cognitive-based exercises. *The integration of an internet intervention with face-to-face treatment is an example of a guided (blended) intervention.*

Factors Influencing the Effectiveness of Internet-Based Interventions

When using an IBI, providers must be cognizant of the role played by user engagement, defined as the length of time users are willing to visit a website and complete the intervention. Content delivery and intervention length can significantly impact user engagement when the face-to-face component is removed (Iloabachie, 2011; Kohl, Crutzen, & de Vries, 2013). Research of IBIs indicates that consumer engagement is a barrier in measuring effectiveness (Kohl et al., 2013) and positive outcomes. This particular relationship has been difficult to research because the main purpose of much of the research is often focused on evaluating the intervention when used (Mouthaan et al., 2013). This research design often forces completion of the intervention with incentives or mechanisms (e.g., supervised classroom-based delivery) that limit moving through the intervention until all the parts are completed (Champion, Newton, Stapinski, & Teesson, 2016; Litz et al., 2014). Thus, an understanding of real-world consumer engagement in the IBI is often lacking. Relatedly, longer treatment duration also appeared to bolster treatment effects, with greater symptom reduction associated with ICBT programs lasting longer than eight weeks (Sijbrandij, Kunovski, & Cuijpers, 2016).

Several techniques increase patient engagement in IBIs. Whereas personal reminders like phone calls, emails, and face-to-face interactions can improve rates of completion (Calear & Christensen, 2010; Christensen et al., 2014), this approach may make an intervention more expensive to implement because of the labor required. Other effective user engagement strategies include leveraging interactive content, gaming with a reward system, homework that can be completed both online and offline, shorter interventions, more focused content that is directly relevant to the intervention, peer forums, and introduction and follow-up by providers (Calear & Christensen, 2010; Iloabachie et al., 2011; Mouthaan et al., 2013; Van Voorhees et al., 2009, 2011). A systematic review of web-based mental health literacy conducted by Brijnath and colleagues (2016) found that these interventions were more likely to be successful if they included a structured program with guidance through steps tailored to a specific population (e.g., military service members, young adults with depressive symptoms) and demographic variables (e.g., gender, age), delivering evidenced-based content and promoting interactivity and experiential learning. Another engagement strategy is to integrate technology into face-to-face or videoconferencing connections vs. stand-alone messaging, particularly with high-risk patients (Novotny, 2017). Baumeister and colleagues (2014) noted that further study is needed to determine more precisely the amount of the guidance-type dosage that is needed and suggested a clinical approach that provides more guidance at the outset of the internet-based intervention, gradually moving toward increased self-management. However, depending on the availability of resources (e.g., in a public health setting) and where the presenting problem is subacute, an unguided intervention may be a better choice (Baumeister et al., 2014).

The benefits of IBI notwithstanding, a few other implementation factors should be noted. For example, internet-based treatment programs carry development costs that include updating content and ongoing maintenance (Donker et al., 2015). The cost for provider involvement (e.g., in the case that email reminders or provider follow-up is used) may be high, depending on the time commitment and the provider's qualifications. Conversely, ICBT has also demonstrated considerable reductions in clinician's time, which may be translated to cost-savings (Arnberg et al., 2014; Baumeister et al., 2014; Erbe et al., 2017; Pihlaja et al., 2018). If content is not maintained, then even formally researched IBI may become unavailable. For example, one evaluation found that out of 268 IBI studies with RCTs, less than a quarter of them (21.3%) had functional websites or that a viable means to publicize the internet's effectiveness in helping with health problems to the consumer was lacking (Rogers et al., 2017). Videoconferencing (e.g., via Skype), a synchronous form of communication and thought to be similar to face-to-face therapy (Berger, 2017), also may counteract potential disadvantages in internet-based treatment such as the lack of nonverbal cues that are available during face-to-face clinical encounters, and differences interpreting a text message vs. an actual verbal communication (Ybarra & Eaton, 2005).

Patient-Generated Data and Security

Advancing capabilities can pose new and interesting challenges, particularly with respect to patient-generated data. Data gathered online via a modules-based internet program has features that make it ideal in an evidenced-based culture. Digital data is easy to read and share among a geographically dispersed treatment team, consumer self-reporting can be done in a timely manner, and data can be graphed in either a dashboard-like personal health record or an enterprise-level medical record. Providers can be notified of a data-based concern and connect with the patient accordingly (Skiba, 2014). These benefits notwithstanding, a common concern for providers is how best to review and secure user-generated data. Further, clinicians who are accustomed to physically securing patient files must be cognizant of security issues when managing digital data. When sites are accessed via mobile devices, encouraging patients to use their own device places ownership of the data with patients and allows them to share only the sections that they choose. When considering how best to receive and store data transmissions from patients, providers need to be guided by existing policies and guidance regarding the protection of patient health data included in the Health Insurance Portability and Accountability Act (HIPAA, 1996; HIPAA, 2003) and the Health Information Technology for Economic and Clinical Health Act (HITECH, 2009). These foundational policies provide excellent guidance for providers to ensure the protection of patient health information and are applicable regardless of the platform.

Barriers to Internet Access

Though as many as 89% of Americans are online (Pew Research Center, 2019), concerns remain regarding barriers to internet access. Access can be affected by low socioeconomic status, living in a rural setting, and being over age 65 (Internet Live Stats, 2019). Because IBIs can have a non-response rate ranging between 30%–65% for particular patient groups (El Alaoui, Ljótsson, Hedman, Svanborg, Kaldo, & Lindefors, 2016; Berger et al., 2011; Høifødt et al., 2015; Johansson, Andersson, et al., 2012; Vernmark et al., 2010), it is important for clinicians to be aware of potential factors and patient characteristics that may predict better outcomes. Studies evaluating severity of illness as a potential predictor to response to IBIs were mixed (Andersson et al., 2005; Proudfoot et al., 2003; Ruwaard et al., 2009). Low-risk populations were less likely to complete interventions that were designed for high-risk populations (Beintner, Jacobi, & Taylor, 2012; Mouthan et al., 2013). An evaluation of an online prevention intervention, HEAL, for prolonged grief, found that if participants used the intervention too early in their grieving process it might circumvent the natural course of healing (Litz et al., 2014). Another study found a significant age effect, with a younger age predicting better outcomes (Donker et al., 2013). In another study comparing two different IBIs for depression, the strength of preference of treatment type was a predictor of response to treatment (Johansson, Sjöberg, et al., 2012).

Practice Considerations

Clinicians recommending the vast resources of the internet during clinical encounters should be attuned to several considerations. Determining when in the course of treatment to introduce an internet-based intervention will depend on the purpose of the recommendation. The internet can be used to help educate patients regarding their presenting complaints: "Before the next session, log on to the National Center for PTSD website and read the following." In this instance, patients can be referred to a website for informational support anytime the clinician has a clear understanding of the patient's diagnosis and level of understanding.

Alternatively, patients can be referred to a site that specializes in skills development where they can practice a mindfulness exercise to help with stress and then report their experience to the clinician at the next session. In this scenario, the timing of the intervention would be similar to an information-only internet prescription. In both cases, it behooves the clinician to check on the patient's compliance with the homework assignment and any questions about web use or difficulty with access or comprehension of the materials.

Alternatively, a site with modules-based content can support or replace in-office sessions. Again, clinical judgment is indicated as to when to introduce the modules. A modules-based website (patient transits linearly through several interactive modules devoted to symptom-reduction and skills development) places higher demand on the patient and should be introduced with periodic therapeutic guidance and encouragement. In cases in which there is difficulty with the content, patients can be encouraged to repeat a module. As with treatments that do not involve the internet (or some other form of technology such as mobile apps), recurrent difficulty with content or failure to complete homework assignments should receive the therapist's attention. The individual's commitment to the treatment plan should be discussed and areas that are impeding progress resolved. Where user engagement with the website is problematic, the clinician might consider bolstering the internet intervention with other forms of support, including phone contacts, emails and, of course, scheduling in-person sessions. An alternative to an in-the-office session might include videoconferencing, which allows the patient and the therapist to directly engage visually.

Internet-based interventions have shown effectiveness with a range of psychological conditions, and the literature suggests that IBIs seem particularly well suited to a cognitive-behavioral model of treatment, though other clinical models (e.g., psychodynamic) have been studied. Clinicians should routinely review a site's quality and accuracy, and when applicable (e.g., a modules-based site), whether the site is grounded in an evidenced-based theoretical model. Clinicians should not assume that the web development team is refreshing the site's content on a regular basis.

Regarding patient-generated data, the patient will want to know how to use a site's assessment tools and how frequently they should take an assessment; if the data are stored on the site and if so how secure the site is; and whether the data can be transmitted directly to the clinician or uploaded to an electronic health record. Knowing how others have coped with a similar condition (peer support) may help a patient adjust to a newly diagnosed condition. Providers should be mindful of the risk of overuse of personal technologies, a circumstance in which an individual is spending an inordinate amount of time on the internet to their detriment.

There are other general considerations: Does the patient have internet access and if so how versed is she in using the internet for informational or potentially skills-building purposes? Has the patient used the internet previously to learn about a health condition, and what was the experience like? Does the patient express willingness to incorporate health technology into the treatment plan or is there skepticism? Perhaps the patient expresses concern that an internet-based intervention might be a barrier to developing a healthy therapeutic relationship with the provider. Between sessions, how frequently should the patient log on to the site? Does the site require registration and an access fee? Is the website transdiagnostic (include information about multiple health conditions) or condition-specific (PTSD, substance abuse, depression, etc.). If the site contains multiple conditions, the clinician should help the patient navigate to the targeted information; guiding the user through the site could be done in the office setting, with clear instructions about next steps.

Health technologies such as websites and mobile apps might not be suitable for individuals with physical or cognitive impairments, or for those with technology-centered delusions. A patient's age may be a limiting factor: in addition to possible disabilities, the older patient may lack the necessary technical equipment or comfort level necessary to engage with internet-oriented interventions.

Future Directions: Web 3.0

Two foundational changes are altering the way health care teams and patients use internet resources: the merging of internet and mobile technologies and the maturity of Web 3.0. Patients will be able to interact with internet and mobile resources in ways that extend the reach of providers and provide additional avenues for care. The merging of web and mobile technology and the broad integration of Web 3.0 will help health care teams increase patient engagement and overcome some barriers to care. This section addresses these transformations and what they mean for health care in the coming years.

While several valuable resources and interventions are still only available on a website or only available on a mobile application, web and mobile technologies are merging and eliminating the need for patients to choose between the two. The digital health applications that patients access on smartphones and tablets often store data to cloud-based (i.e., internet-based) servers. Many of these apps are mobile-friendly views of internet websites. In other words, a mobile app user may in fact be using a website with the look and feel of a mobile app. Many online interventions now include companion mobile apps (see chapter 4 for a larger discussion of mobile apps to promote patient health). However, instead of differentiating between websites and mobile apps, it is preferable to focus on the type of digital content that will provide the most benefit and then prescribing the fitting form. Increasingly, digital content will be available on multiple platforms.

Web 3.0 is a label for another important change: the growing use of artificial intelligence and increases in the effectiveness of machine-led information processing and data mining (Aziz & Madani, 2015; Rudman & Bruwer, 2016; Yang, Xie, & Chen, 2018). Users will first observe these changes in improved search results. Currently, if a patient conducts an internet search for a clinical symptom, standard search engines will return the most common results about the symptom and may provide references to resources and emergency assistance. With Web 3.0, the search engine may return results such as the contact information for the patient's health care team, reminders for the patient's upcoming appointments, directions to the closest pharmacy, or even potential causes for the symptom due to other factors the system mined about the patient.

Technologies such as machine learning and artificial intelligence are still emerging. For example, when chatting with a virtual assistant on a website to purchase a product, most users can clearly detect that they are interacting with a machine. However, as natural language searching and data mining mature, so will virtual assistants. Indeed, users will have difficulty detecting when they are interacting with a digital tool. This change will result in more realistic digital health interventions and better search results, but may also cause more user distrust (Anderson, Rainie, & Luchsinger, 2018). For example, patients may question whether an electronic message from a provider is truly a personal communication or instead a form of artificial intelligence. To increase patient trust as Web 3.0 expands, it is incumbent on health systems and providers to identify when patient-facing tools are leveraging artificial intelligence. These topics are discussed fully in chapter 14.

Conclusion

Technology is transforming the way that health care is delivered. Going forward, digital health tools will provide consumers with "always-on access to care" (Healthcare Information and Management Systems Society, 2019, p. 5). Clinical practice in an age of connectivity involves several important developments: an educated consumer who is more fully integrated into the treatment plan; the popularity of social networks and crowd-sourcing as a means to consume and evaluate health information; the advent of wearable sensors that allow users to track exercise and nutrition regimens and obtain physiological feedback; advancements in user interfaces (a "conversational exchange" with the software); files that can upload from a device directly into an electronic health record; "virtual" clinics; and synchronous and asynchronous communication methods (email, texting, instant messaging) that will significantly alter traditional notions about appointment scheduling and the office setting. The future therapist will have "a traditional office and an e-office, an online space for internet therapy," wherein treatment "will be offered both online and offline" (Ybarra & Eaton, 2005, p. 85).

There is good reason for clinicians to turn to the internet to support treatment planning: consumers use websites to obtain information about health conditions, and studies show positive outcomes for internet-based interventions across a range of behavioral concerns. In fact, at the time of the writing of this chapter (mid-2019), there were over 200 controlled studies (and possibly 300, including unpublished studies) evaluating the internet as a platform for health-type information (Andersson, 2018).

Despite the evidence for internet-based interventions, a caveat is warranted. Research participants recruited into a study will be engaged in a rigorous protocol and may be incentivized with rewards or money for participation. There is the question, therefore, as to whether the characteristics of a research participant are similar enough to a typical real-world patient commonly seen in an actual clinic (e.g., with respect to demographics, health history, education, and motivation) (Andersson & Titov, 2014). It is important to consider the utility of internet-delivered interventions in actual clinical settings (apart from the typical research protocol) and the need to gather usage data in real-context environments (e.g., percentage that completed a "therapeutic dose" of the intervention) (Fleming et al., 2018).

The Fleming et al. review of unguided self-help internet programs found lower rates of program completion in real-world settings when compared to controlled trials. Users of psychological services in a traditional clinical setting arrive with varying symptoms, expectations, and, especially, knowledge about technology. It is necessary, therefore, to focus on the characteristics of routine care and develop guidelines for the implementation of internet- and mobile-based interventions in those settings (Hennemann et al., 2018).

Finally, internet-based interventions act as "a complement and sometimes as an alternative, but not a replacement of regular therapy services" (Andersson, 2018, p. 184). The core fundamentals of effective practice will continue to be essential in psychological treatments: comprehensive diagnostics, knowing the evidence, treatment planning, and establishing a therapeutic alliance.

Note

The opinions or assertions contained herein are the private views of the authors and are not to be construed as official or reflecting the views of the U.S. Government, the Department of Defense, or the Defense Health Agency.

References

Andersson, G. (2018). Internet interventions: Past, present and future. *Internet Interventions*, *12*, 181–188. doi:10.1016/j.invent.2018.03.008

Andersson, G., Bergström, J., Holländare, F., Carlbring, P., Kaldo, V., & Ekselius, L. (2005). Internet-based self-help for depression: Randomised controlled trial. *The British Journal of Psychiatry*, *187*, 456–461. doi:10.1192/bjp.187.5.456

Andersson, G., Cuijpers, P., Carlbring, P., Riper, H., & Hedman, E. (2014). Guided internet-based vs. face-to-face cognitive behavior therapy for psychiatric and somatic disorders: A systematic review and meta-analysis. *World Psychiatry*, *13*(3), 288–295. doi:10.1002/wps.20151

Anderson, G., Rainie, L., & Luchsinger, A. (2018). *Artificial intelligence and the future of humans.* Pew Research Center. Retrieved January 10, 2019 from www.pewinternet. org/wpcontent/uploads/sites/9/2018/12/PI_2018.12.10_future-of-ai_FINAL1.pdf

Andersson, G., & Titov, N. (2014). Advantages and limitations of internet-based interventions for common mental disorders. *World Psychiatry*, *13*(1), 4–11. doi:10.1002/ wps.20083

Andersson, G., Titov, N., Dear, B. F., Rozental, A., & Carlbring, P. (2019). Internet-delivered psychological treatments: From innovation to implementation. *World Psychiatry*, *18*(1), 20–28. doi:10.1002/wps.20610

Andrews, G., Cuijpers, P., Craske, M. G., McEvoy, P., & Titov, N. (2010). Computer therapy for the anxiety and depressive disorders is effective, acceptable and practical health care: A meta-analysis. *PLoS One*, *5*(10), e13196.

Arnberg, F. K., Linton, S. J., Hultcrantz, M., Heintz, E., & Jonsson, U. (2014). Internet-delivered psychological treatments for mood and anxiety disorders: A systematic review of their efficacy, safety, and cost-effectiveness. *PLoS One*, *9*(5), e98118. doi:10.1371/ journal.pone.0098118

Aziz, H. A., & Madani, A. (2015). Evolution of the web and its uses in healthcare. *Clinical Laboratory Science, 28*(4), 245–249.

Baumeister, H., Reichler, L., Munzinger, M., & Lin, J. (2014). The impact of guidance on Internet-based mental health interventions—A systematic review. *Internet Interventions, 1*(4), 205–215. doi:10.1016/j.invent.2014.08.003

Beintner, I., Jacobi, C., & Taylor, C. B. (2012). Effects of an internet-based prevention programme for eating disorders in the USA and Germany—a meta-analytic review. *European Eating Disorders Review, 20*(1), 1–8.

Berger, T. (2017). The therapeutic alliance in internet interventions: A narrative review and suggestions for future research. *Psychotherapy Research, 27*(5), 511–524. doi:10.10 80/10503307.2015.1119908

Berger, T., Caspar, F., Richardson, R., Kneubühler, B., Sutter, D., & Andersson, G. (2011). Internet-based treatment of social phobia: A randomized controlled trial comparing unguided with two types of guided self-help. *Behaviour Research and Therapy, 49*(3), 158–169.

Bhochhibhoya, A., Hayes, L., Branscum, P., & Taylor, L. (2015). The use of the internet for prevention of binge drinking among the college population: A systematic review of evidence. *Alcohol and Alcoholism, 50*(5), 526–535.

Brijnath, B., Protheroe, J., Mahtani, K. R., & Antoniades, J. (2016). Do web-based mental health literacy interventions improve the mental health literacy of adult consumers? Results from a systematic review. *Journal of Medical Internet Research, 18*(6), e165. doi:10.2196/jmir.5463

Brown, M., Glendenning, A., Hoon, A. E., & John, A. (2016). Effectiveness of web-delievered Acceptance and commitment therapy in relation to mental health and well-being: A systematic review and meta-analysis. *Journal of Medical Internet Research, 18*(8), e221–235. doi:10.2196/jmir.6200

Calear, A. L., & Christensen, H. (2010). Review of internet-based prevention and treatment programs for anxiety and depression in children and adolescents. *Medical Journal of Australia, 192*(11), S12.

Carlbring, P., Andersson, G., Cuijpers, P., Riper, H., & Hedman-Lagerlöf, E. (2018). Internet- based vs. face-to-face cognitive behavior therapy for psychiatric and somatic disorders: An updated systematic review and meta-analysis. *Cognitive Behavior Therapy, 47*(1), 1–18. doi:10.1080/16506073.2017.1401115

Champion, K. E., Newton, N. C., Stapinski, L. A., & Teesson, M. (2016). Effectiveness of a universal internet-based prevention program for ecstasy and new psychoactive substances: A cluster randomized controlled trial. *Addiction, 111*(8), 1396–1405.

Christensen, H., Batterham, P., Mackinnon, A., Griffiths, K. M., Hehir, K. K., Kenardy, J., & Bennett, K. (2014). Prevention of generalized anxiety disorder using a web intervention, iChill: Randomized controlled trial. *Journal of Medical Internet Research, 16*(9).

Christensen, H., & Griffiths, K. (2003). The internet and mental health practice. *Evidence-Based Mental Health, 6*(3), 66–69.

Dölemeyer, R., Tietjen, A., Kersting, A., & Wagner, B. (2013). Internet-based interventions for eating disorders in adults: A systematic review. *BMC Psychiatry, 13*(1), 207. doi:www.biomedcentral.com/1471-244X/13/207

Donker, T., Batterham, P. J., Warmerdam, L., Bennett, K., Bennett, P., Cuijpers, P., Griffiths, K. M., & Christensen, H. (2013). Predictors and moderators of response to internet-delivered interpersonal psychotherapy and cognitive behavior therapy for depression. *Journal of Affective Disorders, 151*(1), 343–351. doi:10.1016/j. jad.2013.06.020

Donker, T., Blankers, M., Hedman, E., Ljotsson, B., Petrie, K., & Christensen, H. (2015). Economic evaluations of Internet interventions for mental health: A systematic review. *Psychological Medicine, 45*(16), 3357–3376. doi:10.1017/S0033291715001427

El Alaoui, S., Ljótsson, B., Hedman, E., Svanborg, C., Kaldo, V., & Lindefors, N. (2016). Predicting outcome in internet-based cognitive behaviour therapy for major depression: A large cohort study of adult patients in routine psychiatric care. *PloS One, 11*(9), e0161191.

Ennis, N., Sijercic, I., & Monson, C. M. (2018). Internet-delivered early interventions for individuals exposed to traumatic events: Systematic review. *Journal of Medical Internet Research, 20*(11). doi:10.2196/jmir.9795

Erbe, D., Eichert, H. C., Riper, H., & Ebert, D. D. (2017). Blending face-to-face and internet- based interventions for the treatment of mental disorders in adults: Systematic review. *Journal of Medical Internet Research, 19*(9). doi:10.2196/jmir.6588

Eysenbach, G. (2008). Medicine 2.0: Social networking, collaboration, participation, apomediation, and openness. *Journal of Medical Internet Research, 10*(3). doi:10.2196/jmir.1030

Fleming, T., Bavin, L., Lucassen, M., Stasiak, K., Hopkins, S., & Merry, S. (2018). Beyond the trial: Systematic review of real-world uptake and engagement with digital self-help interventions for depression, low mood, or anxiety. *Journal of Medical Internet Research, 20*(6). doi:10.2196/jmir.9275

Fox, S., & Duggan, M. (2013). *Health online 2013.* Washington, DC: Pew Research Center. Retrieved from www.pewinternet.org/2013/01/15/health-online-2013/

Grohol, J. M., Slimowicz, J., & Granda, R. (2014). The quality of mental health information commonly searched for on the Internet. *Cyberpsychology, Behavior, and Social Networking, 17*(4), 216–221. doi:10.1089/cyber.2013.0258

Han, B., Compton, W. M., Gfroerer, J., & McKeon, R. (2014). Mental health treatment patterns among adults with recent suicide attempts in the United States. *American Journal of Public Health, 104*(12), 2359–2368. doi:10.2105/AJPH.2014.302163

Healthcare Information and Management Systems Society (HIMSS) (2019). *2019 healthcare trends forecast: The beginning of a consumer-driven reformation.* Retrieved from www. himss.org/sites/himssorg/files/u397813/2019_HIMSSPreviewandPredictions.pdf

Health Information Technology for Economic and Clinical Health (HITECH) Act 2 U.S.C. § 300jj et seq.; § 17901 et seq (2009).

Health Insurance Portability and Accountability Act (HIPAA) Security Rule, 45 C.F.R. Parts 160, 164 (Subparts A and C) (2003).

Health Insurance Portability and Accountability Act (HIPAA), 42 U.S.C. § 300gg; 29 U.S. C. § 1181 et seq.; 42 U.S. C. 1320d et seq (1996).

Hennemann, S., Farnsteiner, S., & Sander, L. (2018). Internet-and mobile-based aftercare and relapse prevention in mental disorders: A systematic review and recommendations for future research. *Internet Interventions, 14*, 1–17. doi:10.1016/j.invent.2018.09.001

Henry J Kaiser Foundation (2018, December 31). *Mental health care health professional shortage areas.* Retrieved from www.kff.org/other/state-indicator/mental-health-care-health-professional-shortage-areas-

Høifødt, R. S., Mittner, M., Lillevoll, K., Katla, S. K., Kolstrup, N., Eisemann, M., Friborg, O., & Waterloo, K. (2015). Predictors of response to web-based cognitive behavioral therapy with high-intensity face-to-face therapist guidance for depression: A bayesian analysis. *Journal of Medical Internet Research, 17*(9), e197. doi:10.2196/jmir.4351

Iloabachie, C., Wells, C., Goodwin, B., Baldwin, M., Vanderplough-Booth, K., Gladstone, T., & Van Voorhees, B. W. (2011). Adolescent and parent experiences with a primary care/Internet-based depression prevention intervention (CATCH-IT). *General Hospital Psychiatry*, *33*(6), 543–555.

Internet Live Stats (n.d). *Internet users in the world*. Retrieved January 7, 2019 from www. internetlivestats.com/internet-users/

Johansson, R., Andersson, G., Ebmeier, Smit, Kessler, Cuijpers, . . . Cuijpers. (2012). Internet-based psychological treatments for depression. *Expert Review of Neurotherapeutics*, *12*(7), 861–870.

Johansson, R., Sjöberg, E., Sjögren, M., Johnsson, E., Carlbring, P., Andersson, T., et al. (2012). Tailored vs. standardized internet-based cognitive behavior therapy for depression and comorbid symptoms: A randomized controlled trial. *PLoS One*, *7*(5), e36905. doi:10.1371/journal.pone.0036905

Joint Task Force for the Development of Telepsychology Guidelines for Psychologists. (2013).

Guidelines for the practice of telepsychology. *American Psychologist*, *68*(9), 791–800. doi:10.1037/a0035001

Jorm, A. F. (2000). Mental health literacy: Public knowledge and beliefs about mental disorders. *The British Journal of Psychiatry*, *177*(5), 396–401.

Karyotaki, E., Riper, H., Twisk, J., Hoogendoorn, A., Kleiboer, A., Mira, A., & Andersson, G. (2017). Efficacy of self-guided internet-based cognitive behavioral therapy in the treatment of depressive symptoms: A meta-analysis of individual participant data. *JAMA Psychiatry*, *74*(4), 351–359. doi:10.1001/jamapsychiatry. 2017.0044

Kohl, L. F., Crutzen, R., & de Vries, N. K. (2013). Online prevention aimed at lifestyle behaviors: A systematic review of reviews. *Journal of Medical Internet Research*, *15*(7).

Lee, K., Hoti, K., Hughes, J. D., & Emmerton, L. (2014). Dr. Google and the consumer: A qualitative study exploring the navigational needs and online health information-seeking behaviors of consumers with chronic health conditions. *Journal of Medical Internet Research*, *16*(12). doi:10.2196/jmir.3706

Litz, B. T., Schorr, Y., Delaney, E., Au, T., Papa, A., Fox, A. B., & Prigerson, H. G. (2014). A randomized controlled trial of an internet-based therapist-assisted indicated preventive intervention for prolonged grief disorder. *Behaviour Research and Therapy*, *61*, 23–34.

Loucas, C. E., Fairburn, C. G., Whittington, C., Pennant, M. E., Stockton, S., & Kendall, T. (2014). E-therapy in the treatment and prevention of eating disorders: A systematic review and meta-analysis. *Behaviour Research and Therapy*, *63*, 122–131.

Mouthaan, J., Sijbrandij, M., de Vries, G. J., Reitsma, J. B., van de Schoot, R., Goslings, J. C., & Olff, M. (2013). Internet-based early intervention to prevent posttraumatic stress disorder in injury patients: Randomized controlled trial. *Journal of Medical Internet Research*, *15*(8).

Novotny, Amy. (2017). A growing wave of online therapy. *Monitor on Psychology*, *48*(2), 48.

Olthuis, J. V., et al. (2016). Therapist-supported Internet cognitive behavioural therapy for anxiety disorders in adults. *Cochrane Database of Systematic Reviews*, *3*.

Pew Research Center. (2019). *Internet use*. Retrieved from https://www.pewresearch. org/internet/chart/internet-use/

Pihlaja, S., Stenberg, J. H., Joutsenniemi, K., Mehik, H., Ritola, V., & Joffe, G. (2018). Therapeutic alliance in guided internet therapy programs for depression and anxiety disorders—a systematic review. *Internet Interventions*, *11*, 1–10. doi:10.1016/j. invent.2017.11.005

Proudfoot, J., Goldberg, D., Mann, A., Everitt, B., Marks, I., & Gray, J. A. (2003). Computerized, interactive, multimedia cognitive-behavioural program for anxiety and depression in general practice. *Psychological Medicine, 33*(2), 217–227.

Richards, D., Richardson, T., Timulak, L., & McElvaney, J. (2015). The efficacy of internet- delivered treatment for generalized anxiety disorder: A systematic review and meta- analysis. *Internet Interventions, 2*(3), 272–282. doi:10.1016/j.invent.2015.07.003

Rogers, M. A., Lemmen, K., Kramer, R., Mann, J., & Chopra, V. (2017). Internet-delivered health interventions that work: Systematic review of meta-analyses and evaluation of website availability. *Journal of Medical Internet Research, 19*(3). doi:10.2196/jmir.7111

Rossi, P. (2006). Medicine in the internet age: The rise of the network society. *Functional Neurology, 21*(1), 9–13.

Rudman, R., & Bruwer, R. (2016). Defining Web 3.0: Opportunities and challenges. *Electronic Library, 34*(1), 132–154. doi:10.1108/EL-08-2014-0140

Ruwaard, J., Schrieken, B., Schrijver, M., Broeksteeg, J., Dekker, J., & Vermeulen, H. (2009). Standardized web-based cognitive behavioural therapy of mild to moderate depression: A randomized controlled trial with a long-term follow-up. *Cognitive Behavior Therapy, 38*(4), 206–221. doi:10.1080/16506070802408086

Sander, L., Rausch, L., & Baumeister, H. (2016). Effectiveness of internet-based interventions for the prevention of mental disorders: A systematic review and meta-analysis. *JMIR Mental Health, 3*(3). doi:10.2196/mental.6061

Sevilla-Llewellyn-Jones, J., Santesteban-Echarri, O., Pryor, I., McGorry, P., & Alvarez-Jimenez, M. (2018). Web-Based mindfulness interventions for mental health treatment: Systematic review and meta-analysis. *JMIR Mental Health, 5*(3), e10278. doi:10.2196/mental.10278

Sijbrandij, M., Kunovski, I., & Cuijpers, P. (2016). Effectiveness of internet-delivered cognitive behavioral therapy for posttraumatic stress disorder: A systematic review and meta- analysis. *Depression and Anxiety, 33*(9), 783–791.

Skiba, D. J. (2014). The connected age: Digital tools for health. *Nursing Education Perspectives, 35*(6), 415–418.

Spijkerman, M. P. J., Pots, W. T. M., & Bohlmeijer, E. T. (2016). Effectiveness of online mindfulness-based interventions in improving mental health: A review and meta-analysis of randomised controlled trials. *Clinical Psychology Review, 45*, 102–114. doi:10.1016/j.cpr.2016.03.009

van Beugen, S., Ferwerda, M., Hoeve, D., Rovers, M. M., Spillekom-van Koulil, S., van Middendorp, H., & Evers, A. W. (2014). Internet-based cognitive behavioral therapy for patients with chronic somatic conditions: A meta-analytic review. *Journal of Medical Internet Research, 16*(3), e88.

Van Voorhees, B. W., et al. (2009). Randomized clinical trial of an internet-based depression prevention program for adolescents (Project CATCH-IT) in primary care: 12-week outcomes. *Journal of Developmental & Behavioral Pediatrics, 30*(1), 23–37.

Van Voorhees, B. W., Mahoney, N., Mazo, R., Barrera, A. Z., Siemer, C. P., Gladstone, T., & Munoz, R. F. (2011). Internet-based depression prevention over the life course: A call for behavioral vaccines. *Psychiatric Clinics of North America, 34*(1), 167–183.

Vernmark, K., Lenndin, J., Bjärehed, J., Carlsson, M., Karlsson, J., Öberg, J., et al. (2010). Internet administered guided self-help versus individualized e-mail therapy: A randomized trial of two versions of CBT for major depression. *Behaviour Research Therapy, 48*(5), 368–376. doi:10.1016/j.brat.2010.01.005

Vigerland, S., Lenhard, F., Bonnert, M., Lalouni, M., Hedman, E., Ahlen, J., . . . Ljots-son, B. (2016). Internet-delivered cognitive behavioral therapy for children and adolescents: A systematic review and meta-analysis. *Clinical Psychology Review, 50*, 1–10. doi:10.1016/j.cpr.2016.09.005

Yang, R., Xie, W., & Chen, D. (2018). A three-layer model on users' interests mining. *Journal of Information Science, 44*(1), 136–144. doi:10.1177/0165551517743645

Ybarra, M. L., & Eaton, W. W. (2005). Internet-based mental health interventions. *Mental Health Services Research, 7*(2), 75–87.

Ziebland, S., & Wyke, S. (2012). Health and illness in a connected world: How might sharing experiences on the internet affect people's health? *The Milbank Quarterly, 90*(2), 219–249. doi:10.1111/j.1468-0009.2012.00662.x

4 Using Mobile Apps in Mental Health Practice

Eric Kuhn and Pearl McGee-Vincent

Using Mobile Apps in Mental Health Practice

It is estimated that over ten thousand mental health-related mobile applications (apps) are now available in the App Store (for the Apple iOS) and Google Play Store (for the Android operating system) (Torous & Roberts, 2017a). Given this tremendous volume, therapists wanting to incorporate such apps into clinical practice can quickly become overwhelmed when trying to find suitable high-quality apps for their needs. This chapter is intended to provide practical clinical advice to mental health therapists considering bringing mobile apps into care. We begin by briefly reviewing the emerging evidence for the efficacy of mobile mental health apps. Next, we discuss how using apps and other smartphone features can improve the delivery, enhance the impact, and address common shortcomings of traditionally delivered psychotherapy. To realize the promise of using apps in psychotherapy, we then offer recommendations for selecting apps and share practical considerations when using them in care. We conclude by highlighting exciting developments in mobile health technology that are poised to continue to improve clinical care well into the future.

Mobile Apps Can Be Helpful for Mental Health Conditions

Soon after modern smartphones (i.e., those handheld devices with touchscreens, connection to the internet, ability to run apps) became available, clinical intervention researchers began developing and pilot testing mental health apps (e.g., DBT Coach; Rizvi, Dimeff, Skutch, Carroll, & Linehan, 2011). Since then, hundreds of studies have been published demonstrating the feasibility and acceptability of such apps; however, far fewer full-scale, rigorous randomized controlled trials (RCTs)—the gold standard experiment for establishing treatment efficacy—have been conducted. Despite the relative dearth of RCTs, what became clear early on was that mental health apps that delivered self-management interventions showed promise for improving mental health symptoms (Donker et al., 2013). More current reviews and meta-analyses of RCTs of mental health apps have validated this initial impression. For example, two recent meta-analyses of RCTs testing the effect of mental health apps on depression (18 studies) and anxiety symptoms (9 studies) found significant benefits of these apps, with stronger effects being evidenced for studies comparing apps to inactive control conditions (e.g., waitlist) vs. active control conditions. (Firth, Torous, Nicholas, Carney, Pratap, et al., 2017; Firth, Torous, Nicholas, Carney, Rosenbaum, & Sarris, 2017). More germane to the primary focus of this chapter is evidence showing that when mobile technology interventions, including personal digital assistants (PDAs), apps, and text messaging services, are incorporated into traditionally delivered psychotherapy and behavioral health interventions, they can improve outcomes above therapy alone. In fact, in a meta-analysis of 24 RCTs of the effects of integrating a range of mobile interventions into such treatments, smartphone apps (7 studies) showed the strongest effects ($d = .57$) (Lindhiem, Bennett, Rosen, & Silk, 2015).

Improving Care With Smartphones and Apps

Challenges of Evidence-Based Psychotherapies

Effective evidence-based psychotherapies (EBTs) are a first-line treatment for many common mental and behavioral health problems, including depression (mild to moderate), anxiety disorders, post-traumatic stress disorder (PTSD), and insomnia. Most EBTs are cognitive-behavioral therapies (CBT), which typically are conducted over 12–16 weeks and highly structured, following manualized protocols. These therapies commonly include a thorough initial assessment and ongoing monitoring of symptoms, provision of psychoeducation about the mental health condition being treated (e.g., how it develops and is maintained), and a strong rationale for the therapy. Intervention components involve skills to change maladaptive cognitions and behaviors and to better regulate problematic emotions (e.g., anxiety, anger, and low mood). To maximize benefit, they also routinely require patients to complete between-session homework in order to engage in therapeutic exercises and reinforce development of skills. For example, many CBT approaches include monitoring and challenging negative cognitions, practicing relaxation techniques, or completing in vivo exposure assignments. CBTs are highly collaborative, with the therapist and patient partnering to set and achieve therapy goals. These common features of CBTs make them ideally suited for enhanced delivery and improved outcomes through patient-facing mobile apps.

However, some parameters of psychotherapy can reduce its availability, breadth, and ultimate public health impact. Unlike pharmacological interventions for mental health conditions, psychotherapy is resource- and time-intensive. Preparation time is required for reviewing session content and gathering patient materials, for example, and for photocopying assessment and homework forms. Patients often complete assessments during valuable session time, requiring the therapist to score measures and graph data to inform care. EBTs typically involve delivery to only one individual or a small group (4–8 patients) at a time, requiring 60 to 90 minutes, or longer. Furthermore, given their foundation in clinical science, EBTs are usually intended to primarily focus on only one presenting problem or mental health diagnosis.

In addition to the structural constraints of psychotherapy, other challenges often arise when delivering treatment. For example, many patients miss sessions without notice, which is associated with a slower rate of improvement and reduced overall benefit (Xiao, Hayes, Castonguay, McAleavey, & Locke, 2017). Moreover, many patients fail to complete therapy (i.e., dropout). In fact, across 115 CBT outcome studies, more than a quarter of participants dropped out (26.2%), with the highest rate being for depression (36.4%; Fernandez, Salem, Swift, & Ramtahal, 2015). Rates of dropout in real-world clinical practice can be even higher (e.g., 38.5%; Kehle-Forbes, Meis, Spoont, & Polusny, 2016). In addition to undermining clinical benefit, such adherence issues squander scarce and costly treatment resources. Unfortunately, even when patients are adherent and complete treatment, they may not have an adequate response. For example, at the completion of EBTs for PTSD, a substantial proportion of veteran patients do not achieve clinically significant improvement (30–51%) and only about a third no longer have a PTSD diagnosis (Steenkamp, Litz, Hoge, & Marmar, 2015)

Incorporating smartphones and mental health apps into psychotherapy could help address these practical challenges and possibly even improve outcomes. It is estimated that 81% of adults in the United States now have smartphones (Pew Research Center, 2019a). Smartphones are truly personal devices, so they are almost always carried or within arm's reach and typically are not shared between individuals. This means they can be used discreetly in the moment of need. As communication devices that are nearly always connected to Wi-Fi or cellular service, they can be used to obtain social support through calls, text messaging, participating in social media, and email.

How Apps Could Improve Psychotherapy

While emerging research is showing the benefit of including apps in care (Lindhiem et al., 2015), an understanding of how patients benefit from using apps is lagging. There are several potential mechanisms through which apps could produce benefits. Upon starting psychotherapy, patients' expectancy that the treatment will result in improvement in symptoms significantly relates to outcome ($d = .24$; Constantino, Arnkoff, Glass, Ametrano, & Smith, 2011). High-quality, professionally designed apps from reputable sources (e.g., government or academia) could increase the therapy's credibility and counter negative patient expectations that therapy will not be effective for them. For example, therapists who delivered PE (Prolonged Exposure) while using PE Coach expressed sentiments that having a professional-looking app legitimized the treatment and improved patient perceptions of its effectiveness (Reger et al., 2017).

Another way in which apps may improve care occurs when an app serves as a cognitive aid. Once therapy is underway, mental health apps could improve care by reducing the number of missed sessions and possibly even preventing dropout. To fully realize the potential benefits of psychotherapy, patients must consistently attend sessions and complete their course of care. As forgetting is the most common reason for missed appointments (Carrion, Swann, Kellert-Cecil, & Barber, 1993), apps can provide appointment reminders to overcome such failures of prospective memory. Through self-monitoring, apps can provide evidence of improvement possibly even before it is noticeable to the patient. This could be helpful, as patients who do not believe they are improving are more likely to drop out (Bados, Balaguer, & Saldaña, 2007). Likewise, app-based assessment and monitoring of therapy engagement could lead to improved and earlier identification of treatment non-adherence, which, if addressed, could reduce the risk of dropout (Lambert, 2017).

Probably the area where mental health apps could have the largest impact is on improving homework completion. Homework is an essential component of most EBTs, with completion of homework being associated with more positive therapy outcomes ($r = .26$; Mausbach, Moore, Roesch, Cardenas, & Patterson, 2010). It is encouraging that even small improvements in homework adherence could lead to substantial benefits; for example, if PE patients complete only two of the seven assigned imaginal exposures each week, they are twice as likely to remit vs. those who complete fewer (Cooper et al., 2017). When mobile apps are included in psychotherapy, most therapists agree that they improve homework adherence (Kuhn et al., 2015; Miller et al., 2017), and findings from a small-scale RCT of the CBT-I Coach app suggest that adherence to therapy recommendations were higher for patients randomly assigned to use the app vs. those who were not ($d = .76$, n.s.; Koffel et al., 2018).

Given this, it is important to consider how apps might improve homework completion so that these mechanisms can be optimized to further improve care. For example, mobile apps could reduce barriers to completing assignments, as they can provide most, if not all, of the necessary supplemental patient materials. This could prevent misunderstanding what is required for homework and how to do it, as well as clarify what requisite materials are available in order to complete assignments. Apps can also deliver psychoeducational and other therapy materials in a more convenient, attractive, and understandable format by employing engaging and interactive audio and visual elements. In traditional CBT, psychoeducation is routinely delivered through text-based handouts. Apps can easily incorporate videos and other interactive teaching aids. In addition, app-based materials allow for more frequent opportunities for review and could include learning checks (e.g., assessments of knowledge acquisition), which could facilitate and reinforce learning. Psychotherapy requires that patients learn material presented during sessions and remember to apply it when suitable contexts are encountered outside of sessions in the real world. As people are now rarely without their smartphones, apps could be used to take advantage of situations when more compelling activities are not available. For example, a patient with homework to complete can unobtrusively wear ear buds while waiting for an appointment, traveling on public transportation, or waiting during a child's sports practice. Since smartphone use is considered normal in public settings, patients may find homework completion easier and more tolerable than using paper-based forms, as it reduces the risk of drawing unwanted attention and disclosing what they are doing. This could result in more efficient use of time, which could be helpful for busy patients. In fact, app-enabled homework has been shown to facilitate assignments being completed throughout the day (Stolz et al., 2018).

Apps could improve homework adherence in other ways as well. For example, since smartphones are ever-present, forgetting to bring homework assignments to session can nearly be eliminated when homework is app-based. Clinicians who routinely use apps in treatment anecdotally report that they almost never encounter a patient who forgets their phone. Apps can also increase accountability through automatically date and time stamping homework completion, validating that assignments were completed. The patient awareness that the therapist will know if and when they did their assignments could enhance accountability, resulting in improved homework adherence. This is not a matter of therapists intruding into patients' private space or keeping tabs on them but rather a means of supporting, reinforcing, and acknowledging the hard work patients are doing outside of sessions. Some apps even include gamification elements that provide timely reinforcement upon task completion. In addition, apps can leverage a host of available smartphone features, such as setting reminders and displaying app-generated notifications. Apps can also increase patients' self-efficacy. As the tasks associated with some CBT homework can be daunting, apps can support a belief that they can do what is being asked of them because of the organized materials and app-based reminders. Apps can improve behavior change and homework efforts with tailored motivational messages to overcome ambivalence, inertia, avoidance, and unhealthy impulses by encouraging patients to complete difficult assignments or tolerate or cope with uncomfortable situations or internal states (e.g., exposure exercises, manage a smoking urge).

Psychotherapy apps could improve other aspects of psychotherapy as well, including the therapeutic alliance. A good therapeutic alliance has been shown to be a substantial contributor to positive patient outcomes ($r = .22$) (Martin, Garske, & Davis, 2000). There is evidence that apps can enhance the therapeutic alliance, with their adoption improving patients' perceptions of the relationship with their therapist (Qudah & Luetsch, 2019). Having the app on the patient's smartphone could create a sense of social presence ("my therapist is always with me"). In addition to the app, brief smartphone-based text messaging between sessions to support therapy adherence could further increase therapy adherence and the connection between the patient and therapist (Clough & Casey, 2018). Apps could further reinforce the col-laborative alignment of therapy goals as materials are standardized on them, possibly increasing therapist and patient fidelity to the treatment, which has been shown to positively relate to outcomes (Marques et al., 2019). Such enhanced support and collaboration could result in increased engagement in treatment and homework completion (Abbasgholizadeh Rahimi, Menear, Robitaille, & Légaré, 2017). Moreover, having such structure and support on the app might also improve therapists' competence, which is related to more positive outcomes as well (Marques et al., 2019).

Other Potential Benefits of Using Apps in Psychotherapy

Apps could have additional benefits as well, including improved efficiency of psychotherapy delivery by reducing the time needed to achieve clini-cal improvement. For example, a six-session group therapy for generalized anxiety disorder had better outcomes when it incorporated a mobile inter-vention than when it did not, and outcomes were not significantly different from the same intervention delivered over 12 sessions (Newman, Prze-worski, Consoli, & Taylor, 2014). Likewise, when a ten-session behavioral activation therapy for depression was compared to a truncated four-session version that also included a smartphone app, results were non-inferior even though it was delivered in six fewer sessions with only about half the thera-pist time (Ly et al., 2015). It is not clear how this enhanced efficiency is accomplished, but it could be through increased exposure to and use of interventions. However, a study that included an app for anger management showed that *less* time was spent on homework (Mackintosh et al., 2017), so it could be that patients are using app-based homework in a more effi-cient, timely, appropriate, and effective manner. In addition, comorbidity is common, and apps could increase the efficiency of care by expanding the scope of treatment by affording other issues to be addressed without add-ing substantial resources. Additional targets could include problems such as insomnia and nicotine addiction, which are common comorbid issues among patients with mental health conditions.

At the completion of treatment, patients are rarely entirely free of symp-toms and many conditions have a chronic and relapsing course (e.g., smok-ing, depression). It is disconcerting that patients have very poor memory for what they learn in treatment, which ostensibly could undermine the long-term benefit of therapy (Harvey et al., 2014). Apps could be help-ful after an episode of care by solidifying treatment gains, providing ongo-ing access to symptom management techniques and CBT psychoeducation, thus preventing relapse of symptoms (Hicks et al., 2017), and facilitating continued improvement (skills generalization).

Selecting Apps for Use in Practice

It is obviously very important that before introducing a mental health app to a patient, the therapist should thoroughly review and understand the app's key features, functionality, and content, possibly by using the app as if the therapist were the patient. Consider what a therapist would do before recommending a book to a patient. The therapist would first read it, verify that the content is consistent with the therapeutic approach being used, determine that the reading level is appropriate for the patient, and have a solid clinical rationale for recommending it. Similar considerations apply before introducing a mental health app. Unlike bibliotherapy, clinical integration of mental health apps requires that the therapist can navigate it, assign app features for between session use, and answer patient questions about its functions. Therefore, the therapist will need to set aside time to explore the app, and the amount of time required to do this will depend on the complexity of the app and its intended use.

There are multiple considerations when selecting an app to bring into practice. Foremost among these are clarifying what purpose the app will serve in care and for what condition it is intended to help. The app's role includes what specific aspects of care the therapist is wishing to accomplish or enhance with it. Apps can be included to address a patient issue through self-management, guided self-management, or as a companion to an EBT protocol. Apps can also be used for more limited or specific purposes or interventions, such as to support anxiety management (breathing retraining, relaxation, and mindfulness exercises), pleasant events scheduling, or symptom monitoring.

Searching for an App

With a clear purpose and condition in mind, a sensible starting point to begin the pursuit of a compatible app would be to search the scientific literature for those that have evidence of efficacy. However, a search of this kind might not be fruitful. As was mentioned earlier, the vast majority of mental health apps have not been evaluated, and many that have been are not available in the app stores. For example, only two of the five apps evaluated in the RCTs of Donker et al.'s (2013) meta-analysis were available to the public. Given this, it might be tempting instead to head directly to the app store to select an app by evaluating app descriptions, ratings, and reviews. However, these sources of information can all be misleading (Larsen et al., 2019; Torous, Luo, & Chan, 2018).

Fortunately, professional organizations have begun offering independent ratings and recommendations of available mental health apps. For example, the Anxiety and Depression Association of America (ADAA) rates mental health apps on their ease of use, effectiveness, personalization, interactive/feedback, research evidence for the underlying treatment, research evidence for the app itself, and overall quality (https://adaa.org/finding-help/mobile-apps). The ADAA has recently partnered with PsyberGuide.org, which is a nonprofit website that was created to provide unbiased reviews of mental health apps to help consumers and providers make informed decisions. PsyberGuide.org rates apps on three criteria: credibility, user experience, and transparency. Credibility ratings are based on the research supporting the efficacy of the app, including whether there are peer-reviewed publications demonstrating its effectiveness and the entity that funded that research. It also includes how specific the interventions are for issues the app is intended to address (more specific being better) and if clinical experts were involved in the app's development. User experience ratings are intended to reflect the quality of the app. These ratings are based on the Mobile App Rating Scale (MARS; Stoyanov et al., 2015) which measures how easy and engaging an app is to use. Finally, the transparency rating is based on how accessible to the user is information explaining the app's data privacy policy, including how data are stored (e.g., are they encrypted?) and collected.

While efforts to rate mental health apps are admirable and clearly valuable, therapists must be careful not to rely on them exclusively. Limitations include that ratings can be based on what the app states rather than verification of what the app actually does (e.g., regarding data protections and sharing), and reviewer ratings themselves may not be reliable (Powell et al., 2016). In addition, ratings might not fully capture important considerations or dimensions with which the therapist is most interested. Furthermore, given how many mental health apps are available, most have not yet been rated. For example, as of June 2019, the ADAA had ratings for only 19 apps and Psychberguide.org had ratings for only 186 apps for a wide range of mental health conditions. Finally, it clearly is a daunting, if not infeasible, task to maintain such a database of mental health app ratings over time, as apps are frequently updated, new apps are released, and many apps disappear entirely from the app marketplaces (Larsen, Nicholas, & Christensen, 2016).

Another valuable source for finding quality mental health apps is searching reputable, trusted app purveyors. For example, the VA and the Department of Defense (DoD) have produced over 20 mental health apps (both self-management and EBT companion apps) that are available for free download to the public (Owen et al., 2018; Gould et al., 2019). These apps include self-management apps that are largely informed by CBTs/EBTs (e.g., behavioral activation, stress inoculation training) and therapy companion apps (e.g., PE Coach, CPT Coach, CBT-I Coach). To date, some have even garnered research evidence for their value (see Gould et al., 2019). What is particularly attractive about these apps, aside from the foundation in EBTs, is that they are built to be accessible to users with various forms of disability (e.g., sight or hearing impairment). They also do not share identifiable user data. However, the VA/DoD app portfolio only includes a limited number of apps for a handful of conditions that are common to veterans and service members (e.g., PTSD, insomnia). And while not sharing data can be advantageous, the potential benefits of passively sharing data cannot be realized and can create additional burden on patients if they have to complete measures outside of the app or print out their data to share it with their therapist.

Given the limitations of each of these approaches, there is no shortcut therapists can take to ensure that the apps they wish to use in care are appropriate. Rather than providing professional ratings and reviews of individual apps, the American Psychiatric Association offers the App Evaluation Model as a practical guide to help therapists in deciding if an app is appropriate for use with patients (www.psychiatry.org/psychiatrists/practice/mental-health-apps). The model includes five steps arranged as hierarchical layers of a pyramid, meaning that if significant concerns are raised at any step, the app should not receive further consideration.

Starting at the base, step 1 (also called Level 1, etc. in the pyramid; see the video at https://www.psychiatry.org/psychiatrists/practice/men tal-health-apps/app-evaluation-model) involves gathering background information on the app to assess its credibility. This is based on criteria such as who developed the app (are they reputable?), how often the app is being updated, and whether it costs anything to download. The second step involves assessing risk of harm in terms of how user data is handled and if disclosure of private information is likely. Like Psychberguide.org, these two pieces of information will have to be based on the app's privacy policy—if there is one. Determining the safety of personal information is guided by questions such as whether sensitive data will be collected and if so, whether it will be protected (e.g., encrypted, de-identified), and whether it will be sold to third parties. Step 3 involves seeking evidence that the app is effective (e.g., peer-reviewed, published evidence) or potentially beneficial (is it based on science?). This step also involves diving into the app to see if claims are supported by what is actually delivered in the app. Using other sources of feedback (i.e., app store reviews, professional ratings) can also be helpful for this step. In step 4, the therapist evaluates the app's usability or ease of use and adherence or likelihood of engaging users, particularly over time. Other considerations at this step include whether the app can be customized, whether its use depends on an internet connection, what mobile platforms it is available on, whether it is accessible for those with disabilities, and whether it is culturally informed. Finally, step 5 evaluates whether the app supports interoperability or meaningful data use and sharing; that is, whether app data can be downloaded or exported (e.g., to be printed) or shared directly with the patient's electronic medical record.

Using Apps With Patients

Developing Knowledge and Expertise

While research on integrating mobile apps into psychotherapy is nascent, and clinical practice guidelines have yet to be developed, guidance manuals for clinicians have begun to emerge (e.g., SAMHSA, 2015; Armstrong et al., 2017). Practical clinical guidance offered here is derived from these existing sources as well as the authors' experience developing mental health apps and leading a community of practice with Department of Veterans Affairs (VA) therapists who are integrating mental health apps into psychotherapy (Owen et al., 2018). It is important to remember that, as with any practice change that requires acquisition of new knowledge and skills, ethical practice dictates that the therapist should have the requisite competency in delivering the novel practice. For example, according to APA's guidelines for the practice of telepsychology, psychologists should "take reasonable steps to ensure their competence with both the technologies used and the potential impact of the technologies on clients/patients, supervisees, or other professionals." (APA, 2013). Therefore, therapists lacking such competence should seek training to develop it.

An example of such training is VA's free webinar series (www.myvaapps. com/pbi-network-ce-lecture-series), which is open to any mental health provider both within and outside of VA who is interested in using technology to support treatment for veterans with PTSD and related concerns. These trainings address technologies such as mobile apps, online interventions, and telehealth for concerns common to those with PTSD, such as anger, substance use, and insomnia. They are hosted by subject matter experts from VA's National Center for PTSD (NCPTSD), Dissemination & Training Division, and feature a different speaker and technology-related topic each month. Past presentations are posted on the site and free continuing education units are available to various professionals.

Considering Patient Factors

In deciding which psychotherapy patients should be offered mobile mental health apps, therapists should consider a patient's access to the required technology (e.g., mobile device and access to Wi-Fi or data plan), proficiency with technology, and preferences. With increased access to smartphones across all demographics (Pew Research Center, 2019a), it is important that the therapist does not make assumptions about limited technology access based solely on patient characteristics. It is true that smartphone ownership still lags for some. For example, 67% of those age 50 years and older (vs. 95% under age 50) and 71% of those living in rural areas (vs. 83% in suburban and urban areas) own smartphones, but these gaps are narrowing

(Pew Research Center, 2019b). It is obviously important that mental health patients have smartphones and that they would be willing to use them in care. Fortunately, it has consistently been found that individuals with mental health conditions own smartphones at levels similar to that of the general population and desire to use them to address their mental health needs (e.g., Ben-Zeev, Davis, Kaiser, Krzsos, & Drake, 2013; Erbes et al., 2014; Torous, Friedman, & Keshavan, 2014). Moreover, it has been shown that some patients prefer using an app (i.e., PE Coach) over traditional means of participating in therapy (Reger, Skopp, Edwards-Stewart, & Lemus, 2015).

To assess smartphone ownership and preferences of patients, the therapist can ask questions during a visit or on intake paperwork (e.g., "Do you own a smartphone or tablet?" "Have you downloaded an app for health or mental health?" "Are you interested in talking to your therapist about mobile apps that can be used to support your treatment goals?"). The Mobile Device Proficiency Questionnaire (Roque & Boot, 2018) can also be used to assess technology proficiency for older adults to determine how much training may be required to help them fruitfully engage with the technology. Patients may need additional support with mobile technology due to lack of familiarity, cognitive limitations, or other issues (e.g., fear of technology, low self-efficacy). The therapist and patient may consider involving a family member, caregiver, peer, or clerk to provide technical assistance. In some cases, the therapist may also determine that a patient needing more technical support than can be accommodated may be better served using traditional methods.

Getting Started Using Apps in Care: Informed Consent

It is important that patients are informed participants in decisions about whether and how mobile apps will be integrated into their treatment (see Torous & Roberts, 2017b; Edwards-Stewart, Alexander, Armstrong, Hoyt, & O'Donohue, 2019). Consistent with the informed consent process for any psychotherapeutic intervention, when a mobile app is introduced as part of psychotherapy, the therapist should offer it as an option, provide a strong rationale for why it is recommended, and discuss any known risks and benefits as well as alternatives. For example, when introducing and obtaining verbal informed consent for one of the publicly available treatment companion apps developed by the VA's National Center for PTSD, a clinician might say something like: "Some patients have found apps like this one helpful for tracking symptoms, practicing skills, or completing homework between sessions. We have research evidence suggesting that mobile mental health apps can help with treatment, but we can't say that the benefit you'll get out of psychotherapy will be greater if you decide to use the app. Either way, the evidence-based psychotherapy I will be providing will be the same. It really comes down to a matter of preference. You can use the app or I can provide you with paper materials for between session assignments. Of course, you can always try out one method and switch later on."

Privacy, security, and confidentiality should also be covered during the informed consent process. As mentioned earlier, the therapist should be familiar with the app's privacy policy prior to recommending it to a patient and should be able to summarize the policy in language that the patient can comprehend. For publicly available VA mental health apps, which abide by a strict privacy policy that does not allow for collection of identifiable data, the therapist can inform the patient that no identifiable information such as name or location is ever shared by the app. If an app allows for data sharing between the patient and therapist through a web-based clinician dashboard, the therapist should set the expectation and make clear when and how the patient's data will be used and responded to. For example, if the therapist does not plan to regularly monitor the patient's data between sessions, this can be communicated by saying something like: "I'm going to ask you to track your symptoms using the app between sessions so that you don't have to rely on memory. Instead, we can look at your data together during our sessions. I will not be regularly reviewing your data between our visits. That means if your symptoms worsen or you experience a crisis, I need you to call the clinic or crisis line so we can provide help." In addition to verbally discussing these matters, some use a written technology policy that is signed at the beginning of treatment to ensure clear communication and manage risk.

Any other known or anticipated risks should also be discussed. The therapist can encourage the patient to secure their device with a passcode if they have not already done so. The therapist should also discuss possible unintentional disclosures and ways to guard against them. For example, if the patient's family members or friends also use their phone (e.g., to look at photos or play games), the patient can be encouraged to use a PIN on the app for added protection, if available. The therapist can also educate the patient on how to disable or mask app notifications that may appear on the home screen.

The patient should be given the opportunity to ask questions and discuss any concerns as well as their expectations for the app. This discussion will allow the therapist the opportunity to provide additional information and address any misassumptions. As with any other aspect of psychotherapy, this discussion can be revisited throughout treatment as part of reviewing informed consent, engaging in shared decision making, and making changes as needed. The informed consent process should always be guided by the standards of the therapist's discipline and setting and should be documented in the patient's chart.

Using Apps During Psychotherapy

As was mentioned earlier, one of the key advantages of using apps in psychotherapy is their potential to augment between-session learning and skills practice. When assigning any type of homework for therapy, the therapist needs to do the following: be clear and specific, ensure that the patient understands what they are being asked to do, address any potential barriers to completion, and state that completed homework is to be brought in to the next session. With a homework assignment involving an app, the therapist may also need to walk the patient through how to use the app and specifically how to access and use the features being assigned. The therapist can demonstrate this on a mobile tablet and have the patient navigate the app on their own device during the session so that they have practice using it and can ask any questions about completing homework with the app. Technical barriers, such as software glitches, can occur with any technology, so a contingency plan for completing homework (e.g. analog tracking of behaviors, symptoms, moods) should be available.

As with any homework assignment, it is important that the therapist consistently follow up on the patient's progress. The therapist should consider how information entered or available in the app will be shared if electronic data sharing is not available. Patients may want to hand their smartphone to their therapist, which could present an awkward situation, especially if materials on the phone (pictures, incoming text messages) disclose unflattering information. The therapist may sit next to the patient and have them show the therapist their completed work, or the therapist may ask the patient to share it verbally. Having the device in "airplane mode" during the session temporarily disables incoming text messages from interfering with homework review. Homework completion should be reinforced through highlighting how it helped and verbal praise should be offered. Issues around homework noncompliance can be addressed through similar methods as when not using apps (e.g., problem solving, motivational interviewing), but issues specifically related to the technology should be explored and resolved. If not already done, reminders can be set on the app or device to help patients remember to complete assignments.

Using Apps After Psychotherapy

The conclusion of a course of psychotherapy does not mark the end of needing to use coping skills and practice self-care. At this juncture, the therapist ideally explores with the patient what they found helpful, what they need to continue to practice and work on, as well as signs that they need additional support in the future. The therapist should recommend ongoing use of an app to support maintenance and continued building of skills learned in therapy and to track symptom changes that might indicate the need for a booster session or additional professional services. The therapist can also recommend use of self-help apps for subclinical or secondary issues (e.g., sleep difficulties, anger management) as well as additional issues for which a patient is not yet ready or willing to seek treatment (e.g., problematic alcohol use). The therapist should educate the patient about potential benefits and weaknesses of self-help apps, including that they do not replace care with a therapist. Guided self-help, in which a therapist offers limited support to supplement app use, has been shown in some instances to be more efficacious than self-help alone (e.g., Possemato et al., 2016). Where available, guided self-help may be an option presented to patients who are ending an episode of psychotherapy but could benefit from additional yet limited support.

Conclusion and Future Directions

Mental health apps offer an exciting new means of improving mental health symptoms as well as the delivery and impact of psychotherapy. Although thousands of untested mental health apps are available, research on the small fraction of apps that have been evaluated is encouraging. However, finding suitable apps, including evidence-based ones, to use with patients remains a challenge as many of the apps that have been tested are not available, and many available apps have not been tested. Fortunately, resources exist that can help guide therapists in the process of identifying apps that are appropriate for use with patients. Likewise, clinical guidance on best practices to ethically integrate apps in care is developing. It is hoped that the recommendations offered in this chapter will assist therapists in the process of finding and using appropriate apps to enhance the services and maximize the benefit they provide to their patients.

With advances in technology and their early applications to mental health, the future of helping those with mental health issues seems very promising. Since its historical beginning more than a century ago, there has been relatively little innovation in the delivery of psychotherapy. Much like with other areas of modern life (e.g., banking, shopping, communicating), technology is poised to disrupt mental health treatment as well. This unique opportunity to reimagine mental health care has the potential to make it more accessible, convenient, patient-centered, and effective. While the focus of this chapter has primarily been on using existing mental health apps in care, other smartphone-based technologies are beginning to show promise in detecting and intervening in mental health issues.

Although it is beyond the scope of this chapter to review all of these developments, a few interesting directions are worth mentioning. This includes using smartphone data and smartphone-based or enabled sensors. Smartphones include accelerometers, ambient light sensors, and GPS. They are also capable of being wirelessly connected to external sensors, such as wearable (e.g., on watches, adhesive patches, chest straps, and belts) and placeable sensors (e.g., in mattresses and pill caps). Data from these sources can be employed to capture behavioral, physiological, and social signals, which can be used to infer clinical states, offering novel opportunities to deliver timely interventions (Mohr, Zhang, & Schueller, 2017). For example, metadata on incoming and outgoing phone calls (i.e., number, duration) and text messages have been shown to be able to detect episodes of mania and depression

(Faurholt-Jepsen et al., 2015). Another exciting area is smartphone-based conversational agents, such as chatbots, to deliver CBT interventions, which can reduce symptoms of depression (Fitzpatrick, Darcy, & Vierhile, 2017). Finally, smartphone-based virtual reality (VR) platforms can provide fail-safe environments for patients to practice skills or complete exposure exercises. For example, a recent RCT of a self-guided, CBT-based, VR smartphone app, used with cardboard goggles, for individuals with acrophobia produced large symptom reductions (Donker et al., 2019).

With continued advancements in smartphone computing power and artificial intelligence (AI) and its subfields of natural language processing and machine learning, an entirely new technology-enabled arsenal of mental health interventions is on the not-so-distant horizon. Much like with mental health apps, the potential implications—both positive and negative—of bringing these into mental health care will require careful consideration. Fortunately, therapists who have already begun integrating mental health apps into practice will be well prepared to navigate the common issues (e.g., data protections) involved in using these emerging interventions, facilitating their more rapid adoption and ultimate benefit to patients.

References

Abbasgholizadeh Rahimi, S., Menear, M., Robitaille, H., & Légaré, F. (2017). Are mobile health applications useful for supporting shared decision making in diagnostic and treatment decisions? *Global Health Action, 10*(Suppl. 3), 1332259. doi:10.1080/1 6549716.2017.1332259

American Psychological Association (2013). Guidelines for the practice of telepsychology. *American Psychologist, 68*, 791–800.

Armstrong, C. M., Edwards-Stewart, A., Ciulla, R. P., Bush, N. E., Cooper, D. C., Kinn, J. T., . . . Hoyt, T. V. (2017). *Department of defense mobile health practice guide* (3rd ed.). Washington, DC: Defense Health Agency.

Bados, A., Balaguer, G., & Saldaña, C. (2007). The efficacy of cognitive—behavioral therapy and the problem of drop-out. *Journal of Clinical Psychology, 63*, 585–592. doi:10.1002/jclp.20368

Ben-Zeev, D., Davis, K. E., Kaiser, S., Krzsos, I., & Drake, R. E. (2013). Mobile technologies among people with serious mental illness: Opportunities for future services. *Administration and Policy in Mental Health, 40*(4), 340–343. doi:10.1007/ s10488-012-0424-x

Carrion, P. G., Swann, A., Kellert-Cecil, H. K., & Barber, M. (1993). Compliance with clinic attendance by outpatients with schizophrenia. *Psychiatric Services, 44*(8), 764–767.

Clough, B. A., & Casey, L. M. (2018). Will patients accept dialy SMS as a communication to support adherence to mental health treatment? *International Journal of Cyber Behavior, Psychology and Learning, 8*, 24–35.

Constantino, M. J., Arnkoff, D. B., Glass, C. R., Ametrano, R. M., & Smith, J. Z. (2011). Expectations. *Journal of Clinical Psychology, 67*, 184–192. doi:10.1002/jclp.20754

Cooper, A. A., Kline, A. C., Graham, B. P. M., Bedard-Gilligan, M., Mello, P. G., Feeny, N. C., & Zoellner, L. A. (2017). Homework "dose," type, and helpfulness as predictors of clinical outcomes in prolonged exposure for PTSD. *Behavior Therapy, 48*, 182–194. http://dx.doi.org/10.1016/j.beth.2016.02.013

Donker, T., Cornelisz, I., van Klaveren, C., et al. (2019). Effectiveness of self-guided app-based virtual reality cognitive behavior therapy for acrophobia: A randomized clinical trial. *JAMA Psychiatry.* doi:10.1001/jamapsychiatry.2019.0219

Donker, T., Petrie, K., Proudfoot, J., Clarke, J., Birch, M. R., & Christensen, H. (2013). Smartphones for smarter delivery of mental health programs: A systematic review. *Journal of Medical Internet Research, 15*(11), e247. doi:10.2196/jmir.2791

Edwards-Stewart, A., Alexander, C., Armstrong, C. M., Hoyt, T., & O'Donohue, W. (2019). Mobile applications for client use: Ethical and legal considerations. *Psychological Services,* (16), 281–285. doi:10.1037/ser0000321

Erbes, C. R., Stinson, R., Kuhn, E., Polusny, M., Urban, J., Hoffman, J. E., Ruzek, J. I., & Thorp, S. (2014). Access, utilization, and interest in mHealth applications among Veterans receiving outpatient care for PTSD. *Military Medicine, 179*(11), 1218–1222.

Faurholt-Jepsen, M., Vinberg, M., Frost, M., Christensen, E. M., Bardram, J. E., & Kessing, L. V. (2015). Smartphone data as an electronic biomarker of illness activity in bipolar disorder. *Bipolar Disorder, 17*, 715–728.

Fernandez, E., Salem, D., Swift, J. K., & Ramtahal, N. (2015). Meta-analysis of dropout from cognitive behavioral therapy: Magnitude, timing, and moderators. *Journal of Consulting and Clinical Psychology, 83*(6), 1108–1122. http://dx.doi.org/10.1037/ccp0000044

Firth, J., Torous, J., Nicholas, J., Carney, R., Pratap, A., Rosenbaum, S., & Sarris, J. (2017). The efficacy of smartphone-based mental health interventions for depressive symptoms: A meta-analysis of randomized controlled trials. *World Psychiatry: Official Journal of the World Psychiatric Association (WPA), 16*(3), 287–298. doi:10.1002/wps.20472

Firth, J., Torous, J., Nicholas, J., Carney, R., Rosenbaum, S., & Sarris, J. (2017). Can smartphone mental health interventions reduce symptoms of anxiety? A meta-analysis of randomized controlled trials. *Journal of Affective Disorders, 218*, 15–22.

Fitzpatrick, K. K., Darcy, A., & Vierhile, M. (2107). Delivering cognitive behavior therapy to young adults with symptoms of depression and anxiety using a fully uutomated conversational agent (Woebot): A randomized controlled trial. *JMIR Ment Health, 4*(2), e19. doi:10.2196/mental.7785

Gould, C. E., Kok, B. C., Ma, V. K., Zapata, A. M. L., Owen, J. E., & Kuhn, E. (2019). Veterans Affairs and Department of Defense mental health apps: A systematic review of the available evidence. *Psychological Services, 16*(2), 196–207.

Harvey, A. G., Lee, J., Williams, J., Hollon, S. D., Walker, M. P., Thompson, M. A., & Smith, R. (2014). Improving outcome of psychosocial treatments by enhancing memory and learning. *Perspectives on Psychological Science, 9*(2), 161–179. doi:10.1177/1745691614521781

Hicks, T. A., Thomas, S. P., Wilson, S. M., Calhoun, P. S., Kuhn, E., & Beckham, J. C. (2017). A preliminary investigation of a relapse prevention mobile application to maintain smoking abstinence among individuals with posttraumatic stress disorder. *Journal of Dual Diagnosis, 13*, 15–20.

Kehle-Forbes, S. M., Meis, L. A., Spoont, M. R., & Polusny, M. A. (2016). Treatment initiation and dropout from prolonged exposure and cognitive processing therapy in a VA outpatient clinic. *Psychological Trauma: Theory, Research, Practice, and Policy,* *8*(1), 107–114.

Koffel, E., Kuhn, E., Petsoulis, N., Erbes, C., Anders, S., Hoffman, J. E., Ruzek, J. I., & Polusny, M. (2018). A pilot study of CBT-I Coach: Feasibility, acceptability, and potential impact of a mobile app for patients in cognitive behavioral therapy for insomnia. *Health Informatics Journal.* doi:10.1177/1460458216656472

Kuhn, E., Crowley, J. J., Hoffman, J. E., Eftekhari, A., Ramsey, K. M., Owen, J. E., Reger, G. M., & Ruzek, J. I. (2015). Clinician characteristics and perceptions related to use of the PE (Prolonged Exposure) Coach mobile app. *Professional Psychology: Research and Practice, 46,* 437–443. doi:10.1037/pro0000051

Lambert, M. J. (2017). Maximizing psychotherapy outcome beyond evidence-based medicine. *Psychotherapy and Psychosomatics, 86,* 80–89.

Larsen, M. E., Huckvale, K., Nicholas, J. Torous, J., Birrell, L., Li, E., & Reda, B. (2019). Using science to sell apps: Evaluation of mental health app store quality claims. *NPJ Digital Medicine, 2.* https://doi.org/10.1038/s41746-019-0093-1

Larsen, M. E., Nicholas, J., & Christensen, H. (2016). Quantifying app store dynamics: Longitudinal tracking of mental health apps. *JMIR Mhealth Uhealth, 4*(3), e96. doi:10.2196/mhealth.6020

Lindhiem, O., Bennett, C. B., Rosen, D., & Silk, J. (2015). Mobile technology boosts the effectiveness of psychotherapy and behavioral interventions: A meta-analysis. *Behavior Modification, 39*(6), 785–804. https://doi.org/10.1177/0145445515595198

Ly, K. H., Topooco, N., Cederlund, H., Wallin, A., Bergström, J., Molander, O., et al. (2015). Smartphone-supported versus full behavioural activation for depression: A randomised controlled trial. *PLoS ONE, 10*(5), e0126559. https://doi.org/10.1371/journal.pone.0126559

Mackintosh, M., Niehaus, J., Taft, C. T., Marx, B. P., Grubbs, K., Leslie, A., & Morland, L. A. (2017). Using a mobile application in the treatment of dysregulated anger among veterans. *Military Medicine, 182,* e1941—e1949. https://doi.org/10.7205/MILMED-D-17-00063

Marques, L., Valentine, S. E., Kaysen, D., Mackintosh, M.-A., Dixon De Silva, L. E., Ahles, E. M., . . . Wiltsey-Stirman, S. (2019). Provider fidelity and modifications to cognitive processing therapy in a diverse community health clinic: Associations with clinical change. *Journal of Consulting and Clinical Psychology, 87*(4), 357–369.

Martin, D. J., Garske, J. P., & Davis, M. K. (2000). Relation of the therapeutic alliance with outcome and other variables: A meta-analytic review. *Journal of Consulting and Clinical Psychology, 68*(3), 438–450. http://dx.doi.org/10.1037/0022-006X.68.3.438

Mausbach, B. T., Moore, R., Roesch, S., Cardenas, V., & Patterson, T. L. (2010). The relationship between homework compliance and therapy outcomes: An updated meta-analysis. *Cognitive Therapy and Research, 34*(5), 429–438. doi:10.1007/s10608-010-9297-z

Miller, K. E., Kuhn, E., Owen, J., Taylor, K., Yu, J., Weiss, B. J., Crowley, J. J., & Trockel, M. (2017). Clinician perceptions related to the use of the CBT-I Coach mobile app. *Behavioral Sleep Medicine.* doi:10.1080/15402002.2017.1403326

Mohr, D. C., Zhang, M., & Schueller, S. M. (2017). Personal sensing: Understanding mental health using ubiquitous sensors and machine learning. *Annual Review of Clinical Psychology, 13,* 23–47.

Newman, M. G., Przeworski, A., Consoli, A. J., & Taylor, C. B. (2014). A randomized controlled trial of ecological momentary intervention plus brief group therapy for generalized anxiety disorder. *Psychotherapy, 51*(2), 198–206.

Owen, J. E., Kuhn, E., Jaworski, B., McGee-Vincent, P., Juhasz, K., Hoffman, J. E., & Rosen, C. (2018). VA mobile apps for PTSD and related problems: Public health resources for veterans and those who care for them. *mHealth*, *4*, 28.

Pew Research Center (2019a, February). *Smartphone ownership is growing rapidly around the world, but not always equally.* Retrieved June 1, 2019 from www.pewresearch.org

Pew Research Center (2019b, May). *Digital gap between rural and nonrural America persists.* Retrieved June 1, 2019 from www.pewresearch.org

Possemato, K., Kuhn, E., Johnson, E., Hoffman, J. E., Owen, J. E., Kanuri, N., De Stefano, L., & Brooks, E. (2016). Using PTSD Coach in primary care with and without clinician support: A pilot randomized controlled trial. *General Hospital Psychiatry*, *38*, 94–98.

Powell, A. C., Torous, J., Chan, S., Raynor, G. S., Shwarts, E., Shanahan, M., & Landman, A. B. (2016). Interrater reliability of mHealth app rating measures: Analysis of top depression and smoking cessation apps. *JMIR Mhealth Uhealth*, *4*(1), e15. doi:10.2196/mhealth.5176

Qudah, B., & Luetsch, K. (2019). The influence of mobile health applications on patient—healthcare provider relationships: A systematic, narrative review. *Patient Education and Counseling*, *102*(6), 1080–1089.

Reger, G. M., Browne, K., Campellone, T., Simons, C., Kuhn, E., Fortney, J., . . . Schacht Reisinger, H. (2017). Barriers and facilitators to mobile application use during PTSD treatment: Clinician use of PE Coach. *Professional Psychology: Research and Practice*, *48*, 510–517.

Reger, G. M., Skopp, N. A., Edwards-Stewart, A., & Lemus, E. L. (2015). Comparison of Prolonged Exposure (PE) Coach to treatment as usual: A case series with two active duty soldiers. *Military Psychology*, *27*(5), 287–296. doi:10.1037/mil0000083

Rizvi, S. L., Dimeff, L. A., Skutch, J., Carroll, D., & Linehan, M. M. (2011). A pilot study of the DBT coach: An interactive mobile phone application for individuals with borderline personality disorder and substance use disorder. *Behavior Therapy*, *42*(4), 589–600. doi:10.1016/j.beth.2011.01.003

Roque, N. A., & Boot, W. R. (2018). A new tool for assessing mobile device proficiency in older adults: The mobile device proficiency questionnaire. *Journal of Applied Gerontology*, *37*(2), 131–156.

Steenkamp, M. M., Litz, B. T., Hoge, C. W., & Marmar, C. R. (2015). Psychotherapy for military-related PTSD: A review of randomized clinical trials. *JAMA*, *314*(5), 489–500. doi:10.1001/jama.2015.8370

Stolz, T., Schulz, A., Krieger, T., Vincent, A., Urech, A., Moser, C., . . . Berger, T. (2018). A mobile app for social anxiety disorder: A three-arm randomized controlled trial comparing mobile and PC-based guided self-help interventions. *Journal of Consulting and Clinical Psychology*, *86*(6), 493–504. http://dx.doi.org.laneproxy.stanford.edu/10.1037/ccp0000301

Stoyanov, S. R., Hides, L., Kavanagh, D. J., Zelenko, O., Tjondronegoro, D., & Mani, M. (2015). Mobile app rating scale: A new tool for assessing the quality of health mobile apps. *JMIR Mhealth Uhealth*, *3*(1), e27. doi:10.2196/mhealth.3422

Substance Abuse and Mental Health Services Administration. Using Technology Based Therapeutic Tools in Behavioral Health Services. (2015). *Treatment improvement protocol (TIP) series 60. HHS publication no. (SMA) 15–4924*. Rockville, MD: Substance Abuse and Mental Health Services Administration.

Torous, J., Friedman, R., & Keshavan, M. (2014). Smartphone ownership and interest in mobile applications to monitor symptoms of mental health conditions. *JMIR mHealth and uHealth*, *2*(1), e2. doi:10.2196/mhealth.2994

Torous, J., Luo, J., & Chan, S. R. (2018). Mental health apps: What to tell patients. *Current Psychiatry*, *17*(3), 21–25.

Torous, J., & Roberts, L. W. (2017a). Needed innovation in digital health and smartphone applications for mental health: Transparency and trust. *JAMA Psychiatry*, *74*(5), 437–438. doi:10.1001/jamapsychiatry.2017.0262

Torous, J., & Roberts, L. W. (2017b). The ethical use of mobile health technology in clinical psychiatry. *The Journal of Nervous and Mental Disease*, *205*(1), 4–8.

Xiao, H., Hayes, J. A., Castonguay, L. G., McAleavey, A. A., & Locke, B. D. (2017). Therapist effects and the impacts of therapy nonattendance. *Psychotherapy*, *54*(1), 58–65.

5 Use of Virtual Reality Exposure Therapy for Anxiety- and Trauma-Related Disorders

*Andrew M. Sherrill, Jessica R. Goodnight,
Mark S. Burton, and Barbara O. Rothbaum*

Introduction

The time delay between initial research evidence and routine clinical practice is about 17 years (Balas & Boren, 2000). The first published study using virtual reality (VR) as an effective modality for exposure therapy to treat any psychiatric or psychological disorder was published in 1995 (Rothbaum et al., 1995). Since then, virtual reality exposure therapy (VRE) has received substantial empirical support for several anxiety- and trauma-related disorders, including specific phobias (heights, flying, and spiders), post-traumatic stress disorder (PTSD), social anxiety disorder, and panic disorder (Opriş et al., 2012). The current evidence, along with dramatically declining costs for VR hardware and software, signals that now is the time for VRE in routine clinical practice. In this chapter, we outline the evidence, theory, and best practices of VRE, with the purpose of helping clinicians use this technology in their work.

Virtual reality is most often utilized in psychotherapy as an augmentation method to enhance exposure therapy for anxiety disorders. Exposure therapy has a large literature base in the basic, translational, and clinical sciences that supports it as a first-line intervention for anxiety-related disorders (see Craske, Hermans, & Vervliet, 2018; Milad, Rosenbaum, & Simon, 2014). Modern exposure therapy is rooted in emotional processing theory (Foa & Kozak, 1986) and is designed to reduce anxiety through presenting feared stimuli without aversive outcomes or the opportunity to avoid. Over repeated exposure trials, the fear associated with the stimulus is reduced through a process known as extinction learning (see VanElzakker, Dahlgren, Davis, Dubois, & Shin, 2014).

In the clinical setting, exposure to feared stimuli traditionally involves *in vivo* ("real life") exposure and/or imaginal exposure. During *in vivo* exposure, the patient encounters the feared stimuli in real life (e.g., encountering a real but safe dog in the case of a dog phobia). During imaginal exposure, patients are guided to imagine their feared stimuli (e.g., imagining a dog sitting in the patient's lap). In the case of PTSD, for which the feared stimuli is a trauma memory, imaginal exposure is typically used; the patient closes his or her eyes and recounts the memory in as much detail as possible (Foa, Hembree, Rothbaum, & Rauch, 2019). The use of VRE can be distinguished broadly into two targets: avoided stimuli and avoided memories. See Table 5.1.

VRE has been tested in multiple randomized clinical trials and has been shown to be as effective as conventional exposure therapies across several meta-analyses and reviews (Carl et al., 2019; Morina, Ijntema, Meyerbroker, & Emmelkamp, 2015; Mishkind, Norr, Katz, & Reger, 2017; Opriş et al., 2012). VRE was first examined as an intervention to reduce fear of heights (Rothbaum et al., 1995). For this early pilot study, the authors designed virtual environments to simulate height exposures, including footbridges at varying heights over water, balconies at varying floor heights, and a glass elevator ride. Those randomized to VRE ($n = 10$) showed significantly reduced fear of heights compared to a waitlist control group ($n = 7$), demonstrating feasibility and efficacy for this then-novel treatment delivery method. Importantly, 7 out of 10 treated participants reported exposing themselves to real-life height situations without being asked to, indicating that experiences in the virtual world can influence behavior in the physical world. Following this initial pilot study, VRE was applied to the treatment of fear of flying (FoF) in a randomized trial that compared VRE to conventional exposure therapy on a real airplane and waitlist control (Rothbaum, Hodges, Smith, Lee, & Price, 2000). Virtual environments included sitting on a parked plane, taking off, landing, and being in a flight in calm and stormy weather. The VRE experience included visual stimuli delivered through a head-mounted display (HMD), audio stimuli delivered through headphones, and vibrations delivered through a bass shaker platform. Conventional exposure environments included being at the actual airport and sitting in an actual parked plane. Results indicated that both VRE and conventional *in vivo* exposure were equally effective and resulted in greater

Table 5.1 Exposure Targets in Conventional Exposure and VRE

Target	Conventional Approach	VRE Approach
Safe but avoided anxiety- and trauma-related stimuli.	*In vivo exposure*: Patients confront safe anxiety- and trauma-related stimuli in the real world.	Patients confront VR-simulated anxiety and trauma-related stimuli.
Safe but avoided trauma memories.	*Imaginal exposure*: Patients recount their traumatic memory with eyes closed.	Patients recount their traumatic memories with eyes open while immersed in a sensory-rich environment as the clinician matches the VR stimuli to facilitate engagement with the traumatic memory.

improvements compared to waitlist. These findings were maintained at a 12-month follow-up (Rothbaum, Hodges, Anderson, Price, & Smith, 2002) and replicated in later studies (Krijn et al., 2007; Rothbaum et al., 2006). VRE was subsequently developed to treat fear of public speaking (FoPS) and compared to group-based exposure and waitlist control in a randomized trial (Anderson et al., 2013). The virtual environments included a virtual podium on which a speech could be uploaded and a virtual audience of anywhere from five to 22 people. Audience members were videos of actual people embedded in the virtual environment, and their reaction to the speech could be manipulated by the therapist (e.g., showing boredom). Group-based exposure involved giving speeches live in front of the other group members. Similar to the FoF study, results indicated that VRE and conventional *in vivo* exposure for FoPS was superior to waitlist without differences between the active treatments. Taken together, these studies indicate that VRE is an effective method for delivering exposure therapy for phobias and is comparable to *in vivo* exposure.

VRE also has been studied for the treatment of PTSD. In a preliminary trial on conducting imaginal exposure within VR, VRE was found to be superior to waitlist control for a sample of 21 survivors of the World Trade Center attack (Difede et al., 2007). In this study, virtual environments included the image of the twin towers and surrounding area from the perspective of someone standing on the ground with different scenarios of the attack (e.g., the plane hitting the building). VRE was also shown to be effective for reducing combat-related PTSD in veterans of the Vietnam (Rothbaum, Hodges, Ready, Graap, & Alarcon, 2001) and Iraq and Afghanistan wars (Rothbaum et al., 2014). Virtual environments included being in a Huey helicopter or landing zone (Vietnam) or Humvee on a convoy and walking through Iraq-like city. The therapist was able to manipulate the simulated environment to match traumatic events (e.g., cause an explosion). Importantly, the Rothbaum et al. (2014) study did not have a non-VRE control condition. A more recent study compared VRE to conventional imaginal exposure (i.e., the standard protocol for prolonged exposure therapy [PE]) for combat-related PTSD (Reger et al., 2016). This study found those who received VRE did just as well as those who received PE at posttreatment. However, PE was related to continued reductions at three- and six-month follow-up while VRE did not. Taken together, studies of VRE for the treatment of PTSD suggest that VR is an effective tool. However, more research is needed, as PE was found to maintain gains better than VRE at follow-up, but VRE was found to be associated with more improvements in psychophysiological responding (Katz et al., 2020).

This research suggests that VRE should be viewed as a clinical tool that can enhance the implementation of evidence-based practice but does not replace effective exposure techniques. For example, some evidence suggests that patients are less avoidant of VRE than conventional exposure (Garcia-Palacios, Botella, Hoffman, & Fabrega, 2007), which may increase the likelihood a patient engages with treatment (but does not necessarily mean that patient will demonstrate greater gains compared to someone receiving conventional exposure). Thus, clinicians working with VRE should have a strong background in conventional exposure techniques (e.g., PE) and be able to skillfully incorporate VR into conventional exposure therapies to enhance patient engagement and treatment efficiency—but not necessarily to increase efficacy of evidence-based treatment.

Virtual Reality Equipment

VR can be broadly defined as any immersive interactive simulated environment. It is a simulation that attempts to mimic reality as closely as possible to allow for an immersive experience. The application of VR to psychotherapy has been demonstrated in the empirical literature for over two decades; however, until recently, cost of VR equipment has been a barrier with respect to implementation in most clinics (Mishkind et al., 2017). One clinician survey indicated monetary expense was the largest concern related to incorporating VR technology into clinical practice (Segal, Bhatia, & Drapeau, 2011). Since that survey, costs of VR equipment have dramatically declined, which increases the likelihood that cost may be offset by the savings of providing effective and efficient treatment. To get started in offering VRE to patients, a clinician will need three things: VR hardware, VR software, and appropriate training in exposure therapy and VRE.

VR Hardware

Most VRE systems include an HMD (head-mounted display) with binocular screens for stereoscopic images and a head tracker so that movements of the head are replicated in the virtual environment. Some VRE systems support a dual monitor display so the clinician can control the activation of stimuli on one and also see the patient's view through the HMD on the other. Although visual stimulation is likely the most important component for immersion, other sensory experiences may also be important for the purposes of VRE, depending on patient needs. The most comprehensive systems include rich sound files delivered through stereo headphones usually with directional sound, vibrations delivered through platforms, and olfactory cues delivered through scent machines. These additional stimuli may aid in the exposure process, depending on which stimuli are most activating of anxiety for a particular patient. Patient and practice needs should drive functionality of the VR hardware.

VRE systems require a visual component: an image of some kind that is viewed through an HMD. The quality of the visual component of a VRE system may vary substantially. Three factors are important to consider: image quality, latency, and degrees of freedom. First, image quality is an important but often overestimated component. Early VRE trials used comparatively primitive graphics and still produced clinically significant effects. Recent advances to image displays and computer graphics have made this an area of less concern with respect to clinical effectiveness. Image quality and detail are likely more important to a gaming population than a patient population. The mere presence of fear cues is often enough to have a fearful patient feel immersed in a virtual environment.

Second, latency is the delay between actual movements and image updates that reflect those movements. The shorter the latency, the more immersive the experience. In instances of longer latency, the body will move but brain will not, which can potentially cause motion sickness or "simulator sickness." Latency is largely determined by computing power, which like graphics displays is rapidly improving.

Third, the system should be responsive to the user's movement to allow for an immersive experience; this is referred to in the VR world as "degrees of freedom." There are a total of six degrees of freedom that alter our field of vision in real-life three-dimensional space: heave (move body up and down like jumping), surge (move body forward and backward like walking), sway (move body side to side like sidestepping), pitch (lifting head from ground to sky like nodding "yes"), yaw (turning head horizontally from side to side to indicate "no"), and roll (bending head from shoulder to shoulder like attempting to remove water from ears). The higher number of degrees of freedom that a VR system replicates, the more immersive the user experience. Only in recent years have some commercially available HMDs been equipped with the capacity for all six degrees of freedom.

Higher-end VR systems such as the Oculus Rift and HTC Vive need to be tethered (wirelessly or with wires) to a computer system with considerable computing power and graphics capabilities. These systems provide a high-quality display with short latency and a highly immersive experience due to their capacity to provide six degrees of freedom and interactivity within the virtual environment. Additionally, through their connected PCs, they can allow the therapist to view what the patient is viewing and manipulate the environment, making it easier to guide a VRE session.

Clinicians looking to start offering VRE may consider smartphone-based HMDs as a relatively inexpensive option. These systems can be described as an HMD shell in which otherwise built-in technology is replaced by contemporary smartphones. These devices allow the clinician's or patient's smartphone to function as a VR hardware system that includes stereoscopic images, motion sensors, and speakers (or headphones). The ubiquity of smartphones means that most clinicians and their patients will need very little to get started in accessing VR. Research indicates that these low-cost approaches are effective and can be applied in numerous ways to enhance therapy (Lindner et al., 2017). Smartphone-based HMDs, however, have disadvantages. First, most smartphone-based HMDs only support three degrees of freedom; although some applications include simple and primitive options for moving within environments, most only allow the patient to look around the environment while remaining stationary. Second, a therapist cannot view what the patient is viewing or control the stimulus in any way once the simulation has begun. And third, other than turning their heads to view more of the simulated scene, the patient typically cannot interact with embedded stimuli or experience other sensory simulations (e.g., smell, temperature, and vibration). Most of the literature on the efficacy of VRE was conducted on higher-end (not smartphone) applications, so we may not be able to extrapolate those findings to cost-effective smartphone applications.

VR Software

Regardless of the specific hardware used, it will need to connect with VR software of some kind. Commercially produced VRE software has proliferated in recent years. Most software packages include VR environments useful for common anxiety disorders such as bridges at varying heights, thunderstorms at varying severity, and all stages of air travel (i.e., the terminal, the jet way, and sitting in the seat before, during, and after takeoff). Some PTSD-specific software packages include VR environments of high base-rate traumatic events such as roadside bombs in the Middle East, urban terrorist attacks, and the inside of bedrooms. Importantly, VRE-specific software is designed so that the clinician can control the delivery of feared stimuli while simultaneously monitoring what the patient is experiencing and how the patient is reacting.

Not all software marketed as VR is VR, as we define it. Most notably, 360-degree videos are often marketed as VR despite not offering an interactive simulated environment. The distinction is unclear to consumers because the same hardware is used for 360-degree videos and VR. However, simply put, 360-degree videos are just videos with user-controlled field of view (i.e., the pitch, yaw, and roll degrees of freedom). Many videos, whether static or 360-degree, can function as *in vivo* exposure tools. What makes VR distinct from videos is the ability to interact with a simulated environment (e.g., move in three-dimensional space, manipulate objects, and cue changes in avatars). By our definition, in true VR, the user is active and "behind the wheel," deciding where to go and what to do. In 360-degree videos, the user is passive and "along for the ride." Compared to 360-degree video, true VR has considerably greater clinical utility due to greater patient immersion and clinician control.

Although 360-degree videos might have less utility than true VR, they are highly accessible, and clinicians trained in VRE have little difficulty incorporating them into treatment when appropriate. Online video players such as YouTube typically contain a repository of hundreds of videos that may be useful stimuli for exposure. A YouTube search of "360 flying video," for example, results in many videos that could be useful for a fear of flying *in vivo* exposure. High-quality videos exist for many other common exposure targets such as snakes, heights, driving, crowds, and public speaking. YouTube videos can be easily accessed with a smartphone-based HMD by navigating the YouTube app. Further, clinicians can capture their own videos using a 360 camera such as the 360fly or GoPro Fusion and then upload the videos to YouTube for the patients to use during and between sessions. See Table 5.2 for a presentation of the different functions of 360-degree video and two true VR systems.

Table 5.2 Functions of 360° Video and Two Different VRE Systems

		Example Systems (Software and Hardware)		
		YouTube 360° video of snakes with iPhone	Bravemind with VISIONHMD	Fear of Flying (Virtually Better, Inc.) with Vive
		360° video	Interactive VR	Interactive VR
Sensory Elements	Images	Yes	Yes	Yes
	Sounds	Yes	Yes	Yes
	Smells	No	Yes	Yes
	Vibrations	No	Yes	Yes
Patient Functions	Patient can explore environment	No	Yes	Yes
	Patient can interact with stimuli	No	Yes	Yes
	Patient can move position w/ controller	No	Yes	Yes
Clinician Functions	Clinician can control stimuli	No	Yes	Yes
	Clinician can see patient's perspective	No	Yes	Yes
	Clinician can move patient position	No	Yes	Yes
Degrees of Freedom: Position Factors	Heave (jumping)	No	No	Yes
	Surge (walking)	No	No	Yes
	Sway (sidestepping)	No	No	Yes
Degrees of Freedom: Orientation Factors	Pitch (nodding "yes")	Yes	Yes	Yes
	Yaw (moving head side to side to indicate "no")	Yes	Yes	Yes
	Roll (removing ear water)	Yes	No	Yes

VRE Training

Attempting VRE without appropriate training would be practicing outside the bounds of competence, even if the provider were trained in the general use of VR (Rizzo, Schultheis, & Rothbaum, 2003). Training in VRE is three-fold: mastery of the equipment, mastery of VRE, and mastery of exposure therapy. First, it is critical to have familiarity with each component of the hardware and software. Despite technological advancements, there is always potential for technical issues (e.g., glitches, coding bugs, wiring problems, and wear-and-tear), so it is important to have a good working relationship with equipment vendors who can assist with troubleshooting that is beyond the capabilities of the clinician. The clinician needs to have an intimate understanding of the software, especially the environments to be explored by patients and the clinician controls. Some environments are simple (e.g., a rooftop for fear of heights) whereas other environments are complex and dynamic (e.g., an Iraqi city used for imaginal exposure to treat PTSD). Clinicians should be especially familiar with complex, dynamic environments to respond flexibly to specific patient needs during an exposure.

Second, after learning the equipment, clinicians need to skillfully operate it while still being an attentive and responsive clinician. Experientially based workshops, supervision, and consultation with VRE experts are excellent ways to learn to operate VR equipment in a therapeutic manner. Clinicians new to VR should role-play administering VRE with a confederate to gain familiarity with shifting attention between the patient, the simulation, and the clinician controls, all while writing observations to be discussed later with the patient after the exposure. Third, as in any therapy, the clinician should remain 100% attentive to the patient and what would make a therapeutic exposure. Bad VRE therapy is just bad therapy.

Best Practices in VRE

Patient Selection

Who is a good candidate for VRE? Traditional rule-outs for conventional exposure therapy apply (e.g., inadequate reality testing, uncontrolled mania, severe substance dependence, and active safety risk). Comorbid psychosis should be monitored closely and may rule out the patient because difficulty discerning reality from psychotic processes may interfere with therapeutic learning in a virtual (not real) environment. In one study of PE vs. VRE for post-9/11 active duty soldiers with PTSD, preliminary evidence for VRE found the best outcomes for younger patients, those with no history of taking antidepressants, and those with higher hyperarousal symptoms as compared to PE (Norr et al., 2018). However, no clear rule-outs specific to using VRE have been identified. Much more work is needed to identify the most appropriate patients.

The decision to use VRE should be primarily determined by the likelihood that VR stimuli will adequately address patient needs. That is, if the patient reports a fear of storms, the decision to use VR should be based on whether the clinician can find stimuli that will activate the patient's fear. If adequate stimuli are available, VR seems to be widely acceptable. One study found that for specific phobia, VRE was refused by 3% of patients while conventional *in vivo* exposure was refused by 27% of patients (Garcia-Palacios et al., 2007).

In the past, a unique rule-out of VRE was susceptibility to simulation sickness. However, symptoms of anxiety are very similar to simulator sickness, and a recent study found that VR did not account for any differences in self-reported simulator sickness among soldiers receiving the same exposure therapy with or without VR (Reger, Smolenski, Edwards-Stewart, et al., 2019). If a patient has experienced simulation sickness in another context, that past reaction may not be unique to VR itself but to behaviors that would make many people dizzy (e.g., playing overly stimulating VR video games, taking glasses off and on repeatedly during a 3D film, not using equipment properly). Well-trained VRE clinicians minimize actions that would promote simulation sickness and ensure equipment is used properly. Some of these include minimizing looking around quickly in VR, limiting head movement, preventing overly warm clothes, keeping the room cool, and remaining in the virtual environment too long (over 40 minutes).

Rationale Delivery

A well-delivered rationale is important to every exposure therapy. Patients need to understand why they are doing all exposure tasks through a treatment rationale linked to psychoeducation of the disorder and how avoidance of feared stimuli maintains pathology. The clinician should present the conventional exposure therapy protocol and then describe VR as a tool that may be used within the context of that protocol. Conventional exposure therapy and VRE should not be presented as two distinct treatments. The rationale for conventional exposure therapy follows emotional processing theory (Foa & Kozak, 1986), which argues fear-based pathology manifests from a cognitive structure that includes certain stimuli, responses, and meanings of these stimuli and responses. To change the cognitive structure, it must be activated and modified with new elements such as knowledge that stimuli and responses do not signal danger and that one can handle distress. Patients should understand that to change fear symptoms, they have to be willing to approach and experience fear in a therapeutic context. The patient should anticipate that only through experience in exposure will his or her mind and body learn that the stimulus is not dangerous, the stimulus is tolerable, the stimulus no longer elicits certain responses, and the stimulus no longer means certain conclusions (e.g., danger) about the patient and the world. After the patient articulates this understanding, the clinician should present VRE as a means for facilitating emotional processing due to its potential for activating and modifying the fear-based cognitive structure with an immersive experience that is highly controllable and safe.

Patients will need to consent to VR. When discussing whether the patient believes VR will help, the clinician needs to assess the patient's understanding of the treatment. For example, if the patient declines VRE because it will be too stressful, the patient may not understand that a goal of exposure therapy is to learn that objectively safe situations (e.g., VR simulations) are indeed safe. If, on the other hand, a patient declines VRE because they do not believe the VR will activate fear, this indicates good understanding of the rationale and may open further discussion of identifying activating exposure stimuli. At times, patients may underestimate the stimulation a VR environment offers, and they may need to interact with the VR to determine whether VRE will be therapeutic. For example, many patients with the fear of flying ask how VRE can help when they will not actually leave the ground. The therapist should explain that the fear cues presented in VR typically activate the fear, and with continued therapeutic exposure, the fear and distress decrease with treatment. Even in the rare cases in which the patient cannot suspend judgment to engage emotionally with the virtual airplane, once on an actual airplane, they describe that the last memory that their bodies had on an airplane (i.e., the virtual airplane) were not fearful memories and that translated to the actual airplane.

Conducting VRE

When conducting VRE, the treatment structure mirrors that of conventional exposure therapies. In fact, the treatments should be nearly identical in their major components. Most protocols start with (1) assessment of clinical presentation, including avoidance strategies, (2) psychoeducation on the specific disorder, and (3) treatment rationale that connects the patient's specific presentation to the overall therapeutic model. The clinician then discusses advantages and disadvantages of using VR as applied to the patient's presentation and goals. Next, the clinician and patient develop a hierarchy of exposures using VR, starting with moderately difficult tasks and culminating in very challenging but still objectively safe tasks.

Conveniently, most VRE software includes built-in exposure tasks that were preselected due to high base rates of reported tasks for a given disorder (e.g., for fear of flying: sitting in the airport gate area, walking down the Jetway, walking down the airplane aisle, sitting down in the airplane, taxiing to runway, taking off, flying with and without turbulence, and landing). After the hierarchy is developed, each session includes at least one exposure to an item on that hierarchy followed by a homework assignment, which may involve conventional *in vivo* exposure or VRE, if the patient has access to a smartphone-based HMD at home, or practice of anxiety management skills such as cognitive restructuring. Extinction is tracked during each exposure using self-reported anxiety ratings. After each exposure, the patient and clinician discuss what was learned and how to continue making progress consistent with the patient's goals.

Administering the VR environment is an active process that requires that the clinician have mastery of the stimulus presentation while simultaneously paying as much attention to the patient's experience and behavior as one would in conventional exposure therapy. The clinician must encourage the patient and provide prompts to facilitate emotional engagement. Additionally, the clinician must monitor any maladaptive safety behaviors, which are unneeded distress management behaviors (e.g., hypervigilance and holding lucky objects) and cognitive routines (e.g., self-soothing statements and distraction) meant to calm the patient but ultimately interfere with extinction learning. After each exposure, it is critical that the clinician process the meaning of the experience so that learning generalizes beyond the VR environment.

Conducting Imaginal Exposure Within VR

The structure of imaginal exposure within VR mirrors that of conventional imaginal exposure (e.g., Foa et al., 2019). The focus of this section is on VRE applied to the treatment of PTSD, which is largely based on the treatment protocol for PE (Sherrill, Rothbaum, McSweeney, & Rothbaum, 2019). Conventional imaginal exposure is described to patients as an effective way to process traumatic memories that requires the patient to close his or her eyes and, for 30 to 45 minutes at a time, use the present tense to describe all actions, sensations, thoughts, and emotions experienced during the traumatic event. In VRE, the treatment rationale is the same, with the addition of an explanation of how VR hardware and software operate as a tool to achieve therapeutic goals.

Why would a patient select VRE? Some clients may have difficulty with imaginal visualization and/or may engage in subtle cognitive avoidance strategies (e.g., distraction and minimization) that indicate a need for additional tools to allow for emotional engagement in the trauma memory. By definition, patients with PTSD have well-rehearsed avoidance repertoires and may be unable or unwilling to retrieve important parts of the trauma memory. Unfortunately, the inability to engage the memory predicts negative treatment outcomes (Jaycox, Foa, & Morral, 1998). A recent study found that VR-facilitated imaginal exposure, compared to conventional imaginal exposure, did not evoke greater levels of subjectively reported distress (Reger, Smolenski, Norr, et al., 2019). Thus, VRE may be best used for patients who may be especially unable to fully engage in their trauma memory (e.g., under-engagers and highly avoidant clients), and it may not be necessary for all patients with PTSD. See Table 5.3 for example scripts VRE clinicians use to explore the possibility of using VR to facilitate imaginal exposure.

Table 5.3 Example Clinician Scripts to Help Patient Decide to Use VR

Concern	Script
Introducing rationale for exposure therapy	"For as long as you avoid the stimulus, you will never learn it is safe. Therefore, to change your mind and body's fearful reaction to the stimulus, you must be willing to approach the fear in an objectively safe context. With repeated exposure, your body and mind will learn through experience that you can handle the stimulus and that the stimulus evokes less fear over time. As the distress goes down over the course of treatment, you will gain a new perspective of the stimulus that will help you move forward in life."
Introducing VRE	"To achieve the goals of exposure therapy, we have the option of using virtual reality to approach fear without leaving the office. This immersive and interactive technology was built with the specific purpose of activating fear in a highly controlled manner, allowing patients stay in contact with the stimulus for long enough to truly learn the stimulus is safe."
Providing rationale to use VR for imaginal exposure	"The traumatic event seems to have been dangerous and your emotional response during the event would be expected. However, the memory of the event is objectively safe and yet you have a strong fear response. This is common among those with PTSD. To learn the memory is safe, you need to be willing to revisit it repeatedly until the fear response diminishes. Some people have difficulty staying engaged with trauma memories, so we provide an option of using immersive virtual reality experiences keep the memory activated and block attempts to think of other things. It is a tool to engage all your senses and to help you retell your experience in a controlled manner, which will help your mind and body truly learn the memory is safe."
Patient expresses doubt VR can help activate and sustain their memories.	"Consider how it might be difficult to accurately recall your high school days. If you and I were somehow to go to your high school on a Sunday, it would make it make it easier to visualize your classmates, what they did, and how you felt. VR can be used in that way, as a background that will help you remember what happened."

Once the patient decides to use VR, the clinician must always remember that the aim of VRE for PTSD is to emotionally process the actual memory. The VR simulation is a tool to engage the patient in this process. The aim is not for the VR simulation to replace the trauma memory, nor is the aim to desensitize the patient to the VR simulation. Patients with PTSD are fearful and avoidant of their trauma memory, so that is always the target for extinction learning and processing (see Table 5.1).

The process of VRE is consistent with conventional imaginal exposure: the patient repeatedly describes the traumatic memory from beginning to end, focusing mostly on the most difficult parts. However, unlike conventional imaginal exposure, patients will keep their eyes open as they recount the memory. The clinician matches the VR simulation as the patient describes the sequence of events. The clinician is not aiming to include all the elements, only enough of the elements to help the patient remain engaged with the memory, using a "less is more" approach. For example, when a sexual assault perpetrator is involved, the patient should imagine the perpetrator rather than use an avatar, as it is important to extinguish fear responses to the memory (e.g., the actual perpetrator's face).

The patient should remain in the environment for at least 30 minutes but no more than 45 minutes while revisiting the trauma memory. Following the imaginal exposure, the clinician and patient process the experience, the meaning of the event, and how the patient has responded to it, and the patient's beliefs of the self, other, and world. A more detailed overview of post-exposure processing can be found in the PE manual (Foa et al., 2019).

Common Challenges

Imperfect Stimuli

A common worry among clinicians who are unfamiliar with VRE is that VR stimuli does not perfectly approximate feared stimuli. However, VRE benefits from a sense of presence, not a sense of realness. According to emotional processing theory, fear is the product of a cognitive representation of certain stimuli, which can become highly generalized and can be cued up without an actual real-life presentation (e.g., imagining a disgusting scenario for contamination fear). Thus, any environment (whether VR or in real life) that cues up the fear structure will be sufficient for emotional engagement in exposure therapy. When using VRE for PTSD, mismatches between the trauma memory and the VR simulation are ubiquitous but almost always trivial and the substantial body of literature reviewed earlier illustrates the effectiveness of VRE despite these mismatches. Typically, the most meaningful components of the trauma memory are usually imagined (e.g., seeing dead bodies, performing first aid, running away from perpetrator). In rare cases that a nontrivial mismatch causes an emotional reaction, the clinicians can still benefit from helping the patient understand that reaction and then collaborate with the patient to make improvements to the simulation.

Technology Failure During Session

Clinicians need to become very familiar with their VR systems and address as many potential technical problems before ever seeing their first patient. For example, as discussed previously, if a clinician has not purchased computing hardware sufficient to run the VR software, "glitches" or problems with image quality and latency can occur that could impact patient experience, therapeutic rapport, or therapy fidelity. Since VR is utilized as an adjunct to conventional therapies, traditional clinical skills can be utilized to manage VR technical difficulties. For example, during imaginal exposure using VR, if an unexpected power issue occurs, and the VR environment loses quality or shuts down completely, a patient may be abruptly pulled out of their virtual experience. In this case, the therapeutic response is simple and requires no technical know-how: just instruct the patient to continue revisiting the traumatic memory with his or her eyes closed. Therapy can proceed almost seamlessly. When the virtual environment is up and running again, match it to where the patient is in the recounting and instruct the patient to open his or her eyes and continue recounting.

Noncompliance

If a patient is noncompliant with VR, for example, by taking off the headset during exposure, clinicians should address this as they would any safety behavior or avoidance experienced in conventional exposure therapy. They could say, for example, "I know this is tough, but as we talked about before, this treatment only works if you stick with the memory. Let's finish the exposure and then talk more about the frustration after. Tell me what's happening now." As in PE, conversations during exposure should be avoided. These conversations will be much better received by the patient if the clinician has provided strong psychoeducation about exposure therapy.

Conclusion

Since the first study on VRE (Rothbaum et al., 1995), VR has shown great promise as a useful tool for enhancing and expediting exposure therapy. Clinicians may feel intimidated by the technical aspects of this technology. However, as outlined in this chapter, this technology has evolved to be much more affordable and user-friendly, and most of the issues related to VR-assisted therapy can be addressed with the same clinical skills that enhance conventional exposure therapy. Although more empirical work is needed in understanding how to select patients, optimize delivery, and leverage unique mediators (e.g., sense of presence), the time is now for routine implementation for interested clinicians who can commit to monitoring the empirical literature and pursuing appropriate training and consultation.

Clinicians should always remember that VRE equipment is only a tool. Functionally, VR is no different than low-tech stimuli that exposure therapists have used for decades. Technologically, however, these tools are impressive and can be very appealing to even the most anxious patients. In particular, many patients from the millennial generation seem to be especially eager to use cutting-edge technologies to help address their mental health needs. The quick adoption of technologies is an attribute of current young adults and likely the next generation as well. Improved equipment is always on the horizon, and some advances are impossible to predict. Clinicians can soon expect major clinical innovations in the areas of augmented reality and mixed reality as well as new functionality supported by broadband internet. With such great excitement in the field, clinicians must be careful to not let their own enthusiasm put the tool in front of the actual therapy. Good VRE always starts with case conceptualization and then asking how VR might be helpful within the context of the patient's goals. Good VRE therapy is primarily good therapy.

References

Anderson, P. L., Price, M., Edwards, S. M., Obasaju, M. A., Schmertz, S. K., Zimand, E., & Calamaras, M. R. (2013). Virtual reality exposure therapy for social anxiety disorder: A randomized controlled trial. *Journal of Consulting and Clinical Psychology*, *81*(5), 751–760.

Balas, E. A., & Boren, S. A. (2000). Managing clinical knowledge for health care improvement. *Yearbook of Medical Informatics*, *9*, 65–70.

Carl, E., Stein, A. T., Levihn-Coon, A., Pogue, J. R., Rothbaum, B., Emmelkamp, P., . . . Powers, M. B. (2019). Virtual reality exposure therapy for anxiety and related disorders: A meta-analysis of randomized controlled trials. *Journal of Anxiety Disorders*, *61*, 27–36.

Craske, M. G., Hermans, D., & Vervliet, B. (2018). State-of-the-art and future directions for extinction as a translational model for fear and anxiety. *Philosophical Transactions of the Royal Society B: Biological Sciences*, *373*, 20170025.

Difede, J., Cukor, J., Jayasinghe, N., Patt, I., Jedel, S., Giosan, C., & Hoffman, H. (2007). Virtual reality exposure therapy for the treatment of posttraumatic stress disorder following September 11, 2001. *Journal of Clinical Psychiatry*, *68*, 1639–1647.

Foa, E. B., Hembree, E., Rothbaum, B. O., & Rauch, S. A. M. (2019). *Prolonged exposure therapy for PTSD: Emotional processing of traumatic experiences* (2nd ed.). New York: Oxford University Press.

Foa, E. B., & Kozak, M. J. (1986). Emotional processing of fear: Exposure to corrective information. *Psychological Bulletin*, *99*, 20–35.

Garcia-Palacios, A., Botella, C., Hoffman, H., & Fabregat, S. (2007). Comparing acceptance and refusal rates of virtual reality exposure therapy vs in vivo exposure by patients with specific phobias. *Cyberpsychology and Behavior*, *10*, 722–724.

Jaycox, L. H., Foa, E. B., & Morral, A. R. (1998). Influence of emotional engagement and habituation on exposure therapy for PTSD. *Journal of Consulting and Clinical Psychology*, *66*, 185–192.

Katz, A. C., Norr, A. M., Buck, B., et al. (2020). Changes in physiological reactivity in response to the trauma memory during prolonged exposure and virtual reality exposure therapy for posttraumatic stress disorder. *Psychological Trauma: Theory, Research, Practice, and Policy*. Advance Online Publication.

Krijn, M., Emmelkamp, P. M., Ólafsson, R. P., Bouwman, M., Van Gerwen, L. J., Spinhoven, P., . . . Van der Mast, C. A. (2007). Fear of flying treatment methods: Virtual reality exposure vs. cognitive behavioral therapy. *Aviation, Space, and Environmental Medicine*, *78*, 121–128.

Lindner, P., Miloff, A., Hamilton, W., Reuterskiöld, L., Andersson, G., Powers, M. B., & Carlbring, P. (2017). Creating state of the art, next-generation virtual reality exposure therapies for anxiety disorders using consumer hardware platforms: Design considerations and future directions. *Cognitive Behaviour Therapy, 46*, 404–420.

Milad, M. R., Rosenbaum, B. L., & Simon, N. M. (2014). Neuroscience of fear extinction: Implications for assessment and treatment of fear-based and anxiety related disorders. *Behaviour Research and Therapy, 62*, 17–23.

Mishkind, M. C., Norr, A. M., Katz, A. C., & Reger, G. M. (2017). Review of virtual reality treatment in psychiatry: Evidence versus current diffusion and use. *Current Psychiatry Reports, 19*, 80.

Morina, N., Ijntema, H., Meyerbroker, K., & Emmelkamp, P. M. G. (2015). Can virtual reality exposure therapy gains be generalized to real-life? A meta-analysis of studies applying behavioral assessments. *Behaviour Research and Therapy, 74*, 18–24.

Norr, A. M., Smolenski, D. J., Katz, A. C., Rizzo, A. A., Rothbaum, B. O., Difede, J., . . . Reger, G. M. (2018). Virtual reality exposure versus prolonged exposure for PTSD: Which treatment for whom? *Depression and Anxiety, 35*, 523–529.

Opriş, D., Pintea, S., García-Palacios, A., Botella, C., Szamosközi, Ş., & David, D. (2012). Virtual reality exposure therapy in anxiety disorders: A quantitative meta-analysis. *Depression and Anxiety, 29*, 85–93.

Reger, G. M., Koenen-Woods, P., Zetocha, K., Smolenski, D. J., Holloway, K. M., Rothbaum, B. O., . . . Mishkind, M. (2016). Randomized controlled trial of prolonged exposure using imaginal exposure vs. virtual reality exposure in active duty soldiers with deployment-related posttraumatic stress disorder (PTSD). *Journal of Consulting and Clinical Psychology, 84*, 946–959.

Reger, G. M., Smolenski, D., Edwards-Stewart, A., Skopp, N. A., Rizzo, A. S., & Norr, A. (2019). Does virtual reality increase simulator sickness during exposure therapy for post-traumatic stress disorder? *Telemedicine and e-Health, 25*, 859–861.

Reger, G. M., Smolenski, D., Norr, A., Katz, A., Buck, B., & Rothbaum, B. O. (2019). Does virtual reality increase emotional engagement during exposure for PTSD? Subjective distress during prolonged and virtual reality exposure therapy. *Journal of Anxiety Disorders, 61*, 75–81.

Rizzo, A., Schultheis, M. T., & Rothbaum, B. O. (2003). Ethical issues for the use of virtual reality in the psychological sciences. In S. S. Bush & M. L. Drexler (Eds.), *Ethical issues in clinical neuropsychology* (pp. 243–280). Lisse, NL: Swets and Zeitlinger Publishers.

Rothbaum, B. O., Hodges, L., Anderson, P. L., Price, L., & Smith, S. (2002). Twelve-month follow-up of virtual reality exposure therapy for the fear of flying. *Journal of Consulting and Clinical Psychology, 70*, 428–432.

Rothbaum, B. O., Hodges, L., Anderson, P. L., Zimand, E., Lang, D., & Wilson, J. (2006). Virtual reality exposure therapy and standard (in vivo) exposure therapy in the treatment of fear of flying. *Behavior Therapy, 37*, 80–90.

Rothbaum, B. O., Hodges, L., Kooper, R., Opdyke, D., Williford, J. S., & North, M. (1995). Effectiveness of computer-generated (virtual reality) graded exposure in the treatment of acrophobia. *The American Journal of Psychiatry, 152*, 626–628.

Rothbaum, B. O., Hodges, L., Ready, D., Graap, K., & Alarcon, R. D. (2001). Virtual reality exposure therapy for Vietnam veterans with posttraumatic stress disorder. *The Journal of Clinical Psychiatry, 62*, 617–622.

Rothbaum, B. O., Hodges, L., Smith, S., Lee, J. H., & Price, L. (2000). A controlled study of virtual reality exposure therapy for the fear of flying. *Journal of Consulting and Clinical Psychology, 68*, 1020–1026.

Rothbaum, B. O., Price, M., Jovanovic, T., Norrholm, S. D., Gerardi, M., Dunlop, B., . . . Ressler, K. J. (2014). A randomized, double-blind evaluation of D-cycloserine or alprazolam combined with virtual reality exposure therapy for posttraumatic stress disorder in Iraq and Afghanistan War veterans. *American Journal of Psychiatry, 171,* 640–648.

Segal, R., Bhatia, M., & Drapeau, M. (2011). Therapists' perception of benefits and costs of using virtual reality treatments. *Cyberpsychology, Behavior, and Social Networking, 14,* 29–34.

Sherrill, A. M., Rothbaum, A. O., McSweeney, L., & Rothbaum, B. O. (2019). Virtual reality exposure therapy for posttraumatic stress disorder. *Psychiatric Annals.* Advance Online Publication.

VanElzakker, M. B., Dahlgren, M. K., Davis, F. C., Dubois, S., & Shin, L. M. (2014). From Pavlov to PTSD: The extinction of conditioned fear in rodents, humans, and anxiety disorders. *Neurobiology of Learning and Memory, 113,* 3–18.

6 Mental Health Practice and Social Media

Greg M. Reger and Noah Hammer

People are innately relational, and technologies that facilitate social connections with others are some of the most widely adopted in the digital age. Social media is one prominent example. Social media refers to the collection of online platforms where individuals create personally tied accounts, share electronic content with others, and engage with others in online communities. Shared content can include a range of media, including personally written text, photos, videos, or content created by others (such as web pages, news, or others' social media posts). Features available in social media platforms vary, but common features include *status updates* that share content (e.g., text, photos, videos) with one's network to inform them of what you are currently doing or items of interest, *check-ins* that provide one's network with your current location, *buying/selling* items in an online garage sale type of format, or posting a *poll or question*. Some social media content is shared for limited periods of time. For example, users might share content in a manner that makes it accessible to others for only 24 hours (e.g., Your Story in Instagram). Social networks include people whose social media *friend* or *follow* request is granted. Many social media platforms will assist users in identifying people to add to their social networks through a search of phone contacts or recommending individuals linked to existing social network members. Social media platforms typically enable users to create groups from a subset of users to form community around a shared interest. Groups can be open to anyone, or access may be limited by a moderator or might be granted by any individual already in the group. Finally, many social media platforms afford users the opportunity to directly message another user or group of users in a manner similar to instant messaging.

The communities to which users share content can vary broadly based on the social media platform used and decisions made by users. Social media is commonly used to share information with friends and family, but some users post in an open, public manner. Users can also post to groups that may or may not include their own social network, making the content available to that community regardless of who in that community is in their personal social network.

Social media has become a routine part of many Americans' lives. As of February 2019, 72% of Americans use some form of social media (Pew Research Center, 2019). Rates of use are particularly high among young adults. Among Americans aged 18–29, 90% use at least one social media platform. The percentage of users declines with the age of the cohort, with 40% use of at least one social media site among those 65 and older (Pew Research Center, 2019). Table 6.1 presents some of the most frequently used social media platforms and their core features.

Social media is a particularly relevant technology to mental health given the critical role of relationships in mental health treatment and support. The interpersonal relationship between the mental health clinician and their client has been a focus of interest since the inception of helping professions. Furthermore, the relationships clients have with others can have a meaningful impact on the development and course of mental health difficulties. In addition, social media has the potential to extend one's connections well beyond traditional communities via the ability to share content broadly with remarkable speed and efficiency. This chapter will review some of the most common and significant issues that arise related to the use of social media in the context of mental health practice.

Social Media Support Groups and Peer Support

The power of relationships for those experiencing mental health difficulties is well established, and has been for decades (e.g., Kessler, Price, & Wortman, 1985). Social support buffers the effects of trauma (e.g., Ozer, Best, Lipsey, & Weiss, 2003), and most studies have found social support protects children, adolescents, and adults from depression (Gariepy, Honkaniemi, & Quesnel-vallee, 2016). Accordingly, it is not surprising that users of social media often reach out to one another for support, advice, and understanding. Indeed, social media users often organize themselves into subgroups of users who share a common experience and aggregate online to offer support to one another on social media. A simple search of "support group" in any social media platform will generate scores of results. These groups have the potential to offer unique means of support to some. Those living in rural areas may not have access to face-to-face social support groups and social media may provide flexible times and places for support. Users can access social media support from such groups when they need it and from any location that they have an internet connection. They can also contribute to the well-being of others and provide support when they feel able to do so. Anonymity can be enhanced, relative to traditional support groups, through the use of non-identifying accounts. Users of such groups appear to feel that social media support group interactions support their positive change, and they value contact with others (Griffiths, Reynolds, & Vassallo, 2015). Social media groups on matters related to health enable patients to share their personal experiences with others, ask

Table 6.1 Social Media Platforms and Features

Reddit	A collection of communities based on common interests of users.	Can post: Text, images, videos and share links from other websites. Users upvote or downvote posts and comments, which determines the order content is displayed.
Facebook (Messenger)	Users create profiles with their personal info and can add other users as friends.	Users can post photos, videos, text and share with all of their friends, a select subsection, or with specific individuals.
Instagram	Users share images with their network of followers.	Can follow others, like and comment on posts, directly message groups or individuals.
YouTube	The largest video sharing platform. Anyone can post and watch videos for free.	Can post videos as open, which can be found by anyone, or private, which can only be viewed by those you share with.
Tik Tok	A Chinese based application for short-form video content.	Edit and share videos, comment on videos, like videos.
LinkedIn	A social media site for professional networking.	Create a profile, add users to your network, search for jobs, individuals, and companies.
Twitter	A micro-blogging service where posts are maxed at 280 characters.	Tweet (post text with a maximum character count of 280), re-tweet (share another user's post), like tweets.
Foursquare	A location-based social networking site to get personalized recommendations and reviews of nearby attractions.	Check-in: Will notify friends on the platform where and when you checked in, app will recommend attractions based on your location.
WhatsApp	A cross-platform messaging service with end-to-end encryption.	Direct Message, Create group, Message group, Send text, pictures, videos.
Pinterest	A visual discovery site where users share primarily visual posts and create their own boards filled with posts shared by themselves and others.	Can Post (Pin) images, GIFs and links to your board, Save Pins made by others to your board, browse pins by topics, visit other users' boards.
Snapchat	A media sharing app where users can send pictures, video, and text directly to others and choose how long they will display for.	Direct message friends. Post to your Story. View friends' stories.
Tinder	A dating app where users swipe left or right on profiles to indicate their interest. Users are matched and can then message when both users swipe right on each other.	Create profile, view other profiles, swipe, message.
Bumble	A dating app (similar to Tinder) where users swipe left or right on each other's profiles to indicate interest. If two users match, the female user must send the first message.	Create profile, view other profiles, swipe, message.

questions, and receive direct feedback from peers (Sawesi, Rashrash, Phala-kornkule, Carpenter, & Jones, 2016).

However, several concerns have also emerged around the use of social media peer support groups. Given the open nature of participation, content posted by users can be wide ranging and can reflect both helpful and maladaptive suggestions. There is no guarantee that content on social media support groups will reflect adaptive coping strategies or evidence-supported recommendations or treatments. Consider the following hypothetical example based on representative experiences of a veterans' social media support group post.

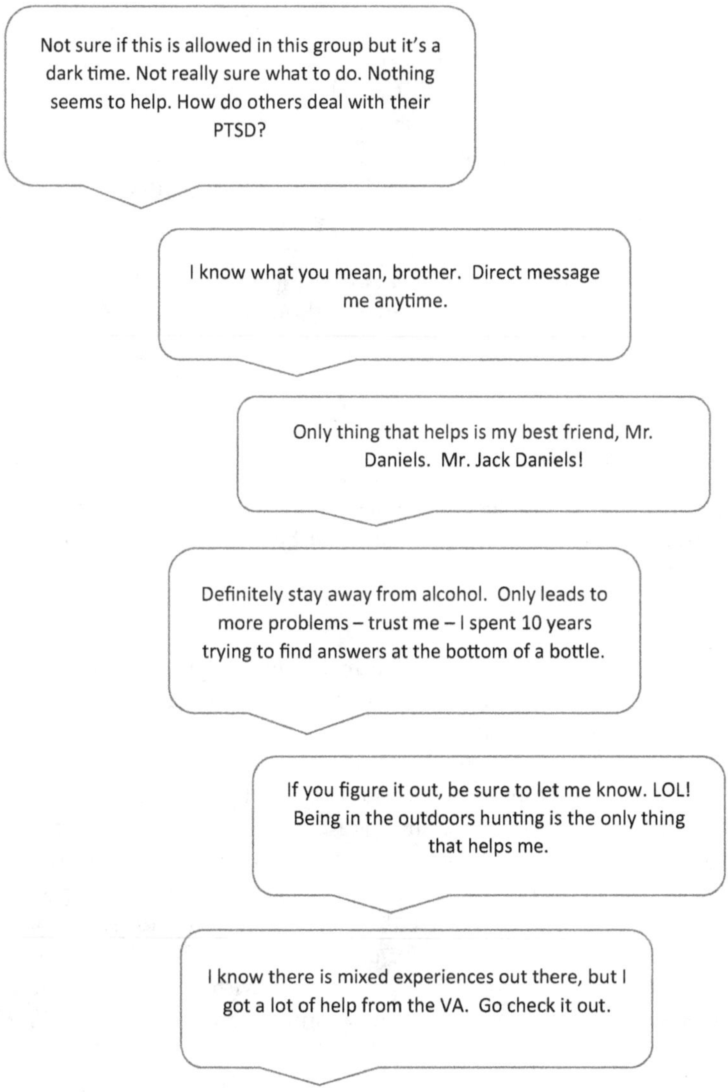

Figure 6.1 Hypothetical Social Media Post in Veterans Outdoor Group

In this example, users' recommendations to cope by using alcohol and those whose responses reflect limited optimism contrast with responses offering direct contact/support and recommendations to seek treatment. Considering the range of effectiveness of support among peers on social media support groups, some have found it useful to distinguish between moderated and non-moderated social media peer groups. Moderated groups have an individual or group of individuals who review and approve content submitted prior to posting to the group. Moderators can serve a variety of functions, including censoring inappropriate content and establishing the rules and boundaries of the discussion. A technical expert panel on behavioral intervention technologies was organized by the Agency for Healthcare Research and Quality and the National Institute of Mental Health (Mohr, Burns, Schueller, Clarke, & Klinkman, 2013). Regarding social media support groups, the panel observed that research evaluations have been limited but existing evidence is disappointing, particularly for unmoderated social media peer groups (e.g., Kaplan, Salzer, Solomon, Brusilovskiy, & Cousounis, 2011; Salzer et al., 2010). Although there may be promise for the development of social media support groups that incorporate evidence-based skills and which promote adaptive peer interactions, clinicians might avoid recommending unmoderated social media support groups, pending more evidence. See chapter 9 for brief thoughts on social media among those with eating disorders and chapter 12 for reflections on social media among those at risk for suicide.

Identity Authentication

When mental health professionals communicate with clients via technology, including social media, consideration must be given to how the identity of the social media user will be authenticated. Take the following hypothetical case as an example:

> Dr. Smith had been seeing Ms. Taylor approximately weekly for four months. Ms. Taylor was having marital problems and depressed mood. She was anxious about her husband's anger and the ways in which she felt controlled by him. She knew he was aware that she was unhappy, but he didn't seem ready to talk about their problems and she did not have the courage to bring it up. She had not yet disclosed to him that she was going to therapy. Dr. Smith routinely used text messages or direct messages from his professional social media account to provide appointment reminders. Dr. Smith received a direct message from Ms. Taylor to his social media account asking for confirmation on the scheduled time for her next appointment. Dr. Smith replied with the date and time and was surprised and horrified to get an immediate reply reading "WHAT IS SHE SAYING ABOUT ME!?"

As this vignette illustrates, using technology to communicate with patients, including direct messaging in social media, presents risks to patient privacy and confidentiality. Authentication of the identity of social media communications can be challenging. Many people remain logged into their social media accounts even when not in use, making the accounts available to those who gain access to their device. The American Psychological Association has developed guidelines for technology use (2013) and pointed out the need to consider potential risks related to the use of telecommunication technologies, including social media. They note that psychologists are recommended to inform clients of the risks to possible disclosure of confidential information during electronic communications. Furthermore, psychologists are encouraged to obtain written informed consent about unique concerns regarding technology-based communications. In the situation discussed, upfront consent about how social media would be used to communicate, the unique privacy/confidentiality considerations, and the boundaries around social media use might have helped to mitigate the risk. Other professional organizations have recommended using means of identity authentication, such as the establishment of code words, a number, or other nondescript identifiers (American Counseling Association, 2014).

Privacy/Confidentiality

The practice of psychotherapy and other mental health services can be stressful. Professionals can encounter a range of painful client histories, difficult interpersonal interactions, organizational or bureaucratic challenges, or patient tragedies such as suicide. It is natural to want to reach out during occupational stress. Social media provides immediate access to one's social network to share such experiences, process difficult emotions, and receive support. However, such posts, even when well-intentioned and with limited identifying information, carry risks to patient privacy as well as the public trust in mental health providers. Wells, Lehavot, and Isaac (2015) discuss mental health providers' social media posts about work-related situations. They note that even when identifying information is omitted from social media posts of clinicians, the content posted can disclose personal information to a digital audience of unknown (and uncontrollable) size without client consent. Further, such posts can risk unintentional disclosure of the client's identity when non-identifying details are considered together. Even in the absence of specific identifiers, circumstances and situational details can reveal identities. This is a particular risk in small communities or when the case discussed is familiar to a large group of people or covered by the media. Wells and colleagues also point out that posted content can undermine the public trust in the field given the potential impacts of a social media post on the public's perceptions of privacy. Maintaining the public trust is an important consideration in the helping professions generally.

Indeed, it is worth noting that the public trust can also be affected by one's personal social media posts unrelated to work. The National Organization for Human Services Ethical Standards has taken this into account and states in Standard 33 that "Human service professionals make careful decisions about disclosing personal information while using social media, knowing that they reflect the profession of human services" (National Organization for Human Service Professionals, 2015, p. 7).

Boundaries, Disclosure, and Multiple Relationships via Social Media

The following hypothetical, but representative, case example illustrates the risk to traditional boundaries via information available through social media.

> Ms. Bower was seeing Tonya for marital problems and for treatment of her moderately depressed mood. Tonya had a history of boundary problems in relationships and Ms. Bower carefully self-monitored her style of counseling to ensure an appropriate professional relationship. She was surprised when Tonya came into a session reporting how pleased she was that Ms. Bower and Tonya shared the same political affiliation, and Tonya expressed appreciation for Ms. Bower's concern for the homeless. Ms. Bower was puzzled until Tonya reported that she had found Ms. Bower's social media account. She commented on a couple of the social media groups Ms. Bower followed and stated that she was a bit surprised that Ms. Bower earned enough as a therapist to afford a home in her upper middle-class neighborhood. Ms. Bower realized that Tanya had located public records online about her home address and that her social media privacy settings allowed non-friends to view the groups she followed, though they could not see her status updates.

In the course of providing mental health services, various information about the provider is disclosed to the client and this includes both intentional disclosure and unintentional disclosure (Zur, 2007). When information is intentionally disclosed, it may be done so thoughtfully and in the service of supporting treatment, whereas unintentional or inadvertent disclosure can occur through observable characteristics, such as an observable physical disability or wearing a wedding ring. Social media can inadvertently or unintentionally disclose information to clients who find their mental health clinician's profile and information online.

Mental health professionals should review their social media accounts and their privacy settings. This process is not always intuitive, and multiple sets of privacy setting menus may need to be reviewed in order to ensure appropriate preferences. Different settings may be required for different types of content, such as status updates, shared posts, photos, posts about you by others, or profile pictures. In addition, when clinicians post to subgroups of users with a shared interest, that content will typically be viewable by members of the group, likely including those outside of their personal network. The postings to some groups may be publicly available. Rural areas may be at particular risk of specialized groups that are geographically organized, facilitating the risk of mutual belonging among mental health clinicians and their clients. Furthermore, regardless of settings, the private information shared on a social media platform resides on servers not in control of the patient or provider. Privacy policies and user agreements should be reviewed by clients and clinicians with careful consideration of the implications of use.

The relationships between mental health providers and their patients is, by definition, a professional relationship in which the clinician is paid to provide a service that is designed to support the well-being of the client or patient. Many disciplines have an explicit commitment to the value of beneficence and non-maleficence. That is, we aim to use our expertise and skills to support the welfare of others and to do no harm. When mental health providers enter a second type of relationship with a patient, other than a professional one, this multiple relationship has the potential to interfere with the patient's ability to effectively receive services and/or the ability of clinician to effectively provide services. One of the most frequently discussed aspects of social media in mental health is the potential it creates for multiple relationships.

When a mental health professional receives and accepts a client's social media "follow" or "friend" request, the clinician risks entering a multiple relationship. It is difficult to predict the client's understanding of a social media connection and the client may start to view the relationship as more personal or intimate than professional. In almost every case, a mental health professional should not accept a client request to join their personal social media network. When social media connections occur with a professional page or account, therapists must decide what to do with client posts or communications, and client expectations about the expediency of clinician review come into play. Many factors can be considered regarding a social media client friend request. Zur and Walker (n.d.) highlight a number of issues to consider, such as the type of therapist social media page or account, the information available on the page, the context of treatment and type of services being provided, the nature of the client's background and difficulties, and the meaning of the request to the client and the therapist.

Because of the risks, some professional organizations explicitly expect professionals who elect to have a professional and personal social media account to use separate profiles and clearly distinguish between the two (American Counseling Association, 2014). This approach is a starting point to keeping a professional social media presence focused on content and connections associated with one's occupation and separate from one's personal information and social relationships. Regardless, mental health practitioners must ensure their personal social media account is appropriately secured. A helpful strategy may be to search for oneself via an account that is not a part of your friend network to see what is viewable by others. Even content available on professional social media accounts, such as LinkedIn, should be viewed through the lens of patient access to available information.

Although not the focus of this chapter, a similar strategy might be used for personal information available online, outside of social media, and on the internet generally. Use of an internet search engine such as Google can reveal what personal information might be discovered through a client's internet search. Websites such as truepeoplesearch.com and spokeo.com aggregate public records and offer basic information only (name, age, city of residence) for free to anyone online. Mental health providers can go to these websites to request that their record be removed. Common types of information available online might include a personal home address and phone number, home purchase price, previous occupational affiliations and jobs, biographies from previous teaching in the community, family relations, public information or content posted by family members, media interviews, and any public court proceedings. Obviously, some of this information is a part of marketing one's practice. Nonetheless, considering how clients view personal and professional information is important when considering social media's impact on boundaries.

Clients Searching for Therapists

In the context of clients searching for information about their therapists, a review of research describing such searches is of interest. A study was conducted of 332 individuals who had been in psychotherapy within the previous year and had found personal and professional information about their therapist online (Kolmes & Taube, 2016). Eighty-seven percent of those who found personal information about their therapist on the internet sought it out intentionally. The most common type of information found was family information (61%), followed by age/birthday (55%), education (51%), and home address (46%). The primary reason for searching for this information was sheer curiosity (81%), and only 28% told their therapist about their search. The study also points out an anecdote highlighting the additional information available to clients about therapists through the postings of therapists' children and spouses. On the one hand, searching for some information about health care providers online may be a sign of a good consumer. On the other hand, some information discovered could negatively impact the treatment relationship. At an extreme end of the continuum, rare cases of client stalking of mental health clinicians do occur (e.g., Soliman, Haque, & George, 2007), and information available online can be used against victims with malintent (Sheridan & Grant, 2007).

Therapists Searching for Clients on Social Media

Data on clients searching for therapists is likely of great interest to behavioral health providers but the search bar is available to all—therapists can just as easily search for their clients. Mental health providers are often in an assessment role, gathering data about client behavior, including corroborating information, in some cases. For some helping professionals, the accuracy and validity of client reports can be questionable at times, particularly when assessment and/or treatment is court mandated or when it is associated with child protective activities. Ashby and colleagues (2015) discuss a range of reasons psychiatrists might think about an online search of a patient, including exploring concerns about falsified information, to learn whether a patient is involved in dangerous behavior, to obtain collateral information in order to inform diagnostic formulation, or to monitor symptoms and treatment effectiveness over time. Regardless of the purpose, the authors point out that such a search poses risk because it bypasses the therapeutic relationship, can negatively affect trust, and may be an invasion of privacy. Should mental health clinicians search for clients on social media? According to a recent article in the London, England, newspaper, *The Times* (Bridge, March 22, 2019), such searches do occur. The paper reported a Lancaster University study that observed field work of child-protective teams. According to the report, social workers would routinely view profiles of parents of at-risk children, at times creating fake Facebook accounts to "friend" parents when their social media activity was not public. The social workers believed that the behavior was justified to help keep children safe.

How often do mental health providers search for clients and why? A survey of 227 psychotherapists (Kolmes & Taube, 2014) found that 48% intentionally searched for information about current clients who were not in crisis. Although internet search engines were the most common tool for these searches (76%), it is interesting to note that 40% used Facebook to search. Most searches were reportedly treatment-related or to verify information shared during treatment. Sixty-one percent of psychotherapists considered the search a slight-to-small boundary crossing and 17% considered it a more significant boundary issue. Interestingly, the behavior may be more common among trainees. In a study of 783 doctoral students who had seen clients and were enrolled in a clinical, counseling, or school psychology program in the United States or Canada, DiLillo and Gale (2011) found that 94% had searched for at least one client's information using social media. This is particularly interesting, given that 77% of the sample reported that it was either never acceptable or usually not acceptable to search for client information.

An important issue associated with the social media searches of clients by therapists is if and how they elect to use the information and how they do or do not discuss the search with their client. Even if clinicians believe they have an appropriate or at least defensible reason for the search, if disclosed to the client there is no guarantee they will agree. The search may be regarded as a significant breach of trust and risks negatively impacting the working relationship. Accordingly, a therapist may not disclose the search but are then placed in the uncomfortable and difficult position of trying to remember what was learned during the search in order to avoid inadvertently disclosing it to the client. These kinds of mental gymnastics would obviously be challenging to employ, and when they fail would present significant risks to the professional relationship on their own.

Professional organizations have begun to develop ethics standards on searching for clients on social media. For example, the National Association of Social Workers Code of Ethics (2017) has a standard requiring social workers to obtain client consent before conducting an electronic search of the client. There are exceptions for searches related to serious, imminent harm or other compelling professional reasons to conduct a search, but the role of client consent as an ethical obligation for social workers is noteworthy. Others have produced thoughtful questions to support ethical decision making prior to a search of a client (e.g., Clinton, Silverman, & Brendel, 2010).

Accuracy of Psychological Information on Social Media

The ability to easily share content with other users is a clear advantage of social media, but the accuracy of this content is, for the most part, unregulated. Accordingly, social media users can easily disseminate information broadly regardless of its accuracy. Individual cases, anecdotes, personal experiences, opinions, or misinformation can receive more attention than they merit. Social media users with large numbers of followers have substantial influence, regardless of mental health expertise. Any topic on which celebrity social media users post can be viewed by millions of people. In contrast, it is interesting to note that well-designed empirical studies that help move our knowledge of behavioral health forward rarely get disseminated broadly and can take years to impact clinical practice.

Social Media Posting and "Practicing"

Mental health professionals often use social media to share content relevant to the treatment or assessment of mental illness or to discuss their own opinions about these matters. Some mental health professions require a license to "practice" in their state, with corresponding legal definitions of what it means to practice. For example, in the State of Washington, psychological practice is defined as follows:

> the observation, evaluation, interpretation, and modification of human behavior by the application of psychological principles, methods, and procedures for the purposes of preventing or eliminating symptomatic or maladaptive behavior and promoting mental and behavioral health. It includes, but is not limited to. . . . (c) Counseling and guidance,

psychotherapeutic techniques, remediation, health promotion, and consultation within the context of established psychological principles and theories.

(Revised Code of Washington, n.d.)

In this context, one can wonder about the extent to which social media posts providing advice to others based on one's training could be constituted psychological practice, a concerning thought given the individuals seeking assistance may reside outside the state in which one is licensed.

A relevant example is available from social media blogs, the contemporary online forum for newspaper advice columns. A syndicated advice columnist with a master's degree and a North Carolina license as a psychological associate received a letter from the Kentucky Board of Examiners after a retired psychologist complained about advice the columnist disseminated. According to ABC News (Rudra, 2013), the author was asked to cease and desist his columns because his columns constituted the practice of psychology, for which he was not licensed in Kentucky. The complaint also included concerns about how the columnist represented his credentials, but for the purposes of this chapter, the dissemination of psychological opinions online, specifically, on social media is an interesting consideration. Follow-up news reporting indicates that the columnist ultimately triumphed in court (Kocher, 2015). However, this case highlights unique risks that emerge as mental health professionals engage with clients and the community via social media. This state of affairs is particularly noteworthy, given an increasingly divisive culture and a wide range of reactions to posted material. Some have observed the use of "weaponized ethics complaints" against clinicians who post views or opinions with which others take issue (Ley, 2019). While such complaints may or may not carry merit, the sheer time, energy, and stress of legally defending oneself is not without cost.

Summary of Steps to Manage the Risks Associated With Social Media Use

Mental health providers should start their risk management with a thorough understanding of the laws guiding the boundaries of technology and social media use in the state in which they are licensed, the policies within their organization, and the ethics codes and clinical guidance documents for their discipline. These laws and guiding documents are updated over time, and a process of continuous learning should be engaged. Mental health providers have long applied ethical decision-making frameworks to complex situations with competing professional obligations (e.g., Cottone & Claus, 2000). Some such frameworks may prove useful in thoughtfully considering options in the course of ethical decision making associated with social media use.

In this context, current practice-based considerations follow:

- Clinicians should consider adopting a social media policy that is shared with clients as part of informed consent. Such a practice places clear information about how social media will and will not be used at the outset of the professional relationship. A widely cited sample social media policy available for download and edit is generously made available by Dr. Keely Kolmes at https://drkkolmes.com/social-media-policy.
- Clinically, use of social media support groups is fraught with potential danger. Some clients may find support from such a group, but mental health providers might be cautious in recommending such groups, particularly unmoderated groups.
- Use of technology to communicate with clients carries long-standing challenges to identity authentication—how can you be sure you are interacting with your client or patient and not someone else? This is relevant to social media because of the opportunities for direct messaging or other opportunities for communications. Health care providers have moved toward the use of brief technology-based appointment reminders. These reminders may carry more risk for mental health providers and organizations, however, given the sensitivity and potential stigma effects for some in treatment. Careful and thoughtful review of the unique risks to any form of technology-based communication and informed consent can help mitigate risk.
- Mental health professionals who choose to have a social media presence should ensure that they have separate accounts for personal and professional use.
- Given the risk of unintentional disclosure of client identity or negatively impacting the public perception of the profession, mental health clinicians should be cautious about posting information about individual situations. There may be other more appropriate and more effective ways of processing emotionally difficult work-related situations, such as through a supervisor, group supervision, or appropriate consultation.
- Unintentional disclosure of information about the therapist to a client via information available on social media can pose risks to the professional relationship in some cases. A careful review of privacy settings can help manage the risk of unintentional/unplanned disclosure of personal information to clients.
- Mental health clinicians can review personal and professional information available about themselves online, seeking to limit potentially problematic information when possible.
- Mental health providers may encounter situations where they are considering searching for a client or patient on social media. Review of relevant ethical codes, laws, and organizational policies is important. Decision-making frameworks may be helpful in thinking through such decisions (e.g., Clinton et al., 2010)

Social media is one of the most ubiquitous technology innovations in the digital age, and there are incredible opportunities to improving the mental health of individuals and populations as innovation proceeds (see chapters 14 and 15). In contemporary mental health practice, social media offers opportunities as well as pitfalls. Application of appropriate and thoughtful safeguards can help mental health providers leverage the potential and reduce the risk associated with social media.

References

American Counseling Association (2014). *2014 ACA code of ethics*. Retrieved from www.counseling.org/resources/aca-code-of-ethics.pdf

Ashby, G. A., O'Brien, A., Bowman, D., Hooper, C., Stevens, T., & Lousada, E. (2015). Should psychiatrists "Google" their patients? *BJPsych Bulletin, 39*(6), 278–283.

Bridge, M. (2019, March 22). Social workers "spying" on families through facebook. *The Times*. Retrieved from www.thetimes.co.uk/article/social-workers-spying-on-families-through-facebook-tkt5kwhxh

Clinton, B. K., Silverman, B. C., & Brendel, D. H. (2010). Patient-targeted googling: The ethics of searching online for patient information. *Harvard Review of Psychiatry, 18*(2), 103–112.

Cottone, R. R., & Claus, R. E. (2000). Ethical decision-making models: A review of the literature. *Journal of Counseling & Development, 78*(3), 275–283.

DiLillo, D., & Gale, E. B. (2011). To Google or not to Google: Graduate students' use of the Internet to access personal information about clients. *Training and Education in Professional Psychology, 5*(3), 160.

Gariepy, G., Honkaniemi, H., & Quesnel-Vallee, A. (2016). Social support and protection from depression: Systematic review of current findings in Western countries. *The British Journal of Psychiatry, 209*(4), 284–293.

Griffiths, K. M., Reynolds, J., & Vassallo, S. (2015). An online, moderated peer-to-peer support bulletin board for depression: User-perceived advantages and disadvantages. *JMIR Mental Health, 2*(2), e14.

Joint Task Force for the Development of Telepsychology Guidelines for Psychologists (2013). Guidelines for the practice of telepsychology. *American Psychologist, 68*, 791–800.

Kaplan, K., Salzer, M. S., Solomon, P., Brusilovskiy, E., & Cousounis, P. (2011). Internet peer support for individuals with psychiatric disabilities: A randomized controlled trial. *Social Science & Medicine, 72*(1), 54–62.

Kessler, R. C., Price, R. H., & Wortman, C. B. (1985). Social factors in psychopathology: Stress, social support, and coping processes. *Annual Review of Psychology, 36*(1), 531–572.

Kocher, G. (2015, October 1). *Federal judge rules in favor of John Rosemond in lawsuit against psychology board*. Lexington Hearld Leader. Retrieved from www.kentucky.com/living/family/article42629730.html

Kolmes, K., & Taube, D. O. (2014). Seeking and finding our clients on the Internet: Boundary considerations in cyberspace. *Professional Psychology: Research and Practice, 45*(1), 3.

Kolmes, K., & Taube, D. O. (2016). Client discovery of psychotherapist personal information online. *Professional Psychology: Research and Practice, 47*(2), 147.

Ley, D. J. (2019, July 19). Weaponized ethics complaints against clinicians. *Psychology Today*. Retrieved from www.psychologytoday.com/us/blog/women-who-stray/201907/weaponized-ethics-complaints-against-clinicians

Mohr, D. C., Burns, M. N., Schueller, S. M., Clarke, G., & Klinkman, M. (2013). Behavioral intervention technologies: Evidence review and recommendations for future research in mental health. *General Hospital Psychiatry, 35*(4), 332–338.

National Association of Social Workers (2017). *Code of ethics*. Retrieved from www.socialworkers.org/About/Ethics/Code-of-Ethics/Code-of-Ethics-English

National Organization for Human Service Professionals (2015). *Ethical standards for human service professionals*. Retrieved from www.nationalhumanservices.org/ethical-standards-for-hs-professionals

Ozer, E. J., Best, S. R., Lipsey, T. L., & Weiss, D. S. (2003). Predictors of posttraumatic stress disorder and symptoms in adults: A meta-analysis. *Psychological Bulletin, 129*(1), 52.

Pew Research Center (2019). *Social media fact sheet*. Retrieved from www.pewresearch.org/internet/fact-sheet/social-media/

Revised Code of Washington (n.d.). Retrieved from https://app.leg.wa.gov/RCW/default.aspx?cite=18.83

Rudra, G. (2013, July 21). Kentucky orders end to parenting column, says columnist not state-licensed psychologist. *abcNews*. Retrieved from https://abcnews.go.com/US/parenting-columnist-claims-kentucky-censorship/story?id=19714678

Salzer, M. S., Palmer, S. C., Kaplan, K., Brusilovskiy, E., Ten Have, T., Hampshire, M., et al. (2010). A randomized controlled study of Internet peer-to-peer interactions among women newly diagnosed with breast cancer. *Psycho-Oncology, 19*, 441–446.

Sawesi, S., Rashrash, M., Phalakornkule, K., Carpenter, J. S., & Jones, J. F. (2016). The impact of information technology on patient engagement and health behavior change: A systematic review of the literature. *JMIR Medical Informatics, 4*(1), e1.

Sheridan, L. P., & Grant, T. (2007). Is cyberstalking different? *Psychology, Crime & Law, 13*(6), 627–640.

Soliman, S., Haque, S., & George, E. (2007). Stalking and Huntington's disease: A neurobiological link? *Journal of Forensic Sciences, 52*(5), 1202–1204.

Wells, D. M., Lehavot, K., & Isaac, M. L. (2015). Sounding off on social media: The ethics of patient storytelling in the modern era. *Academic Medicine, 90*(8), 1015–1019.

Zur, O. (2007). Self-disclosure. In O. Zur (Ed.), *Boundaries in psychotherapy: Ethical and clinical explorations* (149–165). Washington, DC: American Psychological Association.

Zur, O, & Walker, A. (n.d.). *To accept or not to accept? How to respond when clients send "friend request" to their psychotherapist or counselors on Facebook, Linkedin, Twitter or other social networking sites*. Retrieved from www.zurinstitute.com/socialnetworking/

7 Innovative and Evolving Mobile Mental Health Technologies for the Treatment of Serious Mental Illness

Michael Hsu, Jessica Lipschitz, Robert Boland, and John Torous

Introduction

Approximately one in 25 Americans experiences serious mental illness (SMI) such as major depressive disorder (MDD), bipolar disorder, and schizophrenia in a given year (NIMH, 2019). Functional impairment related to SMI has resulted in a public health crisis and $139.2 billion in lost earnings in the United States (NIMH, 2019). However, despite the significant burden of disease and growing public health awareness of mental illness, access to care continues to be problematic for many with SMI. In a National Comorbidity Survey conducted between 2001 and 2003, just 40% of respondents with an active mental illness reported receiving any treatment, with only 21.7% treated by a specialty mental health provider (Wang et al., 2005).

Many patients with a psychiatric illness only interface with the health care system once they become severely symptomatic. For patients with schizophrenia, this might mean seeking care only when they experience relapse or are unable to care for themselves. For patients with depression, this might mean seeking care only after they have developed significant neurovegetative symptoms or endorsed suicide intent and plan. A combination of stigma, lack of preventative measures, inaccessibility of services, and shortage of mental health workers contributes to such crisis–centered care, which results in increased health care costs, drainage of personnel resources, and ultimately poor patient outcomes (Cagney, 2015; Paton et al., 2016). In the traditional model, patients often present through an emergency department and are subsequently hospitalized, only later entering outpatient care (Blonigen et al., 2017). However, as we begin to consider novel care models that instead gravitate toward preventative health and screening tools, innovative methods are needed to identify high-risk patients before they reach a crisis.

Increasing computing power and capabilities in mobile smartphones provide an opportunity for clinicians to gather clinical insights about patients at scale. In other words, mobile technologies enable clinicians to gather a large volume of data on many patients without a significant burden on clinician time and energy. Approximately 225 million people in the United

States have a smartphone, and many predict this figure to increase (Poushter, Bishop, & Chwe, 2018). The concept of a digital divide is diminishing as mobile phones have become available to more individuals regardless of socioeconomic status (Torous, Rodriguez, & Powell, 2017). Smartphone usage among those with serious mental illness is also on the rise: one series of studies showed that smartphone usage in a state Department of Mental Health (DMH) clinic increased from 49% to 66% between 2014 and 2018 (Torous et al., 2014; Torous, Wisniewski, Liu, & Keshavan, 2018). In parallel with increasing smartphone users, the number of mobile applications related to mental health and wellness has rapidly surged, with over 10,000 apps available with functions ranging from self-help to tele-psychiatry to mindfulness (Torous & Roberts, 2017). However, quantity and prevalence of technology does not always equate to efficacy, safety, and cost savings.

In this chapter, we focus on the advent of three scalable smartphone technologies that demonstrate potential to address gaps in access for the diagnosis and treatment of SMI: ecological momentary assessments (EMAs), digital phenotyping, and mobile health peer support (Torous, Kiang, Lorme, & Onnela, 2016). After describing these technologies, we apply the five-step American Psychiatric Association (APA) App Evaluation Model and offer a framework for incorporating digital psychiatry into clinical practice (APA, 2019b; Torous et al., 2019).

Ecological Momentary Assessments

The current model of ambulatory psychiatric evaluation relies on infrequent in-person interviews that are not systematized and may be susceptible to inherent recall bias. Further, patients with SMI or substance use often do not consistently follow up with outpatient care (Marino et al., 2016). One solution is the use of daily symptom diaries, which allow patients to record aspects of their mood, psychosocial environment, behaviors, or thoughts with more granularity than intermittent in-person visits.

Daily diaries are an imperfect tool, however, as they do not account for recall bias or fluctuations in emotional state throughout the course of the day. In comparison, ecological momentary assessments (EMAs) can utilize technologies such as a patient's personal smartphone to deliver intermittent assessments throughout the day to collect a more detailed and timely understanding of patients' thoughts, affect, cognition, and behaviors (Figure 7.1). For example, suicidality is traditionally measured during in-person or over-the-telephone interfaces between patients and providers. With EMA, patients are able to rate their level of suicidality at multiple time points during the day, using the same prompt questions, which offers themselves and their providers a more accurate sense of suicidal thought triggers and burden. If assessing suicidality or self-harm with EMA, it is important to note that responses may not be real-time and clinicians should educate patients to still seek help through traditional channels.

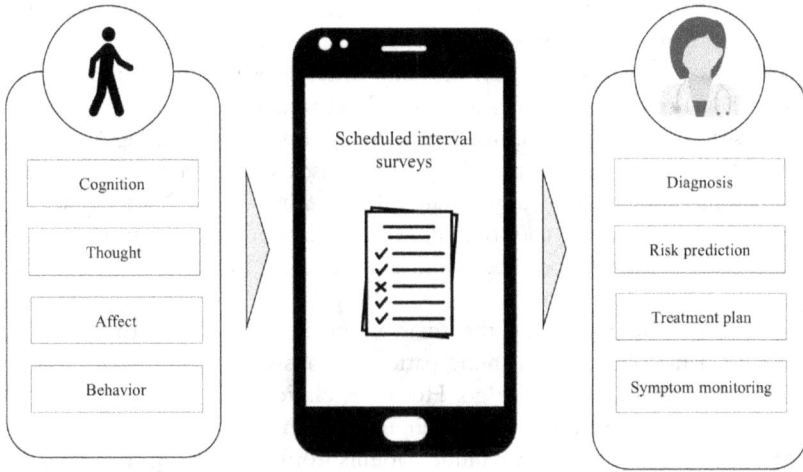

Figure 7.1 Ecological m-Momentary Assessments Utilize Scheduled Interval Surveys to Assess Patients' Cognition, Thoughts, Affect, and behavior to Inform Clinical Assessment

The effectiveness of EMAs depends on patients' willingness to complete the built-in tasks and questions. Early evidence based on paper versions of EMAs suggests that patients of varying psychiatric illnesses and dimensions are amenable to completing repeated surveys. In one study, patients with borderline personality disorder completed a 50-item survey in a 10-day span to track affect, substantiating the notion that patients experiencing impulsivity may be amenable to paper EMAs (Moskowitz & Young, 2006; Stein, 1996). Patients with a history of aggression completed 50 surveys in a week for a study on associations between violence and cholesterol levels (Hillbrand, Waite, Miller, Spitz, & Lingswiler, 2000). Adolescents with attention deficit hyperactivity disorder logged their behavior, mood, and social context twice an hour for four days in two intervals in a study that explored associations between disease severity, behavioral patterns, and substance use (Whalen, Jamner, Henker, Delfino, & Lozano, 2003). Patients with eating disorders have undergone multiple paper EMA studies (Steiger, Gauvin, Jabalpurwala, Séguin, & Stotland, 1999). Although some of the studies just mentioned may have had increased participation because research participants received payment, the studies still reinforce the concept that regardless of diagnosis or presence of ongoing psychiatric symptoms, patients are willing and able to log symptoms to better understand their own disease as well as to provide their providers with useful clinical data for managing their care. Patients' adherence to EMA can be improved if they understand its clinical value and that survey results will be reviewed periodically during clinic visits.

Additionally, emerging research suggests that EMAs may open the door for more accurate self-disclosure of symptoms than clinician interviews. For example, Torous and colleagues (2015) found that patients reported more severe symptoms of depression on daily EMA assessments of mood symptoms than they did via paper and pencil versions of the same questions at in-person clinic visits (Torous et al., 2015). Lucas and colleagues (2014) found that patients are more willing to self-disclose to an automated system than a human provider (Lucas, Gratch, King, & Morency, 2014). EMA can be a powerful, scalable tool that allows clinicians to accurately understand nuances of patient mood, cognition, and behavior in order to make more informed clinical decisions.

Implementing EMAs on the smartphone facilitates an automated and seamless data collection, enabling patients to answer brief survey questions at home, at work, or on the go. However, clinicians should be aware that utilizing mobile EMA may be challenging for some patients with SMI. Poor cognition or illiteracy can preclude patients from completing surveys independently or in a timely manner. Some patients with SMI may provide pushback if surveys include potentially uncomfortable questions such as asking about suicidal thoughts or behaviors (Bajaj et al., 2008). Some patients may have demanding jobs or other environmental factors that can make it difficult for them to complete multiple surveys each day. Clinicians should address any barriers to complying with mobile EMA and collaborate with patients to devise a feasible mobile EMA plan.

Digital Phenotyping

A major challenge in addressing SMI is the inability to detect when a patient is at elevated risk in a timely fashion. The field does not have the tools or data to predict, at scale, when a person with depression might be at elevated risk for a suicide attempt, when a person with schizophrenia may be at elevated risk for symptom relapse, or when a patient with bipolar disorder may become manic. Instead, providers work with clinical data derived from questionnaires or interviews of patients that are staggered in time and convey only a snapshot of a patient's affect and behavior. Digital phenotyping may help identify patients with elevated risk by discovering patterns through observing continuous, dynamic clinical data.

Before further describing the concept of digital phenotyping, we must first establish the two types of data that smartphones collect: active and passive. Active data collection requires patient input. An example of active data is EMA, for which patients answer a series of questions to assess mood or behavior at certain times of the day. Passive data, on the other hand, is gathered continuously by the smartphone's internal microprocessors or sensors without requiring any patient input. Examples of passive data include usage of data from social media and text messaging, user movement patterns via accelerometer, or voice sampling through microphone (Onnela & Rauch,

2016). The breadth of passive data continues to expand with increasing processing speed and capabilities.

Defined as the "moment-by-moment quantification of the individual-level human phenotype *in situ* using data from personal digital devices" (Torous et al., 2015; p. 3), digital phenotyping uses existing data to inform clinical assessment and decision making. The advances in smartphone processing speed and the ubiquity of microprocessors and sensors capture a breadth of patient data not previously attainable (see Figure 7.2). With the appropriate analytical tools, sensory data can improve clinicians' understanding of behavioral health dynamics and drive timely, personalized assessments and interventions.

The types of data often utilized in digital phenotyping include daytime mobility (steps, number of distinct GPS locations, time spent at home or work), sleep duration and quality, number of outgoing and incoming calls, number of outgoing and incoming text messages, natural language processing of text and email content, duration and type of app use (e.g., social media), and number of instances of smartphone use (screen on/off occurrences). The key is applying advanced longitudinal data analysis algorithms to dynamically evaluate the personalized utility of such data for predicting clinical deterioration and improvement for each individual patient over time.

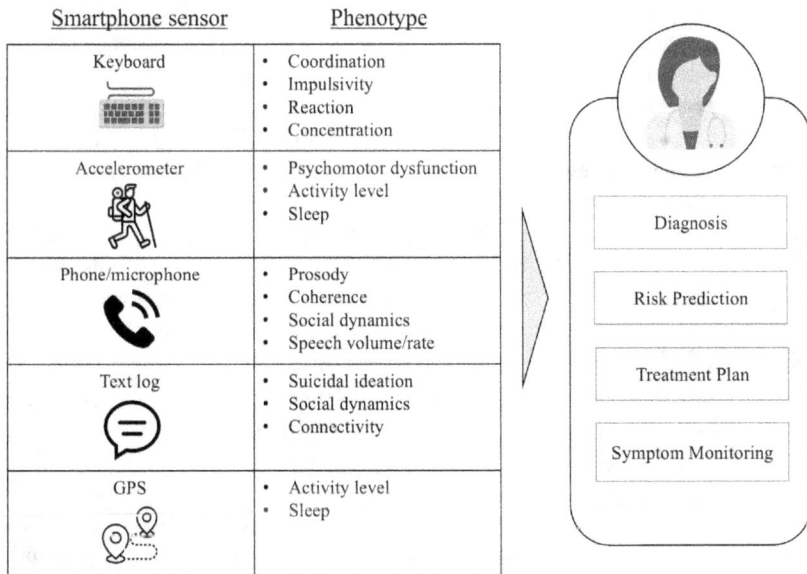

Smartphone sensor	Phenotype
Keyboard	• Coordination • Impulsivity • Reaction • Concentration
Accelerometer	• Psychomotor dysfunction • Activity level • Sleep
Phone/microphone	• Prosody • Coherence • Social dynamics • Speech volume/rate
Text log	• Suicidal ideation • Social dynamics • Connectivity
GPS	• Activity level • Sleep

Diagnosis

Risk Prediction

Treatment Plan

Symptom Monitoring

Figure 7.2 Digital Phenotyping Utilizes Passive Data From Smartphone Sensors to Characterize Patients' Behavioral Phenotype to Inform Clinical Assessments

Compared to EMA, digital phenotyping appears to be more advantageous in assessing behavior for two main reasons. First, gathering real-time clinical data via patients' smartphones eliminates the need for active input and is less burdensome for patients. This factor may be especially pertinent when considering mobile technologies for patients with cognitive impairment, illiteracy, or other characteristics that could make engaging with smartphone apps more challenging. Second, large-scale clinical trials may be easier to conduct and less costly with digital phenotyping, given widespread smartphone use and automated collection of sensory data. Digital phenotyping is admittedly an emerging phenomenon, and clinicians will need to be informed on how to best use this technology for the welfare of patients. To date, there is need for replication studies to validate this technology for widespread use. Clinicians should consider digital phenotyping as potentially useful but still experimental at this point and not a standard of care. Further ethical and privacy challenges will be discussed later in this chapter.

Smartphone-Based Peer Support

A growing body of evidence points to the utility of peer support, defined as support from an individual with shared experience of mental illness, in mental health recovery. A number of feasibility studies conducted in the 1990s and early 2000s indicated non-inferiority when comparing peer to non-peer support for patients with SMI (Clarke et al., 2000; Davidson, Bellamy, Guy, & Miller, 2012). A 2013 Cochrane review of 11 studies comparing groups with consumer-providers as an adjunct to professional care and groups receiving usual care by health professionals alone found no significant differences in quality of life, function, social relations, hospital use, or in the numbers of people withdrawing from the study (Pitt et al., 2013). Subsequent studies suggested that peer support programming performs better than non-peer-support counterparts along several outcome measures, especially among the most disengaged clients (Sells, Davidson, Jewell, Falzer, & Rowe, 2006). Specifically, peer-to-peer support is associated with decreased hospitalizations, reduced length of stay, and decreased substance use in those with SMI and comorbid substance use disorders (Landers & Zhou, 2011; Naslund, Aschbrenner, Marsch, & Bartels, 2016; Rowe et al., 2007). In addition to clinical outcomes, peer support has been shown to provide a sense of hope for recipients as they are given examples of individuals who have experienced similar issues and have overcome them (Solomon, 2004).

One challenge of peer support is finding a place to meet and keeping in close contact with peer providers. In rural areas, there may also be a limited pool of peers. Utilizing smartphone technologies can be helpful to this end, given that most people actively use their phones for health care and non-health care purposes. Smartphones not only resolve geographic constraints but could augment and expand the capacities of peer support.

Prior to recommending mobile peer support, it may be useful for clinicians to ask patients with serious mental illness if they are using peer support channels like Facebook, YouTube, or online forums. Clinicians should also explore with patients about how they plan to use the support toward recovery. Using the app evaluation model delineated in the next section, we evaluate the evidence for mobile health peer support.

App Evaluation Model

Using smartphones to assess real-time symptoms via EMA, digital phenotyping, and smartphone-based peer support is an emerging area of research. Given an incipient body of research, evolving privacy and ethical issues around using smartphone data in health care, regulatory changes concerning using software (e.g., apps) as a medical device, and continual software updates in commercial marketplaces, recommending any single app for patients with SMI is a challenge at this time (Wisniewski et al., 2019). Instead, to increase understanding of this field and help readers make informed decision about apps, we apply the App Evaluation Model published by the APA (Torous et al., 2014; Torous, Chan, et al., 2018). This model comprises five factors for clinicians and patients to consider when assessing an app: (1) background information, (2) privacy and security, (3) evidence, (4) ease of use, and (5) interoperability. The following section provides a framework to guide and inform clinicians on how to use these steps to guide decision making on what interventions to use for particular subsets of patients with SMI.

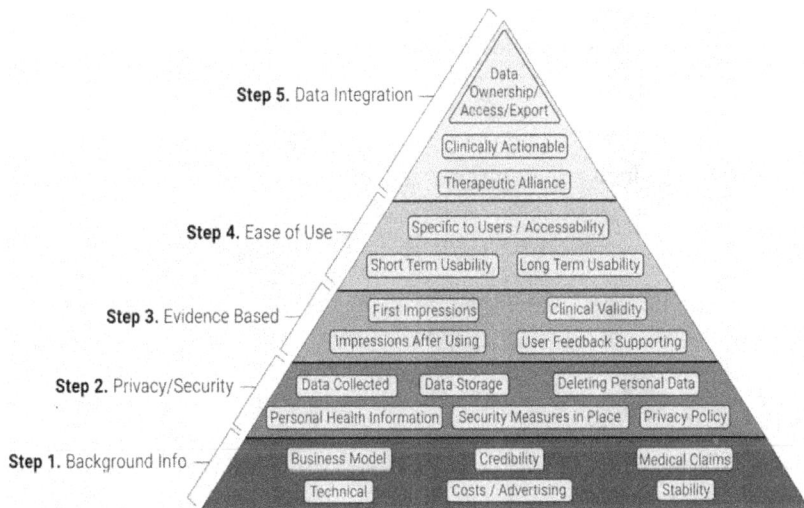

Figure 7.3 App Evaluation Model Published by the American Psychiatric Association (APA)
Source: APA, 2019b.

Step 1: Background Information

Gathering background information about an app is essential for evaluating its usefulness and fit within a given clinical practice and patient population. The following is a list of questions pertaining to general background information.

- **Cost:**
    - Is the app free to download and use?
    - Does the app directly charge users?
    - Does the app charge institutions through a licensing model?
    - Does the app generate revenue through other means such as through advertising, app add-ons, or selling user data?
    - What training is required for patients and providers in order to use the app?

- **Developer:**
    - Is the developer a private company or academic center?
    - Does the developer claim that the application is for medical use, self-help, or general health? (Note: Applications deemed for medical purposes have a responsibility to protect patient privacy under the Health Insurance Portability and Accountability Act (HIPAA). Self-help or general health applications on the other hand are not under such conditions)

- **Platform:**
    - What operating system(s) can the application run on (Apple, Android, etc)?
    - Can the app run on a personal computer?
    - Does the app require internet access?

- **Time commitment:**
    - How much time will patients need to spend using the app on a daily basis?
    - Does the application drain the user's battery quickly?

Given the answers to thesequestions, clinicians can evaluate the potential risks and benefits of utilizing an app with SMI patients. Clinicians need not answer every question, but should answer enough to consider a broad range of potential factors that would influence how patients with SMI may be affected by usage of the app.

Step 2: Risk/Privacy and Security

There are several privacy concerns when it comes to using smartphone apps for mental health in patients with SMI (O'Loughlin, Neary, Adkins, &

Hueller, 2018). Depending on where personal data is stored, certain policy and security measures are necessary. Data stored on a phone or cloud service is vulnerable to security threats, especially if passwords are compromised. Data that is uploaded to an electronic medical record (EMR) system is vulnerable to third-party access (White, 2013). Patients should also be made aware of what an app's privacy agreement says about how their data can be distributed to third parties. However, it should be noted that apps may transmit data to third parties without direct disclosure through a privacy policy (Huckvale, Torous, & Larsen, 2019).

Passive sensing data such as text messages, GPS, and emails may seem innocuous, but third parties may be able to identify individuals based on such raw data (Grundy et al., 2019). As such, patients should be informed of the potential risk they are exposed to. Martinez-Martin and colleagues suggested that passive data could be further categorized into data that is "free of semantic content, such as physiologic measures or keystroke patterns" as opposed to data that is "semantic" such as "text or speech" with specific policies targeting the collection of each data type (Martinez-Martin, Insel, Dagum, Greely, & Cho, 2018). In addition to privacy and security, smartphone app transparency is an important issue both to the end user and to clinicians. This may be a challenge, as the methods or algorithms employed by mobile applications may be proprietary.

Privacy and transparency of mobile applications can have real implications when it comes to patient welfare, therapeutic alliances with providers, and patient buy-in to care. Per survey data published by Rock Health, 92% of consumers agree with the statement "I should be in control of who has access to my health data." Only 8% of consumers in this survey would be comfortable sharing their health data with technology companies (Gandhi & Wang, 2015). In a 2019 survey study of 211 participants, respondents were significantly more comfortable sharing their personal or health data with their doctor as opposed to their family or an EHR system (Nicholas et al., 2019). Furthermore, respondents were significantly more comfortable sharing health information than they were sharing personal data (Nicholas et al., 2019). Yet data privacy and transparency in digital health is lacking (Cummings, Allen, Clennon, Ji, & Druss, 2017). One study in 2014 looking at the 600 most often used mobile health apps on Apple and Android revealed that only about 30% have a discrete privacy policy (Sunyaev, Dehling, Taylor, & Mandl, 2015).

The same privacy issues that face general digital health are also a concern for digital psychiatry. In a study of 72 applications targeting medical and health needs of patients with dementia, only 46% of apps had a privacy policy, of which just 58% pertained to the specific application. Many of the privacy policies lacked clarity (Rosenfeld, Torous, & Vahia, 2017). Despite the lack of privacy policies, many countries do not have nationwide laws to protect user data as of this writing. For example, the United States does not have a federal law requiring privacy policies for smartphone apps. However, the state of California instituted the California Online Privacy Protection Act, which applies to any smartphone applications that may put California residents at risk. Some companies have been proactive in creating their own policies; for example, Apple has confirmed that as of October 2018, all apps that utilize personal user data must have a privacy policy (Apple, 2018). Some patients with serious mental illness may have cognitive deficits that make understanding terms and conditions more challenging. Clinicians should thus invest time to ensure that patients understand the potential risks of allowing third-parties to access their data.

Clinicians and users should investigate whether an app has a privacy policy and to what extent this policy protects user data. Privacy policies can be found in various places depending on the phone operating system. For iOS, privacy policies can often be found through a privacy policy link in the "information" section of the mobile app. These policies can also be found on non-mobile websites on the app page. For Android, privacy policies can typically be found via a link in the Google Play Store app listing. When perusing a privacy policy, some basic information that should be gathered may include:

(1)   What type of data is gathered (e.g. tracking, sensing, user input)?
(2)   Where is the data stored?
(3)   What third parties are involved with the data collection process?
(4)   Is the data de-identified?
(5)   Who has access to the data?
(6)   How is the data used?
(7)   Can you delete your personal data?
(8)   What security measures or encryptions are in place to protect personal data?
(9)   Does the app purport HIPAA compliance?

Step 3: Evidence

Evidence for digital psychiatry technologies can be broken down into feasibility studies, initial efficacy studies, and robust efficacy studies. Feasibility (acceptability) studies establish the likelihood that patients will be willing to adhere to using an app in the clinical setting. Patients may be hesitant to use mental health apps due to time or resource costs, digital literacy, or privacy risks. Initial efficacy (pilot) studies can help identify potential positive or negative outcomes resulting from implementing a digital psychiatric technology. Robust efficacy studies focused on target populations are often used to establish the effectiveness of a technology under the best circumstances and help inform clinical recommendations and guidelines. However, robust efficacy evidence may not be required to use digital technologies per se. For example, some technologies can be used to augment a clinician's assessment of patient's sleep, appetite, or cognition. In this case, feasibility, acceptability, and cost-effectiveness are factors to consider. Clinicians need to customize the app experience based on their knowledge of SMI and the needs of the patient.

Unfortunately, evidence for individual mental health apps is scarce overall. In a 2019 study examining the evidence claims of 73 highly ranked mental health apps in two major app stores, 64% of apps had claims regarding their positive effectiveness. Yet only 53% of these apps actually cited evidence from academic literature and a mere 2.7% had direct evidence to back their efficacy claims (Larsen et al., 2019). Thus, providers cannot rely on efficacy claims made by app developers but must individually assess evidence to support a mental health app through their own investigative efforts. As an example, in the next section we examine the evidence of using scalable technologies (EMA, digital phenotyping, mobile peer support) for patients with psychosis. It should be noted that this is by no means intended to be an exhaustive inventory of evidence.

Psychosis

Though larger studies are still needed, initial studies on use of mHealth-based EMAs for psychosis and schizophrenia have suggested preliminary support for feasibility, acceptability, and initial efficacy (Bell, Lim, Rossell, & Thomas, 2017). One 2008 study by Granholm and colleagues examined outpatients with either schizoaffective disorder or schizophrenia who completed standard questionnaires four times a day over the course of a week through a personal digital assistant (PDA) in order to assess functioning and clinical outcomes. Compliance was acceptable (87%), with an overall positive user experience (Granholm, 2007). Kimhy and colleagues (2006) implemented a methodology similar to EMA, Experience Sampling Method (ESM) via PDAs, to compare ten inpatient schizophrenia patients to healthy controls with respect to functional and clinical outcomes (Kimhy et al., 2006). As expected, the cohort of schizophrenia patients scored higher than the healthy controls on a number of psychiatric findings, including auditory and visual hallucinations, suspiciousness, ideas of thought control, and preoccupation. Additionally, healthy controls were noted to have a less challenging time completing the assessments. Another study is currently underway to examine smartphone-based EMAs for assessment and intervention for patients with auditory hallucinations (Bell et al., 2018).

The application of digital phenotyping to schizophrenia evaluation and monitoring is potentially impactful given the importance of early detection and intervention. Up to 40% of hospitalized schizophrenia patients will have relapsed in the initial year following discharge (Hogarty & Ulrich, 1998). Results from a Cochrane meta-analysis suggest that patients with early intervention based on clinical warning signs had significantly less relapse with increased time to relapse and reduced re-hospitalization rates (Morriss, Vinjamuri, Faizal, Bolton, & McCarthy, 2013). Given these promising findings, despite being novel in concept, digital phenotyping for use in psychosis patients has shown some initial feasibility, acceptability, and efficacy.

In 2016, Wang et al. described CrossCheck, a smartphone system that implemented both passive sensing and EMA to study a group of outpatient schizophrenia patients. The aim of the initial feasibility study was to discover associations between sensory and EMA data to multiple dimensions (severity, symptom presentation) of mental health. Study results suggested a link among decreased physical activity, decreased conversations, and sleeping later with negative mental health as well as waking up earlier with positive mental health (Wang et al., 2016). A follow-up study in 2017 by Ben-Zeev and colleagues used CrossCheck to describe predictive sensory and EMA data (Ben-Zeev et al., 2017). The study qualitatively and quantitatively described five schizophrenia patients who later relapsed and the characteristics of their clinical and digital phenotype course.

Another study that implemented digital phenotyping to predict relapse in schizophrenia was a small pilot study of 15 patients who used the Beiwe app with biweekly surveys and passively collected GPS, accelerometer, and anonymized text and call data (Barnett et al., 2018). Five of the 15 patients sampled subsequently relapsed, three of whom had enough data to detect an "anomaly." It was shown that among relapsed patients, the number of anomalies in the two weeks leading up to a relapse was 71% higher than the average prior to those two weeks (Barnett et al., 2018).

Peer support technologies have also been used in some feasibility and initial efficacy studies for psychosis. In general, studies have suggested that incorporating moderators, or third party individuals who can observe and guide peer-to-peer interactions, into digitally driven peer-to-peer support can improve retention, engagement, and efficacy (Biagianti, Quraishi, & Schlosser, 2018). One particular intervention which utilized unmoderated internet peer support for treatment of schizophrenia and schizoaffective disorder actually resulted in higher reported distress; patients with positive experiences using the peer support website actually had higher psychosocial distress than those with negative experiences (Kaplan, Salzer, Solomon, Brusilovskiy, & Cousounis, 2011). The HORYZON study performed by Alvarez-Jimenez et al. utilized the "moderate online social therapy" with individually tailored psychosocial interventions and incorporation of peer and expert moderation. Twenty patients from the Early Psychosis Prevention and Intervention Centre (EPPIC) in Australia were recruited; 60% of the patients used the system for the entire four-week intervention, and 70% used it for at least three out of four weeks. Seventy-five percent of participants reported a "positive" experience, with 90% stating that they would recommend the program to others (Alvarez-Jimenez et al., 2013). Follow-up analysis of safety, privacy, and security outcomes revealed that 90% of the first-episode psychosis participants reported feeling safer using the intervention due to the peer support nature (Gleeson et al., 2014).

Data Quality

It is also imperative to ensure that data collected is of good quality; that is, that it is as free of bias as possible. Any implicit or explicit biases inherent in the data processed will inevitably be reflected in the actionable outputs. For example, "decreased smartphone activity" suggested by less EMA input or lack of passive sensory data may reflect poor compliance in some patients but for others may be due to a dead battery or amotivation (indicating possible worsening of underlying psychiatric process). If studies for digital psychiatry are too narrow in scope, such as primarily of one gender, socio-economic class, or comorbidity, then generalizability of results can be in question. Such limitations can ultimately impact patient welfare. As of this writing, there are no requirements in place to ensure data is free of bias, and there is no standardized means of assessing for bias on artificial intelligence (Dutchen, 2019). Although one study has looked at the quality of acceler-ometer and GPS data in patients with schizophrenia, there needs to be more research in this area with larger sample sizes to optimize quality of passive data (Torous, Staples, et al., 2018).

Another aspect of data quality is the reliability of patient input. Patients may be dishonest in survey answers or manipulate passive data (i.e., have a friend walk around with a phone to alter accelerometer data). Although largely unavoidable, there are currently no built-in mechanisms to prevent users from manipulating their data (as is the case for in-person clinical assess-ments) to please clinicians or form desired impressions. Furthermore, it will be important to determine optimal resolution of data collected. For exam-ple, having an accelerometer or GPS tracker running at all times may not necessarily result in improved data quality, though it would certainly drain the device's battery. Before making clinical decisions based on smartphone data, clinicians need to be confident that data quality is high and to trust the sensors and algorithms underlying the clinical output.

Limitations

EMA, digital phenotyping, and smartphone-enabled peer support are all promising technologies that may enhance diagnostic clarity and enable timely interventions. However, there are three limitations to consider. First, acceptability is a major concern. This is reflected by the fact that despite the myriad of mobile mental health technologies available, there have been very few, if any, that have been widely adopted. One acceptability study with col-lege students in the UK revealed that users are hesitant about digital pheno-typing, given concerns with third party access to data, loss of autonomy, and lack of improvement to self-efficacy (Rooksby, Morrison, & Murray-Rust, 2019). Second, clear benefits to patient care have largely not been estab-lished due to the paucity of robust evidence. Tracking behaviors through smartphone apps does not necessarily translate into meaningful clinical outcomes (Laing et al., 2014). Further studies are needed to determine the relevant data to collect for particular psychiatric conditions. Third, smartphone applications have the potential to do harm to patients. For example, some applications label patients with a psychiatric disorder which may be stigmatizing and lead to poor outcomes (Bakker, Kazantzis, Rickwood, & Rickard, 2016; Moses, 2009). Some smartphone apps are not evidence-based and may recommend maladaptive behavior (APA, 2019a). Further studies are needed to explore the potential negative impact these technologies have on patients.

Step 4: Ease of Use

Ease of use for EMA can be described in terms of intuitiveness and survey burden, among other factors. Intuitiveness will depend on the relationship between the patient's experience with technology and the app's user interface. For example, a younger patient with significant smartphone experience may not need as much guidance in finding, downloading, or using the application, whereas an elderly patient with his/her first smartphone may require frequent guidance. Survey burden, that is the frequency and duration of surveys that patients are required to complete, may influence compliance with the study or intervention. Although there are no established standards, one study on use of EMAs to motivate weight loss suggested having less than five random EMA prompts over the course of a day, training each user on how to use the phone and app, and ensuring trained staff are available to answer patient questions (Burke et al., 2017). Patients with SMI, especially those with cognitive deficits, may find it especially challenging to engage with apps, and thus special consideration with respect to intuitiveness and survey burden may be needed.

An advantage of digital phenotyping, specifically with passive data collection, in use with patients with SMI, is that it requires minimal user input. As mentioned earlier, digital phenotyping may thus be especially beneficial for patients who find other forms of mobile mental health technologies such as mobile EMAs burdensome. One main challenge is to assist the user in downloading the app and educating the user on what type of data is collected. Another is ensuring the data quality is high, as missing data (e.g., the phone turns certain sensors off) can render passive data meaningless. Implications from a privacy standpoint are also important and cannot be ignored.

Step 5: Interoperability

One of the challenges with adopting digital psychiatry is the issue of interoperability; today's digital data can often not be transferred among devices, medical records, and hospital systems. Interoperability is essential so that data and output from digital technologies can be easily accessible to providers to optimize workflow, prevent fragmentation of care, and allow for ease of use in making clinical decisions. Interoperability has historically been a challenge because app development platforms and EMR systems have operated in siloed environments. More recently, however, there have been efforts to address this issue. Health Level Seven (HL7), an international nonprofit group, has developed FHIR (Fast Healthcare Interoperability Resources), which is a framework that allows for standardized health care data exchange. Third parties can build upon "resources" which are exchangeable content to allow for safe, high-quality exchange of health care data. SMART, which is based at Boston Children's Hospital and Harvard University, is another platform that allows developers to create apps that can seamlessly integrate with EMR systems. Similarly, App Orchard is an arm of EPIC, a widely used EMR system, which allows third-party developers to build apps that integrate with EPIC's operating system.

Evaluating app interoperability requires inspecting the development platform and determining how seamlessly it integrates with the clinician's EMR. Other specific questions to ask include:

1. Who "owns" the data?
2. Can the data be shared with an EMR?
3. Can the data be exported or downloaded?
4. Can the data be shared with Fitbit, Apple, or another device?

Conclusion

EMA, digital phenotyping, and mHealth peer support are examples of scalable technologies with the potential to address inadequate access to SMI care. These technologies can provide clinical insights to enable more precise diagnosis and timely interventions. However, as with any digital technology, there are risks associated with implementation. Smartphone applications can place patient privacy at risk, have low acceptability, and may not demonstrate clinical benefit. Clinicians need to be equipped with the proper framework to evaluate said technologies before recommending them to patients with SMI. The APA App Evaluation Model as described in this chapter provides the needed steps to ensure efficacy and safety when applying any smartphone technology to a patient population.

References

Alvarez-Jimenez, M., Bendall, S., Lederman, R., Wadley, G., Chinnery, G., Vargas, S., . . . Gleeson, J. F. (2013). On the HORYZON: Moderated online social therapy for long-term recovery in first episode psychosis. *Schizophrenia Research, 143*(1), 143–149. https://doi.org/10.1016/j.schres.2012.10.009

APA (2019a). *Why rate mental health apps?* American Psychiatric Association. Retrieved 2019, from www.psychiatry.org/psychiatrists/practice/mental-health-apps/why-rate-mental-health-apps

APA (2019b). *App evaluation model*. American Psychiatric Association. Retrieved from www.psychiatry.org/psychiatrists/practice/mental-health-apps/app-evaluation-model

Apple. (2018). *Upcoming privacy policy requirement*. Apple Developer. Retrieved 2018, from https://developer.apple.com/app-store-connect/whats-new/

Bajaj, P., Borreani, E., Ghosh, P., Methuen, C., Patel, M., & Joseph, M. (2008). Screening for suicidal thoughts in primary care: The views of patients and general practitioners. *Mental Health in Family Medicine, 5*(4), 229–235.

Bakker, D., Kazantzis, N., Rickwood, D., & Rickard, N. (2016). Mental health smartphone apps: Review and evidence-based recommendations for future developments. *JMIR Mental Health, 3*(1), e7. https://doi.org/10.2196/mental.4984

Barnett, I., Torous, J., Staples, P., Sandoval, L., Keshavan, M., & Onnela, J.-P. (2018). Relapse prediction in schizophrenia through digital phenotyping: A pilot study. *Neuropsychopharmacology, 43*(8), 1660–1666. https://doi.org/10.1038/s41386-018-0030-z

Bell, I. H., Fielding-Smith, S. F., Hayward, M., Rossell, S. L., Lim, M. H., Farhall, J., & Thomas, N. (2018). Smartphone-based ecological momentary assessment and intervention in a coping-focused intervention for hearing voices (SAVVy): Study protocol for a pilot randomised controlled trial. *Trials, 19*(1), 262. https://doi.org/10.1186/s13063-018-2607-6

Bell, I. H., Lim, M. H., Rossell, S. L., & Thomas, N. (2017). Ecological momentary assessment and intervention in the treatment of psychotic disorders: A systematic review. *Psychiatric Services, 68*(11), 1172–1181. https://doi.org/10.1176/appi.ps.201600523

Ben-Zeev, D., Brian, R., Wang, R., Wang, W., Campbell, A. T., Aung, M. S. H., Merrill, M., Tseng, V. W. S., Choudhury, T., Hauser, M., Kane, J. M., & Scherer, E. A. (2017). CrossCheck: Integrating Self-Report, Behavioral Sensing, and Smartphone Use to Identify Digital Indicators of Psychotic Relapse. *Psychiatric Rehabil J, 40*(3), 266-275. doi:10.1037/prj0000243

Biagianti, B., Quraishi, S. H., & Schlosser, D. A. (2018). Potential benefits of incorporating peer-to-peer interactions into digital interventions for psychotic disorders: A systematic review. *Psychiatric Services, 69*(4), 377–388. https://doi.org/10.1176/appi.ps.201700283

Blonigen, D. M., Macia, K. S., Bi, X., Suarez, P., Manfredi, L., & Wagner, T. H. (2017). Factors associated with emergency department use among veteran psychiatric patients. *Psychiatric Quarterly, 88*(4), 721–732. doi:10.1007/s11126-017-9490-2

Burke, L. E., Shiffman, S., Music, E., Styn, M. A., Kriska, A., Smailagic, A., Siewiorek, D., Ewing, L. J., Chasens, E., French, B., Mancino, J., Mendez, D., Strollo, P., & Rathbun, S. L. (2017). Ecological Momentary Assessment in Behavioral Research: Addressing Technological and Human Participant Challenges. 19(3), e77. https://doi.org/10.2196/jmir.7138

Cagney, H. (2015). Depression: An economic and moral case to tackle the crisis. *The Lancet Psychiatry, 2*(1), 20. doi:10.1016/s2215-0366(14)00136-9

Clarke, G. N., Herinckx, H. A., Kinney, R. F., Paulson, R. I., Cutler, D. L., Lewis, K., & Oxman, E. (2000). Psychiatric hospitalizations, arrests, emergency room visits, and homelessness of clients with serious and persistent mental illness: Findings from a randomized trial of two ACT programs vs. usual care. *Mental Health Services Research, 2*(3), 155–164. https://doi.org/10.1023/A:1010141826867

Cummings, J. R., Allen, L., Clennon, J., Ji, X., & Druss, B. G. (2017). Geographic access to specialty mental health care across high- and low-income US communities. *JAMA Psychiatry*. https://doi.org/10.1001/jamapsychiatry.2017.0303

Davidson, L., Bellamy, C., Guy, K., & Miller, R. (2012). Peer support among persons with severe mental illnesses: A review of evidence and experience. *World Psychiatry : Official Journal of the World Psychiatric Association (WPA)*, *11*(2), 123–128.

Dutchen, S. (2019). *The importance of nuance.* Harvard Medicine. Retrieved 2019, from https://hms.harvard.edu/magazine/artificial-intelligence/importance-nuance?utm_source=Silverpop&utm_medium=email&utm_term=field_news_item_3&utm_content=HMNews02252019

Gandhi, M., & Wang, T. (2015). Digital health consumer adoption: 2015. In *Rock health.* Rock Health. Retrieved from https://rockhealth.com/reports/digital-health-consumer-adoption-2015/

Gleeson, J. F., Lederman, R., Wadley, G., Bendall, S., McGorry, P. D., & Alvarez-Jimenez, M. (2014). Safety and privacy outcomes from a moderated online social therapy for young people with first-episode psychosis. *Psychiatric Services*, *65*(4), 546–550. https://doi.org/10.1176/appi.ps.201300078

Granholm, E., Loh, C., & Swendsen, J. (2007). Feasibility and validity of computerized ecological momentary assessment in schizophrenia. *Schizophrenia Bulletin, 34*(3). https://doi.org/10.1093/schbul/sbm113

Grundy, Q., Chiu, K., Held, F., Continella, A., Bero, L., & Holz, R. (2019). Data sharing practices of medicines related apps and the mobile ecosystem: Traffic, content, and network analysis. *BMJ, 364*, l920. https://doi.org/10.1136/bmj.l920

Hillbrand, M., Waite, B. M., Miller, D. S., Spitz, R. T., & Lingswiler, V. M. (2000). Serum cholesterol concentrations and mood states in violent psychiatric patients: An experience sampling study. *The Journal of Behavioral Medicine, 23*(6), 519–529. https://doi:10.1023/a:1005551418922

Hogarty, G. E., & Ulrich, R. F. (1998). The limited effects of antipsychotic medication on schizophrenia relapse and adjustment and the contributions of psychosocial treatment. *Journal of Psychiatric Research, 32*(3–4), 243–250. https://doi.org/10.1016/S0022-3956(97)00013-7

Huckvale, K., Torous, J., & Larsen, M. E. (2019). Assessment of the data sharing and privacy practices of smartphone apps for depression and smoking cessation. *JAMA Network Open, 2*(4), e192542. https://doi.org/10.1001/jamanetworkopen.2019.2542

Kaplan, K., Salzer, M. S., Solomon, P., Brusilovskiy, E., & Cousounis, P. (2011). Internet peer support for individuals with psychiatric disabilities: A randomized controlled trial. *Social Science & Medicine, 72*(1), 54–62. https://doi.org/10.1016/j.socscimed.2010.09.037

Kimhy, D., Delespaul, P., Corcoran, C., Ahn, H., Yale, S., & Malaspina, D. (2006). Computerized experience sampling method (ESMc): Assessing feasibility and validity among individuals with schizophrenia. *Journal of Psychiatric Research, 40*(3), 221–230. https://doi.org/10.1016/j.jpsychires.2005.09.007

Laing, B., Mangione, C. M., Tseng, C.-H., Leng, M., Vaisberg, E., Mahida, M., . . . Bell, D. S. (2014). Effectiveness of a smartphone application for weight loss compared with usual care in overweight primary care patients: A randomized, controlled trial. *Annals of Internal Medicine, 161*(10 Suppl.), S5–12. https://doi.org/10.7326/m13-3005

Landers, G. M., & Zhou, M. (2011). An analysis of relationships among peer support, psychiatric hospitalization, and crisis stabilization. *Community Mental Health Journal, 47*(1), 106–112. https://doi.org/10.1007/s10597-009-9218-3

Larsen, M., Huckvale, K., Nicholas, J., Torous, J., Birrell, L., Li, E., & Reda, B. (2019). Using science to sell apps: Evaluation of mental health app store quality claims. *NPJ Digital Medicine, 2*(1), 18. https://doi.org/10.1038/s41746-019-0093-1

Lucas, G. M., Gratch, J., King, A., & Morency, L.-P. (2014). It's only a computer: Virtual humans increase willingness to disclose. *Computers in Human Behavior*, *37*, 94–100. https://doi.org/10.1016/j.chb.2014.04.043

Marino, L., Wissow, L. S., Davis, M., Abrams, M. T., Dixon, L. B., & Slade, E. P. (2016). Predictors of outpatient mental health clinic follow-up after hospitalization among Medicaid-enrolled young adults. *Early Intervention in Psychiatry*, *10*(6), 468–475. https://doi.org/10.1111/eip.12206

Martinez-Martin, N., Insel, T. R., Dagum, P., Greely, H. T., & Cho, M. K. (2018). Data mining for health: Staking out the ethical territory of digital phenotyping. *NPJ Digital Medicine*, *1*(1), 68. https://doi.org/10.1038/s41746-018-0075-8

Morriss, R., Vinjamuri, I., Faizal, M., Bolton, C. A., & McCarthy, J. P. (2013). Training to recognise the early signs of recurrence in schizophrenia. *Cochrane Database of Systematic Reviews*, (2). https://doi.org/10.1002/14651858.cd005147.pub2

Moses, T. (2009). Self-labeling and its effects among adolescents diagnosed with mental disorders. *Social Science & Medicine*, *68*(3), 570–578. https://doi.org/10.1016/j.socscimed.2008.11.003

Moskowitz, D. S., & Young, S. N. (2006). Ecological momentary assessment: What it is and why it is a method of the future in clinical psychopharmacology. *Journal of Psychiatry & Neuroscience*, *31*(1), 13–20. Retrieved from www.ncbi.nlm.nih.gov/pubmed/16496031

Naslund, J., Aschbrenner, K., Marsch, L., & Bartels, S. (2016). The future of mental health care: Peer-to-peer support and social media. *Epidemiology and Psychiatric Sciences*, *25*(2), 113–122. https://doi.org/10.1017/S2045796015001067

Nicholas, J., Shilton, K., Schueller, S., Gray, E., Kwasny, M. J., & Mohr, D. C. (2019). The role of data type and recipient in individuals' perspectives on sharing passively collected smartphone data for mental health: Cross-Sectional questionnaire study. *JMIR Publications*, *7*(4).

NIMH (2019). *Mental illness*. National Institute of Mental Health. Retrieved from www.nimh.nih.gov/health/statistics/mental-illness.shtml

O'Loughlin, K., Neary, M., Adkins, E. C., & Hueller, S. (2018). Reviewing the data security and privacy policies of mobile apps for depression. *Internet Interventions*, *15*(Behav. Ther. 35 4 2012), 110–115. https://doi.org/10.1016/j.invent.2018.12.001

Onnela, J.-P., & Rauch, S. L. (2016). Harnessing smartphone-based digital phenotyping to enhance behavioral and mental health. *Neuropsychopharmacology*, *41*(7), 1691. https://doi.org/10.1038/npp.2016.7

Paton, F., Wright, K., Ayre, N., et al. (2016). Improving outcomes for people in mental health crisis: A rapid synthesis of the evidence for available models of care. *Health Technology Assessment*, *20*(3), 1–162. https://doi:10.3310/hta20030

Pitt, V., Lowe, D., Hill, S., Prictor, M., Hetrick, S. E., Ryan, R., & Berends, L. (2013). Consumer-providers of care for adult clients of statutory mental health services. *Cochrane Database of Systematic Reviews*, *3*(3), CD004807. https://doi.org/10.1002/14651858.CD004807.pub2

Poushter, J., Bishop, C., & Chwe, H. (2018). Social media use continues to rise in developing countries but plateaus across developed ones. In *Pew research center*. Pew Research Center. Retrieved from www.pewresearch.org

Rooksby, J., Morrison, A., & Murray-Rust, D. (2019). Student Perspectives on Digital Phenotyping: The Acceptability of Using Smartphone Data to Assess Mental Health. 1–14. https://doi.org/10.1145/3290605.3300655

Rosenfeld, L., Torous, J., & Vahia, I. V. (2017). Data security and privacy in apps for dementia: An analysis of existing privacy policies. *The American Journal of Geriatric Psychiatry: Official Journal of the American Association for Geriatric Psychiatry, 25*(8), 873–877. https://doi.org/10.1016/j.jagp.2017.04.009

Rowe, M., Bellamy, C., Baranoski, M., Wieland, M., O'Connell, M. J., Benedict, P., Davidson, L., Buchanan, J., & Sells, D. (2007). A Peer-Support, Group Intervention to Reduce Substance Use and Criminality Among Persons With Severe Mental Illness. *Psychiatric Services, 58*(7), 955–961. https://doi.org/10.1176/ps.2007.58.7.955

Sells, D., Davidson, L., Jewell, C., Falzer, P., & Rowe, M. (2006). The treatment relationship in peer-based and regular case management for clients with severe mental illness. *Psychiatric Services, 57*(8), 1179–1184. https://doi:10.1176/ps.2006.57.8.1179

Solomon, P. (2004). Peer support/peer provided services underlying processes, benefits, and critical ingredients. *Psychiatric Rehabilitation Journal, 27*(4), 392. https://doi.org/10.2975/27.2004.392.401

Steiger, H., Gauvin, L., Jabalpurwala, S., Séguin, J. R., & Stotland, S. (1999). Hypersensitivity to social interactions in bulimic syndromes: Relationship to binge eating. *Journal of Consulting and Clinical Psychology, 67*(5), 765. https://doi.org/10.1037/0022-006X.67.5.765

Stein, K. (1996). Affect instability in adults with a borderline personality disorder. *Archives of Psychiatric Nursing, 10*(1), 32–40. https://doi.org/10.1016/S0883-9417(96)80084-7

Sunyaev, A., Dehling, T., Taylor, P. L., & Mandl, K. D. (2015). Availability and quality of mobile health app privacy policies. *Journal of the American Medical Informatics Association, 22*(e1), e28–e33. https://doi.org/10.1136/amiajnl-2013-002605

Torous, J., Andersson, G., Bertagnoli, A., Christensen, H., Cuijpers, P., Firth, J., Haim, A., Hsin, H., Hollis, C., Lewis, S., Mohr, D. C., Pratap, A., Roux, S., Sherrill, J., & Arean, P. A. (2019). Towards a consensus around standards for smartphone apps and digital mental health. *World Psychiatry, 18*(1), 97–98. https://doi.org/10.1002/wps.20592

Torous, J., Chan, S., Gipson, S., Kim, J., Nguyen, T.-Q., Luo, J., & Wang, P. (2018). A hierarchical framework for evaluation and informed decision making regarding smartphone apps for clinical care. *Psychiatric Services, 69*(5), 498–500. https://doi.org/10.1176/appi.ps.201700423

Torous, J., Chan, S., Tan, S., Behrens, J., Mathew, I., Conrad, E. J., Hinton, L., Yellowlees, P., & Keshavan, M. (2014). Patient Smartphone Ownership and Interest in Mobile Apps to Monitor Symptoms of Mental Health Conditions: A Survey in Four Geographically Distinct Psychiatric Clinics. *JMIR Mental Health, 1*(1), e5. https://doi.org/10.2196/mental.4004

Torous, J., Kiang, M. V., Lorme, J., & Onnela, J.-P. (2016). New tools for new research in psychiatry: A scalable and customizable platform to empower data driven smartphone research. *JMIR Mental Health, 3*(2), e16. https://doi.org/10.2196/mental.5165

Torous, J., & Roberts, L. (2017). Needed innovation in digital health and smartphone applications for mental health: Transparency and trust. *JAMA Psychiatry.* https://doi.org/10.1001/jamapsychiatry.2017.0262

Torous, J., Rodriguez, J., & Powell, A. (2017). The new digital divide for digital biomarkers. *Digital Biomarkers, 1*(1), 87–91. https://doi.org/10.1159/000477382

Torous, J., Staples, P., Barnett, I., Sandoval, L. R., Keshavan, M., & Onnela, J.-P. (2018). Characterizing the clinical relevance of digital phenotyping data quality with applications to a cohort with schizophrenia. *NPJ Digital Medicine, 1*(1), 15. https://doi.org/10.1038/s41746-018-0022-8

Torous, J., Staples, P., Shanahan, M., Lin, C., Peck, P., Keshavan, M., & Onnela, J.-P. (2015). Utilizing a personal smartphone custom app to assess the patient health questionnaire-9 (PHQ-9) depressive symptoms in patients with major depressive disorder. *JMIR Mental Health*, 2(1), e8. https://doi.org/10.2196/mental.3889

Torous, J., Wisniewski, H., Liu, G., & Keshavan, M. (2018). Mental health mobile phone app usage, concerns, and benefits among psychiatric outpatients: Comparative survey study. *JMIR Mental Health*, 5(4), e11715. https://doi.org/10.2196/11715

Wang, P. S., Lane, M., Olfson, M., Pincus, H. A., Wells, K. B., & Kessler, R. C. (2005). Twelve-Month use of mental health services in the United States: Results from the national comorbidity survey replication. *Archives of General Psychiatry*, 62(6), 629–640. https://doi.org/10.1001/archpsyc.62.6.629

Wang, R., Aung, M. S. H., Abdullah, S., Brian, R., Campbell, A. T., Choudhury, T., Hauser, M., Kane, J., Merrill, M., Scherer, E. A., Tseng, V. W. S., & Ben-Zeev, D. (2016). CrossCheck: toward passive sensing and detection of mental health changes in people with schizophrenia. 886–897. https://doi.org/10.1145/2971648.2971740

Whalen, C. K., Jamner, L. D., Henker, B., Delfino, R. J., & Lozano, J. M. (2003). The ADHD spectrum and everyday life: Experience sampling of adolescent moods, activities, smoking, and drinking. *Child Development*, 73(1), 209–227. https://doi.org/10.1111/1467-8624.00401

White, R. (2013). *Electronic health records: Balancing progress and privacy*. The Hastings Center. Retrieved 2021, from www.thehastingscenter.org/electronic-health-records-balancing-progress-and-privacy/

Wisniewski, H., Liu, G., Henson, P., Vaidyam, A., Hajratalli, N., Onnela, J.-P., & Torous, J. (2019). Understanding the quality, effectiveness and attributes of top-rated smartphone health apps. *Evidence Based Mental Health*, 22(1), 4. https://doi.org/10.1136/ebmental-2018-300069

8 Technology-Based Interventions for Substance Use Disorders

Patrick Dulin,[1] Anayansi Lombardero, Robyn Mertz, and Diane K. King

Technology-based interventions, including telephone applications and web-based programs targeting hazardous alcohol and substance use, have the potential to provide alternative intervention options to millions of individuals in need and to reduce the public health burden associated with hazardous alcohol and substance use[2]. Hazardous use of substances and substance addiction includes a range of unhealthy use patterns, including drinking or drug use over safe limits to "binging" to serious dependence on alcohol and drugs. Incidences of hazardous use increases the risk of a variety of individual and societal issues, including accidents, absenteeism, alcohol-related emergency department admissions, violence, suicidality, and infectious diseases (Esser et al., 2014; Grucza et al., 2018), contributing to significant health, social, and economic burdens (Degenhardt & Hall, 2012). In the United States, hazardous alcohol use is responsible for one in ten deaths among adults aged 20–64 and together with other substance use costs the nation approximately $530 billion per year (Stahre, Roeber, Kanny, Brewer, & Zhang, 2014).

One key factor that leads to substance abuse being so damaging is that while prevalence rates for substance use disorders are relatively high, rates of treatment are very low. For example, the National Epidemiological Survey on Alcohol and Related Conditions (NESARC) found that drug use disorder affects approximately 10% of the U.S. population but only about 25% of that number receive any type of treatment (Grant et al., 2016). This same study also found that the lifetime prevalence for an alcohol use disorder was 30% and 12-month prevalence was 8.5% (Hasin, Stinson, Ogburn, & Grant, 2007). This survey similarly found that treatment utilization for Alcohol Use Disorder was low, with only 14.6% of those who met criteria for Alcohol Use Disorder reporting any type of prior treatment (Cohen, Feinn, Arias, & Kranzler, 2007).

Technology-Based Interventions Address Common Barriers to Treatment

There are a number of personal, contextual, and treatment-related barriers to engaging in traditional face-to-face substance use treatment, including the lack of adequate and available services, inadequate insurance coverage, the high cost of services, and pragmatic issues such as the need for childcare during treatment, work-related complications, and transportation problems (Cohen et al., 2007; Grant, 1997). Another substantial barrier to addiction treatment relates to concerns regarding stigma associated with attending alcohol and drug treatment facilities (Saunders, Zygowicz, & D'Angelo, 2006). Many individuals appear to have difficulty admitting to others, even in a treatment context, that they have a substance problem. Finally, one of the most commonly cited reasons for not seeking treatment among those with a substance use disorder is the belief that one should be strong enough to handle their problem alone, which leads to unsuccessful, unsupported attempts to quit or cut down on substance use (Cohen et al., 2007). Technology-based interventions for alcohol and drug problems have the potential to address the barriers to access, cost, and stigma by removing the need for the individual to travel to a treatment facility and by eliminating or reducing costs associated with delivery of in-person services while preserving individual privacy. Mobile technology in particular has the potential to provide timely intervention in the actual environment in which substance abuse occurs when other forms of traditional help are not available. For example, an individual may experience a substance craving at 1:00 a.m. or may enter a bar in which they have abused alcohol in the past and find themselves with limited to no options regarding accessing traditional treatment. An app or web-based intervention, however, could be immediately available that provides in-the-moment help.

Acceptance of technology-based alcohol and drug interventions is also increasing among potential users of such services (Choo, Ranney, Wong, & Mello, 2012), and there is an indication that for some problems, treatment seekers would prefer to receive technology-based services than traditional face-to-face counseling (Gandhi, Welsh, Bennett, Carreño, & Himelhoch, 2009). Technology-based interventions for substance use problems also show promise for reducing health disparities, given their potential to reach groups that are often underrepresented in face-to-face treatment due to the access, cost, or pragmatic barriers described earlier (Postel et al., 2011). For example, VanDeMark et al. (2010) indicated that women and adults with children were more interested and engaged with technologically based interventions for substance abuse, a finding that also was reported for individuals with an alcohol problem.

Technology-Based Interventions May Be Stand-Alone, Clinician-Monitored, or Offered as Extensions to Treatment

There are numerous technologically delivered intervention systems available for a variety of substance use problems that are gaining traction among individual users and within health care systems (Bedrouni, 2018; Holmes, van Agteren, & Dorstyn, 2018; Nesvåg & McKay, 2018; Ramsey, Satterfield,

Gerke, & Proctor, 2019). In this chapter, we cover what the authors have found to be the most current, technology-delivered intervention systems that were developed from empirically based protocols and have empirical support for their efficacy in reducing hazardous alcohol, cannabis, stimulants, and opioid use. We also discuss technology-delivered treatment systems that are oriented towards providing post-treatment abstinence-based support. The interventions described include stand-alone treatment programs that substitute for face-to-face care, interventions that include varying levels of clinician or treatment program support or monitoring, and interventions offered post-treatment to support maintenance of healthy behaviors and prevent relapse. We acknowledge that this is not a comprehensive list of available and upcoming interventions for hazardous substance use, but we chose to highlight those interventions that have empirical support and are at a developmental stage in which they are available for use by interested clinicians and individuals with a need for substance use intervention.

Stand-Alone Technology-Based Treatment

Step Away

Step Away is a stand-alone smartphone-based alcohol intervention system that was developed by Dulin and colleagues (Dulin, Gonzalez, King, Giroux, & Bacon, 2013). It has been in existence for approximately ten years and is now in its fourth major iteration (V 4.0). Step Away is oriented toward enhancing motivation to reduce or abstain from drinking by enhancing awareness of drinking and related problems, facilitating setting of a specific drinking goal (abstinence or moderation), and providing tools to manage drinking-related problems when they occur, such as having a craving to drink. The original version of Step Away was called the Location-Based Monitoring and Intervention System for Alcohol Use Disorders (LBMI-A) and was the first stand-alone alcohol intervention smartphone app with demonstrated empirical support (Dulin, Gonzalez, & Jones, 2014). Step Away is informed by three theoretical constructs that, after more than three decades of empirical testing and clinical application, are considered the most important "active ingredients" for person-centered, behavioral-based intervention and treatment in addictions: i.e., (1) Motivational Enhancement (Miller, 1999), (2) Relapse Prevention (Marlatt & Donovan, 2005), and (3) Community Reinforcement (Meyers, Villanueva, & Smith, 2005).

Motivational Enhancement (ME) integrates principles of behavior change and motivational psychology (Miller & Rollnick, 2013) to increase self-efficacy and coping. Its primary goal is to help people develop motivation to change in a nonjudgmental, facilitative manner without providing overt pressure to change. In keeping with ME principles, Step Away provides numerous options for users to choose from to provide encouragement and supportive feedback regardless of whether they indicate continued drinking.

Step Away integrates Relapse Prevention by identifying high-risk situations for continued drinking, including assessment of mood and cravings, and providing strategies for coping with situational triggers when they cannot be avoided. Community Reinforcement, an approach that emphasizes intervention in multiple domains of a client's life to change their patterns and reinforce coping strategies, also informed the design of Step Away. Specifically, Step Away proactively encourages the user to identify and include supportive others in treatment; to identify and plan non-drinking, recreational activities; and to develop other non-drinking lifestyle skills and strategies.

The latest version of Step Away contains seven modules that are oriented toward four overarching goals: enhancing awareness of drinking and drinking-related problems, establishing and monitoring progress toward a drinking goal, managing triggers and other problems using in-the-moment tools, and connecting users with other types of support. Step 1, Assessment & Feedback, provides assessment and feedback on drinking relative to age-specific norms, peak blood alcohol level, alcohol dependence severity, drinking-related problems, and weekly monetary costs of drinking. Step 2, Goal Setting, offers users a choice of abstinence or moderation as a goal and provides input on the likelihood of success if moderation is chosen based on alcohol dependence severity, as well as information regarding what constitutes low-risk drinking. Step 3, Cravings, provides information about coping with cravings and offers six different in-the-moment interventions for coping with cravings (e.g., urge surfing), in keeping with the relapse prevention model. Step 4, Moderation or Abstinence Strategies, provides simple behavioral strategies tailored to whether a user selected moderation or abstinence as a goal. For instance, if abstinence is the chosen goal, users are provided with strategies to support abstinence, such as removing alcohol from the home. Step 5, New Activities, discusses the importance of replacing drinking with non-drinking activities to further increase self-efficacy and community reinforcement to avoid drinking. It provides functionality to schedule the activities and reminders/alerts within the smartphone calendar. Step 6, Support Persons, in keeping with the Community Reinforcement approach, provides tools for connecting with supportive persons when additional support is needed. Step 7, Reminders, encourages users to create verbal and visual reminders for changing their drinking. For instance, functionality is provided to load photos from their phone that remind them of their desire to change.

In addition to the steps just outlined, Step Away provides ongoing assessment and feedback. At a user-specified time of day, Step Away prompts users to complete a brief questionnaire on drinking and cravings during the prior 24 hours. It then uses this information to provide weekly feedback, highlighting progress toward goals, drinking patterns, and ongoing craving triggers experienced throughout the prior week. Feedback includes strategies for managing common alcohol triggers and a feature for users to enter future "high-risk events" that might negatively influence their drinking goals. If a high-risk event is entered, Step Away sends a reminder 30 minutes before the scheduled time, which includes users' chosen drinking goals and their reminders for change.

Step Away also provides timely intervention options. When a user indicates a need for help, they are provided with strategies for managing cravings or negative emotions (i.e., engage in a pleasurable activity or listen to a progressive muscle relaxation audio file), working through a problem via a problem-solving algorithm, calling for help (i.e., a support person or a contact), and contacting a national treatment finder service to receive help finding in-person treatment in their area.

Several studies have evaluated Step Away in various populations. The first version of Step Away, the LBMI-A, was evaluated in a sample of adults who met criteria for Alcohol Use Disorder and were interested in making a change to their drinking. Results from this study indicated that users of the system evidenced a 60% reduction in hazardous drinking and a 55% increase in days abstinent during the six weeks participants used the system (Dulin et al., 2014). This study also indicated that the amount of system utilization was predictive of alcohol outcomes, with more utilization resulting in better outcomes (Gonzalez & Dulin, 2015). A recent study that utilized Step Away with a sample of U.S. veterans who were drinking hazardously and not in VA treatment suggested that participant hazardous drinking days dropped by approximately 45% over six months of Step Away use and that the app helped users to become more motivated to make a change in their drinking (Hawkins et al., 2019). A New Zealand-specific version of Step Away was created and studied among a sample of heavy-drinking New Zealanders over six months. Results suggested that heavy-drinking days dropped by approximately 70% and that users reported reductions in drinking-related problems (Walker et al., 2019). Recent analysis of user retention has shown substantial user retention in the app, with approximately 90% user retention at two weeks and 60% and 30% retention at three and six months, respectively. Results from the aforementioned studies suggest that Step Away can produce meaningful change among heavy-drinking individuals at a level that is roughly equivalent to the effect of in-person treatment. Results suggest that a primary factor in Step Away's success is the regular prompted interviews and the feedback Step Away provides regarding progress over time (Dulin et al., 2014; Hawkins et al., 2019). Users report that these features, combined with goal setting, provide them with awareness of their specific problem with alcohol and the motivation to keep trying to change. The Step Away app is available for download on iOS and Android devices. Step Away is available for individual users to download the app through iTunes and Google Play Store. Users can utilize the entire system for free for one week to determine if the system is a match for their needs, but ongoing use requires a monthly subscription. Step Away is also available for organizations to utilize in order to reduce problematic drinking among their constituents (see Stepaway.biz for more information).

CheckUp & Choices

This program has different elements (a CheckUp and a Choices Program) for individuals who want to reduce or abstain from alcohol, stimulants, opioids, or marijuana. For the alcohol program, an individual can choose from three different options: The first option (CheckUp only program) consists of a one-time, 40-minute-long motivational intervention that provides assessment and feedback regarding alcohol use. Based on this program, the individual can get clarification on the impact of alcohol on their lives, whether they want to change their drinking, and if so, whether they want to reduce or abstain from alcohol use. A CheckIn has been added recently (2019) that is a three-month follow-up to the CheckUp. It provides feedback on the individual's current level of drinking (or abstinence) and alcohol-related problems. It then compares their baseline to their follow-up status on those variables. If the person decides to change their drinking, they can opt for the Choices elements of the program, which are available as a three- or 12-month subscription (and a money back guarantee). These "action stage" programs include strategies based on whether the individual wants to moderate (The Moderate Program, only available for alcohol) or abstain (The Abstain Programs). The choices include: Moderate Alcohol, Abstain Alcohol, Abstain Marijuana, Abstain Opioids, and Abstain Stimulants. The Moderate programs consist of the following components: Goal-setting, tracking of drinking, identifying and managing triggers for heavy drinking, developing healthy alternatives to overdrinking, problem solving, mood monitoring and maximizing chances of success with a Change Plan and customized emails and text messages.

A randomized clinical trial (Hester, Delaney, & Campbell, 2011) examined the outcomes of the Moderate Drinking Program (MD, www.moderatedrinking.com), the content of which has now been integrated into the CheckUp & Choices program. It compared MD plus use of the resources online at Moderation Management (MM, www.moderation.org). MM offers face-to-face and online meetings, a self-help book, educational materials, a forum, and a listserv. The control condition was using MM only. This study provided data for 75 participants with follow-up assessments at three, six, and 12 months. Both groups demonstrated reductions in alcohol-related problems during follow-up assessments. The experimental group demonstrated higher percentages of abstinent days at follow-up assessments, and only a subset of participants, less heavy drinkers, demonstrated reductions in drinking levels and alcohol-related problems.

The Abstain program follows the same protocol as the Moderate without the goal setting for reduced drinking. It was also developed in collaboration with SMART Recovery and its four-point program for achieving and maintaining sobriety. An RCT of the Overcoming Addictions (OA, the content of which has been integrated into the CheckUp & Choices program) compared the use of the Abstain protocol plus use of the resources of SMART Recovery (www.smartrecovery.org) to use of SMART Recovery by itself (Campbell, Hester, Lenberg, & Delaney, 2016). Both intent-to-treat analyses and the actual-use analyses showed significant improvement from baseline to follow-ups for all three groups. Mean within-subject effect sizes were large ($d>0.8$) overall with no significant differences between groups. The actual use analysis consisted of groups who used both the OA and SMART Recovery meetings, used SMART Recovery meetings alone, or used the OA app alone and did not attend any meetings. Non-significant differences between these groups led the researchers to conclude that "Web-based interventions can help even those individuals with lengthy histories of heavy drinking to make clinically significant reductions in their consumption and related problems."

The drug protocols follow the same protocol for alcohol but are tailored to the differences inherent in each drug. They were developed in consultation with experts in their respective fields. For instance, the opioid module supports medication-assisted treatment (MAT). The stimulant module consists of CBT, information about detox, including advice to consult a primary care provider about detox options prior to beginning the program, and addressing cravings and triggers. The Marijuana "CheckUp" module is under development, but the program offers the "Choices" module which consists of CBT and Motivational Enhancement. The evidence cited on the CheckUp & Choices website is based solely on alcohol research, so clinicians and potential users of this online program for cannabis, opioid, and stimulant use should take this into account when considering the program. CheckUp & Choices offers a free screening and feedback module, but access to the suite of tools requires a fee. Individuals and organizations can assess this treatment system. More information about access can be found at www. checkupandchoices.com.

Technology-Based Interventions With Clinician or Treatment Program Support

CBT4CBT

Cognitive-Behavioral Therapy (CBT) is widely recognized as an empirically supported treatment for substance use disorders (Carroll & Kiluk, 2017; Dutra et al., 2008; Magill et al., under review; Magill & Ray, 2009), but it has proven challenging to move CBT to clinical practice with high levels of fidelity. Thus, in an effort to develop a form of CBT that was inexpensive, high-quality, and broadly accessible, Carroll and colleagues (Carroll et al., 2008) developed CBT4CBT, or Computer Based Training for Cognitive-Behavioral Therapy, with NIDA and NIAAA support. The CBT4CBT programs are web-based and focus on teaching core cognitive-behavioral strategies (functional analysis, coping with craving, decision making, recognizing and changing thoughts, problem solving skills, assertiveness skills) in an engaging way through use of multiple brief videos. Each video demonstrates use of a behavioral strategy by an actor playing an individual with a substance use problem. The programs use animations, interactive exercises, short quizzes, and narration to reinforce skills training and encourage patients to practice skills outside of sessions. The programs collect no identifying information from the user, require only a third-grade reading level (all activities are audio-driven), require no previous computer experience, and can be used on a variety of devices (laptops, tablets, smartphones).

There are currently five versions available: CBT4CBT-Drugs; CBT4CBT-Alcohol, CBT4CBT-Spanish-Drugs, and CBT4CBT-Alcohol, and CBT4CBT-Buprenorphine. The program targets adults with a broad range of substance use disorders (alcohol, marijuana, opioids, stimulants) and has been shown to be effective even among samples with significant psychiatric comorbidity (Paris et al., 2018). Seven independent studies in a range of settings have demonstrated CBT4CBT is associated with significant and sustained reductions in drug and alcohol use both during and following treatment compared to treatment as usual (Carroll et al., 2008; Carroll et al., 2014; Carroll, Nich, DeVito, Shi, & Sofuoglu, 2017; Kiluk et al., 2016; Kiluk et al., 2018; Paris et al., 2018; Shi, Henry, Dwy, Orazietti, & Carroll, in press). These studies have demonstrated that CBT4CBT is effective as a stand-alone treatment with brief monitoring or as an adjunct to standard clinician care (Kiluk et al., 2016; Kiluk et al., 2018). That is, CBT4CBT only required brief (10 minute) regular clinical monitoring by a clinician to ensure that this level of care is appropriate. Thus, CBT4CBT can easily be used in a range of settings to provide a robust dose of skill training to help individuals learn and implement these skills to reduce their drug and alcohol use. Information for clinicians regarding access to the program and a brief demo video are available through www.CBT4CBT.com. All versions of CBT4CBT are available for a fee and clinicians can access the service through the CBT4CBT website.

ReSET

ReSET is a mobile app that is currently approved by the U.S. Food and Drug Administration: www.resetforrecovery.com/. It was originally tested under the name Therapeutic Education System (TES) as a computer program, and was then modified to be available as a mobile app. The developers of this mobile app argue that although the app itself has not been tested in a randomized clinical trial, its content is equivalent to the desktop version, which was found to be effective at improving abstinence rates among people with alcohol, cannabis, and stimulant use disorders in a large clinical trial among patients receiving treatment for SUDs (Campbell et al., 2016; De

Novo, 2017). It is based on principles of the Community Reinforcement Approach and includes elements of cognitive-behavioral therapy. It encourages individuals to form habits of substituting their use of substances with other social activities. The original TES that was tested featured interactive online modules to work on skills such as managing harmful thoughts and negative moods, refusal skills, and developing new patterns of behavior. The modules also focused on harm reduction, specifically in reducing behaviors that place the individual at risk for HIV or STIs (Marsch & Dallery, 2012; Marsch et al., 2014).

When tested in clinical trials, participants who used TES were found to have significantly greater rates of abstinence than treatment as usual, and when tested with patients undergoing methadone maintenance, those receiving TES with treatment showed increased rates of abstinence and less attrition rates (Bickel, Marsch, Buchhalter, & Badger, 2008; Campbell et al., 2014; Marsch et al., 2014). The adapted version of TES, reSET, is available via prescription and downloadable as a mobile app on the iTunes store. It is designed as an adjunct to standard care for people with the substance use disorders described earlier. This mobile app is not meant for use by individuals who are not enrolled in a SUD treatment program. The developers of reSET have recently released reSET-O, a version of the app intended to increase retention of patients with opioid use disorder. Similar to the traditional reSET, there is no evidence for the actual reSET-O app, but the internet-delivered treatment from which the app seems to be based was tested in a study by Christensen et al. (2014) in which participants receiving the internet-based Community Reinforcement Approach, Contingency Management, and Buprenorphine had reduced dropout rates and approximately ten more days of abstinence compared to participants receiving Contingency Management and Buprenorphine. There is a brief instruction pamphlet for clinicians accessible through the reSET website: www.resetforrecovery.com/pdf/reSET%20Brief%20Summary%20Instruc tions%20Clinician%20Information.pdf. Full clinician directions are also available through the clinician dashboard of the mobile app.

The goal of the reSET app is to increase abstinence rates while patients are engaged in treatment as well as to increase retention among individuals in outpatient treatment settings. As described in the brief summary instructions for clinicians, once a prescription for reSET is given to the patient by a licensed clinician, the patient is contacted by a patient care specialist from reSET Connect™ by Pear Therapeutics, Inc. The patient care specialist then guides the patient in downloading the phone app, entering the access code and email address, and setting up a password. During the 12-week program, the patient is engaged in a Contingency Management (CM) system that provides them with opportunities to earn rewards for negative drug screens and completed lessons. There are also quiz questions and reporting of triggers, cravings, and use of substances. The program contains a clinician dashboard where the clinician is able to monitor progress made by the patient, use of the app, and patient report on triggers, substance use, and cravings. In addition, the clinician has the ability to input results from drug screens and adherence to appointments, which should take place every 30 days. If the client fails to attend appointments, they lose access to the CM reward portion of the app. Access can be gained again if the clinician enters a visit on the clinician dashboard.

Technology-Based Interventions as Treatment Extenders

A-CHESS

A-CHESS (Addiction—Comprehensive Health Enhancement Support System) is a smartphone-based recovery support system designed originally to function in the traditional addiction treatment system with patients leaving residential treatment for alcohol use disorder (AUD). A-CHESS consists of tools and services designed to address addiction in ways that are both appealing and effective. For example, when patients receive the app, they can record a video of themselves describing why they want to recover— something they can watch when they face difficult times in the future. They can also enter into A-CHESS risky locations, such as a bar they used to frequent, so the app will warn them when they approach those places. The three most frequently used services in A-CHESS are the discussion board and private messaging, Help with Cravings, and Games and Relaxation. The discussion board allows patients to communicate with others in the same situation, but anonymously (patients create usernames when they start using the app), and private messaging allows similar communication between two patients. These forms of peer support are the most frequently used services in A-CHESS, and the source of testimonials about people getting just the help they need at the moment they most needed it. Help with Cravings—also called the Panic Button in some iterations of A-CHESS— allows patients facing a craving to talk to someone supportive, find directions to the closest Alcoholics Anonymous or Narcotics Anonymous meeting, do relaxation exercises, or view motivations for staying clean. Games and Relaxation provides ready distraction. This service provides links to game apps such as Angry Birds and Candy Crush and relaxation techniques from audio recordings of various meditation and relaxation clips.

The theoretical basis of A-CHESS is self-determination theory, which holds that helping people meet three basic needs improves their adaptive functioning: being perceived as competent, feeling related to others, and feeling internally motivated and not coerced in one's actions (Ryan & Deci, 2000). A clinical trial of A-CHESS used by patients leaving residential treatment for AUD showed a 57% reduction in risky drinking days among patients with A-CHESS vs. the control group without A-CHESS (Gustafson et al., 2014). Patient use of A-CHESS was high, with 58% of patients in the intervention group using the system in the last week of the eight-month intervention period. Data from the clinical trial were also used to develop and test a Bayesian network model to predict relapse, which showed promising results (Chih et al., 2014).

Since its initial use with patients leaving residential treatment for AUD, A-CHESS has evolved and been studied in other contexts and to address specific SUD issues. For example, A-CHESS was shown to increase the odds that patients receive outpatient treatment after residential treatment (Glass et al., 2017). A-CHESS has also been studied as a means of treating addiction in primary care (Quanbeck et al., 2018). Two other studies are currently underway. In one, patients recovering from SUDs are randomized to one of four groups: (1) telephone monitoring, (2) A-CHESS, (3) telephone monitoring plus A-CHESS, and (4) usual care. The other study tests A-CHESS for patients recovering from opioid use disorder. In this study, patients are randomized to two groups: (1) A-CHESS, or (2) A-CHESS plus medication-assisted treatment. A-CHESS will likely continue to be modified and improved to meet the needs of patients with SUDs in various contexts. A-CHESS is typically adopted at the clinic or treatment facility level. At the time of this writing, it is not available for individuals to download. More information about how to integrate A-CHESS into a clinical practice can be found at www.chess.health.

Clinical Practice Considerations

There are currently a multitude of technologically delivered interventions available for substance use disorders, and there are surely many in the works that will bring exciting and helpful tools to individuals in need of help with a drug or alcohol problem. While considering these options, clinicians should understand several important factors uniquely related to substance use that are somewhat consistent across the diversity of substance use problems. These factors include motivation, addiction severity, safety, and relapse. The next sections will discuss these factors and provide recommendations to clinicians who are considering technology delivered intervention or have patients engaged with a technology delivered intervention.

Motivational Factors

Perhaps one of the largest issues related to whether or not an individual will benefit from any type of intervention for substance use disorders relates to their motivation to engage in treatment. In fact, Motivational Interviewing (MI), a highly influential and efficacious substance use treatment modality, focuses heavily on enhancing an individual's motivation to change. MI practitioners believe that increased motivation to change is itself an important and beneficial outcome of treatment (Miller & Rollnick, 2013). It was once thought that individuals with a substance use disorder who did not express a desire to change should "come back when they are ready or have hit rock bottom," but this has changed with the advent of MI, as research has shown that it is possible to help an individual become more motivated to change their substance use (Sellman, 2010). In the world of technologically delivered substance interventions, if an individual has no motivation to change and no motivation to engage in the intervention (and to subsequently download the software), they will obviously not receive benefit. However, some of the interventions mentioned have an explicit focus on enhancing motivation to change (CheckUp & Choices and Step Away), even amongt individuals with a low level of awareness of a substance use problem. For example, in one Step Away study, participants were recruited to "evaluate a health app" and were not aware of its focus on reducing alcohol consumption. The participants did not come into the study because of a desire to change their drinking. Results suggested that the majority of these participants (all of whom met criteria for hazardous drinking) indicated that the app enhanced their awareness of an alcohol problem and that it motivated them to make a change in their drinking (Hawkins et al., 2019). This study suggests that Step Away, and other similarly focused interventions, can help people who have low initial motivation to engage in treatment to develop motivation to change their substance use. For clinicians, the takeaway message is that encouraging a client who has a low level of awareness of a drug or alcohol problem to "just give the app a try" has potential to produce helpful clinical outcomes in the form of increased motivation to change alcohol or drug use. However, clinicians are advised to exercise caution when prescribing technological intervention strategies to individuals with low motivation, particularly for intervention systems that assume an individual is already motivated to engage in treatment.

Safety and Severity

Addiction severity, the extent to which an individual is physiologically and psychologically dependent on alcohol or drugs, is another key issue when considering technologically delivered intervention services. In cases in which an individual has a high degree of addiction severity and is physiologically dependent on a substance (opioids and alcohol in particular), the process of withdrawal can be dangerous and even fatal (Mayo-Smith et al., 2004; Kampman & Jarvis, 2015). Determination of addiction severity is a complicated process that requires an extensive in-person assessment by trained clinicians. There are useful tools, however, that can help to identify potential alcohol and drug dependence such as the Alcohol Use Disorders Identification Test (AUDIT) and the Drug Abuse Screening Test (DAST) for alcohol and drugs, respectively. The AUDIT is a 10-item, free and publicly available screening test that is valid as a screening tool for identifying the presence and severity of an alcohol use disorder (Reinert & Allen, 2007). The DAST can also be helpful in determining if an individual is appropriate for brief intervention or needs referral to specialized treatment for drug addiction. It is also a 10-item, free and publicly available questionnaire that has been extensively studied and been shown to have robust psychometric properties (Yudkho, Lozhinka, & Fouts, 2007). If these instruments, in combination with the clinician's judgment, suggest that the patient has a high degree of addiction severity, it is recommended for safety reasons that they be followed by a medical professional during any type of intervention, especially during the first month of abstinence. In these cases, stand-alone technology intervention systems such as Step Away and CheckUp & Choices should be avoided or be utilized in combination with traditional, in-person addiction support services. Other systems, such as A-CHESS and reSET are, by design, integrated with a clinical team and are used as adjuncts to traditional services.

Encouraging System Utilization

As alluded to earlier, research has shown that the clinical effectiveness of technologically delivered interventions is partly driven by the extent to which users engage with the technological intervention (Gonzalez & Dulin, 2015; Gustafson et al., 2014). The more fully users engage with system features and especially with ongoing monitoring and feedback, the greater the chances that they will reduce or even abstain from alcohol or drugs.

Clinicians can play a key role in encouraging utilization in the initial stages of system utilization by discussing with patients the pros and cons of using the chosen intervention system to develop patient motivation to utilize the tool. In the case of an ambivalent patient, an approach that encourages experimentation with a technological tool could be useful. For example, a clinician may suggest a trial period or an "experiment" if the patient is unsure if they want to utilize a given technological intervention system. The message from the clinician in this case could be something like: "How about if you use (System A) for a few weeks and see what it has to tell you. I'd be happy to discuss how it went for you during our next meeting." In later stages, once a patient has "bought in" to utilizing the system, reviewing feedback reports with a patient can be a very useful approach, especially with technological tools that provide ongoing assessment and feedback. This approach has the benefit of providing the clinician with information about usage patterns (and environmental and emotional triggers in Step Away) that are more accurate and reliable than patient retrospective self-report, as patients often have poor recall about their use over time and sometimes underreport due to concerns about how the clinician may view them (Shiffman, Stone, & Hufford, 2007).

Clinicians can also play a role in helping patients determine the appropriate time to cease use of a technology-based intervention system. These systems were neither designed nor intended for use into perpetuity and often rely on users to determine for themselves when to stop use. A clinician can help a patient to process their overall progress and to assess their confidence in their ability to manage their substance use problem independently. They can also provide recommendations for either ceasing use of the intervention or continuing for a certain amount of time.

Relapse

Resuming drinking or drug use during or following treatment is a substantial and highly prevalent problem. Relapse rates are often shown to be in the 40% to 60% range, with some studies suggesting rates as high as 80% (Moos & Moos, 2006). Relapse is so prevalent that some theorists believe it should be considered a normal or expected aspect of treatment for substance use disorders (Marlatt & Donovan, 2005). Thus, if an individual engaged in a technology delivered intervention goes back to or resumes alcohol or drug use (or resumes heavy drinking in the case of moderation-based intervention), the intervention system should not necessarily be considered to be a failure, as high relapse rates are common even after intensive in-person treatment for alcohol and drug problems (Moos & Moos, 2006). In these cases, it can be helpful for the clinician to consider the resumed substance use as a normal part of the process and to help the patient to view the relapse as a learning experience and not evidence of a weak will or a personal failure. It is also advisable that the clinician discuss reengagement with the technology-delivered intervention as a way to restart the therapeutic process. Most technologically delivered interventions (the ones based on clinical science) have resumed drinking or drug use woven into the fabric of the system. For example, if a user of the Step Away system who has chosen an abstinence goal indicates that they have resumed drinking, the system provides reassuring messages that relapse is not uncommon and that the most important thing is to start again and reengage with the process.

One potential benefit of technology-delivered interventions is that it may be easier for an individual to report to the system that they have resumed alcohol or drug use than it would be for that person to admit the same to a therapist who they fear may judge them for the relapse. The system can then help the individual to immediately reengage and not wait until they are ready or have mustered the courage to tell their clinician. As mentioned previously, people are frequently more honest when reporting substance use to apps or web-based systems than they are to a fellow human being. For clinicians who are following a patient who is utilizing a technology-delivered intervention, it is important to keep a vigilant eye out for signs of relapse (missed appointments, increased negative emotions, poor self-care, isolation, etc.) while maintaining and communicating a nonjudgmental stance, and to use the assessment features of a technology-delivered intervention system to provide accurate, real-time monitoring for resumed alcohol or drug use.

Summary/Conclusions

Technology-based interventions address many of the barriers to obtaining treatment for hazardous alcohol and substance use, and yet the availability of evidence-based technological interventions for alcohol and substance use lags behind the wealth of effective interventions addressing other types of health behavior, such as diet, physical activity, and chronic disease self-management (Yang & Van Stee, 2019). We identified and reviewed eight examples of diverse technology-based interventions that have demonstrated feasibility and acceptability to users, as well as some level of efficacy. Most are available for use through direct marketing to consumers, clinician prescription or referral, or worksites. All of the interventions we identified have been evaluated using experimental study designs, albeit some with small samples. The interventions made use of older and newer technology, including web, telephone, and smart-phone. All of the interventions reviewed were theoretically based and included intervention(s) that were deemed appropriate in the literature for the specific population and substances they targeted. Interventions fell into three broad categories of use: (1) as stand-alone substitutes for face-to-face treatment, (2) as adjuncts to clinician or treatment program care, or (3) as post-treatment support for behavior-change maintenance and relapse prevention. It is interesting to note that most of these interventions continue to undergo development and testing, adding new features as the technology changes (Step Away), or expanding their use to intervene on a growing list of substances (A-CHESS; CheckUp and Choices).

Regardless of whether an intervention is intended to be used as a stand-alone substitute for in-person treatment, an adjunct to in-person treatment, or a post-treatment support, clinicians can play an important role in assisting patients to select programs that are appropriate to their motivational stage, severity, and maintenance support needs. Specific recommendations for clinicians are that they (1) use motivational interviewing techniques to assess patient awareness of their need and motivation to change their alcohol or drug use patterns, (2) screen patients for severity using standardized tools, such as the AUDIT or DAST, (3) advise patients to try out mobile apps that are not only science-based but include motivational enhancement principles, if motivation to change is low, (4) schedule a two- or three-week follow-up call or appointment with patients who agree to try out the mobile app, (5) reinforce their continued use of the program by reviewing feedback reports with them at future visits, and (6) accept relapse as a part of the recovery process and encourage patients to talk about what triggered the relapse and to use what they learned to reengage with the app. In the alternative, the clinician can recommend a different app for them to try.

The interventions described in this chapter were developed for adult populations, but there is a recognized need for developing effective technology-based interventions for substance-using youth (Carreiro et al., 2018). Also, given the increased recognition that alcohol and substance use are often comorbid with other conditions, including trauma and numerous psychiatric disorders, the need for interventions that also address these comorbidities is a growing area for research (Gilmore, Wilson, Skopp, Osenbach, & Reger, 2017; Sugarman, Campbell, Iles, & Greenfield, 2017). Finally, innovations in mobile health technology, such as wearable clothing and devices

Table 8.1 Intended Use and Components of Available Technology-Based Interventions

Available Technology-Based Interventions	Source (url or contact information)	Substance	Intended Use	Intervention Strategies and Components
Stand-Alone Interventions				
Step Away—Phone App	Stepaway.biz	Alcohol	Stand-alone	Clinical Strategies: Motivational Enhancement; Relapse Prevention; Community Reinforcement Components/Steps: • Assessment and Feedback • Goal Setting • Cravings • Moderation or Abstinence Strategies • New Activities • Support Persons Reminders to Change Drinking
CheckUp & Choices—web-Based	checkupandchoices.com	Alcohol; opioids; cannabis (under develop-ment); stimulants	Stand-alone or as an adjunct to treatment. Available for individuals or organizations.	Clinical Strategies: Brief Motivational Treatment Components: • Screening • Goal-Setting • Self-Monitoring • Feedback
Clinician or Treatment Supported Interventions				
CBT4CBT-Alcohol—web-based	www.cbt4cbt.com	Alcohol	With brief clinician monitoring	Clinical Strategies: CBT Components: • Functional Analysis • Coping with Cravings • Decision Making • Recognizing and Changing Thoughts • Problem-Solving Skills • Assertiveness Skills

CBT4CBT-Drugs	www.cbt4cbt.com	Cannabis; stimulants	With brief clinician monitoring	Clinical Strategies: CBT Components: • Functional Analysis • Coping with Cravings • Decision Making • Recognizing and Changing Thoughts • Problem-Solving Skills • Assertiveness Skills
CBT4CBT-Bupenophrine	www.cbt4cbt.com	Opioids	With brief clinician monitoring	Clinical Strategies: CBT Components: • Functional Analysis • Coping with Cravings • Decision Making • Recognizing and Changing Thoughts • Problem-Solving Skills • Assertiveness Skills
reSET—Phone App	www.resetforrecovery.com/	Alcohol; cannabis; stimulants;	Prescription only adjunct treatment, as an adjunct to outpatient therapy and to contingency management	Clinical Strategies: CBT Components: • Patient Application • Clinician Dashboard
Treatment Extender Interventions				
A-CHESS—Phone App	www.chess.health/solutions/	Alcohol	Recovery support system for patients leaving residential treatment	Clinical Strategies: Self-determination theory Components: • Discussion Board and Private Messaging • Help with Cravings • Games and Relaxation

Note: For alcohol and opioid use disorders, medication evaluations/management should be conducted as serious withdrawal symptoms can occur, including death. Clinical Practice Guidelines also recommend referral to specialty SUD care for clients who meet diagnostic criteria and are willing to engage in specialty treatment.

that passively collect real-time data (Arnrich et al., 2017; Selvam, Muthuku-mar, Kamakoti, & Prasad, 2016) and devices that use artificial intelligence, have great potential to provide proactive feedback and intervention as well as coaching and support (Connor, Symons, Feeney, Young, & Wiles, 2007). Such advances will expand the reach and potential public health impact of technology-based interventions to prevent and address hazardous alcohol and substance use.

Note

1. Patrick Dulin discloses his financial interest in Step Away as an owner of the company.
2. Special thanks to Kathleen Carroll, Reid Hester, and Andrew Quanbeck for their contributions to sections on CBT4CBT, Checkup & Choices, and A-CHESS, respectively.

References

Arnrich, B., Ersoy, C., Mayora, O., Dey, A., Berthouze, N., & Kunze, K. (2017). Wearable therapy—detecting information from wearables and mobiles that are relevant to clinical and self-directed therapy. *Methods of Information in Medicine, 56*(1), 37–39. doi:10.3414/ME17-14-0001

Bedrouni, W. (2018). On the use of digital technologies to reduce the public health impacts of cannabis legalization in Canada. *Canadian Journal of Public Health, 109*(5–6), 748–751. doi:10.17269/s41997-018-0117-7

Bickel, W. K., Marsch, L. A., Buchhalter, A. R., & Badger, G. J. (2008). Computerized behavior therapy for opioid-dependent outpatients: A randomized controlled trial. *Experimental and Clinical Psychopharmacology, 16*(2), 132. doi:10.1037/1064-1297.16.2.132

Campbell, A. N., Nunes, E. V., Matthews, A. G., Stitzer, M., Miele, G. M., Polsky, D., . . . Wahle, A. (2014). Internet-delivered treatment for substance abuse: A multisite randomized controlled trial. *American Journal of Psychiatry, 171*(6), 683–690. doi:10.1176/appi.ajp.2014.13081055

Campbell, W., Hester, R. K., Lenberg, K. L., & Delaney, H. D. (2016). Overcoming addictions, a web-based application, and SMART Recovery, an online and in-person mutual help group for problem drinkers, part 2: Six-month outcomes of a randomized controlled trial and qualitative feedback from participants. *Journal of Medical Internet Research, 18*(10), e262. doi:10.2196/jmir.2565

Carreiro, S., Chai, P. R., Carey, J., Lai, J., Smelson, D., & Boyer, E. W. (2018). mHealth for the detection and intervention in adolescent and young adult substance use disorder. *Current Addiction Reports, 5*(2), 110–119. doi:10.1007/s40429-018-0192-0.

Carroll, K. M., Ball, S. A., Martino, S., Nich, C., Babuscio, T. A., Nuro, K. F., . . . Rounsaville, B. J. (2008). Computer-assisted delivery of cognitive-behavioral therapy for addiction: A randomized trial of CBT4CBT. *American Journal of Psychiatry, 165*(7), 881–888. doi:10.1176/appi.ajp.2008.07111835

Carroll, K. M., & Kiluk, B. D. (2017). Cognitive behavioral interventions for alcohol and drug use disorders: Through the stage model and back again. *Psychology of Addictive Behaviors, 31*(8), 847–861. doi:10.1037/adb0000311

Carroll, K. M., Kiluk, B. D., Nich, C., Gordon, M. A., Portnoy, G. A., Marino, D. R., & Ball, S. A. (2014). Computer-assisted delivery of cognitive-behavioral therapy:

Efficacy and durability of CBT4CBT among cocaine-dependent individuals maintained on methadone. *American Journal of Psychiatry, 171*(4), 436–444. doi:10.1176/appi.ajp.2013.13070987

Carroll, K. M., Nich, C., DeVito, E. E., Shi, J. M., & Sofuoglu, M. (2017). Galantamine and computerized cognitive behavioral therapy for cocaine dependence: A randomized clinical trial. *Journal of Clinical Psychiatry, 79*(1). doi:10.4088/JCP.17m1166.

Chih, M. Y., Patton, T., McTavish, F. M., Isham, A. J., Judkins-Fisher, C. L., Atwood, A. K., & Gustafson, D. H. (2014). Predictive modeling of addiction lapses in a mobile health application. *Journal of Substance Abuse Treatment, 46*(1), 29–35. doi:10.1016/j.jsat.2013.08.004

Choo, E. K., Ranney, M. L., Wong, Z., & Mello, M. J. (2012). Attitudes toward technology-based health information among adult emergency department patients with drug or alcohol misuse. *Journal of Substance Abuse Treatment. 43*(4), 397–401. doi:10.1016/j.jsat.2012.09.005

Christensen, D. R., Landes, R. D., Jackson, L., Marsch, L. A., Mancino, M., Chopra, M. P., & Bickel, W. K. (2014). Adding an internet-delivered treatment to an efficacious treatment program for opioid dependence. *Journal of Consulting and Clinical Psychology, 82*(6), 964–972. doi:10.1037/a0037496

Cohen, E., Feinn, R., Arias, A., & Kranzler, H. R. (2007). Alcohol treatment utilization: Findings from the national epidemiologic survey on alcohol and related conditions. *Drug and Alcohol Dependence. 86*(2–3), 214–221. doi:10.1016/j.drugalcdep.2006.06.008

Connor, J. P., Symons, M., Feeney, G. F. X., Young, R. M., & Wiles, J. (2007). The application of machine learning techniques as an adjunct to clinical decision making in alcohol dependence treatment. *Substance Use & Misuse, 42*(14), 2193–2206. doi:10.1080/10826080701658125

Degenhardt, L., & Hall, W. (2012). Extent of illicit drug use and dependence, and their contribution to the global burden of disease. *The Lancet, 379*(9810), 55–70. doi:10.1016/S0140-6736(11)61138-0

De Novo Classification Request for reSET. DEN160018 (2017, May 16). Retrieved from www.accessdata.fda.gov/cdrh_docs/reviews/DEN160018.pdf

Dulin, P., Gonzalez, V. M., & Jones, K. (2014). Results of a pilot test of a self-administered smartphone-based treatment system for alcohol use disorders: Usability and early outcomes. *Substance Abuse, 35*, 168–175. doi:10.1080/08897077.2013.821437

Dulin, P., Gonzalez, V. M., King, D., Giroux, D., & Bacon, S. (2013). Development of a smartphone-based, self-administered intervention system for alcohol use disorders. *Alcoholism Treatment Quarterly, 31*, 321–336. doi:10.1080/07347324.2013.800425

Dutra, L., Stathopoulou, G., Basden, S. L., Leyro, T. M., Powers, M. B., & Otto, M. W. (2008). A meta-analytic review of psychosocial interventions for substance use disorders. *American Journal of Psychiatry, 165*(2), 179–187. doi:10.1176/appi.ajp.2007.06111851

Esser, M. B., Hedden, S. L., Kanny, D., Brewer, R. D., Gfroerer, J. C., & Naimi, T. S. (2014). Prevalence of alcohol dependence among US adult drinkers, 2009–2011. *Preventing Chronic Disease, 11*. doi:10.5888/pcd11.140329

Gandhi, D., Welsh, C., Bennett, M., Carreño, J., & Himelhoch, S. (2009). Acceptability of technology-based methods substance abuse counseling in office based buprenorphine maintenance for opioid dependence. *American Journal on Addictions. 18*(2), 182–183. doi:10.1080/10550490902772553

Gilmore, A. K., Wilson, S. M., Skopp, N. A., Osenbach, J. E., & Reger, G. (2017). A systematic review of technology-based interventions for co-occurring substance use and trauma symptoms. *Journal of Telemedicine and Telecare, 23*(8), 701–709. doi:10.1177/1357633X16664205

Glass, J. E., McKay, J. R., Gustafson, D. H., Kornfield, R., Rathouz, P. J., McTavish, F. M., . . . Shah, D. (2017). Treatment seeking as a mechanism of change in a randomized controlled trial of a mobile health intervention to support recovery from alcohol use disorders. *Journal of Substance Abuse Treatment, 77*, 57–66. doi:10.1016/j.jsat.2017.03.011

Gonzalez, V. M., & Dulin, P. L. (2015). Comparison of a smartphone app for alcohol use disorders with an Internet-based intervention plus bibliotherapy: A pilot study. *Journal of Consulting and Clinical Psychology, 83*(2), 335–345. doi:10.1037/a0038620

Grant, B. F. (1997). Barriers to alcoholism treatment: Reasons for not seeking treatment in a general population sample. *Journal of Studies on Alcohol, 58*(4), 365–371. doi:10.15288/jsa.1997.58.365

Grant, B. F., Saha, T. D., Ruan, W. J., Goldstein, R. B., Chou, S. P., Jung, J., . . . Hasin, D. S. (2016). Epidemiology of DSM-5 drug use disorder: Results from the national epidemiologic survey on alcohol and related conditions-III. *JAMA Psychiatry, 73*(1), 39–47.

Grucza, R. A., Sher, K. J., Kerr, W. C., Krauss, M. J., Lui, C. K., McDowell, Y. E., . . . Bierut, L. J. (2018). Trends in adult alcohol use and binge drinking in the early 21st-Century United States: A meta-analysis of 6 National Survey Series. *Alcoholism: Clinical and Experimental Research, 42*(10), 1939–1950. doi:10.1111/acer.13859

Gustafson, D. H., McTavish, F. M., Chih, M. Y., Atwood, A. K., Johnson, R. A., Boyle, M. G., . . . Isham, A. (2014). A smartphone application to support recovery from alcoholism: A randomized clinical trial. *JAMA Psychiatry, 71*(5), 566–572. doi:10.1001/jamapsychiatry.2013.4642

Hasin, D. S., Stinson, F. S., Ogburn, E., & Grant, B. F. (2007). Prevalence, correlates, disability, and comorbidity of DSM-IV alcohol abuse and dependence in the United States: Results from the national epidemiologic survey on alcohol and related conditions. *Archives of General Psychiatry, 64*(7), 830–842. doi:10.1001/archpsyc.64.7.830

Hawkins, E., Danner, A., Lott, A., Malte, C., Dulin, P., Fortney, J., . . . Baer, J. (2019). Evaluating a mobile application for self-management of unhealthy alcohol use. (manuscript in progress).

Hester, R. K., Delaney, H. D., & Campbell, W. (2011). ModerateDrinking.Com and moderation management: Outcomes of a randomized clinical trial with non-dependent problem drinkers. *Journal of Consulting and Clinical Psychology, 79*(2), 215–224. doi:10.1037/a0022487

Holmes, N. A., van Agteren, J. E., & Dorstyn, D. S. (2018). A systematic review of technology-assisted interventions for co-morbid depression and substance use. *Journal of Telemedicine and Telecare, 25*(3), 131–141. doi:10.1177/1357633X17748991

Kampman, K., & Jarvis, M. (2015). American society of addiction medicine (ASAM) national practice guidelines for the use of medications in the treatment of addiction involving opioid use. *Journal of Addiction Medicine, 9*(5), 358–367. doi:10.1097/ADM.0000000000000166

Kiluk, B. D., Devore, K. A., Buck, M. B., Nich, C., Frankforter, T. L., LaPaglia, D. M., . . . Carroll, K. M. (2016). Randomized trial of computerized cognitive behavioral therapy for alcohol use disorders: Efficacy as a virtual stand-alone and treatment add-on compared with standard outpatient treatment. *Alcohol Clinical Experimental Research, 40*(9), 1991–2000. doi:10.1111/acer.13162

Kiluk, B. D., Nich, C., Buck, M. B., Devore, K. A., Frankforter, T. L., LaPaglia, D. M., . . . Carroll, K. M. (2018). Randomized clinical trial of computerized and clinician-delivered CBT in comparison with standard outpatient treatment for substance use disorders: Primary within-treatment and follow-up outcomes. *American Journal of Psychiatry*, *175*(9), 853–863.doi:10.1176/appi.ajp.2018.17090978

Magill, M., & Ray, L. A. (2009). Cognitive-behavioral treatment with adult alcohol and illicit drug users: A meta-analysis of randomized controlled trials. *Journal of Studies on Alcohol and Drugs*, *70*(4), 516–527. doi:10.15288/jsad.2009.70.516

Magill, M., Ray, L. A., Kiluk, B. D., Hoadley, A., Bernstein, M., Tonigan, J. S., & Carroll, K. M. (under review). Cognitive behavioral therapy and relapse prevention for alcohol and other drug use disorders: A meta-analysis.

Marlatt, G. A., & Donovan, D. M. (2005). *Relapse prevention: Maintenance strategies in the treatment of addictive behaviors* (2nd ed.). New York: Guilford Press.

Marsch, L. A., & Dallery, J. (2012). Advances in the psychosocial treatment of addiction: The role of technology in the delivery of evidence-based psychosocial treatment. *Psychiatric Clinics*, *35*(2), 481–493. doi:10.1016/j.psc.2012.03.009

Marsch, L. A., Guarino, H., Acosta, M., Aponte-Melendez, Y., Cleland, C., Grabinski, M., . . . Edwards, J. (2014). Web-based behavioral treatment for substance use disorders as a partial replacement of standard methadone maintenance treatment. *Journal of Substance Abuse Treatment*, *46*(1), 43–51. doi:10.1016/j.jsat.2013.08.012

Mayo-Smith, M. F., Beecher, L. H., Fischer, T. L., Gorelick, D. A., Guillaume, J. L., Hill, A., . . . Melbourne, J. (2004). Management of alcohol withdrawal delirium: An evidence-based practice guideline. *Archives of Internal Medicine*, *164*(13), 1405–1412. doi:10.1001/archinte.164.13.1405

Meyers, R. J., Villanueva, M., & Smith, J. E. (2005). The community reinforcement approach: History and new directions. *Journal of Cognitive Psychotherapy*, *19*(3), 247–260. doi:10.1001/archinte.164.13.1405

Miller, W. R. (Ed.). (1999). *Enhancing motivation for change in substance abuse treatment. treatment improvement protocol (TIP) series, no. 35*. Rockville, MD: Center for Substance Abuse Treatment.

Miller, W. R., & Rollnick, S. (2013). *Motivational interviewing: Preparing people for change* (3rd ed.). New York: Guildford Press.

Moos, R. H., & Moos, B. S. (2006). Rates and predictors of relapse after natural and treated remission from alcohol use disorders. *Addiction*, *101*(2), 212–222. doi:10.1111/j.1360-0443.2006.01310.x

Nesvåg, S., & McKay, J. R. (2018). Feasibility and effects of digital interventions to support people in recovery from substance use disorders: Systematic review. *Journal of Medical Internet Research*, *20*(8), e255. doi:10.2196/jmir.9873

Paris, M., Silva, M., Anez-Nava, L., Jaramillo, Y., Kiluk, B. D., Gordon, M. A., . . . Carroll, K. M. (2018). Culturally adapted, web-based cognitive behavioral therapy for Spanish-speaking individuals with substance use disorders: A randomized clinical trial. *American Journal of Public Health*, *108*(11), 1535–1542. doi:10.2105/AJPH.2018.304571

Postel, M. G., de Haan, H. A., Ter Huurne, E. D., van der Palen, J., Becker, E. S., & de Jong, C. A. (2011). Attrition in web-based treatment for problem drinkers. *Journal of Medical Internet Research*, *13*(4), 120–133. doi:10.2196/jmir.1811

Quanbeck, A., Gustafson, D. H., Marsch, L. A., Chih, M. Y., Kornfield, R., McTavish, F., . . . Shah, D. V. (2018). Implementing a mobile health system to integrate the treatment of addiction into primary care: A hybrid implementation-effectiveness study. *Journal of Medical Internet Research, 20*(1), e37. doi:10.2196/jmir.8928

Ramsey, A. T., Satterfield, J. M., Gerke, D. R., & Proctor, E. K. (2019). Technology-based alcohol interventions in primary care: Systematic review. *Journal of Medical Internet Research, 21*(4), e10859. doi:10.2196/10859

Reinert, D., & Allen, J. P. (2007). The alcohol use disorders identification test: An update of research findings. *Alcoholism: Clinical and Experimental Research, 31*(2), 185–199. doi:10.1111/j.1530-0277.2006.00295.x

Ryan, R. M., & Deci, E. L. (2000). Self-determination theory and the facilitation of intrinsic motivation, social development, and well-being. *American Psychologist, 55*(1), 68–78. doi:10.1016/j.jsat.2006.01.002

Saunders, S. M., Zygowicz, K. M., & D'Angelo, B. R. (2006). Person-related and treatment-related barriers to alcohol treatment. *Journal of Substance Abuse Treatment, 30*(3), 261–270. doi:10.1016/j.jsat.2006.01.003

Sellman, D. (2010). The 10 most important things known about addiction. *Addiction, 105*(1), 6–13. doi:10.1111/j.1360-0443.2009.02673.x

Selvam, A. P., Muthukumar, S., Kamakoti, V., & Prasad, S. (2016). A wearable biochemical sensor for monitoring alcohol consumption lifestyle through Ethyl glucuronide (EtG) detection in human sweat. *Scientific Reports, 6*, 23111. doi:10.1038/srep23111

Shi, J. M., Henry, S., Dwy, S. L., Orazietti, S. A., & Carroll, K. M. (in press). Randomized pilot trial of online cognitive behavioral therapy adapted for use in office-based buprenorphine maintenance. *Substance Abuse.*

Shiffman, S., Stone, A. A., & Hufford, M. R. (2007). Ecological momentary assessment. *Annual Review of Clinical Psychology, 4*, 1–32.

Stahre, M., Roeber, J., Kanny, D., Brewer, R. D., & Zhang, X. (2014). Contribution of excessive alcohol consumption to deaths and years of potential life lost in the United States. *Prevention of Chronic Disease, 11.* doi:10.5888/pcd11.130293

Sugarman, D. E., Campbell, A. N., Iles, B. R., & Greenfield, S. F. (2017). Technology-based interventions for substance use and comorbid disorders: An examination of the emerging literature. *Harvard Review of Psychiatry, 25*(3), 123. doi:10.1097/HRP.0000000000000148

VanDeMark, N. R., Burrell, N. R., LaMendola, W. F., Hoich, C. A., Berg, N. P., & Medina, E. (2010). An exploratory study of engagement in a technology-supported substance abuse intervention. *Substance Abuse Treatment, Prevention, and Policy, 5*(1), 10. doi:10.1186/1747-597X-5-10

Walker, N., McCormack, J., Dulin, P., Newxombe, D., Jones, R., & Galea-Singer, S. (2019). Outcomes of a feasibility trial of a mobile-based intervention for hazardous drinking. (manuscript in progress).

Yang, Q., & Van Stee, S. K. (2019). The comparative effectiveness of mobile phone interventions in improving health outcomes: Meta-analytic review. *JMIR mHealth and uHealth, 7*(4), e11244. doi:10.2196/11244

Yudkho, E., Lozhinka, O., & Fouts, A. (2007). A comprehensive review of the psychometric properties of the drug abuse screening test. *Journal of Substance Abuse Treatment, 32*(2), 189–198. doi:10.1016/j.jsat.2006.08.002

9 Utilization of Technologies to Support Patients With Eating Disorders

C. Barr Taylor, Shiri Sadeh-Sharvit,
Ellen E. Fitzsimmons-Craft, Naira Topocco,
Elsa Rojas-Ashe, and Denise E. Wilfley

Introduction

Eating disorders (EDs) are severe psychiatric disorders associated with high morbidity and mortality, marked psychosocial impairment, and poor quality of life (American Psychiatric Association, 2013). A recent meta-analysis found point prevalence rates of eating disorders of about 6% in women and 2% in men in the Western world and also evidence for the disorders influencing individuals across the globe (Galmiche, Dechelotte, Lambert, & Tavolacci, 2019).

Fortunately, effective treatments for EDs are available (Kass, Kolko, & Wilfley, 2013). However, numerous barriers to receiving empirically supported treatments exist (Kazdin, Fitzsimmons-Craft, & Wilfley, 2017). Digital interventions have the potential to improve care for EDs by overcoming barriers to treatment while increasing access and reducing costs (Taylor, Graham, Flatt, & Fitzsimmons-Craft, in press). In this chapter, we review how ubiquitous technologies can be used in clinical practice to treat clients with EDs. We discuss empirically supported, technology-based interventions but also focus on a broader view of how digital practices can be incorporated into treatment to improve care for people with EDs.

The Evidence Base for Technologies Focused On Eating Disorders

Many studies have now been conducted on the effectiveness of internet-based ED treatment programs (Taylor et al., in press). Most of the interventions for EDs, other than those aimed at patients with anorexia nervosa, are based on cognitive-behavioral interventions originally developed for face-to-face delivery and for which the efficacy has been established in randomized efficacy trials using a variety of comparators. Across studies, results suggest that internet-based interventions for EDs are effective with small-to-moderate effect sizes. Little research has directly compared internet-based self-help with guided self-help or blended therapy, and no comparisons have been made directly to face-to-face therapy (Taylor et al., in press). Guided self-help internet-based programs have proved comparable to face-to-face treatment for other mental health problems, but it is unknown if this is the case with EDs.

Most of the controlled, internet-based intervention studies for EDs have focused on outpatients with clinical and subclinical bulimia nervosa and binge eating disorder symptoms. However, internet and digital programs have also been developed to aid individuals with EDs who would not seek help otherwise (Sadeh-Sharvit et al., 2018), such as for clients who have been discharged from hospital or who are in recovery (Bauer, Okon, Meermann, & Kordy, 2012), to prevent relapse, to improve attendance at outpatient clients, and to provide service to individuals waiting for appointments or those living in underserved communities. Other interventions have focused on caregivers and families of patients with anorexia nervosa, the use of virtual reality to provide various aspects of treatment, and the development of non-CBT approaches (e.g., ACT, compassion therapy) provided online (Ferrer-Garcia &

Table 9.1 Overview of Clinician Involvement for Levels of Digital Interventions

Level of Digital Intervention	Clinician Involvement	Example
Referral to digital resources clients use independently, e.g., Psychoeducation, monitoring, or apps for eating disorders or other ancillary issues.	None to minimal. The clinician may direct, recommend, or review client's use/ understanding of these tools.	"I thought you might find the testimonials on www. theprojecteal.org relevant to what we spoke about last week. I would be happy to talk about your thoughts on our next session."
Guided/moderated/ coached	Virtual coaches/ moderators/ clinicians guide the intervention remotely, with minimal or no face-to-face contact; intervention content delivered digitally.	Programs such as The Healthy Body Image program, everyBody, etc. See Case 1 for further demonstration.
Blended treatment	A combination of some clinician-led intervention (face-to-face or delivered via web-conferencing), with interaction of internet based program/ teletherapy, perhaps managed using a clinician "dashboard" to help review client's progress.	Meeting clients regularly in your clinic, and implementing a specialized app for eating disorders, such as Recovery Record. See Case 2 for illustration.

Gutiérrez-Maldonado, 2012). The clinician should stay alert to the development of programs in this area that may prove useful for practice. While a number of studies have shown the negative effects of online groups that promote EDs (e.g., Juarascio, Shoaib, & Timko, 2010; Sowles et al., 2018), it is likely that other online groups, including those on social media, more supportive of recovery, and perhaps monitored by mental health experts, might benefit patients.

Table 9.1, adapted from Muñoz (2016), presents a useful framework for considering the role of the clinician in driving digital activities. After presenting some general considerations about digital practice for eating and other disorders, we consider (a) self-help and psychoeducational approaches that do not necessarily involve the therapist, (b) coached programs (provided only online; supported by the client's own in-person therapist or another supporter); and (c) blended treatment approaches (a combination of face-to-face and internet programs directed by the patient's therapist). We will also describe a number of digital practices, like texting/messaging or revisiting social media use, that can be provided or recommended by therapists.

Preparing Your Client

Clinicians should allocate some time during early evaluation of a new client to determine the client's digital behaviors and interests, including current and past use of mental health apps, social networking sites, online support groups, internet games, dating apps, etc., as well as their interest in incorporating a focus on internet behavior and use of supportive apps in treatment. We have developed a basic survey that assesses the client's media use and interests. The survey takes only a few minutes to complete and is available on the Center for m2Health website at www.m2health.paloaltou.edu/resources. More detailed and rigorously evaluated scales, including the 60-item Media and Technology Usage and Attitudes Scale (Rosen, Whaling, Carrier, Cheever, & Rokkum, 2013) which has been shown to be valid and reliable, are also available for this purpose and can be found at the same website.

It is important also to assess the client's experience with other internet programs and their perceptions about their possible benefit, particularly if they are considering a program you recommend. A recent study found that individuals with high expectations of improvement from self-help programs did much better than those with lesser expectations (Mira et al., 2019). For clients who have agreed to use an app, a useful question is: "On a scale of 100% confidence that you will use it to 0% sure you won't use it, how confident are you that you will use the app at least once?" It is our experience that clients who report less than 70% confidence may not use the app at all, and lower scores can help generate a dialogue about their concerns with the technology.

Downloading apps and other programs can be a challenge and users often forget their passwords. If such activities use up time in session, it can negatively influence the client's as well as your own perception of the usefulness of technology in treatment. In our experience, it is sometimes better to go over the basics of the app and installation briefly and then to provide a handout with clear instructions so that the client can download the recommended app at home.

Before recommending any ED or other apps to clients, it is a good idea to try them out yourself first. This way, you will be better able to assess potential issues and to explain the use of the app better to your clients. For instance, apps are often promoted in ways that oversell their content and ease of use; many offer a "free version" but then charge for more useful functionalities, and some apps for EDs can be harmful (Rouleau & von Ranson, 2011).

Using Digital Diagnosis and Screening Tools

Several online instruments are currently available to assist with identifying risk and diagnosis of EDs: The Eating Disorder Assessment for DSM-5 (EDA-5) is a semi-structured interview designed to aid clinicians in evaluating individuals for feeding- and eating disorder-related conditions that is available in the public domain at EDA5.org (requires Google Chrome to use). The instrument has shown high rates of agreement with clinical interviews (Sysko et al., 2015). This interview is intended for use by clinicians on their computer as they are interviewing a client, and offers a printout summarizing the interview. The interview provides you with prompts to guide your client assessment and then uses the data you input to determine likely DSM-5 ED diagnoses. The interview is available in English and Spanish (and Norwegian), and adult and youth-specific versions (ages 8–14) exist.

We have developed an eating disorder screen called the Stanford-Washington University Eating Disorders Screen (SWED; Graham et al., 2019), which has demonstrated high sensitivity and specificity for most diagnoses. The SWED is freely available at the Center for m2Health website, but it requires an algorithm to interpret. Thus, it is best used when programmed as an online survey. The same screen can also be completed through the National Eating Disorders Association (NEDA) (www.nationaleatingdisorders.org/screening-tool). The screen is intended for use by individuals aged 13 and older, stratifies respondents into *risk for* or *possible ED categories*, provides feedback on results, and makes recommendations for seeking intervention as indicated (Fitzsimmons-Craft et al., 2019). In clinical practice, the client can take the questionnaire provided by NEDA prior to, or even in the session, and you can discuss the results and what symptoms may have led to the NEDA feedback as well as your client's reactions to that feedback.

Psychoeducation and Self-Help

Psychoeducation

A simple and important use of digital technology to facilitate the treatment of EDs is to provide psychoeducation. Excellent materials are available from NEDA and from the National Institute of Mental Health (NIMH) as well as from client organizations such as Project HEAL and Recovery Warriors. There are also several inspiring videos that might provide valuable, non-triggering information and help clients with motivation to overcome their resistance to treatment. For example, we have had good success with sharing the "Dove Evolution" video with clients to educate them about how the media heavily doctors images. Table 9.2 illustrates some resources our team has found useful in our practice.

If you decide to recommend these videos or others, review them first to determine their fit with your values and treatment approach and if they might be appropriate for your client. It is also useful to review the client's experience with the video.

Table 9.2 Recommended Online Resources for Psychoeducation to Clients Experiencing Shape and Weight Concerns or Eating Disorders

Source/Background	Website Address
National Eating Disorder Association (NEDA)	www.nationaleatingdisorders.org/
National Institute of Mental Health (NIMH)	www.nimh.nih.gov/health/topics/eating-disorders/index.shtml
Project Heal: a nonprofit organization aimed at supporting individuals with eating disorders through advocacy and community resources	www.theprojectheal.org
Recovery Warriors: resources for individuals struggling with depression, anxiety, and eating disorders	www.recoverywarriors.com/
"Dove Evolution" video	www.youtube.com/watch?v=iYhCn0jf46U
Jameela Jamil talks about her iWeigh movement: a part of body positivity movement against diet culture; mainly concerns women	www.youtube.com/watch?v=oBbpWLWJsIg
Videos in which participants react to being called beautiful by stranger or share something beautiful about themselves. All include representation of most body types, genders, and ethnicities, and end on a positive note	www.youtube.com/watch?v=B256AxNCe_Q www.youtube.com/watch?v=jg-O7f_1Ngc www.youtube.com/watch?v=CTf9x0DB8M4

Self-Help

While there are innumerable weight loss and fitness apps available—and they are widely used by clients with EDs, sometimes with detrimental effects as discussed later—we are aware of only three commercially available apps focusing on self-help for EDs, and of these, we have only used Recovery Record.

The Recovery Record (www.recoveryrecord.com) app was designed with input from ED experts to support recovery. The Recovery Record app allows self-monitoring of meals, thoughts, and feelings and provides customized meal plans and coping tactics. The program can also be linked with a treatment provider so that a therapist can have access to their client's data. The program has been widely downloaded (Tregarthen, Lock, & Darcy, 2015) and has demonstrated high acceptability (Kim et al., 2018). A controlled trial has been conducted but not yet published. In 2019, Recovery Record has a credibility rating of 2.86/5 on PsyberGuide, a freely available online resource that evaluates available mobile mental health apps (see more information later in this chapter); a user experience rating of 2.90/5; and transparency rated as unacceptable. However, we have found the program useful in clinical practice and present a case example later in the chapter.

We are aware of two other apps that can be used as self-help, Jourvie (www.jourvie.com) and Rise Up + Recover (www.recoverywarriors.com/app/). We could find no empirical studies on their use and have not used them ourselves. The reader is referred to other sections of this book that discuss how to choose and evaluate these and other apps if they wish to do so.

Based on our clinical experience, weight loss and fitness apps are commonly used by individuals with EDs. Since food restriction/avoidance and over-exercise are significant problems in EDs, and many apps promote both, the clinician needs to carefully monitor their clients' use of apps for potential negative effects and in general consider how they are helping/hindering ED treatment. For example, Honary, Bell, Cinch, Wild, and McNaney (2019) interviewed a number of people, aged 18 to 25 and mostly males with body image concerns, to determine the potential impact of weight loss/fitness apps on maladaptive behaviors and attitudes. The most common problems reported by the sample were becoming obsessed about counting behaviors, guilt about food restriction, reducing time available for social activities, and failing to meet goals. Several of their respondents mentioned that the app use was making their ED worse.

The clinician may want to consider additional apps for comorbidities and other issues. EDs are highly comorbid with depressive, anxiety, substance abuse, and other disorders. Thus, in formulating a treatment plan, it is worthwhile to consider what other apps might also be useful for a client—in addition to or even instead of—apps the client is already using. The types of supplemental apps we have most commonly recommended include ones focusing on stress management/mindfulness and insomnia, and we have had our choices guided by reviews on PsyberGuide.org and Mindtools.io, as well as by our own experience.

Self-Monitoring of EDs Using Digital Tools

Self-monitoring is a common component of ED treatment: most evidence-based programs include self-monitoring tools which involve tracking behaviors related to the intervention (e.g., meal planning and tracking, monitoring ED and related behaviors, monitoring maladaptive cognitions). In theory, digital self-monitoring tools have advantages over paper and pencil ones in terms of data management (e.g., graphing the data, interactivity, time stamps), but integrating self-monitoring data from clients into practice can be cumbersome depending on how a clinician sets up their practice for digital services and digital communication regulations of the provider's workplace. One option to consider is to have your client share their feedback screen from their phone, which keeps their data private and on their own devices. (However, clinicians and clients need to be comfortable having the phone passed back and forth). The information can then be summarized in the clinical note based on this review in session. Another option is for the client to share their data with their clinician—this functionality is available in some existing apps (e.g., Recovery Record as demonstrated in Case 2). Some clinicians may wish to incorporate use of more general self-monitoring tools (e.g., mood triggers, [www.nicholasjacobson.com/project/mood-triggers/] as opposed to tools that only assess ED symptoms.

Guided Self-Help Programs for Eating Disorders

In recent years, guided/coached self-help programs have been developed to provide online interventions for individuals with EDs. The general rationale for the development of these programs is their scalability compared to traditional in-person treatment and that they have the potential to provide accessible, affordable, evidence-based care to anyone, anywhere. Although privacy is certainly an issue, they also can be less stigmatizing. These programs could work as a stand-alone intervention or in parallel with other clinical face-to-face efforts, e.g., to allow therapists to facilitate the client receiving care for ED symptoms while they address other issues, such as self-harm or trauma.

Guided self-help interventions have evidenced acceptability and efficacy with individuals with ED symptoms (Taylor et al., in press). Our team developed such an intervention for college women with eating disorders, called Student Bodies-Eating Disorders, which was designed based on two small-scale efficacy trials that suggested it would be effective (Jacobi, Völker, Trockel, & Taylor, 2012; Saekow et al., 2015). The intervention was based on the core components of CBT for EDs, including reducing disordered eating behaviors (e.g., via self-monitoring, promotion of regular eating, conducting behavioral chain analyses); improving body image (e.g., decreasing importance of weight and shape on self-esteem); changing behavior (e.g., reintroducing forbidden foods); regulating emotions; addressing shape checking and avoidance; challenging negative automatic thoughts; and preventing relapse. The program included psychoeducational content as well as meal planning and tracking tools, self-monitoring logs, and other interactive tools (e.g., texting platform facilitating coach-user communication; Fitzsimmons-Craft et al., under review). The final program was designed to comprise 40 core sessions, requiring about 10–15 minutes each to complete, and was offered via mobile app in addition to web browser access. Users were provided access to the intervention for eight months, and each user was assigned a personal online coach to guide them through the intervention. Coaches, mostly psychology graduate students who underwent extensive training, used a clinical management "dashboard" to efficiently monitor multiple users at one time (for more detail, see Fitzsimmons-Craft et al., under review). The dashboard provided information on users' goals, progress, and intervention use, as well as the ability to message users.

We have recently completed a large-scale randomized controlled trial (RCT) evaluating the efficacy of this program. In this study, 690 college women with EDs from 28 universities were randomized to the intervention or a control group (i.e., referral to usual care at the college counseling/health center). For the primary outcome of ED psychopathology (measured by the Eating Disorders Examination-Questionnaire [EDE-Q] Global Score), there was a significantly greater reduction in the intervention compared to control at post-intervention ($d=-0.40$; $p<0.001$), as well as over follow-up ($d=-0.35$; $p<0.001$). The intervention was associated with significantly greater reductions than control in binge eating (Rate: 0.82 [0.70–0.96]; $p=0.016$), compensatory behaviors (Rate: 0.68 [0.54–0.86]; $p<0.001$), depression ($d=-0.22$; $p=0.009$), and clinical impairment ($d=-0.21$; $p=0.011$) at post-intervention, with these gains sustained through follow-up for all outcomes except binge eating (Fitzsimmons-Craft et al., under review).

Unfortunately, we know of no stand-alone coached ED programs currently available for clinicians who may want to refer clients for ancillary, parallel coached self-help treatment. The program evaluated in our long-term NIMH trial was migrated to the SilverCloud platform and renamed *Space from Body and Eating Concerns*. We are currently evaluating the program as part of a large NIMH-sponsored trial, but results will not be available for some time. We anticipate the program to be equally effective on the Silver-Cloud platform to the previous version. Hopefully, coached programs will be available in the near future.

The following case illustrates the use of coached guided self-help program to treat EDs.

Case Example 1

Gabby was a 20-year-old Latina college student. She had always been physically active in high school (she was on the swim team) and maintained a normal weight. However, upon beginning college, she found herself having less time for physical activity, as she was quite stressed about maintaining a high GPA in order to keep her scholarship, so she spent every minute she could focused on her schoolwork. This, combined with her increased alcohol intake (which made her feel less anxious at parties) and consumption of many less healthy food options available in the dining hall led to her gaining about 10 pounds over the course of her freshman year. At the beginning of her sophomore year, after her family had given her a lot of trouble about her weight over the summer, Gabby began strict dieting, including skipping many meals, in an attempt to lose the weight she'd gained. But after a couple of weeks of this, she found that oftentimes in the evenings after her classes, she would become totally famished and then binge eat in her dorm room on whatever she and her roommate had around—she felt like she could not stop eating once she started and would feel totally disgusted by herself after eating. This pattern went on for several months, and Gabby kept feeling worse and worse about her body as she gained more weight and also became really down. One day Gabby's college sent out an email informing students about an opportunity to take a mental health screen and gain access to resources. She was not sure about the idea of going to the counseling center (she didn't want her friends to find out about her issues) but figured it couldn't hurt to take the screen to see what it said about her issues and what her options were. The screen informed her that her symptoms may be suggestive of an ED, which was upsetting to Gabby but also helped her to see that her symptoms were "real." Her feedback also informed her that she may be struggling with some symptoms of anxiety and depression. Gabby was informed about a coached mobile program available on her campus she might find useful. Gabby signed up right away and was assigned to her coach, Michelle. She was informed that Michelle would be available to communicate with Gabby weekly to support her through the program using a messaging feature available in the app.

Gabby had not talked about her issues with eating with anyone, not even her family, and was skeptical that a mobile app could help her, but she decided she had little to lose by trying it out. Gabby's coach was very welcoming and helped her solidify her goals, which were to feel more in control of her eating and feel better about her body. Gabby made a goal to log into the program a few times a week, and when she did, she would spend about 15 minutes with it. There was new content available each time she logged in, and usually there was a mix of content to read, videos to watch, quizzes to take, and/or interactive activities to complete (see Figure 9.1 sample screenshots depicting some mobile app features). She could squeeze the

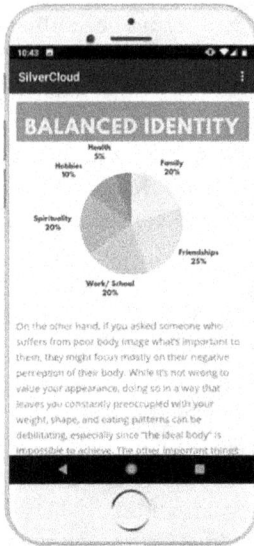

Session psycho-education

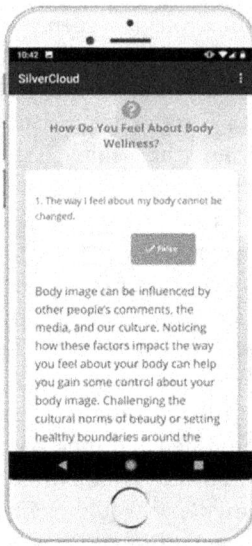

Psycho-educational quizzes

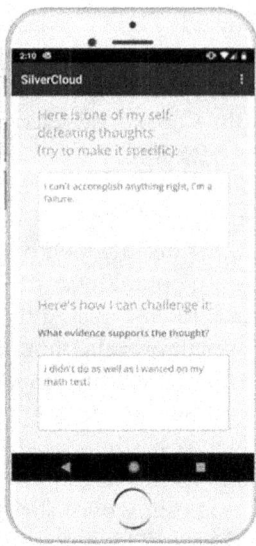

Interactive tools to learn skills

Coaches send users reviews to foster engagement, help users practice skills in daily life, and reflect on progress.

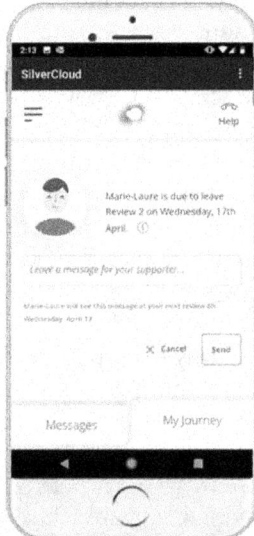

Users leave messages for their coach to ask questions, reflect on content, etc.

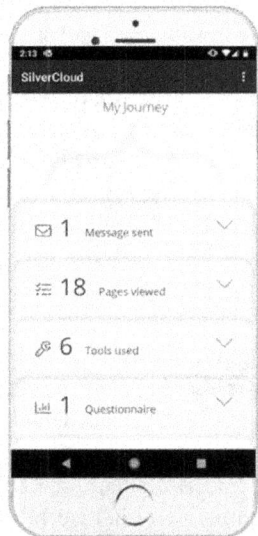

Users can keep track of their progress with the program.

Figure 9.1 Mobile App Features

program in between things—and she got in the habit of doing it in between her classes when she had a few minutes to spare.

The program started out by teaching Gabby about the importance of regular eating for gaining more control over her eating, which she had not really appreciated before. She decided to try eating three meals and a snack or two a day, to see if that improved her binge eating. She was worried this approach would make her gain even more weight, which she expressed to Michelle, but Michelle was able to provide some assurance this was not typically the case and that with this strategy, most users usually maintain a healthy weight. The program also helped Gabby recognize other triggers for binge eating (feeling really anxious or stressed about school) and come up with alternative, more adaptive coping strategies, like calling her sister, taking a shower, or going for a quick walk. In addition, the program helped Gabby reevaluate the importance she was placing on weight and shape and helped her to reduced behaviors that were making her focus even more on her weight and shape, like weighing herself every day and constantly checking her body in the mirror. Gabby really liked how Michelle helped personalize the program to her exact needs. Because Gabby struggled with some symptoms of depression and anxiety, her coach was able to guide her toward modules specific to helping her improve these issues. Michelle also always helped Gabby to see how the various skills she was learning could help her work on not only her eating disorder symptoms but also her anxiety and depression.

Gabby really liked the symptom-tracking features available in the mobile app, which let both her and her coach easily see how she was doing symptom-wise (see Figure 9.2). For example, during the middle of her time in the program, Gabby suffered the loss of a family member, which triggered her binge eating to spike, but she and her coach were able to quickly pick up on this pattern, and Michelle helped Gabby figure out which strategies she could use to get back on track.

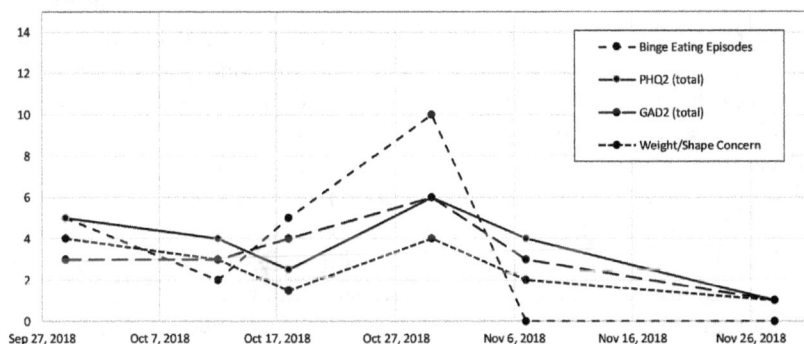

Figure 9.2 Symptom-Wise Tracking Features

After a couple of months in the program, Gabby was not only feeling much more in control of her eating but she was also feeling better about her body, less anxious, and less depressed. Michelle was also able to work with Gabby to come up with some strategies for maintaining her progress, particularly as the holiday break came up, including being more open with her mom about what she had been experiencing and talking with her mom about the types of comments she had been making about her body that were only making Gabby feel worse.

Email and Texting Correspondence With Clients

Human interactions and relationships are no longer limited to the physical constraints of face-to-face interactions. Teletherapy, or the provision of therapy or other clinical services by a clinician using telecommunication technologies that include visual, audio, or email/text message contact with a client (American Psychological Association, 2013), has changed the landscape of clinical work. Most individuals who are 16–24 years old and those with graduate education report an inclination to send or receive emails to or from their doctor, nurse, or health care organization, and those with greater health problems report more frequent email correspondence than their counterparts (Newhouse, Lupiáñez-Villanueva, Codagnone, & Atherton, 2015). About a third of individuals with EDs report not confiding in anyone about their symptoms (Sadeh-Sharvit et al., 2018), therefore they may lack significant support resources other than their therapist. Some empirically supported approaches to treating EDs, such as cognitive-behavioral therapy and dialectical behavioral therapy, include routine email communication as part of the treatment package (Sadeh-Sharvit, 2019). Further, in a recent RCT, a maintenance program post hospitalization, which included one text message exchange once a week between patients and their therapists, was associated with higher ED remission rates. Over the course of 16 weeks after discharge, the patient sent a message to their therapist who responded in a text that was adapted to the patient's message. Patients receiving texts had less ED symptoms and better functioning than controls (Bauer et al., 2012).

Text and email messages can benefit clients with EDs but do require thoughtful consideration of privacy and ethics and some preparations. The provider should educate their client about important issues such as privacy, confidentiality, and the type of messages the provider is able to respond to via email or text (e.g., the client should be advised to avoid using this channel in case of crisis or suicidal threats). Appropriate safety plans for alternative client support should be developed to support urgent needs, should they occur. Further, the provider should explicitly clarify expectations for availability and response time. Organization and workplace policies about texting and emailing clients also need to be considered, and text and email correspondence should be added to routine informed consent forms. Therapists should develop a plan for how messages will be saved in health records. When responding to messages, we recommend that providers keep their texts succinct and focused on the issue at hand, and refocus the client to information and skills already discussed in the session.

Reviewing clients' self-monitoring and providing support via text can be quite straightforward. Figures 9.3 and 9.4 illustrate simple strategies to two examples of how a therapist can monitor target behaviors. On the other hand, texting should augment the treatment effects and not become a channel through which the client constantly engages the therapist in daily

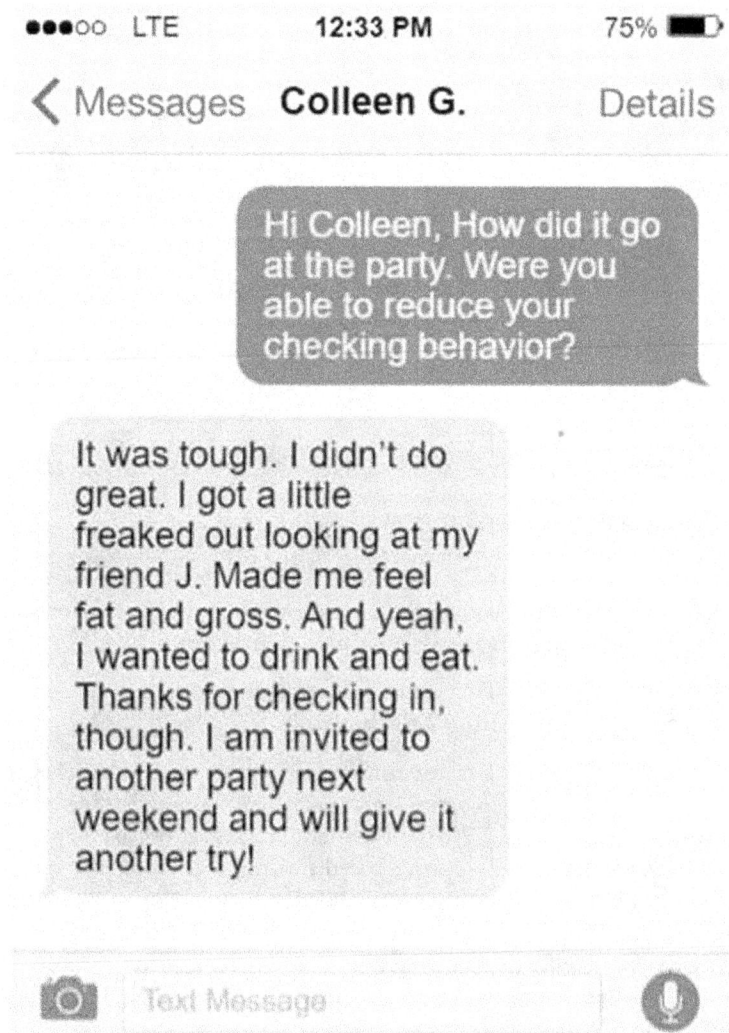

Figure 9.3 Reviewing Clients' Self-Monitoring and Providing Support via Text

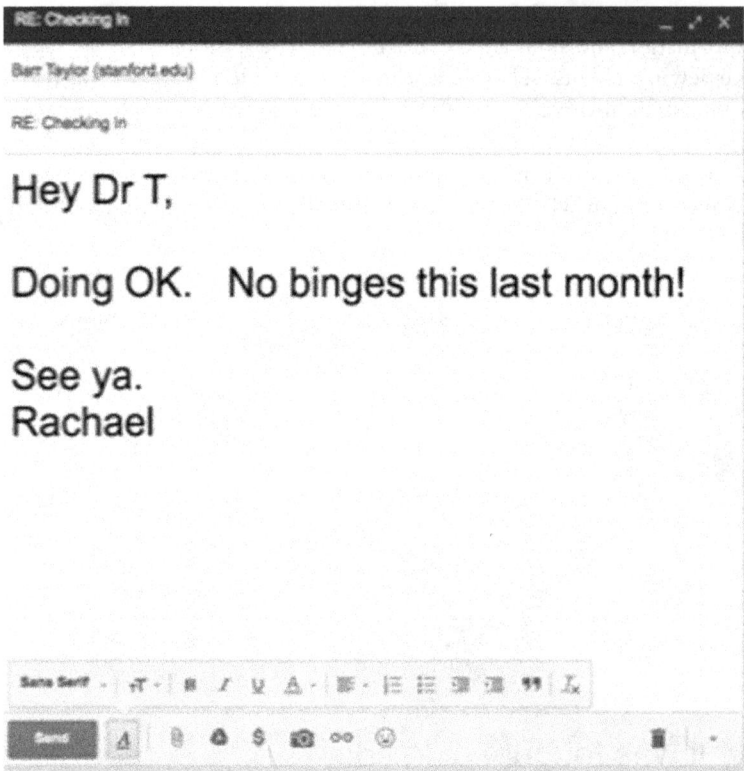

RE: Checking In

Barr Taylor (stanford.edu)

RE: Checking In

Hey Dr T,

Doing OK.   No binges this last month!

See ya.
Rachael

Figure 9.4 Texting to Augment the Treatment Effects

decisions. As always, we recommend relying on your clinical judgment and experience in addressing between-sessions communications.

Blended Therapy (Including Teletherapy)

"Blended treatment" approaches are emerging to combine the benefits of traditional and online psychological treatment concurrently, using teletherapy tools (Kleiboer et al., 2016). Blended treatments use elements of both face-to-face sessions and internet-based treatment components, combined in an integrated or sequential manner (Erbe, Eichert, Riper, & Ebert, 2017). Depending on the preferences and needs of the client, online components can be included either between therapist sessions, prior to sessions, or following standard face-to-face treatment as a form of supplementary post-intervention.

Most clinicians are already providing aspects of blended therapy through messaging and even phone calls. Blended formats may better suit the regular practice and skills of clinicians and help integrate technology in treatment in a way that meet clients and clinician needs and desires, as well as meeting the ethical and professional guidelines (Childress, 2000; Kemmeren et al., 2019). Blended therapy mirrors the gradual integration of technology seen in daily life and clinical practice (Eonta et al., 2011) and may thus facilitate acceptance. Blended therapy is in line with findings on the importance of guidance to provide clinical effect and maintain engagement in online interventions (Baumeister, Reichler, Munzinger, & Lin, 2014; Johansson & Andersson, 2012). It may also significantly reduce therapist sessions compared to standard treatment (e.g., Thase et al., 2018) while retaining qualities of increased availability by means of saved travel time. In addition, it may allow clients to process treatment at their own pace and can help ensure that standard treatment quality criteria are met and prevent therapist drift in treatment (e.g., Erbe et al., 2017; Urech, 2018).

Both guided and blended therapies often involve some teletherapy. We are aware of only two studies that have evaluated the use of teletherapy for EDs (Anderson, Byrne, Crosby, & Le Grange, 2017; Mitchell et al., 2008). In Mitchell et al. (2008), 128 individuals were randomized to 20 sessions of manual-based CBT for bulimia nervosa either delivered face-to-face or via telemedicine. Retention and abstinence rates were not significantly different between the two conditions. Anderson et al. (2017) tested the feasibility and preliminary effects of family-based treatment for adolescents with anorexia nervosa delivered via telehealth. Participants were retained for the course of treatment, and adolescents' weight and ED psychopathology significantly improved from baseline to end of treatment and six-month follow-up. Spoch and Anderson (2019) have provided an excellent overview of issues related to clinician-delivered teletherapy for EDs.

The following case describes the use of Recovery Record to provide blended therapy.

Case Example 2

Haley was a 23-year-old woman. After graduating from college, she began work as a flight attendant. She lived with her boyfriend, a medical student, in a small apartment in an urban area. Haley sought treatment due to her bulimia nervosa symptoms. She reported that her parents and siblings all had obesity and that she had struggled with eating and weight management issues growing up. Haley reported feeling highly influenced by negative messages from peers about her weight and obesity growing up, causing her to feel ashamed of her body, and eat in secret. But it was not until college that she started experiencing binge eating episodes followed by vomiting, three times a week. Haley attributed these symptoms to the stressful student life, living far from home, and availability of foods high in sugar and processed fat in her dorms. Although she had confided in a childhood friend about her situation, it was not until about six months after college that she decided to turn to a therapist. In the first session, Haley described that her work hindered her from maintaining a routine meal schedule, and that serving food for a living was also worsening her binge eating. She also disclosed feeling concerned about being stigmatized due to her eating behaviors. She maintained that all the women she knew shared similar body image concerns.

Haley's therapist provided psychoeducation about the connection between thin ideal internalization, negative mood intolerance, and EDs. When she presented the concept of regular eating, Haley first seemed reluctant to follow a schedule that she perceived as confining and inflexible. She was also worried that she would not have access to a notebook to record her eating and purging behaviors. The therapist introduced a mobile app (Recovery Record) to assist in treatment, and Haley was pleased with the idea that she could record her information on her phone and that the app would prompt her to eat her scheduled meals and snacks according to her meal plan. Haley downloaded the app during the session, and experimented with it in session. The therapist used this onboarding process as an opportunity to discuss and set realistic expectations about time, content, and place of planned meals and snacks. When the therapist mentioned that the app allowed Haley to connect with the therapist, Haley responded that she would like to start on her own and inform the therapist in the next session how that past week had gone. The following appointment, Haley reported that the past week went well. She had fewer binge eating episodes and no purging, but she was having a hard time identifying triggers to her binges. Haley pulled out her phone, opened the app, and showed the therapist her weekly graph. The two discussed the implication that in the past week, Haley marked that she was very hungry after most of her meals, i.e., "8" on a scale of 1–10. Haley disclosed that she had completely forgotten about feeling hungry after meals. Despite perceiving herself for many years as "someone with too big of an appetite," Haley was surprised to realize that her meals and snacks were not sufficient and satiating. Relieved to realize that the joint review was less intimidating and more helpful than she had initially assumed, Haley asked whether the therapist could connect with her on the app so that she could have her own printout of Haley's progress throughout the week. Before the next session, the therapist accessed the separate Recovery Record app for clinicians, and reviewed Haley's progress (see Figure 9.5 for screenshots of the client's self-monitoring on the app and the therapist's review of Haley's weekly self-monitoring. When Haley entered the clinic, her therapist was already aware of how Haley's urges to binge spread over the week, and the two spent the session discussing the successes and pitfalls of the past week. This process continued for a few weeks, and Haley made significant progress. After about a month, Haley informed her therapist that due to her work schedule, she would not be able to attend any sessions in the last two weeks of August. She inquired if the therapist could continue supporting her remotely, using the app. The therapist suggested that she would check

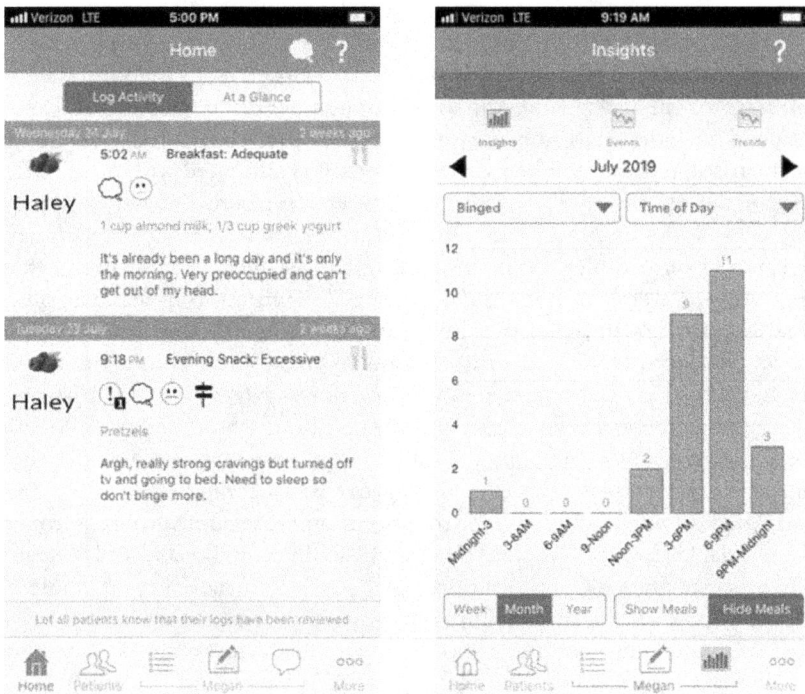

Figure 9.5 Haley's Weekly Self-Monitoring

in on Haley twice a week during this period and send her suggestions for coping skills via the app.

When their meetings resumed regularly, Haley thanked the therapist and said that knowing that the therapist was reviewing her logs made her more accountable. Both Haley and the therapist felt that using the app during this time strengthened their therapeutic alliance as well. The therapist also saw this event as an opportunity to bring up Haley's shame and guilt about her eating behaviors and to discuss the implications of her not seeking help from her support network. Haley agreed that this was an important issue and decided to confide in her boyfriend and share her struggles with him. Over the next few months, Haley continued making progress in treatment. She reduced her use of the app, however, in times of relapse, but she found that planning and recording her meals on the app helped her get quickly back on track.

Social Media and Online Groups

It is important to evaluate clients' social media use, particularly for clients with EDs, and to consider both how such use may be negatively affecting clients and how it might be used in a more positive fashion. To study the impact of interacting with Facebook for individuals with EDs, we recruited 415 individuals who had been in ED treatment in a group setting (Saffran et al., 2016). The respondents reported having 10–19 Facebook friends from treatment and spending up to 30 minutes per day interacting on Facebook with individuals from treatment or ED-related organizations. More comparison to treatment peers on Facebook was associated with greater ED psychopathology and ED-related impairment. Of note was that few participants (19.5%) reported that a therapist asked about the impact of clients' media use on pathology (Saffran et al., 2016). A meta-analysis found that exposure to websites promoting anorexia (known as "pro-ana" websites) was associated with high body image dissatisfaction, dieting, and negative affect (Rodgers, Lowy, Halperin, & Franko, 2016). Furthermore, the use of often digitally altered images online allows for negative body comparisons. It can be enlightening for clinicians to learn about who their clients follow on social media (e.g., Instagram, Twitter, blogs, Snapchat) and how they use social media in other ways (e.g., for negative social comparisons).

Clinicians might also consider the use of online support groups. Groups are available through Reddit, treatment facilities, and many other ways. However, online groups, at least unsupervised by clinicians, have the potential to expose clients to individuals supporting psychopathology, to potentially harmful practices and ideas, and potentially to being exploited by commercial entities. For example, our work has indicated the presence of such pro-ED groups on Reddit and that the majority of participants in these groups are supportive of ED behaviors (Sowles et al., 2018). Furthermore, we could find no studies that evaluated the effectiveness of online ED treatment groups, even potential risk/benefit for participants. For these reasons we do not refer clients to online support groups. Please refer Chapter 6 for more details on the use of social media in clinical practice.

Setting Up Your Office

In some settings, therapists may sit at desk with a computer positioned so that they can share the screen with the client. This setup makes the use of internet activities fairly straightforward. In settings where therapists prefer to face their clients directly, it is possible to use tablets to do such activities, such as writing notes, examining online client activities, completing standardized assessments, and sharing screens. Tablets are not more intrusive than the traditional notepad and paper. If you have not done so, take a minute to consider how you have or might set up your office for digital practice.

Training

One issue for clinicians who decide to provide guided self-help or blended therapy is how to be trained to do so. Most of the companies that provide services suitable for blended therapy (e.g., SilverCloud, Recovery Record) offer at least minimal training in its use and it is likely that training programs will become more available for interested clinicians. As part of the Center for m2Health at Palo Alto University, we offer training in digital technology and have developed Continuing Education courses provided by the American Psychological Association (see m2Health website).

Privacy/Ethics/Reimbursement

Internet therapies involve important and complicated issues related to privacy, local, state and national practice guidelines, and licensing and reimbursement. As these issues are covered elsewhere in the book, we will not go into them here in detail other than to reiterate that when they deploy digital tools in their work, clinicians should always rely on the practice guidelines of their professional organization, their clinical experience and knowledge in adapting interventions to clients, and their personal preferences.

Conclusion

Behavioral interventions are embedded in a practical framework. Clinicians are asked to move with the times and offer their clients empirically supported treatments that are also up to date, and that their clients would find useful, accessible, adapted to their lifestyle when possible, and engaging. Providers willing to explore digital tools and strategies would likely learn that technology augments their current services to individuals with EDs and facilitates additional support to their clients when they need it the most.

References

American Psychiatric Association. (2013). *Diagnostic and statistical manual of mental disorders* (5th ed.). APA: Washington, DC.
American Psychological Association. (2013). *Guidelines for the practice of telepsychology*. Retrieved from www.apa.org/practice/guidelines/telepsychology
Anderson, K. E., Byrne, C. E., Crosby, R. D., & Le Grange, D. (2017). Utilizing telehealth to deliver family-based treatment for adolescent anorexia nervosa. *International Journal of Eating Disorders, 50*(10), 1235–1238. doi:10.1002/eat.22759
Bauer, S., Okon, E., Meermann, R., & Kordy, H. (2012). Technology-enhanced maintenance of treatment gains in eating disorders: Efficacy of an intervention delivered via text messaging. *Journal of Consulting and Clinical Psychology, 80*(4), 700–706. doi:10.1037/a0028030
Baumeister, H., Reichler, L., Munzinger, M., & Lin, J. (2014). The impact of guidance on Internet-based mental health interventions—A systematic review. *Internet Interventions, 1*(4), 205–215. doi:10.1016/j.invent.2014.08.003
Childress, C. A. (2000). Ethical issues in providing online psychotherapeutic interventions. *Journal of Medical Internet Research, 2*(1), E5. doi:10.2196/jmir.2.1.e5

Eonta, A. M., Christon, L. M., Hourigan, S. E., Ravindran, N., Vrana, S. R., & Southam-Gerow, M. A. (2011). Using everyday technology to enhance evidence-based treatments. *Professional Psychology: Research and Practice, 42*(6), 513–520.

Erbe, D., Eichert, H. C., Riper, H., & Ebert, D. D. (2017). Blending face-to-face and Internet-based interventions for the treatment of mental disorders in adults: Systematic review. *Journal of Medical Internet Research, 15*(19(9)), e306. doi:10.2196/jmir.6588

Ferrer-Garcia, M., & Gutiérrez-Maldonado, J. (2012). The use of virtual reality in the study, assessment, and treatment of body image in eating disorders and non-clinical samples: A review of the literature. *Body Image, 9*(1), 1–11. doi:10.1016/j.bodyim.2011.10.001

Fitzsimmons-Craft, E. E., Balantekin, K. N., Graham, A. K., Smolar, L., Park, D., Mysko, C., . . . Wilfley, D. E. (2019). Results of disseminating an online screen for eating disorders across the US: Reach, respondent characteristics, and unmet treatment need. *International Journal of Eating Disorders, 52*(6), 721–729. doi:10.1002/eat.23043

Fitzsimmons-Craft, E. E., Taylor, C. B., Graham, A. K., Sadeh-Sharvit, S., Balantekin, K. N., Eichen, D. M., . . . Wilfley, E. E. Effects of a digital cognitive-behavior therapy guided self-help intervention for college women with eating disorders: A cluster randomized clinical trial, under review.

Galmiche, M., Dechelotte, P., Lambert, G., & Tavolacci, M. P. (2019). Prevalence of eating disorders over the 2000–2018 period: A systematic literature review. *American Journal of Clinical Nutrition, 109*(5), 1402–1413. doi:10.1093/ajcn/nqy342

Graham, A. K., Trockel, M., Weisman, H., Fitzsimmons-Craft, E. E., Balantekin, K. N., Wilfley, D. E., & Taylor, C. B. (2019). A screening tool for detecting eating disorder risk and diagnostic symptoms among college-age women. *Journal of American College Health, 67*(4), 357–366. doi:10.1080/07448481.2018.1483936

Honary, M., Bell, B. T., Cinch, S., Wild, S. E., & McNaney, R. (2019). Understanding the role of healthy eating and fitness mobile apps in the formation of maladaptive eating and exercise behaviors in young people. *Journal of Medical Internet Research Mhealth Uhealth, 18*(7(6)), e14239. doi:10.2196/14239

Jacobi, C., Völker, U., Trockel, M. T., & Taylor, C. B. (2012). Effects of an Internet-based intervention for subthreshold eating disorders: A randomized controlled trial. *Behaviour Research and Therapy, 50*(2), 93–99. doi:10.1016/j.brat.2011.09.013

Johansson, R., & Andersson, G. (2012). Internet-based psychological treatments for depression. *Expert Review of Neurotherapeutics, 12*(7), 861–869. doi:10.1586/ern.12.63

Juarascio, A. S., Shoaib, A., & Timko, C. A. (2010). Pro-eating disorder communities on social networking sites: A content analysis. *Eating Disorders, 18*(5), 393–407. doi:10.1080/10640266.2010.511918

Kass, A. E., Kolko, R. P., & Wilfley, D. E. (2013). Psychological treatments for eating disorders. *Current Opinions in Psychiatry, 26,* 549–555. doi:10.1097/YCO.0b013e328365a30e

Kazdin, A. E., Fitzsimmons-Craft, E. E., & Wilfley, D. E. (2017). Addressing critical gaps in the treatment of eating disorders. *International Journal of Eating Disorders, 50*(3), 170–189. doi:10.1002/eat.22670

Kemmeren, L. L., van Schaik, A., Smit, J. H., Ruwaard, J., Rocha, A., Henriques, M., . . . Riper, H. (2019). Unraveling the black box: Exploring usage patterns of a blended treatment for depression in a multicenter Study. *Journal of Medical Internet Research Mental Health, 6,* e12707. doi:10.2196/12707

Kim, J. P., Sadeh-Sharvit, S., Darcy, A. M., Neri, E., Vierhile, M., Robinson, A., . . . Lock, J. D. (2018). The utility and acceptability of a self-help smartphone application for eating disorder behaviors. *Journal of Technology in Behavioral Science, 3*(3), 161–164.

Kleiboer, A., Smit, J., Bosmans, J., Ruwaard, J., Andersson, G., Topooco, N., . . . Riper, H. (2016). European COMPARative effectiveness research on blended depression treatment versus treatment-as-usual (E-COMPARED): Study protocol for a randomized controlled, non-inferiority trial in eight European countries. *Trials, 17*(1), 387. doi:10.1186/s13063-016-1511-1

Mira, A., Soler, C., Alda, M., Baños, R., Castilla, D., Castro, A., . . . Botella, C. (2019). Exploring the relationship between the acceptability of an Internet-based intervention for depression in primary care and clinical outcomes: Secondary analysis of a randomized controlled trial. *Frontiers of Psychiatry, 10*, 325. doi:10.3389/fpsyt.2019.00325

Mitchell, J. E., Crosby, R. D., Wonderlich, S. A., Crow, S., Lancaster, K., Simonich, H., . . . Myers, T. C. (2008). A randomized trial comparing the efficacy of cognitive-behavioral therapy for bulimia nervosa delivered via telemedicine versus face-to-face. *Behaviour Research and Therapy, 46*(5), 581–592. doi:10.1016/j.brat.2008.02.004

Muñoz, R. F. (2016). The efficiency model of support and the creation of digital apothecaries. *Clinical Psychology: Science and Practice, 24*(1), 46–49.

Newhouse, N., Lupiáñez-Villanueva, F., Codagnone, C., & Atherton, H. (2015). Patient use of email for health care communication purposes across 14 European countries: An analysis of users according to demographic and health-related factors. *Journal of Medical Internet Research, 17*(3), e58. doi:10.2196/jmir.3700

Rodgers, R. F., Lowy, A. S., Halperin, D. M., & Franko, D. L. (2016). A meta-analysis examining the influence of pro-eating disorder websites on body image and eating pathology. *European Eating Disorders Review, 24*(1), 3–8. doi:10.1002/erv.2390

Rosen, L. D., Whaling, K., Carrier, L. M., Cheever, N. A., & Rokkum, J. (2013). The media and technology usage and attitudes scale: An empirical investigation. *Computers and Human Behavior, 29*, 2501–2511.

Rouleau, C. R., & von Ranson, K. M. (2011) Potential risks of pro-eating disorder websites. *Clinical Psychology Review, 31*(4), 525–531. doi:10.1016/j.cpr.2010.12.005

Sadeh-Sharvit, S. (2019). Use of technology in the assessment and treatment of eating disorders in youth. *Child & Adolescent Psychiatric Clinics of North America, 28*(4), 653–661. doi:10.1002/eat.23077

Sadeh-Sharvit, S., Kim, J. P., Darcy, A. M., Neri, E., Vierhile, M., Robinson, A., . . . Lock, J. D. (2018). Subgrouping the users of a specialized app for eating disorders. *Eating Disorders, 26*(4), 361–372. doi:10.1080/10640266.2018.1440043

Saekow, J., Jones, M., Gibbs, E., Jacobi, C., Fitzsimmons-Craft, E. E., Wilfley, D., & Taylor, C. B. (2015). StudentBodies-eating disorders: A randomized controlled trial of a coached online intervention for subclinical eating disorders. *Internet Interventions, 2*(4), 419–428.

Saffran, K., Fitzsimmons-Craft, E. E., Kass, A. E., Wilfley, D. E., Taylor, C. B., & Trockel, M. (2016). Facebook usage among those who have received treatment for an eating disorder in a group setting. *International Journal of Eating Disorders, 49*(8), 764–777. doi:10.1002/eat.22567

Sowles, S. J., McLeary, M., Optican, A., Cahn, E., Krauss, M. J., Fitzsimmons-Craft, E. E., . . . Cavazos-Rehg, P. A. (2018). A content analysis of an online pro-eating disorder community on Reddit. *Body Image, 24*, 137–144. doi:10.1016/j.bodyim.2018.01.001

Spoch, L. E., & Anderson, K. P. (2019). Clinician-delivered teletherapy for eating disorders. *Psychiatric Clinics of North American, 42*, 243–252. doi:10.1016/j.psc.2019.01.008

Sysko, R., Glasofer, D. R., Hildebrandt, T., Klimek, P., Mitchell, J. E., Berg, K. C., . . . Walsh, B. T. (2015). The Eating Disorder Assessment for DSM-5 (EDA-5): Development and validation of a structured interview for feeding and eating disorders. *International Journal of Eating Disorders, 48*(5), 452–463. doi:10.1002/eat.22388

Taylor, C. B., Graham, A. K., Flatt, R. E., & Fitzsimmons-Craft, E. E. (in press). Current state of scientific evidence on Internet-based interventions for the treatment of depression, anxiety, eating disorders, and substance abuse: An overview of systematic reviews and meta-analysis. *European Journal of Public Health*.

Thase, M. E., Wright, J. H., Eells, T. D., Barrett, M. S., Wisniewski, S. R., Balasubramani, G., . . . Brown, G. K. (2018). Improving the efficiency of psychotherapy for depression: Computer- assisted versus standard cbt. *American Journal of Psychiatry*, *175*(3), 242–250. doi:10.1176/appi.ajp.2017.17010089

Tregarthen, J. P., Lock, J., & Darcy, A. M. (2015). Development of a smartphone application for eating disorder self-monitoring. *International Journal of Eating Disorders*, *48*(7), 972–982. doi:10.1002/eat.22386

Urech, A. (2018). A patient post-hoc perspective on advantages and disadvantages of blended cognitive behavior therapy for depression: A qualitative content analysis. *Psychotherapy Research*, *31*, 1–13.

10 Mobile Technology for Tobacco Cessation

Ellen Herbst, Eric Kuhn, and Janice Tsoh

Case Example

Sam is a 26-year-old United States Marine Corps (USMC) veteran who served two combat tours in Afghanistan. Midway through his first tour, he started smoking cigarettes, increasing to a pack a day within several months. He also initiated smokeless tobacco ("dip") after a smokeless tobacco manufacturer hosted a "free giveaway" event on his forward-operating base in Afghanistan. Sam said that he smoked and dipped to relieve stress and boredom while on deployment. After returning home from his second deployment, he tried to quit tobacco use on his own using electronic cigarettes ("vapes"), but continued to smoke and chew tobacco ("dip"), with especially heavy use when reminded of traumatic experiences. Upon the advice of his Veteran Affairs (VA) physician, he downloaded *Stay Quit Coach* (https://mobile.va.gov/app/stay-quit-coach), the VA's mobile application for smoking cessation, from the Apple (iOS) App Store. He used the app in conjunction with nicotine replacement therapy (NRT) and supportive coaching from his therapist to quit smoking. Two months later, Sam was able to quit smoking, vaping, and dipping. Sam told his providers that the combination of NRT, coaching sessions, and the app all contributed to his success in quitting. He cited the app's mobile messaging (i.e., notifications), money-saved calculator, and evidence-based information about quitting to be the most beneficial features in helping him quit. Sam has since encouraged friends from his USMC unit to try to quit.

Overview

In this chapter we discuss recent trends in tobacco and nicotine use, both in the general population and in high-risk groups. This is followed by a brief review of current clinical practice guidelines for tobacco cessation interventions as well as currently available evidence-based treatments. Next, we review the evidence for and outline key features and categories of mobile technology interventions for tobacco cessation, including text messaging, apps, and interventions offered on social media and social messaging platforms such as Facebook and WhatsApp. During this review, we highlight apps designed to be used as self-management vs. those used as adjunctive treatments to complement existing evidence-based treatments. Examples of both freely available, public domain products and fee-for-service mobile interventions are discussed. We also highlight specific mobile technology interventions designed for high-priority populations and novel smartphone-compatible sensor technologies. Most, but not all, of the mobile interventions reviewed are based on resources available and studies conducted in the United States (U.S.). We conclude by discussing where future work is needed for continued progress in improving tobacco cessation efforts using mobile interventions.

Current Trends in Tobacco and Nicotine Use

Cigarette Use Declining, But Not in High-Risk Groups

Tobacco use remains the leading preventable cause of death worldwide. Cigarette smokers lose an estimated decade or more of life compared with nonsmokers. Fortunately, this risk can be reduced by 90% through cessation before age 40 and 40% through cessation before age 60 (Jha et al., 2013). Cessation as early in life as possible is critical, and substantial health benefits of quitting are observed at all ages. In the United States, cigarette use has been declining in the general public, in large part due to public health initiatives and increased treatment access.

Despite great strides in reducing tobacco-related diseases, tobacco-related health disparities persist in high-risk groups. Young adults; members of certain racial and ethnic groups (Martell, Garrett, & Caraballo, 2016); members of the lesbian, gay, bisexual, and transgender (LGBT) community (Fallin, Goodin, Lee, & Bennett, 2015); and those with lower socioeconomic status (Chen, Machiorlatti, Krebs, & Muscat, 2019) continue to disproportionately face health disparities related to tobacco use. Individuals with mental disorders such as post-traumatic stress disorder (PTSD), depression, substance use disorders (SUD), and serious mental illnesses (SMI), such as schizophrenia and bipolar disorder, have the highest smoking rates and more frequent relapse than those without these conditions (Prochaska, Das, & Young-Wolff, 2017). Women smoke at lower rates than men, but given the well-known risks of smoking during pregnancy and the cardiovascular risks associated with concurrent oral contraceptive and cigarette use, as well as the relatively high rate of tobacco use during pregnancy compared with other substances (Oh, Reingle Gonzalez, Salas-Wright, Vaughn, & DiNitto, 2017), women of reproductive age are another high-priority population.

U.S. military service members and veterans also smoke at higher rates than the civilian population (Little et al., 2016), likely due in part to occupational exposure during military service and deployment, permissive attitudes toward tobacco use in military culture, and high-stress experiences encountered in military service, particularly during combat deployments. Veterans with mental illness, including PTSD, and/or SUD have higher prevalence rates of tobacco use disorder and more frequent relapse than those without these conditions (Crum-Cianflone, Powell, LeardMann, Russell, & Boyko, 2016). Service members also use smokeless tobacco at higher rates than their civilian counterparts (Odani, Agaku, Graffunder, Tynan, & Armour, 2018).

Regional differences in tobacco have been observed in the United States and worldwide. Tobacco use is more common in Southern states and in rural areas, whereas states and municipalities with public health initiatives such as higher taxes and educational programs have observed a decline in smoking rates (Sharbaugh et al., 2018). With declining smoking rates in the United States, tobacco manufacturers have expanded markets to developing nations, where tobacco legislation is relatively permissive and smoking prevalence rates are rising (Savell et al., 2015).

Concerningly, individuals in high-risk groups are often least likely to receive access to evidence-based smoking cessation services. Epidemiological evidence indicates that in the United States, delivery of physician advice to quit smoking and receipt of prescription smoking cessation medications are lowest among men, younger adults, uninsured individuals, racial/ethnic minority groups, and those without smoking-associated medical comorbidities (Tibuakuu et al., 2019).

Electronic Nicotine Delivery Systems

Another trend in nicotine use is the recent emergence and proliferation of electronic cigarettes, or electronic nicotine delivery systems (ENDS; "e-cigarettes," "e-cigs," "vapes," "vape pens"). Some ENDS devices have refillable tanks and nicotine liquid, whereas "pod mod" products, such as JUUL (Altria, Inc.), are ENDS that use pre-filled pods of nicotine liquid rather than refillable tanks. Over the past decade, ENDS products have gained popularity among nicotine-naïve populations, adolescents, and young adults. Epidemiologic surveys have shown an alarmingly rapid escalation in ENDS in adolescents since 2013 (Gentzke et al., 2019) and an association between ENDS use and initiation of other tobacco products in teens (Berry et al., 2019), leading the Centers for Disease Control and Prevention (CDC) to declare an ENDS epidemic in adolescents (Walley, Wilson, Winickoff, & Groner, 2019). In 2019, the USPTF (United States Preventive Services Task Force) issued draft guidelines to prevent initiation of ENDS use in children and adolescents (United States Preventive Services Task Force, 2019).

Heated tobacco vape pens such as IQOS (Philip Morris, Inc.), which heat and vaporize tobacco rather than burn it, are new products that are available internationally and are expected to be available in the United States in the near future. In contrast to ENDS devices that vaporize nicotine liquid, heated tobacco devices such as IQOS contain tobacco.

ENDS use is associated with cardiovascular morbidity and mortality (Darville & Hahn, 2019) and is difficult to quit due to nicotine withdrawal (Walley et al., 2019). Recent data show that "dual users" of ENDS and combustible cigarettes may experience a higher level of pulmonary toxicity (Goniewicz et al., 2018) and may have more severe nicotine dependence and face greater challenges quitting than users of either product alone (Choi, Inoue-Choi, McNeel, & Freedman, 2019). ENDS use has been associated with seizures, and has been implicated in cases of acute lung injury and pulmonary-related deaths (Christiani, 2019). Limited long-term safety data is also of great concern (Huang et al., 2019). Despite these risks, it is generally believed that for established tobacco users, ENDS is less harmful than combustible cigarette use (Darville & Hahn, 2019). ENDS use may promote smoking cessation in adult chronic cigarette users who have tried and failed FDA-approved medications for cessation (Hajek et al., 2019), although this approach is controversial (Kulik, Lisha, & Glantz, 2018) and is not standard clinical care at this time.

ENDS manufacturers are facing increased regulation by local and state authorities as well as the Food and Drug Administration (FDA), given that added flavors appeal to younger users (i.e., dessert, candy, and fruit flavorings) and the products were initially sold to teens with minimal to no warning labels and marketed on social media platforms (Soneji, Knutzen, & Villanti, 2019). At the time of this writing, several states and municipalities implemented flavored ENDS bans, and the FDA announced plans to ban flavored ENDS products throughout the United States (Sharpless, 2019). In contrast, public health agencies in the United Kingdom and New Zealand emphasize the relatively lower risks associated with ENDS use as compared with conventional combustible cigarettes in adults, potential of ENDS as a cessation aid in treatment-refractory smokers, and need for further study. ENDS devices are not currently recommended by USPTF or CDC as aids for smoking cessation treatment for adults. It is predicted that as combustible cigarette use continues to decline in the general population, ENDS use may increase.

Cigars and Smokeless Tobacco

In the United States, the prevalence of cigar use was 4.8% of all adults and 7.9% of men in 2016, increasing in adolescents, and more common in co-users of other substances such as cannabis (Centers for Disease Control and Prevention, 2019b). Public health experts have raised concern that flavorings added to newer cigar products may appeal to young users.

Use of smokeless tobacco, including chewing tobacco and snuff or dip, declined in the U.S. general population from 1986 to 2000, but has been increasing since that time (Centers for Disease Control and Prevention, 2019a). High school students, young adult men, Non-Hispanic American Indians/Alaska Natives, and residents of rural states such as Wyoming and West Virginia are particularly at risk. Military service members and athletes use smokeless tobacco at higher rates than the general population. It is estimated that 3.9% of young adults are dual users of chewing tobacco and other tobacco products (Centers for Disease Control and Prevention, 2019a).

Evidence-Based Treatment for Tobacco Cessation: Current Models of Care

Access to evidence-based treatment for tobacco cessation substantially improves quit rates, both in the general population and in vulnerable, high-risk groups. Twelve-month smoking cessation rates without the use of evidence-based treatment approaches are dismal; 95–97% of those who quit without assistance relapse within the first year (Hughes, Keely, & Naud, 2004). The USPTF has established guidelines for interventions based on multiple high-quality randomized controlled trials (RCTs) for tobacco cessation treatment, including behavioral counseling, pharmacological aids (nicotine replacement therapy, Wellbutrin [Zyban], varenicline [Chantix]), or both (United States Preventive Services Task Force, 2015). Outcomes for tobacco cessation are superior when pharmacotherapy is combined with counseling. USPTF clinical practice guidelines include implementation of the Five A's when conducting counseling for tobacco cessation: (1) Ask about tobacco use, (2) Advise to quit through clear, personalized messages, (3) Assess willingness to quit, (4) Assist in quitting, and (5) Arrange follow-up and support (United States Preventive Services Task Force, 2015).

Current models of cognitive-behavioral treatment (CBT) enhance the odds of cessation (Hartmann-Boyce, Hong, Livingstone-Banks, Wheat, & Fanshawe, 2019) and primarily utilize face-to-face counseling or telephone quitline delivery methods. CBTs typically include setting of a quit date, highlighting the rewards and benefits of quitting, and recommending behavioral changes before, during, and after the quit date. In addition to CBT, other widely accepted evidence-based approaches for smoking cessation include acceptance and commitment therapy (ACT; Bricker et al., 2014) and contingency management (CM; Secades-Villa, García-Rodríguez, López-Núñez, Alonso-Pérez, & Fernández-Hermida, 2014). ACT is a psychological intervention that incorporates mindfulness and acceptance-based strategies to increase psychological flexibility and tolerance to a range of experiences. CM is a behavioral therapy which delivers positive reinforcement, often financial, in the setting of objective evidence of positive behavioral change.

Mobile Technology for Tobacco Cessation

Mobile technology offers a scalable, cost-effective, and convenient means of treatment delivery for tobacco cessation. Smartphone usage continues to increase in the United States, with 81% reporting smartphone ownership in 2019 (Pew Research Center, 2019). Several of the highest risk groups for tobacco use are also high utilizers of smartphone technology. For example, 96% of Americans aged 18–29 own a smartphone (Pew Research Center, 2019). One in five Americans relies on a smartphone as their sole computing device; this is more common among young adults, individuals with lower income, and people of color (Pew Research Center, 2019). Smartphone usage is more common in advanced economies than in emerging economies; however, smartphone utilization is expanding globally.

Given the high penetration of smartphone usage in the general population, particularly among youth and young adults, mobile technology may be a powerful approach to rapidly expanding access to evidence-based behavioral interventions for smoking cessation to those in need. Mobile technology affords several advantages. Mobile apps for smoking cessation are free or low-cost, can be accessed at any time the user has urges to smoke, and can be used to deliver evidence-based behavioral strategies outside of usual clinic or quitline hours.

Mobile health interventions for smoking cessation have shown great promise to date. A 2018 systematic review examining 108 studies and 110,372 participants found that smoking cessation interventions using mobile health platforms and individually tailored text messages resulted in significantly higher success in achieving smoking abstinence than usual care (Do et al., 2018). Despite the promise of mobile health in supporting cessation goals, app quality varies substantially. At the time of this writing in 2019, there are over 550 apps that claim to help with smoking cessation in the App Store and Google Play Store. However, recent content analyses of general apps for adults (Rajani, Weth, Mastellos, & Filippidis, 2019) and adolescents (Robinson et al., 2018) reveal that not all apps include evidence-based content for tobacco cessation as described by USPTF and other health agencies.

In the following sections we explore a range of currently available treatment modalities delivered through mobile technology, including (1) mobile messaging platforms, (2) smartphone apps, (3) novel sensor technologies, and (4) social media-delivered interventions. Due to the large volume of available apps, we emphasize that this is not a comprehensive review, as mobile interventions evolve rapidly.

Text Messaging and Push Notifications

Mobile messaging has demonstrated efficacy in improving smoking cessation outcomes, both incorporated in apps and as a stand-alone intervention. This intervention typically involves delivery of motivational text messages or notifications with reminders and encouragement pertaining to smoking cessation goals. A 2016 meta-analysis of 20 studies examining 22 text messaging interventions found that they were associated with improved quit rates and reductions in cigarette use (Scott-Sheldon et al., 2016). Similarly, a 2016

Cochrane review of 12 studies concluded that text messaging programs are associated with improved six-month smoking abstinence rates, including six studies with bioverification of abstinence (Whittaker, McRobbie, Bullen, Rodgers, & Gu, 2016), which is considered the gold-standard method of verification of cessation.

Although mobile messaging programs have demonstrated efficacy in improving smoking outcomes, it is not fully understood what message content might be most effective in assisting with quitting. Mobile messaging programs vary substantially in the degree of personalization and interactivity; the most basic programs offer simple push notification reminders to users, whereas others aim to deliver interactive chats with users (Luk et al., 2019). Researchers are actively investigating the content, nature, and timing of messages for different populations, and the extent to which external treatments such as medication and counseling mediate the treatment effect observed with text messaging programs (Hoeppner, Hoeppner, & Abroms, 2017). Evidence to date suggests that mobile messaging programs with tailored messages may be more effective than generic messages and that multiple daily messages may not be better than less frequent messaging (Do et al., 2018). Text messaging programs that allow the user to set time and frequency of messages and personalize content may enhance acceptability.

Several accessible, publicly available mobile messaging programs exist for those interested in quitting. The National Cancer Institute's (NCI) *SmokefreeTXT* (available at www.SmokeFree.gov) includes text messaging programs designed to send motivational messages, advice, and reminders about cessation goals, using messaging consistent with clinical practice guidelines. Smokefree.gov and *SmokefreeTXT* offers tailored text messaging and apps available to specific populations, including *SmokefreeVET* (a platform offered in partnership with the U.S. Department of Veteran Affairs); *SmokefreeWomen; SmokefreeTeen; SmokefreeEspanol;* and *Smokefree60+*. SmokefreeTXT also includes *DipFreeTXT*, which is intended to help users of chewing tobacco, snuff, and other smokeless tobacco products quit using them. The Truth Initiative, a U.S.-based nonprofit public health organization, offers *This is Quitting* (www.thetruth.com/articles/hot-topic/quit-vaping) and *BecomeAnEx* (www.becomeanex.org/), free text messaging programs for those aiming to quit e-cigarettes. Content is tailored to the age range of the user and is available to those as young as 13 as well as to adults of all ages.

In addition to the programs just described, callers to the national quitline number, 1–800-QUIT-NOW, may access *Text2Quit*, a national mobile messaging program offered free of charge in some states as adjunctive treatment to the quitline. In a RCT of 503 participants, use of *Text2Quit* was associated with a higher bioverified point prevalence quit rate than use of paper self-help materials (Abroms, Boal, Simmens, Mendel, & Windsor, 2014). Multiple RCTs are currently examining text messaging programs to promote smoking cessation in specific populations, including adolescents, women of reproductive age, and economically disadvantaged individuals

(Hoeppner et al., 2019; Kurti et al., 2019; Thomas, Bendtsen, Linderoth, & Müssener, 2018; Vidrine et al., 2019).

Mobile Applications (Apps)

Mobile apps for tobacco cessation are a widely available but relatively under-studied treatment vehicle. As noted previously, apps vary widely in content and focus. Some apps are designed to be used on their own as a smoking cessation aid, whereas others are intended to complement existing behavioral health treatments. Some apps are designed to target high-risk groups, such as individuals with mental illness or marginalized communities. A small number aim to assist with quitting smokeless tobacco (i.e., *DipQuit* on iOS App Store and Google Play Store and *Stop Smokeless Tobacco* available in the UK). Apps such as *Vapertrack* and *Vapemate*, available on iOS on App Store and Google Play Store, aim to assist quitting combustible cigarettes through the use of ENDS, a non-FDA approved harm reduction approach. The VA app *Stay Quit Coach 2.0* to be released in late 2019 allows for tracking reduction and cessation of ENDS, smokeless tobacco, and cigars in addition to combustible cigarettes.

Although a wide range of apps exist for smoking cessation, a relatively small number have been empirically studied. A 2017 review of eight studies examining heterogeneous mobile apps delivering a range of interventions, including ACT, CBT, and other behavioral change-based approaches, found that the following app features were most accepted and utilized by smokers: (1) audiovisual features followed by a quit plan; (2) tracking features (e.g. tracking progress with reducing and quitting), and (3) sharing features (e.g., sharing progress with friends or others trying to quit; Regmi, Kassim, Ahmad, & Tuah, 2017). However, use of these features were not consistently positively associated with smoking cessation. Authors also noted bias in the majority of studies reviewed and highlighted a need for RCT with mobile apps to elucidate which app features, if any, are positively associated with cessation.

A 2019 review examined 33 freely available mobile apps that have undergone peer-reviewed research (Vilardaga, Casellas-Pujol, McClernon, & Garrison, 2019). The review identified commonly implemented features used across a range of apps, including (1) psychoeducation about tobacco use and treatment, (2) self-tracking features to monitor smoking behaviors during quitting, (3) personalized feedback based on user characteristics and data, (4) social support via social media or networking, (5) rewards or badges for achieving behavioral milestones, (6) digital distractions, including video game tasks, to cope with smoking urges, (7) geolocation to track user location and ecological momentary assessment to anticipate cue-based cravings, (8) skills acquisition apps that prompt the user to acquire skills to promote cessation, (9) sensor features that provide immediate biofeedback, such as CO levels or hand gestures, to the user to deter smoking, and (10) machine learning to tailor or deliver app content. Reviewers observed that the majority of apps used three or more basic features, most commonly psychoeducation (76%) and self-tracking (70%). Personalized feedback (42%), social support (36%) and reward systems (36%) were used less often. Geolocation (9%), sensors (6%), and machine learning features (3%) were used the least.

A 2019 review evaluated the 67 freely available, most highly-rated smoking cessation apps from the App Store and Google Play Store. The study utilized the Mobile App Rating System (MARS), a validated self-report measure that rates mobile apps on key aspects of app quality on a 5-point scale (1-Inadequate, 2-Poor, 3-Acceptable, 4-Good, 5-Excellent) and established a coding system to determine how well these apps adhered to the USPTF's Five A's (Ask, Advise, Assess, Assist, Arrange Follow-Up; Lee et al., 2019). Inter-rater reliability was established with two independent coders who reviewed and scored app content and quality. The mean MARS score was 16.2 of a possible 20.0: apps scored highest on Functionality (4.4/5.0), Aesthetics (4.0/5.0), and Engagement (3.3/5.0), and relatively lower on Information (2.6/5.0). Reviewed apps were only inconsistently adherent to the Five A's: Ask (n = 44), Advise (n = 54), Assess (n = 30), Assist (n = 62), and Arrange Follow-Up (n = 0).

Freely Available Apps in the Public Domain

As mentioned previously, there are well over 550 apps available in the two major app marketplaces claiming to support smoking cessation. Given this volume, it is beyond the scope here to review all of these apps. Instead, we advise potential users and clinicians who are searching for quality, effective apps to consider the reputation of the developer of an app, among other things (see the APA App Evaluation Model; www.psychiatry.org/psychiatrists/practice/mental-health-apps). For example, in addition to text messaging programs, NCI's Smokefree.gov offers free mobile apps for iOS and Android devices, including *QuitGuide* and *quitSTART*. *QuitGuide* helps users gain insight into their smoking patterns by tracking cravings, mood, and smoking triggers. The *quitSTART* app is intended to help smokers prepare to quit by offering tailored tips, inspiration, and challenges (e.g., to resist a craving to smoke). In both apps, users can track cravings by time of day and location and can get motivational messages and tips at these times and places (using geolocation) in the future. They also allow for sharing of progress on social media sites.

Lee and colleagues' (Lee et al., 2019) recent review of smoking cessation apps provides an excellent resource that can serve as a point of departure in the search for top-rated, available, free apps that are most adherent to the USPTF's Five A's. None of the apps reviewed included all five, but 25 included four of the five, including the NCI's apps reviewed earlier. The *Smoke Free* app (available at the iOS App Store and Google

Play Store) was also among these, and as reviewed later, is one of only a handful of apps (available or not) that has evidence demonstrating its efficacy in a large-scale RCT.

Apps for Specific Populations

A range of apps for high-priority populations exist that are currently under development and investigation, and only a small minority of apps have undergone RCTs to examine efficacy, though results to date suggest mobile technology may support quitting in disadvantaged groups (Boland et al., 2018). Examples of apps for specific groups include the Canadian app *Crush the Crave* (available for Android and iOS platforms) and *REQ-Mobile* (available on Windows platforms) for young adults; *Stay Quit Coach* for military veterans, including veterans with PTSD, that incorporates NCI *Smoke-freeTXT* messages as local notifications (Herbst et al., 2018, 2019; Hicks et al., 2017); *See Me Smoke Free*, a research app for women available on Google Play Store; *SmokeFree Baby* (iOS and Android) for pregnant women; *Kick.it* (research build; Lawn et al., 2018) and *Learn to Quit* (research build; Vilardaga et al., 2018) for individuals with serious mental illness; *Smokerface* (iOS App Store and Google Play Store) for adolescents and young adults and *Smokerface-HIV* for HIV positive individuals; *QuitIT* for smokers diagnosed with cancer (Krebs et al., 2019); *Smart-Treatment (Smart-T;* Businelle et al., 2016) for individuals of low socioeconomic status.

Many currently available apps apply evidenced approaches such as CBT, ACT, and CM. Many apps were designed to be used independent of any other treatment, whereas some apps *(Smart-T, QUIT4EVER, Stay Quit Coach, Pivot)* are designed to complement behavioral counseling. *Quit Genius* is a fee-for-service app that provides CBT for smoking cessation coupled with in-app coaching and is marketed to consumers and employers.

Apps for Use in Primary Care Setting

Given that 70% of smokers have a clinical encounter with a health care provider yearly (Kruger, O'Halloran, Rosenthal, Babb, & Fiore, 2016), mobile interventions have been developed and tested within primary care or other health care settings. These mobile apps aim to engage both smoking patients and their health care providers at point-of-care to facilitate patients' receipts of the Five A's as recommended by the USPTF to promote smoking cessation. Examples included a computer-facilitated Five A program (*CF5A's*), delivered on a mobile tablet given to patients in the waiting room right before seeing their providers. *CF5A's* assess patients' smoking status and intention for quitting and generates a tailored handout for patients with a clinical guide for providers on giving advice and smoking cessation medication dosing (Satterfield et al., 2018). It delivers intervention in English and Spanish (Satterfield et al., 2018). An RCT of *CF5A's* with 961 patients at two primary care clinics and one HIV clinic across 221 providers showed that intervention patients reported higher receipt of Ask, Advise, Assess, and Assist (70% to 84%) compared to the usual care patients (57% to 77%; Satterfield et al., 2018). The *Interactive Mobile Doctor (iMD)*, which delivers interactive and tailored video messages on an Android mobile tablet, aims to enhance patients' motivation for quitting and encourages them to discuss tobacco use at the clinical encounter. The *iMD* also generates a handout summary printout for both the patient and the provider to enhance their discussions on the patient's readiness to quit, concerns about quitting, and a list of recommendations such as quitline referrals and medication options (Tsoh et al., 2018). The *iMD* has the capacity for delivery in English and multiple Asian languages (Tsoh et al., 2018).

In addition, other mobile apps have been developed to enhance adherence to smoking cessation medications, which appear to mostly target varenicline adherence. Examples include the *My Mobile Advice Program (MyMAP)* that provides self-report monitoring of varenicline use along with timed and tailored advice and messaging with a cessation counselor or a health care provider following a clinical encounter with a prescription of varenicline (J. B. McClure, Anderson, Bradley, An, & Catz, 2016). The *RxCoach*, an iPhone app, includes barcoding scanning to input medication regimen, provides medication-taking reminders and tracking, tailored adherence feedback and a "one-touch" feature to call patients' prescribing physician and pharmacy for side effects management (Gordon et al., 2017).

Incorporating Sensor and Geotracker Technologies

"Just-in-time" interventions aim to provide support to users through mobile messaging or novel, sophisticated interventions such as geolocation trackers or carbon monoxide (CO) sensors to deter smoking at the time cravings arise. Geotracker apps such as *Q Sense, MapMySmoke*, and others (McQuoid, Thrul, & Ling, 2018) aim to use ecological momentary assessment data input by smokers in their everyday naturalistic environment, paired with geographical tracking data, to identify contextual triggers to smoke. Wearable sensor devices with compatible mobile apps have recently been developed and tested for objective monitoring of cigarette smoking based on tracking of hand gestures, breathing, or cigarette lighting events (V. Senyurek, M. Imtiaz, P. Belsare, S. Tiffany, & E. Sazonov, 2019; V. Y. Senyurek, M. H. Imtiaz, P. Belsare, S. Tiffany, & E. Sazonov, 2019). *Pivot* (Carrot, Inc.) incorporates a mobile app with live text messaging by smoking cessation counselors and a CO sensor to track changes in breath CO levels. *Pivot* is adherent with USPTF guidelines and was designed to be offered through medical insurance in employer-based programs. Recent pilot data indicate that the *Pivot* program is engaging and feasible (Marler et al., 2019). Personal use, smartphone-compatible CO monitors are also now available for purchase and provide smokers with objective feedback (breath CO) during quit attempts, which may be combined with mobile messages or other mobile interventions (Krishnan, Elf, Chon, & Golub, 2018; E. A. McClure, Tomko, Carpenter, Treiber, & Gray, 2018).

Social Media and Social Messaging Interventions

Leading social media and social messaging mobile-enabled platforms such as Facebook and WhatsApp have been used to promote readiness to quit, assist with cessation, and provide relapse prevention. Interventions include chat rooms to provide support to those trying to quit or not relapse as well as preprogrammed text messages delivered through social media sites. Results of clinical trials using these interventions have been mixed. An RCT of 500 young adults comparing a Facebook-delivered, tailored tobacco cessation messaging and Facebook-delivered cognitive-behavioral therapy intervention with active control (referral to the NCI website) found higher engagement and improved bioverified cessation rates in the experimental condition at three months, but not at six, nine, or 12 months, compared with the control (Ramo et al., 2018). A relapse prevention intervention delivered via WhatsApp and Facebook social groups to 467 quitters found that engagement was higher, with more frequent sharing of encouragement and information, in the WhatsApp groups than in the Facebook groups (Cheung, Chan, Wang, Li, & Lam, 2017). Lastly, in an RCT of 132 patients entering care in a smoking cessation clinic, receipt of WhatsApp text messages for three months improved six-month cessation rates relative to no messages (Durmaz et al., 2019). Clinical trials are ongoing to elucidate best practices for smoking cessation treatment delivery within social media platforms.

Mobile Apps for Smoking Cessation: Review of Evidence Base

A 2017 systematic review used the Preferred Reporting Items for Systematic Reviews and Meta-Analyses guidelines to review 158 studies related to mobile technology and smoking cessation (Haskins, Lesperance, Gibbons, & Boudreaux, 2017). The purpose of the review was to identify smoking cessation mobile apps that were both (1) highly rated on the iOS App Store and Google Play Store, and (2) had at least one scientific study supporting their use. The review identified six highly rated apps with at least one scientific study demonstrating feasibility, acceptability, and/or potential benefit. Apps varied widely in theoretical basis and approach. They included *SmartQuit 2.0*, a fee-for-service app available for iOS and Android that delivers ACT; *mCM*, an app that can be used in treatment programs in the context of CM; *DistractMe*, an Android app that allows quitters to access and share distractions and tips to cope with cigarette cravings; *SmokeFree28*, a UK-based iOS app which delivers behavior change techniques to resist cravings and adhere to goals; *Craving to Quit* for iOS and Android, which uses a mindfulness approach; and *REQ-Mobile* for Windows, which delivers CBT. Reviewers also found that among the 50 highest rated apps recommended in leading app stores, only two (4%) had any scientific support.

To our knowledge, only four mobile apps have undergone large-scale RCTs to examine efficacy as a stand-alone intervention to improve smoking cessation rates. Of these, two reported higher self-reported three- or six-month cessation rates with app use (BinDhim, McGeechan, & Trevena, 2018; Crane, Ubhi, Brown, & West, 2018) and two reported no discernable effect of app use compared with controls (Baskerville et al., 2018; Garrison et al., 2018). In the *Smartphone Smoking Cessation* application (*SSC* app) trial, 684 daily smokers aged 18 and older were randomized to receive either a control (informational) app or the *SSC* app, a decision-aid app that allowed smokers to choose a quit method through a structured process of weighing the available options and their pros and cons, using a decision-aid design based on the Ottawa Decision Support Framework, an approach that applies behavioral and psychological theory to facilitate decision making (BinDhim et al., 2018). The *SSC* App also includes (1) information about quitting options, with their benefits and harms, (2) daily motivational messages using push notifications, (3) a quitting diary, and (4) a quitting benefits tracker. Use of *SSC* resulted in higher self-reported continuous abstinence from smoking at one, three and six months compared with the information-only app.

A large RCT examined *Smoke Free*, an app available on iOS and Android that delivers evidence-based behavioral techniques as daily "missions" designed to prevent and manage cravings, vs. a basic (control) version of the app that provided information but lacked the behavioral missions (Crane et al., 2018). A sample of 28,112 smokers aged 18+ years who set a quit date were randomly assigned to receive the full *Smoke Free* app or the control app. Missions were delivered as push notifications and were associated with positive reinforcement, such as badges, updates about health benefits of cessation, and positive messages for days smoke-free. Use of the full version of the app resulted in a higher self-reported continuous three-month abstinence rate than use of the control app. Notably, there was significant attrition at follow-up, with fewer than 10% of participants in each group completing self-report measures at three-month follow-up.

Other large RCTs, including one of the *Craving To Quit* mindfulness app in 325 adult smokers (Garrison et al., 2018) and another of *Crush the Crave* app in 1599 young adult smokers (Baskerville et al., 2018), did not demonstrate a benefit of app use in smoking cessation outcomes compared with control interventions. The *Craving To Quit* trial had relatively fewer participants than the other studies, which may have limited its power, and it used bioverified cessation as the primary outcome (Garrison et al., 2018), a more rigorous metric than the self-report data used in other studies. Taken together, data from large-scale RCTs to date suggest that interactive mobile app features that promote behavioral change and assist with decision making may complement mobile messaging to facilitate quitting. It should be noted that small pilot feasibility studies with mobile apps are underpowered to detect a change in smoking cessation rates and that larger adequately powered studies are needed to examine efficacy.

Conclusions

Mobile technology holds great promise as a convenient, scalable, and accessible means of treatment delivery for smoking cessation. Despite this promise, currently available apps range widely in quality and adherence to treatment guidelines. Mobile messaging and push notification programs for smoking cessation are free or low-cost, can be tailored to the target population, and have demonstrated efficacy in improving smoking cessation rates. Future studies are needed to characterize which mobile app features other than mobile messages/push notifications are associated with improved cessation outcomes. Ensuring that mobile app products are adherent with current clinical practice guidelines is also essential.

Replication of findings and bioverification of self-reported cessation outcomes are needed in future trials. In addition, future research may clarify how cessation apps might be used either alone or incorporated into existing evidence-based behavioral and pharmacological treatments. Despite the high prevalence of dual use of nicotine and tobacco products, only a small minority of apps target cessation of multiple nicotine and tobacco products. Future apps may target cessation of ENDS, cigars, and smokeless tobacco products in addition to cigarettes. Sophisticated features such as geolocation, sensor technology, ecological momentary assessment, and machine learning are also promising and understudied areas worthy of future investigation. Finally, the unique needs of vulnerable populations facing health disparities related to tobacco and nicotine use should always be considered when designing, testing, and implementing mobile app interventions.

Note

The views expressed in this chapter do not represent those of the U.S. Government or the Department of Veterans Affairs.

References

Abroms, L. C., Boal, A. L., Simmens, S. J., Mendel, J. A., & Windsor, R. A. (2014). A randomized trial of Text2Quit: A text messaging program for smoking cessation. *American Journal of Preventive Medicine, 47*(3), 242–250. doi:10.1016/j.amepre.2014.04.010

Baskerville, N. B., Struik, L. L., Guindon, G. E., Norman, C. D., Whittaker, R., Burns, C., . . . Brown, K. S. (2018). Effect of a mobile phone intervention on quitting smoking in a young adult population of smokers: Randomized controlled trial. *JMIR Mhealth Uhealth, 6*(10), e10893. doi:10.2196/10893

Berry, K. M., Fetterman, J. L., Benjamin, E. J., Bhatnagar, A., Barrington-Trimis, J. L., Leventhal, A. M., & Stokes, A. (2019). Association of electronic cigarette use with subsequent initiation of tobacco cigarettes in US youths. *JAMA Network Open, 2*(2), e187794. doi:10.1001/jamanetworkopen.2018.7794

BinDhim, N. F., McGeechan, K., & Trevena, L. (2018). Smartphone smoking cessation application (SSC App) trial: A multicountry double-blind automated randomised controlled trial of a smoking cessation decision-aid 'app'. *BMJ Open, 8*(1), e017105. doi:10.1136/bmjopen-2017-017105

Boland, V. C., Stockings, E. A., Mattick, R. P., McRobbie, H., Brown, J., & Courtney, R. J. (2018). The methodological quality and effectiveness of technology-based smoking cessation interventions for disadvantaged groups: A systematic review and meta-analysis. *Nicotine & Tobacco Research, 20*(3), 276–285. doi:10.1093/ntr/ntw391

Bricker, J. B., Mull, K. E., Kientz, J. A., Vilardaga, R., Mercer, L. D., Akioka, K. J., & Heffner, J. L. (2014). Randomized, controlled pilot trial of a smartphone app for smoking cessation using acceptance and commitment therapy. *Drug and Alcohol Dependence, 143*, 87–94. doi:10.1016/j.drugalcdep.2014.07.006

Businelle, M. S., Ma, P., Kendzor, D. E., Frank, S. G., Vidrine, D. J., & Wetter, D. W. (2016). An ecological momentary intervention for smoking cessation: Evaluation of feasibility and effectiveness. *Journal of Medical Internet Research, 18*(12), e321. doi:10.2196/jmir.6058

Centers for Disease Control and Prevention. (2019a). Smokeless tobacco: Health effects. Retrieved from www.cdc.gov/tobacco/data_statistics/fact_sheets/smokeless/health_effects/index.htm.

Centers for Disease Control and Prevention. (2019b). Cigars. Retrieved from www.cdc.gov/tobacco/data_statistics/fact_sheets/tobacco_industry/cigars/index.htm.

Chen, A., Machiorlatti, M., Krebs, N. M., & Muscat, J. E. (2019). Socioeconomic differences in nicotine exposure and dependence in adult daily smokers. *BMC Public Health, 19*(1), 375. doi:10.1186/s12889-019-6694-4

Cheung, Y. T. D., Chan, C. H. H., Wang, M. P., Li, H. C. W., & Lam, T. H. (2017). Online social support for the prevention of smoking relapse: A content analysis of the whatsapp and facebook social groups. *Telemedicine Journal and E Health, 23*(6), 507–516. doi:10.1089/tmj.2016.0176

Choi, K., Inoue-Choi, M., McNeel, T. S., & Freedman, N. D. (2019). Mortality risks of dual- and poly-tobacco product users in the United States. *American Journal of Epidemiology*. doi:10.1093/aje/kwz143

Christiani, D. C. (2019). Vaping-induced lung injury. *New England Journal of Medicine*. doi:10.1056/NEJMe1912032

Crane, D., Ubhi, H. K., Brown, J., & West, R. (2018). Relative effectiveness of a full versus reduced version of the 'Smoke Free' mobile application for smoking cessation: An exploratory randomised controlled trial. *F1000 Research, 7*, 1524. doi:10.12688/f1000research.16148.2

Crum-Cianflone, N. F., Powell, T. M., LeardMann, C. A., Russell, D. W., & Boyko, E. J. (2016). Mental health and comorbidities in U.S. military members. *Military Medicine, 181*(6), 537–545. doi:10.7205/MILMED-D-15-00187

Darville, A., & Hahn, E. J. (2019). E-cigarettes and atherosclerotic cardiovascular disease: What clinicians and researchers need to know. *Current Atherosclerosis Reports, 21*(5), 15. doi:10.1007/s11883-019-0777-7

Do, H. P., Tran, B. X., Le Pham, Q., Nguyen, L. H., Tran, T. T., Latkin, C. A., . . . Baker, P. R. (2018). Which eHealth interventions are most effective for smoking cessation?

A systematic review. *Patient Preference and Adherence, 12,* 2065–2084. doi:10.2147/PPA.S169397

Durmaz, S., Ergin, I., Durusoy, R., Hassoy, H., Caliskan, A., & Okyay, P. (2019). WhatsApp embedded in routine service delivery for smoking cessation: Effects on abstinence rates in a randomized controlled study. *BMC Public Health, 19*(1), 387. doi:10.1186/s12889-019-6727-z

Fallin, A., Goodin, A., Lee, Y. O., & Bennett, K. (2015). Smoking characteristics among lesbian, gay, and bisexual adults. *Preventive Medicine, 74,* 123–130. doi:10.1016/j.ypmed.2014.11.026

Garrison, K. A., Pal, P., O'Malley, S. S., Pittman, B. P., Gueorguieva, R., Rojiani, R., . . . Brewer, J. A. (2018). Craving to quit: A randomized controlled trial of smartphone app-based mindfulness training for smoking cessation. *Nicotine & Tobacco Research.* doi:10.1093/ntr/nty126

Gentzke, A. S., Creamer, M., Cullen, K. A., Ambrose, B. K., Willis, G., Jamal, A., & King, B. A. (2019). Vital signs: Tobacco product use among middle and high school students—United States, 2011–2018. *MMWR Morbidity Mortality Weekly Report, 68*(6), 157–164. doi:10.15585/mmwr.mm6806e1

Goniewicz, M. L., Smith, D. M., Edwards, K. C., Blount, B. C., Caldwell, K. L., Feng, J., . . . Hyland, A. J. (2018). Comparison of nicotine and toxicant exposure in users of electronic cigarettes and combustible cigarettes. *JAMA Network Open, 1*(8), e185937. doi:10.1001/jamanetworkopen.2018.5937

Gordon, J. S., Armin, J. S., Cunningham, J. K., Muramoto, M. L., Christiansen, S. M., & Jacobs, T. A. (2017). Lessons learned in the development and evaluation of RxCoach, an mHealth app to increase tobacco cessation medication adherence. *Patient Education and Counseling, 100*(4), 720–727. doi:10.1016/j.pec.2016.11.003

Hajek, P., Phillips-Waller, A., Przulj, D., Pesola, F., Myers Smith, K., Bisal, N., . . . McRobbie, H. J. (2019). A randomized trial of E-Cigarettes versus nicotine-replacement therapy. *New England Journal of Medicine, 380*(7), 629–637. doi:10.1056/NEJMoa1808779

Hartmann-Boyce, J., Hong, B., Livingstone-Banks, J., Wheat, H., & Fanshawe, T. R. (2019). Additional behavioural support as an adjunct to pharmacotherapy for smoking cessation. *Cochrane Database of Systematic Reviews, 6,* CD009670. doi:10.1002/14651858.CD009670.pub4

Haskins, B. L., Lesperance, D., Gibbons, P., & Boudreaux, E. D. (2017). A systematic review of smartphone applications for smoking cessation. *Translational Behavioral Medicine.* doi:10.1007/s13142-017-0492-2

Herbst, E., McCaslin, S. E., Daryani, S. H., Laird, K. T., Hopkins, L. B., Pennington, D., & Kuhn, E. (2019). A qualitative examination of stay quit coach, a mobile application for veteran smokers with posttraumatic stress disorder. *Nicotine & Tobacco Research.* doi:10.1093/ntr/ntz037

Herbst, E., Pennington, D., Kuhn, E., McCaslin, S. E., Delucchi, K., Batki, S. L., . . . Carmody, T. (2018). Mobile technology for treatment augmentation in veteran smokers with posttraumatic stress disorder. *American Journal of Preventive Medicine, 54*(1), 124–128. doi:10.1016/j.amepre.2017.08.016

Hicks, T. A., Thomas, S. P., Wilson, S. M., Calhoun, P. S., Kuhn, E. R., & Beckham, J. C. (2017). A preliminary investigation of a relapse prevention mobile application to maintain smoking abstinence among individuals with posttraumatic stress disorder. *Journal of Dual Diagnosis, 13*(1), 15–20. doi:10.1080/15504263.2016.1267828

Hoeppner, B. B., Hoeppner, S. S., & Abroms, L. C. (2017). How do text-messaging smoking cessation interventions confer benefit? A multiple mediation analysis of Text2Quit. *Addiction, 112*(4), 673–682. doi:10.1111/add.13685

Hoeppner, B. B., Hoeppner, S. S., Schick, M. R., Milligan, C. M., Helmuth, E., Bergman, B. G., . . . Kelly, J. F. (2019). Using the text-messaging program SmokefreeTXT to support smoking cessation for nondaily smokers. *Substance Use and Misuse*, 1–12. doi:10.1080/10826084.2018.1552300

Huang, J., Feng, B., Weaver, S. R., Pechacek, T. F., Slovic, P., & Eriksen, M. P. (2019). Changing perceptions of harm of e-Cigarette vs cigarette use among adults in 2 US national surveys from 2012 to 2017. *JAMA Network Open, 2*(3), e191047. doi:10.1001/jamanetworkopen.2019.1047

Hughes, J. R., Keely, J., & Naud, S. (2004). Shape of the relapse curve and long-term abstinence among untreated smokers. *Addiction, 99*(1), 29–38.

Jha, P., Ramasundarahettige, C., Landsman, V., Rostron, B., Thun, M., Anderson, R. N., . . . Peto, R. (2013). 21st-century hazards of smoking and benefits of cessation in the United States. *New England Journal of Medicine, 368*(4), 341–350. doi:10.1056/NEJMsa1211128

Krebs, P., Burkhalter, J., Fiske, J., Snow, H., Schofield, E., Iocolano, M., . . . Ostroff, J. S. (2019). The QuitIT coping skills game for promoting tobacco cessation among smokers diagnosed with cancer: Pilot randomized controlled trial. *JMIR Mhealth Uhealth, 7*(1), e10071. doi:10.2196/10071

Krishnan, N., Elf, J. L., Chon, S., & Golub, J. E. (2018). COach2Quit: A pilot randomized controlled trial of a personal carbon monoxide monitor for smoking cessation. *Nicotine & Tobacco Research*. doi:10.1093/ntr/nty182

Kruger, J., O'Halloran, A., Rosenthal, A. C., Babb, S. D., & Fiore, M. C. (2016). Receipt of evidence-based brief cessation interventions by health professionals and use of cessation assisted treatments among current adult cigarette-only smokers: National adult tobacco survey, 2009–2010. *BMC Public Health, 16*, 141. doi:10.1186/s12889-016-2798-2

Kulik, M. C., Lisha, N. E., & Glantz, S. A. (2018). E-cigarettes associated with depressed smoking cessation: A cross-sectional study of 28 European union countries. *American Journal of Preventive Medicine, 54*(4), 603–609. doi:10.1016/j.amepre.2017.12.017

Kurti, A. N., Bunn, J. Y., Nighbor, T., Cohen, A. H., Bolívar, H., Tang, K. J., . . . Higgins, S. T. (2019). Leveraging technology to address the problem of cigarette smoking among women of reproductive age. *Preventive Medicine, 118*, 238–242. doi:10.1016/j.ypmed.2018.11.004

Lawn, S., Van Agteren, J., Zabeen, S., Bertossa, S., Barton, C., & Stewart, J. (2018). Adapting, pilot testing and evaluating the kick.it app to support smoking cessation for smokers with severe mental illness: A study protocol. *International Journal of Environmental Research and Public Health, 15*(2). doi:10.3390/ijerph15020254

Lee, J., Dallery, J., Laracuente, A., Ibe, I., Joseph, S., Huo, J., & Salloum, R. (2019). A content analysis of free smoking cessation mobile applications in the USA. *Journal of Smoking Cessation, 14*(4), 195–202. doi: 10.1017/jsc.2019.6

Little, M. A., Bursac, Z., Derefinko, K. J., Ebbert, J. O., Talcott, G. W., Hryshko-Mullen, A., & Klesges, R. C. (2016). Types of dual and poly-tobacco users in the US military. *American Journal of Epidemiology, 184*(3), 211–218. doi:10.1093/aje/kwv321

Luk, T. T., Li, W. H. C., Cheung, D. Y. T., Wong, S. W., Kwong, A. C. S., Lai, V. W. Y., . . . Wang, M. P. (2019). Chat-based instant messaging support combined with brief smoking cessation interventions for Chinese community smokers in Hong

Kong: Rationale and study protocol for a pragmatic, cluster-randomized controlled trial. *Contemporary Clinical Trials*, 77, 70–75. doi:10.1016/j.cct.2018.12.013

Marler, J. D., Fujii, C. A., Utley, D. S., Tesfamariam, L. J., Galanko, J. A., & Patrick, H. (2019). Initial assessment of a comprehensive digital smoking cessation program that incorporates a mobile app, breath sensor, and coaching: Cohort study. *JMIR Mhealth Uhealth*, 7(2), e12609. doi:10.2196/12609

Martell, B. N., Garrett, B. E., & Caraballo, R. S. (2016). Disparities in adult cigarette smoking—United States, 2002–2005 and 2010–2013. *MMWR Morbidity and Mortality Weekly Report*, 65(30), 753–758. doi:10.15585/mmwr.mm6530a1

McClure, E. A., Tomko, R. L., Carpenter, M. J., Treiber, F. A., & Gray, K. M. (2018). Acceptability and compliance with a remote monitoring system to track smoking and abstinence among young smokers. *American Journal of Drug and Alcohol Abuse*, 44(5), 561–570. doi:10.1080/00952990.2018.1467431

McClure, J. B., Anderson, M. L., Bradley, K., An, L. C., & Catz, S. L. (2016). Evaluating an adaptive and interactive mhealth smoking cessation and medication adherence program: A randomized pilot feasibility study. *JMIR Mhealth Uhealth*, 4(3), e94. doi:10.2196/mhealth.6002

McQuoid, J., Thrul, J., & Ling, P. (2018). A geographically explicit ecological momentary assessment (GEMA) mixed method for understanding substance use. *Social Science and Medicine*, 202, 89–98. doi:10.1016/j.socscimed.2018.02.014

Odani, S., Agaku, I. T., Graffunder, C. M., Tynan, M. A., & Armour, B. S. (2018). Tobacco product use among military veterans—United States, 2010–2015. *MMWR Morbidity and Mortality Weekly Report*, 67(1), 7–12. doi:10.15585/mmwr.mm6701a2

Oh, S., Reingle Gonzalez, J. M., Salas-Wright, C. P., Vaughn, M. G., & DiNitto, D. M. (2017). Prevalence and correlates of alcohol and tobacco use among pregnant women in the United States: Evidence from the NSDUH 2005–2014. *Preventive Medicine*, 97, 93–99. doi:10.1016/j.ypmed.2017.01.006

Pew Research Center. (2019). Mobile Fact Sheet. Retrieved June 4, 2020 from https://www.pewresearch.org/internet/fact-sheet/mobile/

Prochaska, J. J., Das, S., & Young-Wolff, K. C. (2017). Smoking, mental illness, and public health. *Annual Review of Public Health*, 38, 165–185. doi:10.1146/annurev-publhealth-031816-044618

Rajani, N. B., Weth, D., Mastellos, N., & Filippidis, F. T. (2019). Adherence of popular smoking cessation mobile applications to evidence-based guidelines. *BMC Public Health*, 19(1), 743. doi:10.1186/s12889-019-7084-7

Ramo, D. E., Thrul, J., Delucchi, K. L., Hall, S., Ling, P. M., Belohlavek, A., & Prochaska, J. J. (2018). A randomized controlled evaluation of the tobacco status project, a Facebook intervention for young adults. *Addiction*. doi:10.1111/add.14245

Regmi, K., Kassim, N., Ahmad, N., & Tuah, N. (2017, April). Effectiveness of mobile apps for smoking cessation: A review. *Tobacco Prevention & Cessation*, 3, 12. https://doi.org/10.18332/tpc/70088

Robinson, C. D., Seaman, E. L., Grenen, E., Montgomery, L., Yockey, R. A., Coa, K., . . . Augustson, E. (2018). A content analysis of smartphone apps for adolescent smoking cessation. *Translational Behavioral Medicine*. doi:10.1093/tbm/iby113

Satterfield, J. M., Gregorich, S. E., Kalkhoran, S., Lum, P. J., Bloome, J., Alvarado, N., . . . Vijayaraghavan, M. (2018). Computer-facilitated 5A's for smoking cessation: A randomized trial of technology to promote provider adherence. *American Journal of Preventive Medicine*, 55(1), 35–43. doi:10.1016/j.amepre.2018.04.009

Savell, E., Gilmore, A. B., Sims, M., Mony, P. K., Koon, T., Yusoff, K., . . . Chow, C. K. (2015). The environmental profile of a community's health: A cross-sectional study on tobacco marketing in 16 countries. *Bulletin of the World Health Organization*, *93*(12), 851–861G. doi:10.2471/BLT.15.155846

Scott-Sheldon, L. A., Lantini, R., Jennings, E. G., Thind, H., Rosen, R. K., Salmoirago-Blotcher, E., & Bock, B. C. (2016). Text messaging-based interventions for smoking cessation: A systematic review and meta-analysis. *JMIR Mhealth Uhealth*, *4*(2), e49. doi:10.2196/mhealth.5436

Secades-Villa, R., García-Rodríguez, O., López-Núñez, C., Alonso-Pérez, F., & Fernández-Hermida, J. R. (2014). Contingency management for smoking cessation among treatment-seeking patients in a community setting. *Drug and Alcohol Dependence*, *140*, 63–68. doi:10.1016/j.drugalcdep.2014.03.030

Senyurek, V., Imtiaz, M., Belsare, P., Tiffany, S., & Sazonov, E. (2019). Cigarette smoking detection with an inertial sensor and a smart lighter. *Sensors (Basel)*, *19*(3). doi:10.3390/s19030570

Senyurek, V. Y., Imtiaz, M. H., Belsare, P., Tiffany, S., & Sazonov, E. (2019). Smoking detection based on regularity analysis of hand to mouth gestures. *Biomed Signal Processing and Control*, *51*, 106–112. doi:10.1016/j.bspc.2019.01.026

Sharbaugh, M. S., Althouse, A. D., Thoma, F. W., Lee, J. S., Figueredo, V. M., & Mulukutla, S. R. (2018). Impact of cigarette taxes on smoking prevalence from 2001–2015: A report using the Behavioral and Risk Factor Surveillance Survey (BRFSS). *PLoS One*, *13*(9), e0204416. doi:10.1371/journal.pone.0204416

Sharpless, N. (2019). How FDA is regulating e-cigarettes. Retrieved from www.fda. gov/news-events/fda-voices-perspectives-fda-leadership-and-experts/how-fda-regulating-e-cigarettes.

Soneji, S. S., Knutzen, K. E., & Villanti, A. C. (2019). Use of flavored E-cigarettes among adolescents, young adults, and older adults: Findings from the population assessment for tobacco and health study. *Public Health Reports*. doi:10.1177/0033354919830967

Thomas, K., Bendtsen, M., Linderoth, C., & Müssener, U. (2018). mHealth smoking cessation intervention among high-school pupils (NEXit Junior): Study protocol for a randomized controlled trial. *Trials*, *19*(1), 648. doi:10.1186/s13063-018-3028-2

Tibuakuu, M., Okunrintemi, V., Jirru, E., Echouffo Tcheugui, J. B., Orimoloye, O. A., Mehta, P. K., . . . Michos, E. D. (2019). National trends in cessation counseling, prescription medication use, and associated costs among US adult cigarette smokers. *JAMA Network Open*, *2*(5), e194585. doi:10.1001/jamanetworkopen.2019.4585

Tsoh, J. Y., Quach, T., Duong, T. B., Sa Nan Park, E., Wong, C., Huang, S. M., & Nguyen, T. T. (2018). Interactive Mobile Doctor (IMD) to promote patient-provider discussion on tobacco use among Asian American patients in primary care: A pilot study. *Journal of the American Board of Family Medicine*, *31*(6), 869–880. doi:10.3122/jabfm.2018.06.180018

United States Preventive Services Task Force. (2015). Retrieved from www.uspre ventiveservicestaskforce.org/Page/Document/UpdateSummaryFinal/tobacco-use-in-adults-and-pregnant-women-counseling-and-interventions.

United States Preventive Services Task Force. (2019). Retrieved from www.uspreventives ervicestaskforce.org/Page/Document/draft-recommendation-statement/tobacco-and-nicotine-use-prevention-in-children-and-adolescents-primary-care-interventions.

Vidrine, D. J., Frank-Pearce, S. G., Vidrine, J. I., Tahay, P. D., Marani, S. K., Chen, S., . . . Prokhorov, A. V. (2019). Efficacy of mobile phone-delivered smoking cessation interventions for socioeconomically disadvantaged individuals: A randomized clinical trial. *JAMA Internal Medicine, 179*(2), 167–174. doi:10.1001/jamainternmed.2018.5713

Vilardaga, R., Casellas-Pujol, E., McClernon, J., & Garrison, K. (2019). Mobile applications for the treatment of tobacco use and dependence. *Current Addiction Reports, 5.*

Vilardaga, R., Rizo, J., Zeng, E., Kientz, J. A., Ries, R., Otis, C., & Hernandez, K. (2018). User-centered design of learn to quit, a smoking cessation smartphone app for people with serious mental illness. *JMIR Serious Games, 6*(1), e2. doi:10.2196/games.8881

Walley, S. C., Wilson, K. M., Winickoff, J. P., & Groner, J. (2019). A public health crisis: Electronic cigarettes, vape, and JUUL. *Pediatrics, 143*(6). doi:10.1542/peds.2018-2741

Whittaker, R., McRobbie, H., Bullen, C., Rodgers, A., & Gu, Y. (2016). Mobile phone-based interventions for smoking cessation. *Cochrane Database of Systematic Reviews, 4,* CD006611. doi:10.1002/14651858.CD006611.pub4

11 Older Adults and the Utilization of Mobile and At-Home Health Technologies for Mental Health Care

James Phillips, Andrew Shutes-David, and Debby W. Tsuang

Over the past three decades, advances in mobile technologies have transformed the way that most Americans work, play, and function in daily life. Such advances have also transformed the way that health care providers organize work, interface with patients, offer preventive measures, and treat disease. In this chapter, we will specifically consider applying mobile health information technologies in the treatment of older adults seeking mental health care, a population that may be more recalcitrant to such interventions than middle-aged or younger adults and that is steadily growing in number. Indeed, census estimates suggest that over 20% of the U.S. population will be over the age of 65 by 2030, an increase of 7% since 2010 (Ortman, Velkoff, & Hogan, 2014). It is therefore imperative that older adults are included as beneficiaries in the medical technology revolution. Here, we will review the barriers to mobile technology use, emerging mobile health technologies, and condition-specific applications of mobile technology in older adults who require mental health care. See Table 11.1 for a list of the technology tools discussed in this chapter that are currently available to health care providers.

Views Toward Technology and Barriers to Use

Medicine has become one of the fastest growing markets for mobile technology, yet the application of this technology in the geriatric population seems to have lagged behind its application in other populations, and wide implementation has been challenging (Heart & Kalderon, 2013). Chronic mental health and cognitive disorders contribute significantly to this slow adoption of health information technology by older adults. Elderly populations present unique challenges to health care providers, as most elderly Americans have at least one chronic medical condition and many others have neurodegenerative disorders like Alzheimer's disease or Parkinson's disease. Mobile health interventions that target older populations must develop innovative assistive measures that can account for the cognitive, functional, and mobility impairment that are features of these disorders and that are more common among older adults.

Table 11.1 Health Technology for Older Adults

Technology Type	Subtypes or Brand Examples	Are These Examples Publicly Available?	Potential Benefits	Resources to Learn More
Devices				
Fitness tracker	*Fitbit or other wristwatch devices, *Mobile phone apps	Yes	Increase awareness of physical activity with associated improvement in mood/anxiety	O'Brien et al. (2017)
Fall monitor, medical alerts, and GPS trackers	*Wristwatch devices, *Mobile phone apps, *Silver Alert	Yes	Notify emergency services or relatives if patients fall (e.g., for PD) or assist in finding patients with cognitive disorientation that leads to getting lost (e.g., for AD)	www.theseniorlist.com/best-medical-alert-systems/, https://blog.caregiverhomes.com/the-50-best-gps-trackers-for-seniors, or Hadwen, Smallbon, Qing, and D'Souza (2017)
Robotics	*assistive telepresence robot, *remote presence robot	No	Assist in day-to-day tasks and telemedicine	Koceska, Koceski, Beomonte Zobel, Trajkovik, and Garcia (2019) and Vermeersch, Sampsel, and Kleman (2015)
Smart homes	*Microsoft Kinect sensors	No (the sensors are available to developers)	Leverage existing technology and provide a holistic system of monitoring and care (e.g., for AD or PD)	Phillips et al. (2017)
Video-delivered treatments	*BREATHE	No	Provide convenient and mobile treatment for anxiety and other conditions	Gould et al. (2017)
Video games	*NeuroRacer	No	Educate patients and aid in treatments	Anguera, Gunning, and Arean (2017)
Virtual reality headsets	*SocialBike	No	Project immersive environments or tasks with the potential for socialization (e.g., for loneliness, anxiety, or cognitive impairment)	Arlati et al. (2019) and Manera et al. (2016)

Apps				
Cognitive training apps	*Tablet for Healthy Ageing	No	Improve cognition	Vaportzis, Martin, and Gow (2017)
Insomnia apps	*CBT-i; *Cognitive training program	Yes; No	Improve sleep	Horsch et al. (2017) and Haimov (2013)
Social and video apps	*FaceTime; *WeChat; *EDLAH2	Yes; Yes; No	Improve connections with family and friends	Kostopoulos, Kyritsis, Ricard, Deriaz, and Konstantas (2018)
Provider monitoring apps	*FOCUS; *EDLAH2	No	Provide accurate ADLs for improved assessment and alert providers of acute needs or emergencies	Ben-Zeev, Kaiser, et al. (2013) and Kostopoulos et al. (2018)
Self-management apps	*FOCUS	No	Increase patient skills and autonomy in handling symptoms	Ben-Zeev, Kaiser, et al. (2013)
Reminder and medication management apps	*iNephro Medication Plan	No	Improve patient adherence to pharmaceutical regiments	Gatwood, Hohmeier, and Brooks (2019) and Mertens et al. (2016)

Source: For additional examples of wearable motion, environmental, and biometric sensors that are currently available on the market, see King et al. (2017). AD: Alzheimer's disease; ADL: activity of daily living; CBT: cognitive–behavioral therapy for insomnia; GPS: global positioning service; PD: Parkinson's disease.

Another important trend in the adoption of new technology is socio-economic status. The Pew Research Center found that seniors who were more educated and/or are wealthier adopted new technologies far more frequently than seniors who were less educated or wealthy (Anderson & Perrin, 2017). Outreach to poorer and less educated members of the geriatric population is thus critical to effectively integrate mobile health technology, particularly given that such individuals are likely to be the sickest and to have the fewest resources to help them stay healthy and/or access the health care system.

The Center for Research and Education on Aging and Technology Enhancement has also found that accessibility and ease of use are common barriers to widespread adoption of newer technologies for people of all ages (Czaja et al., 2006). These barriers are particularly salient for older adults who did not grow up with computers, who have mental health or cognitive concerns, and who may find such technologies less intuitive. Likewise, in their review of facilitators and barriers to the adoption of mobile health solutions, Kruse et al. highlight the importance of devices that achieve clarity, indicating that the complexity of technology poses the greatest obstacle for elderly patients (Kruse, Mileski, & Moreno, 2017).

Although health information technology developers should take accessibility and ease of use into account when designing mobile technologies for older adults, it is encouraging that older adults appear to be growing in their acceptance of mobile technologies. The Pew Research Center estimates that about 65% of seniors in the United States now own and use their own smartphones (Anderson & Perrin, 2017). Moreover, nearly 60% of elderly populations say that technology has a positive effect on society. This suggests that usability barriers may continue to decline among older adults, making them more likely to benefit from mobile health technologies.

Another sign for optimism regarding the use of mobile technology for health care is that even subpopulations with serious mental illnesses appear to frequently use mobile devices and may be open to their use for health purposes. Ben-Zeev et al. conducted a survey of patients diagnosed with schizophrenia/schizoaffective disorder, bipolar disorder, major depressive disorder, and substance use disorder (N=1,568), and they found that 86% of the patients with mood disorders used a mobile device, as well as 63% of patients with schizophrenia/schizoaffective disorders (Ben-Zeev, Davis, Kaiser, Krzsos, & Drake, 2013). Even more importantly, 81% of the individuals in this study who had a mobile device indicated that they were interested in having their mobile device serve as a conduit for mental health services.

Emerging and Current Technologies

Mobile health care, or e-health, may be the fastest growing field of health information technology. Examples of mobile health technology include apps that are freely available on patient smartphones or tablets, as well as mobile devices that record remote electrocardiograms, blood pressure, serum glucose levels, and sleep. These kinds of devices use Wi-Fi signals or cellular networks to instantaneously upload real-time data to health care providers, and because they are often paired with treatment response software or apps, health care providers are able to analyze and respond to health-related data in an unprecedented fashion. In the subsections that follow, we will provide examples of health technology systems that can incorporate these kinds of devices into their treatment, but first we will provide several examples of the apps on these devices to provide a sense of how mobile phones and/ or tablets are helping to transform mental health care for older adults (see Table 11.1 for examples).

Smartphone and tablet games are one of the more powerful and surprising medical tools to have emerged in this era of mobile health technology. Video games can be used to educate patients on everything from upcoming procedures to relevant medicine information. Such games offer a fun and interactive way for patients to become engaged with the specifics of their medical care. Moreover, as we describe in more detail later (see the "Depressive Disorders" subsection), games can also be used as a treatment tool for specific mental health conditions. It is critical, however, that health care providers recognize that elderly populations will be less familiar with video games and may therefore require additional technical and user support.

In addition to video games, there are a tremendous number of other apps that have been designed for health-related purposes. Indeed, some apps may have specific cognitive or mental health benefits for users. Vaportzis et. al., for example, found that adults who were between the ages of 65 and 76 and

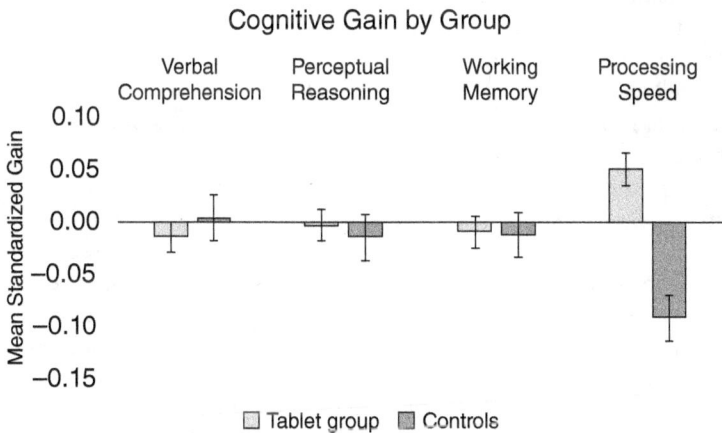

Figure 11.1 Mean Standardized Gain Scores and Standard Error Bars Demonstrating Significant Processing Speed Improvement Due to Tablet Intervention

Source: Licensed for Reuse by Elsevier.

who completed an intervention on a tablet app, showed greater improvements in processing speed ($\eta^2 = 0.10$), which is one of the first cognitive areas affected by the aging process, than controls who did not complete the intervention (Vaportzis et al., 2017).

Other apps, like the FOCUS app, combine guided exercises that improve self-management skills with important monitoring features (Ben-Zeev, Kaiser, et al., 2013). The FOCUS app uses an auditory signal and large visual notifications to prompt users with serious mental illnesses, including schizophrenia, to complete daily mental health-related surveys and provide feedback to their care providers, who receive it as time-stamped data on a secure web page. If any of the assessment targets are flagged as a concern, the FOCUS app encourages the user to engage in management interventions directly related to the relevant issue. Systems like FOCUS can provide an essential link in health-care monitoring that has been previously missing in mental illness health care.

Finally, the EDLAH2 app, a comprehensive app that includes self-entered health care measurements, vitals and exercise notifications, communication with health care providers, and health-related quizzes, provides an example of the ways in which mobile health technology can also encourage socialization (Kostopoulos et al., 2018). That is, in addition to these key functions, the app also encourages users to access its communal media platforms. Not surprisingly, aging populations have difficulty maintaining and fostering new relationships, and apps like EDLAH2 that consider social dimensions could be crucial in bridging that gap.

Telemedicine

Telemedicine is an important form of mobile health care that allows clinicians to remotely diagnose and treat patients using telephones, online communication apps, and other telecommunication services. Indeed, the use of telemedicine is especially beneficial for mental health care, given that mental health care is unlikely to require physical examination and that brief neurological examinations can be conducted remotely if a caregiver or other support is available to assist with patients. Although some patients may prefer in-person visits in the context of mental health care, telemedicine offers clear advantages for older patients who are more likely to experience decreases in mobility or driving skills that limit their willingness or ability to attend hospital or clinic appointments. A large review of mental health treatment that was provided through telemedicine found that older patients reported high levels of satisfaction in 76% of studies that investigated the use of telemedicine (Vedel, Akhlaghpour, Vaghefi, Bergman, & Lapointe, 2013), and another review found that health care delivery via telemedicine decreased emergency room visits and resulted in high patient satisfaction (Narasimha et al., 2017). Given the widespread growth of telemedicine throughout the United States, an entire chapter in this book is dedicated to its use in mental health, and we therefore refer readers Chapter 2 for more details regarding the use of telemedicine.

Robotics

Small studies have begun to investigate the use of robotic assistants in remote health care for the elderly. A study by Koceska et al., for example, investigated using an apparatus with a screen and an arm to assist nursing home residents in day-to-day tasks (e.g., fetching objects, measuring vital signs, and providing reminders) and to communicate with caregivers (Koceska et al., 2019), and a study by Vermeersch et al. explored using a robot to assist off-site nurse practitioners in performing telemedicine (Vermeersch et al., 2015). These small studies (N<50) both reported high patient and/ or caregiver satisfaction with the technological interventions (i.e., > 70%). Neither study specifically evaluated the role of robotics technology to assist in the context of mental health care, but it is likely that as robotics become more sophisticated and affordable, they may be extremely useful in caring for patients with cognitive and/or functional impairment.

Medication Management Technology

Proper medication management is a necessary component to the prevention and treatment of both chronic and acute conditions, and yet the benefits of pharmacology are often unrealized because of errors by medical providers or pharmacists (McKibbon et al., 2011) or because of poor patient adherence (Osterberg & Blaschke, 2005). There is also the risk that dosing inaccuracies or in adherence can lead to life-threatening outcomes. These problems may be compounded in elderly patients who are on multiple medications, particularly if they experience troublesome side effects. Moreover, medication adherence is also reduced in older patients given that they are more likely to experience forgetfulness or confusion.

Medication management technology may be useful to assist clinicians, pharmacists, patients, and caregivers in addressing the challenges related to prescribing and ordering, order communication, dispensing, administration and monitoring, education, and medication reconciliation. A large number of studies in this context have focused on technologies that assist medical providers in prescribing and monitoring medications, and these studies have demonstrated that clinician decision support systems (CDSSs) or computerized provider order entry systems (CPOEs) are likely to increase patient satisfaction and medication adherence (McKibbon et al., 2011).

Other studies have found that mobile phone or tablet apps that set medication reminders for patients or caregivers increase adherence, and these kinds of apps are often incorporated into other technological approaches discussed in this chapter (e.g., see the "Robotics" section just before this section). For example, Mertens et al. investigated iNephro Medication Plan, a tablet app to increase medication adherence in patients with coronary heart disease and no prior experience using tablets, and they found that patients who used the app were more likely to adhere to their medication schedule than patients who used a paper diary or no supporting system at all (Mertens et al., 2016). Furthermore, other studies have suggested that other approaches, like low-cost messaging platforms, can be used by pharmacies to provide patients with individualized support in medication adherence (Gatwood et al., 2019).

Passive Remote Monitoring and Smart Home Systems

Over the past ten years, household items like televisions, computers, refrigerator magnets, and alarm clocks have integrated different forms of technology to streamline performance and ease of use. Recently, some of these items have garnered attention for their ability to assist in medication management, monitor activities of daily living (ADLs), or send alerts to emergency medical services or family members, all of which can be tremendously helpful for older adults who may have mental health concerns. A smart home is a system that makes holistic use of such devices, comprising, for example, cameras that are placed in participants' homes, mobile on-body sensors to monitor vitals, and other wireless home devices to set reminders for medications (Majumder et al., 2017). The sensors are part of a growing trend toward the use of actigraphy devices to measure physical activity (e.g., wristwatches like the Fitbit), which has been shown to be closely connected to cognitive health and the reduction of depressive symptoms in aging (King et al., 2017; Nagamatsu et al., 2014; O'Brien et al., 2017). Likewise, global positioning system (GPS) software, which is commonly available either as a mobile app or on specific devices, provides another movement-related method in the care of older adults, as such systems can be beneficial in monitoring patients who are at risk for falling or for locating individuals with cognitive impairment who may tend to wander or get lost (Hadwen et al., 2017).

In a more particular example of using a holistic home network of systems and devices, investigators from the University of Missouri installed a smart home system in a local senior living facility that used Microsoft Kinect sensors, the same sensors that were previously used for a series of Xbox video games, to generate summaries of resident movements in bed and within the individual residences in order to recommend a better exercise plan for each resident (Phillips et al., 2017). These SMART systems thus creatively repurpose devices and environments that might otherwise only be used for entertainment to enhance family communications and daily activities. By expanding the capabilities of already existing technologies or spaces in this way, they provide clinicians with information that may be more accurate and reliable than information collected by self-report questionnaires or caregiver reports, thereby enabling clinicians to better personalize treatment in older patients (e.g., by tailoring exercise activities to individual patients, in the case of the University of Missouri study) (Lee & Shiroma, 2014). Although these systems offer the possibility of a synchronous health care delivery mechanism that can serve as an adjunct to standardized forms of clinical treatment intervention and that may have great promise for people with neurodegenerative disorders like Alzheimer's or Parkinson's disease, it is important to note that older adult patients and their family members may have legitimate concerns about their privacy with these in-home devices.

The Use of Mobile Health Technologies in Specific Mental Health Syndromes

Each mental health disorder presents its own challenges and opportunities for innovation in the context of mobile technology solutions for health care. Therefore, in the sections that follow, we provide a few specific examples of mobile health technology applications for some of the more common mental health syndromes that are experienced by older adults.

Depressive Disorders

Depression directly affects nearly 7 million Americans who are over the age of 65 (Steinman et al., 2007). Older adults are also more likely to develop depression than individuals in other age groups because the presence of multiple medical comorbidities is a risk factor for depression (Evans et al., 2005). Medication management is one key component in the treatment of depression (see the earlier section "Medication Management Technology"), and older patients are more likely to experience medication side effects due to polypharmacy and medication–medication interactions (Kim & Parish, 2017). Thus, treatment strategies for depression should also include non-pharmacological management, such as cognitive-behavioral treatment, supportive therapy, and problem-solving therapy. In addition, innovative mobile technologies are rapidly developing to assist older people with depression.

One example of these innovative technologies is the video game Neuro-Racer, in which players guide a character through an immersive environment with multitasking challenges that are shaped by an adaptive algorithm (Anguera et al., 2017). In a small randomized trial (N=22) that also included problem-solving therapy, Anguera et al. showed that older players of the game experienced clinical improvements in depression (as measured by the Hamilton Depression Rating Scale and Patient Health Questionnaire) and in cognitive measures of sustained attention and working memory compared to older participants who did not play the game; these improvements occurred as early as four weeks into the intervention and were sustained at eight weeks (Anguera et al., 2017). These results suggest that video games like NeuroRacer may be an effective intervention for depression, but larger studies that include participants with a greater range in cognition will be necessary to truly gauge whether these kinds of video games are beneficial in older adults with major depression.

Anxiety Disorders

Anxiety disorders are another major mental health problem faced by a large number of older Americans (Andreescu & Varon, 2015). Although there are numerous pharmacological and behavioral therapies available for the treatment of anxiety disorders, elderly populations, again, are more likely to develop side effects due to polypharmacy, and thus other strategies are needed to supplement medication use. Some investigators have used mobile technologies like the FOCUS app to address anxiety (see the earlier section "Emerging and Current Technologies"), and others have attempted to treat anxiety by adapting existing therapies into mobile video-delivered applications. For example, in a study of 20 older veterans, Gould et al. tested the efficacy of BREATHE, a video that educates veterans on breathing and relaxation techniques to reduce anxiety (Gould et al., 2017). They found that the veterans reported immediate benefits and that 100% of the participants reported that the breathing and relaxation video instructions were easy to follow. This particular study requires replication in a larger sample of participants with anxiety disorders (e.g., participants with post-traumatic stress disorder), but it clearly points to the ways in which using mobile technology to treat anxiety in older adults is feasible.

Insomnia and Sleep Disorders

Geriatric adults are more likely to experience trouble sleeping than younger adults (Mander, Winer, & Walker, 2017), and the prevalence of late-life insomnia ranges from 20% to 50% (Haimov & Shatil, 2013). Moreover, as adults age, they spend less and less time in the restorative stages of sleep (i.e., slow-wave and rapid eye-movement sleep), which means that their sleep becomes more fragmented, with frequent and longer awakenings. Older adults are also more likely to develop sleep apnea and other sleep disorders, both as primary conditions as well as conditions that are secondary to other comorbid medical and psychiatric conditions (Kaufmann, Susukida, & Depp, 2017; Okuro & Morimoto, 2014). The availability of mobile at-home sleep studies, which often occur through a device that patients can wear on their foreheads, has improved the accurate and timely diagnosis of common sleep disorders in older adults. These at-home tools are particularly valuable because older adults often decline hospital-based sleep laboratory assessments, and the real-time uploading of sleep data allows sleep physicians to easily monitor and adjust treatment without in-person visits. Moreover, some investigators have experimented with performing treatments directly through mobile health technology. For example, Horsch et al. demonstrated in a randomized controlled trial that it is feasible to carry out cognitive-behavioral therapy for insomnia (CBT-i) using fully automated mobile phone apps (Horsch et al., 2017).

Among the many adverse consequence associated with insomnia and sleep disturbances is worsening cognition. Haimov et al. performed a randomized trial of a home-based, personalized, computer cognitive training intervention in participants with insomnia who were between the ages of 65 and 85 (Haimov & Shatil, 2013). After controlling for age, they found that according to sleep diary entries and mobile actigraphy measurements, the participants who were randomized to the intervention (i.e., 34 of 51 participants) showed significant improvements in both sleep onset latency and sleep efficiency. In fact, after the eight-week cognitive training, they found that the participants' sleep latency no longer met criteria for insomnia. The mechanism by which cognitive training may improve sleep is unknown, but this study strongly suggests that the use of at-home cognitive training programs can significantly improve insomnia as measured by mobile health devices.

Social Isolation and Loneliness

Social isolation and loneliness are also common among older adults, affecting between one-third and one-half of the geriatric population (Landeiro, Barrows, Nuttall Musson, Gray, & Leal, 2017). To reverse these trends, many apps and devices are currently used to directly connect older adults with their friends and family, including video mobile apps on popular mobile devices (e.g., FaceTime or WeChat) that can keep elderly subjects in touch with family members who may live far away. Clinical apps like the EDLAH2 app described in the earlier "Emerging and Current Technologies" section) are also attempting to include community-building features.

Virtual or augmented reality technologies, in which users look through a goggle-like headset that projects an immersive, engaging experience, may also be useful mobile tools in helping address social isolation and loneliness, as well as anxiety disorders and cognitive impairment (Manera et al., 2016). Virtual reality headsets can often be linked so that individuals can gather together and virtually explore the projected content, such as a sightseeing destination, which can lead to an improved sense of adventure and connectiveness. Moreover, the social and visual dimensions of virtual reality can also be used as incentives for other tasks. Ariati et al., for example, have designed SocialBike, a multiplayer app in which older patients exercising on stationary bikes can collaboratively or competitively race to recognize various target animals or objects that they see as they pedal along (Arlati et al., 2019). These are some examples of how technology can build community in older individuals who might experience limitations in visual, auditory, and physical domains.

Conclusions

The ubiquity of the internet as a worldwide method of connectivity has opened the door for faster, more efficient, and, in some cases, safer methods of geriatric mental health treatment. If mobile health technology is to flourish and take advantage of this connectivity in geriatric populations, then developers, researchers, and clinicians will need to consider the unique challenges this demographic poses. As we have discussed, numerous studies are considering a wide range of technological advancements to address mental health needs in these populations, and in many cases, they are finding that usability, advanced support, and education are critical if efficacy and significance are to be achieved. Likewise, the increased presence of aging- and disease-related cognitive and sensory impairments in older adults raises the stakes in meeting these challenges.

Larger sample sizes are needed to confirm the effectiveness of many of these mobile health technologies, but our health care system is likely to benefit from implementing these kinds of innovative strategies in the context of mental health care. Indeed, if we are to effectively treat this growing demographic in our society, we will need to keep up with the most usable and effective forms of health care available for patients, which is likely to include mobile health services. Incorporating mobile health technology into all facets of care, from telemedicine to medication management, will save providers and patients millions of dollars in unnecessary clinic or emergency room visits and will help achieve the broader and more important aim of keeping our patients healthy and improving their quality of life. To accomplish these goals, clinicians must take an active role in both prescribing and integrating already available technologies to improve the quality of life of their older patients.

Acknowledgments

This work was supported in part by the U.S. Department of Veterans Affairs.

References

Anderson, M., & Perrin, A. (2017). *Tech adoption climbs among older adults*. Washington, DC: Pew Research Center. Retrieved from https://www.pewresearch.org/internet/2017/05/17/tech-adoption-climbs-among-older-adults/

Andreescu, C., & Varon, D. (2015). New research on anxiety disorders in the elderly and an update on evidence-based treatments. *Current Psychiatry Reports*, 17(7), 53. doi:10.1007/s11920-015-0595-8

Anguera, J. A., Gunning, F. M., & Arean, P. A. (2017). Improving late life depression and cognitive control through the use of therapeutic video game technology: A proof-of-concept randomized trial. *Depression Anxiety*, 34(6), 508–517. doi:10.1002/da.22588

Arlati, S., Colombo, V., Spoladore, D., Greci, L., Pedroli, E., Serino, S., . . . Sacco, M. (2019). A social virtual reality-based application for the physical and cognitive training of the elderly at home. *Sensors (Basel), 19*(2). doi:10.3390/s19020261

Ben-Zeev, D., Davis, K. E., Kaiser, S., Krzsos, I., & Drake, R. E. (2013). Mobile technologies among people with serious mental illness: Opportunities for future services. *Administration and Policy in Mental Health and Mental Health Services, 40*(4), 340–343. doi:10.1007/s10488-012-0424-x

Ben-Zeev, D., Kaiser, S. M., Brenner, C. J., Begale, M., Duffecy, J., & Mohr, D. C. (2013). Development and usability testing of FOCUS: A smartphone system for self-management of schizophrenia. *Psychiatric Rehabilitation Journal, 36*(4), 289–296. doi:10.1037/prj0000019

Czaja, S. J., Charness, N., Fisk, A. D., Hertzog, C., Nair, S. N., Rogers, W. A., & Sharit, J. (2006). Factors predicting the use of technology: Findings from the center for research and education on aging and technology enhancement (CREATE). *Psychology and Aging, 21*(2), 333–352. doi:10.1037/0882-7974.21.2.333

Evans, D. L., Charney, D. S., Lewis, L., Golden, R. N., Gorman, J. M., Krishnan, K. R., . . . Valvo, W. J. (2005). Mood disorders in the medically ill: Scientific review and recommendations. *Biological Psychiatry, 58*(3), 175–189. doi:10.1016/j.biopsych.2005.05.001

Gatwood, J., Hohmeier, K. C., & Brooks, I. M. (2019). Beyond the reminder: The next steps in pharmacist-driven, mHealth patient engagement. *The Journal of the American Pharmacists Association (2003), 59*(2S), S21–S24. doi:10.1016/j.japh.2018.10.003

Gould, C. E., Zapata, A. M. L., Bruce, J., Bereknyei Merrell, S., Wetherell, J. L., O'Hara, R., . . . Beaudreau, S. A. (2017). Development of a video-delivered relaxation treatment of late-life anxiety for veterans. *International Psychogeriatrics, 29*(10), 1633–1645. doi:10.1017/S1041610217000928

Hadwen, T., Smallbon, V., Qing, Z., & D'Souza, M. (2017). Energy efficient LoRa GPS tracker for dementia patients. *Conference Proceedings: Annual International Conference of the IEEE Engineering in Medicine and Biology Society., 2017*, 771–774. doi:10.1109/EMBC.2017.8036938

Haimov, I., & Shatil, E. (2013). Cognitive training improves sleep quality and cognitive function among older adults with insomnia. *PLoS One, 8*(4), e61390. doi:10.1371/journal.pone.0061390

Heart, T., & Kalderon, E. (2013). Older adults: Are they ready to adopt health-related ICT? *The International Journal of Medical Informatics, 82*(11), e209–231. doi:10.1016/j.ijmedinf.2011.03.002

Horsch, C. H., Lancee, J., Griffioen-Both, F., Spruit, S., Fitrianie, S., Neerincx, M. A., . . . Brinkman, W. P. (2017). Mobile phone-delivered cognitive behavioral therapy for Insomnia: A randomized waitlist controlled trial. *The Journal of Medical Internet Research, 19*(4), e70. doi:10.2196/jmir.6524

Kaufmann, C. N., Susukida, R., & Depp, C. A. (2017). Sleep apnea, psychopathology, and mental health care. *Sleep Health, 3*(4), 244–249. doi:10.1016/j.sleh.2017.04.003

Kim, J., & Parish, A. L. (2017). Polypharmacy and medication management in older adults. *Nursing Clinics of North America, 52*(3), 457–468. doi:10.1016/j.cnur.2017.04.007

King, R. C., Villeneuve, E., White, R. J., Sherratt, R. S., Holderbaum, W., & Harwin, W. S. (2017). Application of data fusion techniques and technologies for wearable health monitoring. *Medical Engineering & Physics, 42*, 1–12. doi:10.1016/j.medengphy.2016.12.011

Koceska, N., Koceski, S., Beomonte Zobel, P., Trajkovik, V., & Garcia, N. (2019). A telemedicine robot system for assisted and independent living. *Sensors (Basel)*, *19*(4). doi:10.3390/s19040834

Kostopoulos, P., Kyritsis, A., Ricard, V., Deriaz, M., & Konstantas, D. (2018). Enhance daily live and health of elderly people. *Procedia Computer Science*, *130*, 967–972.

Kruse, C. S., Mileski, M., & Moreno, J. (2017). Mobile health solutions for the aging population: A systematic narrative analysis. *Journal of Telemedicine and Telecare*, *23*(4), 439–451. doi:10.1177/1357633X16649790

Landeiro, F., Barrows, P., Nuttall Musson, E., Gray, A. M., & Leal, J. (2017). Reducing social isolation and loneliness in older people: A systematic review protocol. *BMJ Open*, *7*(5), e013778. doi:10.1136/bmjopen-2016-013778

Lee, I. M., & Shiroma, E. J. (2014). Using accelerometers to measure physical activity in large-scale epidemiological studies: Issues and challenges. *The British Journal of Sports Medicine*, *48*(3), 197–201. doi:10.1136/bjsports-2013-093154

Majumder, S., Aghayi, E., Noferesti, M., Memarzadeh-Tehran, H., Mondal, T., Pang, Z., & Deen, M. J. (2017). Smart homes for elderly healthcare-recent advances and research challenges. *Sensors (Basel)*, *17*(11). doi:10.3390/s17112496

Mander, B. A., Winer, J. R., & Walker, M. P. (2017). Sleep and human aging. *Neuron*, *94*(1), 19–36. doi:10.1016/j.neuron.2017.02.004

Manera, V., Chapoulie, E., Bourgeois, J., Guerchouche, R., David, R., Ondrej, J., . . . Robert, P. (2016). A feasibility study with image-based rendered virtual reality in patients with mild cognitive impairment and dementia. *PLoS One*, *11*(3), e0151487. doi:10.1371/journal.pone.0151487

McKibbon, K. A., Lokker, C., Handler, S. M., Dolovich, L. R., Holbrook, A. M., O'Reilly, D., . . . Raina, P. (2011). Enabling medication management through health information technology (Health IT). *Evidence Report/Technology Assessment (Full Rep)*(201), 1–951.

Mertens, A., Brandl, C., Miron-Shatz, T., Schlick, C., Neumann, T., Kribben, A., . . . Becker, S. (2016). A mobile application improves therapy-adherence rates in elderly patients undergoing rehabilitation: A crossover design study comparing documentation via iPad with paper-based control. *Medicine (Baltimore)*, *95*(36), e4446. doi:10.1097/MD.0000000000004446

Nagamatsu, L. S., Flicker, L., Kramer, A. F., Voss, M. W., Erickson, K. I., Hsu, C. L., & Liu-Ambrose, T. (2014). Exercise is medicine, for the body and the brain. *The British Journal of Sports Medicine*, *48*(12), 943–944. doi:10.1136/bjsports-2013-093224

Narasimha, S., Madathil, K. C., Agnisarman, S., Rogers, H., Welch, B., Ashok, A., . . . McElligott, J. (2017). Designing telemedicine systems for geriatric patients: A review of the usability studies. *Telemedicine Journal and E-Health*, *23*(6), 459–472. doi:10.1089/tmj.2016.0178

O'Brien, J. T., Gallagher, P., Stow, D., Hammerla, N., Ploetz, T., Firbank, M., . . . Olivier, P. (2017). A study of wrist-worn activity measurement as a potential real-world biomarker for late-life depression. *Psychological Medicine*, *47*(1), 93–102. doi:10.1017/S0033291716002166

Okuro, M., & Morimoto, S. (2014). Sleep apnea in the elderly. *Current Opinion in Psychiatry*, *27*(6), 472–477. doi:10.1097/YCO.0000000000000105

Ortman, J., Velkoff, V., & Hogan, H. (2014). *An aging nation: The older population in the United States.* Hyattsville, MD: US Census Bureau.

Osterberg, L., & Blaschke, T. (2005). Adherence to medication. *The New England Journal of Medicine*, *353*(5), 487–497. doi:10.1056/NEJMra050100

Phillips, L. J., DeRoche, C. B., Rantz, M., Alexander, G. L., Skubic, M., Despins, L., . . . Koopman, R. J. (2017). Using embedded sensors in independent living to predict gait changes and falls. *Western Journal of Nursing Research*, *39*(1), 78–94. doi:10.1177/0193945916662027

Steinman, L. E., Frederick, J. T., Prohaska, T., Satariano, W. A., Dornberg-Lee, S., Fisher, R., . . . Late Life Depression Special Interest Project, P. (2007). Recommendations for treating depression in community-based older adults. *The American Journal of Preventive Medicine*, *33*(3), 175–181. doi:10.1016/j.amepre.2007.04.034

Vaportzis, E., Martin, M., & Gow, A. J. (2017). A tablet for healthy ageing: The effect of a tablet computer training intervention on cognitive abilities in older adults. *The American Journal of Geriatric Psychiatry*, *25*(8), 841–851. doi:10.1016/j.jagp.2016.11.015

Vedel, I., Akhlaghpour, S., Vaghefi, I., Bergman, H., & Lapointe, L. (2013). Health information technologies in geriatrics and gerontology: A mixed systematic review. *The Journal of the American Medical Informatics Association*, *20*(6), 1109–1119. doi:10.1136/amiajnl-2013-001705

Vermeersch, P., Sampsel, D. D., & Kleman, C. (2015). Acceptability and usability of a telepresence robot for geriatric primary care: A pilot. *Geriatric Nursing*, *36*(3), 234–238. doi:10.1016/j.gerinurse.2015.04.009

12 Using Technology to Promote Suicide Prevention

Sean M. Barnes, Christine L. Jackson,
Laurel A. Gaeddert, Ryan Holliday,
Lisa A. Brenner, and Sarra Nazem

The rate of suicide within the United States (U.S.) continues to rise, with an approximate increase of 30% in age-adjusted suicide rates from 2000 to 2016 (Hedegaard, Curtin, & Warner, 2018). Suicide is now the tenth leading cause of death (Heron, 2018), with subsets of the general population at heightened risk (e.g., males; Hedegaard et al., 2018). Although several nationwide initiatives have been implemented to address suicide, the changing U.S. sociocultural environment, which is impacted by technological advances, necessitates continued evaluation and evolution to decrease risk and, optimally, prevent suicide.

An overarching challenge in suicide prevention is understanding inherent drivers of suicidal self-directed violence. Although psychiatric diagnoses (e.g., depression) are often associated with increased risk for suicide, suicide is complex and multidetermined, often not deriving from a singular predictor. Instead, extant theories of suicide often conceptualize suicide risk using a transdiagnostic lens, an approach that embraces the dynamic nature of suicide risk, which is often associated with numerous psychosocial stressors and medical/psychiatric diagnoses.

Although many theories of suicide exist, there are a number of common elements across these theories. For instance, negative perceptions of self, including perceptions of being a burden to others (i.e., perceived burdensomeness), and an unmet need to belong (e.g., thwarted belongingness) are inherent to Joiner's Interpersonal-Psychological Theory of Suicide (IPTS; Joiner, 2005; Van Orden et al., 2010). Similarly, in Rudd's Fluid Vulnerability Theory, he posits that negative perceptions of oneself (e.g., "I am broken"), others (e.g., "No one likes or really cares about me"), and the world (e.g., "the world is horrible and this will never get better) are likely to exacerbate one's risk for suicide (Rudd, 2006). Moreover, across a number of theories (e.g., Hopelessness Theory; Abramson et al., 2002), hopelessness regarding one's situation and difficulty coping with this distress are identified as key components in one's risk for subsequently engaging in suicidal self-directed violence (Kleiman, Law, & Anestis, 2014; Rudd, 2006). Evidence-informed novel technological-based strategies that are aimed at (1) the general population (universal interventions), (2) those at increased risk (selected interventions), and (3) individuals at acute risk (indicated interventions) may help to mitigate such drivers. At the same time, exposure to information available via technological sources (e.g., social media) may also increase risk.

As discussed throughout this chapter, the empirical basis of the interrelation between technology and suicide risk prediction and/or prevention is still relatively underdeveloped. This is the case despite the fact that rapid changes in the use of technology have direct relevance to transdiagnostic drivers of suicide risk. For example, access to the internet was rare to nonexistent in the 1990s; however, current rates indicate that the overwhelming majority of individuals in the United States have at least one method of accessing the internet (Ryan & Lewis, 2017). Further, technological changes have resulted in greater access and reliance on technology in one's everyday life, with individuals having increasing access to computers and smartphones among other technological devices, resulting in a quick sociocultural paradigm shift. Due to this unprecedented shift within a relatively short period of time, evidence-informed guidance on, and support for, how to incorporate technology when working with individuals at risk for suicide is not yet available (e.g., VA/DoD Clinical Practice Guidelines; The Assessment and Management of Suicide Risk Work Group, 2019); however, we posit that further clinical consideration and research are warranted based on theoretically informed mechanisms, such as those highlighted previously, which suggest that exposure to information via technology may mitigate or exacerbate risk for suicide.

On one hand, widespread access to others through a myriad of outlets (e.g., social media, online video games) may increase one's sense of belonging and ability to develop a social network, directly targeting and mitigating transdiagnostic suicide risk factors. This may hold especially true in circumstances where connectedness may be difficult (e.g., rurality). Moreover, as detailed in many chapters throughout this book, technology-based health resources (e.g., online health resources, smartphone applications, telehealth) would be expected to increase access to understanding of and treatment for mental health-related symptoms, including suicidal thoughts and behaviors.

On the other hand, a multitude of new issues have emerged secondary to the proliferation of technology. For instance, online bullying and access to resources guiding self-directed violence have received attention as a factor related to increased suicide risk (Aboujaoude, Savage, Starcevic, & Salame, 2015; Biddle, Donovan, Hawton, Kapur, & Gunnell, 2008). Further, despite increasing technology-based health resources, many require further investigation to evaluate their efficacy compared to in-person care, as well as effectiveness (e.g., strategies for integration into routine clinical practice).

This chapter serves as an exploration of the interplay of technology and suicide risk and prevention. Models of understanding how technology can attenuate and exacerbate suicide risk will be discussed utilizing a public health model. Based upon this framework, considerations for implementation or novel risk identification and prevention strategies, as well as associated clinical implications, will be discussed.

Public Health Approaches to Suicide Prevention

Whereas public health approaches have historically been implemented to address infectious diseases (e.g., influenza), more recently they have been adopted to address a broader range of conditions (Berridge & Bourne, 2005). This is in part associated with an increased understanding regarding the complex array of biopsychosocial factors that contribute to the onset of health conditions; factors exist outside the health care system (e.g., social determinants of health) that can both contribute to decreased physical and mental health as well as promote wellness and prevention. At present, there is consensus among policy makers and researchers regarding the importance of adopting public health approaches to prevent suicide (U.S. Department of Health and Human Services, 2012). Such approaches require surveillance, research, and education (U.S. Department of Health and Human Services, 2012) as well as interventions aimed at diverse populations. These include "health promotion to address the needs of the population as a whole" (universal prevention efforts: e.g., to encourage "mental and emotional well-being"); "clinical and community preventive services" to address the needs of those with risk factors for future suicidal behaviors (selected interventions: e.g., interventions to address mental health disorders, such as depression); and, "treatment and support services" for those at highest risk for suicidal behavior or with a past history of self-directed violence (indicated interventions: e.g., evidence-based psychotherapies for suicide prevention; U.S. Department of Health and Human Services, 2012, p. 24). Toward this end, development and implementation of both upstream and downstream interventions are indicated. Upstream approaches are those that affect larger populations (e.g., media campaigns; Brownson, Seiler, & Eyler, 2010). Conversely, downstream approaches (selected/indicated) are focused on addressing individual level behaviors (Brownson et al., 2010). Within this chapter, we will address technological strategies that either have been developed or are being developed to facilitate both upstream and downstream interventions for suicide prevention that may be accessible by the population as a whole or specific individuals. For further discussion of the public health model and suicide prevention, see Caine (2013).

How Technology Can Improve *and* Hinder Suicide Prevention Efforts Among Members of the General Population

Universal interventions involve approaches that encompass the population as a whole and may hold promise given that we now live in a time of unprecedented widespread social connectivity; however, such connectivity also comes with potential peril. Online social networks have increased connectivity between people to the extent that information can spread to millions of people in just minutes (Burnap & Williams, 2015). Social media and micro-blogging websites and applications (Facebook, Twitter, Instagram, Reddit, etc.) have made it possible to interact with a broad and far-reaching audience/peers in a way that drastically augments social interactions relative to previous modes of communication and interaction offered by letter writing, phone calls, and even email. As previously mentioned, connection with others is a key factor in a number of suicide theories (e.g., IPTS; Joiner, 2005; Van Orden et al., 2010), and therefore, in some cases social media has the potential to minimize suicide risk (e.g., via meaningful social connections, social support, suicide risk detection, knowledge of resources, treatment delivery, public messaging). One key difference between social media connections and more traditional approaches, is that they can occur with a high degree of anonymity (Wachs, Wright, & Vazsonyi, 2019) and limited accountability. As such, engaging in misbehavior such as cyberbullying (Kowalski, Giumetti, Schroeder, & Lattanner, 2014) may come with less social risk for the perpetrator despite the fact that those same behaviors increase risk for a wide range of negative mental health outcomes in victims (Pham & Adesman, 2015). Furthermore, information found on social media or the internet may contribute to the normalization of suicide, suicide contagion, and knowledge regarding lethal means.

Allen and colleagues (2014) critically reviewed the literature related to social media and adolescents' sense of belonging and suggest that social media elevates the ease in which individuals may form and create online groups and communities. This creates opportunities for users to interact with others who share similar values, beliefs, and interests and can positively affect perceptions of social integration and bonding (Ko & Kuo, 2009; Quinn & Oldmeadow, 2013). Such communities may in turn protect against the development of a desire for suicide.

Beyond preventing the development of suicide risk, social media presents a unique opportunity for preventing suicide via upstream media campaigns. Social media has been used to destigmatize mental health issues and offer resources to support users who might benefit from psychoeducation or mental health care. Health care organizations (e.g., Veterans Health Administration, Twitter: @VeteransHealth, Facebook: VeteransHealth), suicide prevention organizations (e.g., American Foundation for Suicide Prevention, Twitter: @afspnational, Facebook: AFSPNational; The Suicide Prevention Resource Center, Twitter: @SPRCtweets, Facebook: SuicidePrevention-ResourceCenter), and suicide prevention lifelines (e.g., The Suicide Prevention Lifeline, Twitter: @800273TALK, Facebook: 800273talk) have utilized social media to provide psychoeducation about suicide and support for at-risk individuals and their loved ones. Twitter has partnered with the International Association for Suicide Prevention and the White Swan Foundation to support media campaigns, even developing a special emoji for World Suicide Prevention Day. Some social media platforms have also developed their own suicide prevention resource centers. Facebook features a suicide prevention page ("Facebook's Safety Center" www.facebook.com/ safety/wellbeing/suicideprevention) with resources such as links to crisis lines and guidelines to help young people safely discuss topics like suicide (Matyus, 2019; Robinson et al., 2018).

Social media is clearly useful for promoting suicide prevention; however, the impact of social media use on individual users can also be negative. Cyberbullying has become a significant public health concern that can lead to mental and behavioral health issues and an increased risk of suicide. In fact, cyberbullying is more strongly related to suicidal ideation (OR, 3.12 [95% CI, 2.40–4.05]) compared to traditional bullying (2.16 [2.05–2.28]; Van Geel, Vedder, & Tanilon, 2014), potentially because more people can witness the bullying and the material is stored online, creating the possibility for victims to be reminded of the experiences more often (Patchin & Hinduja, 2006). In addition to amplifying opportunities for peer victimization and undermining social connection, individual social media users sometimes encourage self-directed violence by sharing knowledge about means, creating suicide pacts (Jiang et al., 2017; Lee & Kwon, 2018), or using pro-suicide hashtags (Arendt, 2019). Researchers have documented examples of glorification and normalization of self-harm on Facebook and other social forums (Marchant et al., 2017). The power of social media can be used by individual users to promote suicidal behavior and on a larger community level can create the potential for increasing the chances of individuals acting on suicidal thoughts and plans in response to reports of suicide.

Similar to other forms of media, reports of suicide on social media have the potential for contagion or copycat attempts. Suicide contagion is when one or more suicides are reported or discussed in a way that contributes to another suicide (Stack, 2005). Research has demonstrated that certain types of news coverage can increase the likelihood of suicide in vulnerable individuals (see reportingonsuicide.org for media guidelines for safely reporting on suicide and a full bibliography of relevant research). Communication via social media could theoretically lead to the same iatrogenic effects as print media via normalization, glorification, and oversimplification of reasons for suicide, making users at risk of suicide more likely to engage in suicidal behavior. Research on suicide contagion related to social media is limited. Investigators have examined the impact of reported suicides on posting trends (Karamshuk et al., 2017), and some work suggests that there may be an increase in actual suicidal behavior following celebrity suicides that result in a large reaction from Twitter users (Ueda, Mori, Matsubayashi, Sawada, 2017). To mitigate suicide contagion, it is recommended that users follow social media guidelines for mental health promotion and suicide prevention as well as recommendations for online media reporting (see reportingonsuicide.org).

Reporting on Suicide (2015) states that the:

> Recommendations for Reporting on Suicide also apply to online content including citizen-generated media coverage, social media sites, blogs, and online content from traditional media websites. In fact, following the recommendations for online content is just as important since online articles, blogs, photos, and videos can be shared instantly with millions of people around the world. And we know from research that extensive media coverage of suicide increases risk for contagion.

Recommendations include guidance for not sensationalizing suicide, including excessive detail, or oversimplifying the cause of suicide. It is also recommended including links to suicide prevention and postvention support.

Guidelines have also been developed that are specific to social media platforms and include relevant information for both professionals and individual users. Some recommendations have focused on youth. Robinson and colleagues (2018) conducted a Delphi survey to develop guidelines to support youth communicating about suicide via social media, *#Chatsafe a Young Persons Guide to Communicating Safely Online About Suicide* (Robinson et al., 2018; see reference for download link). The guidelines provide useful information for youth to consider prior to posting about suicide or responding to others' posts about suicide. The American Association for Suicidology also developed *Suicide and Social Media: A Tipsheet for Parents and Providers* (American Association of Suicidology, 2019; see reference for download link). Recommendations include suggestions like discussing and monitoring youths' "digital lives" and including assessment of social media use when performing a crisis intervention safety plan. The tipsheet also includes a list of "parental control tools" to assist in monitoring and/or limiting access to certain websites, social media platforms, and content. Other sets of recommendations target a broader audience. For example, the Veterans Health Administration has developed a *Social Media Safety Toolkit: For Veterans, Their Families, and Friends*, which offers recommendations on recognizing and responding to emotional distress on social media, how to recognize and respond to signs of a potential crisis on social media, and reporting suicidal content on Facebook and Twitter (U.S. Department of Veterans Affairs, n.d.; see reference for download link). The Entertainment Industries Council's TEAM UP also developed *Social Media Guidelines for Mental Health Promotion and Suicide Prevention* (Entertainment Industries Council, n.d.; see reference for download link) and the National Suicide Prevention Lifeline developed recommendations to support digital community managers and social media platforms establish relevant policies (*Support for Suicidal Individual on Social and Digital Media*; National Suicide Prevention Lifeline, n.d.; see reference for download link).

Organizers of social media platforms have made efforts to prevent the potential negative effects of social media without undercutting the potential benefits of using social media to share resources and provide support. Major social media platforms such as Facebook, Twitter, and Instagram all ban posts that glorify or encourage self-harm or suicide. However, there is also a recognized need not to overly censor suicide-related content, as this could promote stigma and prevent healthy communication about suicide (e.g., Brown, 2019). Allowing posts about suicide creates opportunities to leverage universal prevention approaches to identify individuals in need of selected and indicated interventions. With improvement in computerized interventions, social media may be an ideal vehicle for connecting people in need with easily accessible computerized treatment programs. At a minimum, when social media users are identified as being at elevated risk of suicide due to their posts, most social media platforms are able to provide links to relevant resources for accessing additional support. Social media is proving a powerful resource for suicide prevention, and continued efforts will be made to balance the risks and benefits of social media use.

Case Example

You have just completed two sessions with a new client, George, a 19-year-old reporting current stress related to moving to a new city for work. During your intake, George noted that he spends a considerable amount of time online, often on social media sites such as Facebook, Snapchat, and Instagram. To leverage potential universal interventions with George, an important first step would be to assess George's online activity, determining information on what is likely occurring in George's life prior to posting, what the frequency and content are for social media engagement, and what the resulting emotions/thoughts/behaviors are that follow online activity. If your assessment suggests that George's behaviors are occurring as a result of a need to improve social connections, as his therapist, you might work collaboratively with George to identify online communities that could promote a sense of belongingness and discuss limiting social media interactions that are associated with negative emotions. Although he is not reporting any conditions associated with increased suicide risk, and has no history of suicidal ideation, by helping George buffer against social isolation, you are promoting protective factors, like belongingness, which could ultimately help George increase behavioral activation and value living in a new city.

Addressing Potential Drivers of Suicide Among Those at Risk

Selective interventions are developed and implemented to address the needs of those at increased risk for suicide. As there are a wide range of factors that contribute to increased risk, interventions aimed at preventing suicide among such cohorts are also diverse. Two often noted risk factors for suicidal behavior are depression (Hawton, Casanas, Haw, & Saunder, 2013) and sleep disturbances (Perlis et al., 2016). Ferrari and colleagues (2013) evaluated the global burden of disease associated with depressive disorders and found that Major Depressive Disorder explained 16 million suicide-related disability-adjusted life years. In a recent meta-analysis conducted by Pigeon and colleagues (2012), insomnia was associated with an increased relative risk for SI, attempt, and death by suicide (2.84, 95% Confidence Interval (CI), 2.44–3.31). This association remained significant after adjusting for potential confounders, such as depression and anxiety (1.98, 95% CI, 1.63–2.41). As such, computerized Cognitive-Behavioral Therapies (cCBT) for depressed mood and insomnia could offer a potentially efficacious means of delivering depression and insomnia treatments by providing the opportunity to engage in evidence-based treatments (EBT) via computers. cCBTs are modeled on efficacious behaviorally based face-to-face treatments that have been operationalized and transformed for internet delivery (Ritterband et al., 2003). From both a policy and clinical perspective, cCBTs have garnered attention due to their potential to overcome barriers to treatment, including cost, scheduling and travel demands, stigma, and lack of trained EBT clinicians (Cartreine, Ahern, & Locke, 2010). As such, two examples of cCBTs, Beating the Blues (BtB; depression) and Sleep Healthy Using the Internet (SHUTi; insomnia), could be considered key selected suicide prevention interventions that leverage technology to meet treatment needs and demands.

One of the most empirically supported cCBTs for depression is Beating the Blues (BtB). BtB is an eight-session cCBT for depression, comprised of interactive modules that utilize learning exercises, case examples, and homework. A "Care Coordinator" can monitor progress and provide support. BtB was listed on the Substance Abuse and Mental Health Services Administration's (SAMHSA) National Registry of Evidence-Based Programs and Practices (U.S. Department of Health and Human Services, 2015), which was suspended in 2018, and has been offered through the United Kingdom's public health system for over 15 years. The National Institute of Health and Clinical Excellence in the United Kingdom recommends BtB as a gold standard treatment in primary care contexts for mild to moderate symptoms of depression (Learmonth, Trosh, Rai, Sewell, & Cavanagh, 2008; NICE, 2006). BtB has been established as an acceptable intervention in primary care contexts (Cavanagh, Seccombe, & Lidbetter, 2011) and has been associated with reduction in mild to moderate symptoms of depression and anxiety (Ormrod, Kennedy, Scott, & Cavanagh, 2010; Proudfoot et al., 2003; Van den berg, Shapiro, Bickerstaffe, & Cavanagh, 2004). As a testament to its feasibility, BtB has also been established as a cost-effective intervention in randomized controlled trials (RCT; Learmonth et al., 2008, McCrone et al., 2004). Additionally, BtB has been demonstrated as an effective intervention for older adults (McMurchie, Macleod, Power, Laidlaw, & Prentice, 2013). However, the acceptability, feasibility, and effectiveness of BtB for specific populations at risk for suicide is unknown. For example, little is known about the effectiveness of BtB among veterans enrolled in VA care, a critical population given the disproportional burden of suicide in veteran and military populations. Current efforts at the Veterans Affairs Rocky Mountain MIRECC include establishing the acceptability and feasibility of BtB for veterans with mild to moderate depression.

Similar work has been conducted to develop cCBTs for insomnia, with several studies that have supported the efficacy of cCBTs for insomnia (Anderson, Goldsmith, & Gardiner, 2014; Espie et al., 2012). Insomnia treatment is an especially promising suicide prevention approach given that insomnia is an independent risk factor for suicide, a precursor of, and comorbid with, other disorders associated with increased risk for suicide (Pigeon et al., 2012). In a meta-analysis of cCBTs for insomnia, post-treatment mean differences between groups ranged from small to large effect sizes with high treatment adherence (78%; Cheng & Dizon, 2012). One cCBT for insomnia, SHUTi, is a self-guided, interactive, and tailored web-based program modeled on the primary tenets of face-to-face cognitive-behavioral therapy for insomnia. The intervention is delivered through six cores, which include interactive features, including personalized goal-setting, graphical feedback, animations/illustrations to enhance comprehension, quizzes to test knowledge, patient vignettes, and video-based expert explanations. Several SHUTi randomized controlled trials have demonstrated that SHUTi is associated with reductions in insomnia severity as well as comorbid symptoms (e.g., depression), and that these treatment gains maintain in the long term (i.e., six months and one year) when compared to an online patient education program (Christensen et al., 2016; Ritterband, Thorndike, & Ingersoll, 2017). Similar to BtB, no RCTs have examined the acceptability, feasibility, and efficacy of SHUTi in veteran or military populations. Current efforts at the Veterans Affairs Rocky Mountain MIRECC include two RCTs examining the efficacy of SHUTi in reducing insomnia symptoms and improving functioning among veteran populations.

Case Example

You have been working with Marie, a 41-year-old, divorced working mother of two, for about three months. Marie began seeking treatment with you for help with insomnia, chronic pain, and anxiety but has encountered tremendous difficulties with scheduling. She works two jobs and has unreliable childcare, making it extremely tough for her to make therapy sessions during your typical clinic schedule. Given the combination of Marie's sleep difficulties and scheduling challenges, this is a case where you might suggest a cCBT for insomnia. This would allow Marie to more flexibly receive an evidence-based therapy for her primary complaint while allowing you to monitor progress with a combination of clinician portals, phone check-ins, booster sessions, etc. Leveraging technology to meet Marie's treatment need could not only decrease her insomnia symptoms but could also serve to mitigate the likelihood of future suicide risk.

Identifying and Providing Interventions to Mitigate Risk for Those at High Risk for Suicide

Indicated interventions are directed at meeting the needs of those at high risk for future suicidal behavior (e.g., those with suicidal ideation and intent, those with a past history of suicidal behavior). Although much of the suicide prevention work via social media occurs at a universal level, social media also presents opportunities for identifying users who may be at risk for suicide. Suicidologists and other stakeholders have been investigating the possibility of using individuals' social media activity to detect acute increases in suicide risk to overcome limitations of relying primarily on self-reported intentions to engage in suicidal behavior. Most screening for suicide risk is conducted in health care settings, and many people who die by suicide may not be recently engaged in care within these health care settings (Coppersmith, Leary, Crutchley, & Fine, 2018). Furthermore, the time between the onset of a suicidal crisis and suicidal behavior may not allow enough time for contact with health professionals (Coppersmith et al., 2018). Even if individuals interact with health care professionals and have the opportunity to disclose concerns about suicide, many still choose not to disclose this information. Data suggest that many of these same individuals, particularly teens and young adults, do disclose information about suicide risk factors on social media (Pourmand et al., 2018). Pourmand et al. highlight the need for ways to screen for suicide risk outside of health care settings and suggest that social media presents an opportunity for this.

The enormity of data communicated via social media necessitates automated means of monitoring for suicide risk on a large scale. Several groups of researchers have successfully demonstrated the ability to use natural language processing and machine learning to detect expressions of suicide risk (Burnap & Williams, 2015; Coppersmith et al., 2018). Similarly, some social media services such as Facebook use automated algorithms to detect and potentially respond to users expressing suicide risk. Most social media platforms offer individual users the ability to flag posts for suicide-related content to create opportunities for outreach and support. On an individual level, people often provide support and resources to prevent suicide when other social media users make statements indicating increased risk for self-harm. Educational programs have been developed to teach teens and young adults to support others via social media (see Marchant et al., 2017). Additionally, supportive communities have developed via social media specifically to prevent suicide. The social media website Reddit has a subreddit called "SuicideWatch" where people post about suicidal thoughts to receive feedback and support from the community of over 155,000 subscribers (reddit.com/r/SuicideWatch). This subreddit is designed for users to receive "non-judgemental peer support ONLY," while other subreddits, such as /r/ SWResources, focus on providing information about professional resources.

Some attempts have also been made to more formally empower users to monitor social media platforms for suicide-related content as part of an online "safety net." For example, The Samaritan's Radar Twitter plug-in used an algorithm with keywords and phrases to allow Twitter users to monitor each other's posts. When key words were identified, an automated email was sent to the person who had signed up to monitor that account containing information regarding the best way of reaching out and providing support. However, the plug-in was permanently removed from Twitter approximately ten days after it was launched amid privacy and safety concerns because the plug-in did not notify users that their account was being monitored (The Samaritans, n.d.). Concerns were also raised about the potential of making Twitter a less safe space for users to seek support due to self-censoring or use of the plug-in for bullying users who are in distress.

After identifying those at increased risk for suicide, technology can be utilized to deliver interventions that are aimed at preventing future self-directed violence. For example, a number of groups have developed computer-based and smartphone applications to facilitate safety planning, a brief structured personalized effective intervention aimed at mitigating suicide risk (Stanley et al., 2018). As noted by Stanley et al. (2018), safety planning is comprised of six steps:

> (1) identify personalized warning signs for an impending suicide crisis; (2) determine internal coping strategies that distract from suicidal thoughts and urges; (3) identify family and friends who are able to distract from suicidal thoughts and urges and social places that provide the opportunity for interaction; (4) identify individuals who can help provide support during a suicidal crisis; (5) list mental health professionals and urgent care services to contact during a suicidal crisis; and (6) lethal means counseling for making the environment safer.
>
> (p. 896)

As plans are collaboratively developed by patients and providers, and are intended for use outside the medical setting, being able to access as well as revise the plan is paramount. With the goal of potentially reducing time of developing a plan, promoting the quality of safety plans, and enhancing the ability to share developed plans, Boudreaux et al. (2017) developed a web-based self-administered computer application. Initial findings supported the usability of the program, however, "completeness" of the plans entered were varied.

Researchers in Denmark are currently engaged in a clinical trial to evaluate differences between a safety plan delivered as a mobile application vs. by paper in terms of reduction of suicidal ideation (Andreasson et al., 2017). The application (MyPlan) was developed with extensive user input to facilitate uptake (Buus et al., 2019). Individuals in both arms of the trial will complete a safety plan (paper or smartphone application) as well as receive treatment as usual, which consists of 8–10 sessions. Recruitment is underway.

Aside from safety planning, the development of web-based evidence-informed approaches to suicide prevention has been ongoing. Van Spijker, Van Straten, and Kerkhof (2014) have developed and evaluated a web-based intervention based on principles from cognitive-behavioral (Beck, 2011), problem solving (Townsend et al., 2001), mindfulness-based cognitive (Segal, Williams, & Teasdale, 2002), and dialectic behavioral therapies (Linehan, 1993), with the goal of assisting individuals in reducing the severity of their suicidal ideation. The program is comprised of six online modules, and participants are instructed to complete one module per week as well as spend 30 minutes per day engaging with the programmatic content. Each module is comprised of four components: "(1) theory, (2) a weekly assignment, (3) two to three exercises, and (4) optional exercises to help consolidate relevant information and skills" (Van Spijker, Van Straten, & Kerkhof, 2014, p. 2). Compared to those in a waitlist control condition, those who engaged with the web-based program reported statistically significant decreases in suicidal thoughts. Interestingly, findings were more pronounced among those with a history of multiple suicide attempts. However, in a replication trial where pre- and post-symptoms of those participating in "Living with Deadly Thoughts" (the web-based program) were compared to those of individuals in attention control conditions (modular online course regarding lifestyle information [e.g., nutrition]), no between group differences in terms of severity of suicidal thinking were identified. A limitation of the second study noted by authors was a high attrition rate which contributed to the study being underpowered.

To augment traditional CBT therapies for suicide prevention (Rudd, 2006), clinicians have implemented hope boxes (Wenzel, Brown, & Beck, 2009). That is, individuals at high risk are encouraged to place items associated with reasons for living in a box (e.g., shoe box) that can be accessed during periods of crisis. To increase access to such reminders, Bush and colleagues (2017) developed a Virtual Hope Box (VHB) phone application, in which individuals can store individually tailored content (e.g., pictures, music). Post-development, Bush et al. (2017) conducted a RCT to evaluate the efficacy of the VHB. Veterans who reported recent suicidal ideation were randomized to VHB or a control group. Those in the control group received printed materials regarding coping with suicidal thoughts and feelings. Those in the VHB group reported significantly greater ability to cope with unpleasant feelings and thoughts. In addition to these notable findings, the VHB is one of a few suicide-specific apps that meet several proposed criteria for psychological health app quality (Bush, Armstrong, & Hoyt, 2019), further supporting its quality and clinical utility for at-risk populations. The VHB is available for free download on Android and iOS.

Case Example

You have been working with Robert, a 67-year-old, retired veteran for about a month. Robert has experienced long-standing chronic suicidal ideation. Since retirement, Robert has struggled with his suicidal thoughts, noting a lack of purpose. Although he is open to coming to your office, he would prefer less frequent sessions due to transportation concerns. You have noticed that Robert's motivation and engagement in session is terrific, but that he struggles with keeping up momentum between sessions. In particular, he often loses sight of his reasons for living and forgets about coping skills he can utilize when experiencing warning signs. You might recommend augmenting your in-session interventions with the use of app-based safety plans and the VHB, by determining ways to set reminders to review and further develop both app-based programs. To assist with outcome tracking, you could ask Robert to log his level of suicidal ideation (and other targeted behaviors) prior to and after engaging in the apps. This information could be used to help Robert understand the impact his between-session engagement has in helping to regulate emotions and would serve as two technology-based resources that provide individualized reminders of warning signs and reasons for living.

Implementation

In addition to the multitude of barriers facing all forms of help-seeking, there are also unique barriers to accessing technology-based care (e.g., Azarang, Pakyurek, Giroux, Nordahl, & Yellowlees, 2018; Kruse et al., 2018). When utilizing a public health approach to suicide prevention, these barriers are critical to examine given that successful suicide prevention approaches, spanning from universal to indicated interventions, are by definition, directed at every member of the population. For example, for universal social media campaigns designed to destigmatize mental health issues to be the most successful, it is necessary for all individuals to first own technological devices, and second, ensure that those devices are not limited in some fashion (e.g., limited bandwidth or cellphone data) that would lead to systematic differences in the likelihood of receiving campaign information. Because several factors (e.g., financial, geographic) will be associated with differential access to technology, the successful implementation of suicide prevention approaches utilizing technology must ensure that the intended targeted population is characterized by the assumed level of access that would be required to receive full benefit from the intervention. Aside from access, there are other considerations that may impede technology-based suicide prevention approaches. Some individuals who do have the ability to use technological devices may experience difficulties or frustration utilizing those devices. Additionally, socioeconomic and educational disadvantage (Meurk, Leung, Hall, Head, & Whiteford, 2016) could impact patients' lack of familiarity and experience with technology, and concerns about breaches in confidentiality could impede the implementation of technology-based care. Notably, most studies that have assessed the impact of demographic characteristics on acceptability of technology-based care have found no significant relationship between the two, reinforcing the need to utilize an idiographic approach when working with patients (Berry, Lobban, Emsley, & Bucci, 2016). This may be especially true when working with older adults, who may have less familiarity with smartphones and wearable devices and derive less benefit from these approaches when accommodations are not made (e.g., larger, more legible font sizes; Simblett et al., 2018). Addressing these implementation considerations is an incredibly challenging task, one that is critical for the success of public health approaches.

Despite these obstacles, several factors facilitate interest and engagement in technology interventions (Kruse et al., 2018). Patients living in rural areas far from medical centers may benefit from the ease of access provided by technology-based care. This is critical for suicide prevention efforts, given that individuals living in rural areas may have increased risk for suicide, experience greater mental health stigma, and have less access to suicide-specific selected and indicated evidence-based interventions. Utilizing telemedicine can also decrease expenditures associated with travel to medical centers as well as decrease the need for time off work and costly childcare arrangements, especially by improving accessibility to support and interventions that may be not readily available outside of "regular" hours or within usual settings (Luxton, June, & Kinn, 2011; Predmore et al., 2017). These factors often function as barriers that keep individuals from engaging in treatment earlier in the course of distress and illness, suggesting that telemedicine may be an especially effective upstream approach to helping individuals engage in support and care earlier on. Further, many individuals could also benefit from the comfort and privacy of receiving care at home, as well as the personalization and level of autonomy that technological interventions can ultimately provide. This personalization "at home" could also assist with greater family engagement, thereby promoting behavior change that could benefit systems outside of the individual.

Clinical Implications

The clinical implications associated with technological advances in suicide prevention reflect the complex cost-benefit analysis described throughout this chapter thus far. Most importantly, the widespread use and reliance on technology offers unlimited opportunities to extend reach and impact of both upstream and downstream suicide prevention approaches. This expansive ability is exactly what is needed for suicide prevention approaches to achieve the maximized likelihood of effectiveness; solely targeting suicide prevention efforts towards a segment of the population at highest risk will never attain the same level of impact that can be derived from also utilizing universal and selected interventions. Employing a public health framework to technology-based suicide prevention efforts is critical, as there is a growing need for innovative approaches that can meet treatment demands. Leveraging technology to meet these needs is consistent with service delivery models based upon stepped care principles (Witt et al., 2017). Technology allows for new opportunities to provide interventions to large numbers of people in accessible and convenient ways, contributing to greater numbers of individuals receiving treatment and benefit than ever before. This is critical when it comes to suicide prevention, given that the field of suicidology remains theoretically and conceptually challenged in its ability to predict short- and long-term risk, especially due to an inability to prevent all transdiagnostic mechanisms that contribute to risk over time.

Several researchers have also documented that technological approaches to care, such as telemedicine, contribute to increased disclosure and openness (Azarang et al., 2018; Krysinska & De Leo, 2007). Self-report data collected by apps could also be used to enhance engagement in treatment by providing a more efficient way to customize symptom tracking and feedback (Bush et al., 2019). Given the existing stigma around suicidal thoughts, technology may afford opportunities not only to create communities of shared support and healing but also to improve treatment engagement. The successes of the Veterans Crisis Line (VCL) suggest that providing alternatives to crisis support such as telephone, text, and web-based messaging may assist in engaging cohorts of at-risk populations that have been historically difficult to reach (e.g., middle-aged male veterans; Knox, Kemp, McKeon, & Katz, 2012). Notably, qualitative interviews of VCL responders suggest that increased anonymity contributes to users' ease in sharing suicidal ideation and that options such as web chat increases users' ability to engage in crisis care across a variety of settings where telephone options may be limited (e.g., verbal disclosure of distress at work; Predmore et al., 2017). By optimizing the likelihood of disclosure and support-seeking, technological advances such as those developed by the VCL have contributed to improved access to immediate support and resources and serve as one example whereby face-to-face modalities pale in comparison to the sheer numbers that can be served via technology-based interventions.

The clinical implications of technology-based suicide prevention efforts are not without inherent challenges. For example, Murphy and Mitchell (1998) accurately describe the complexities of email contact:

> Despite its two major disadvantages—i.e., asynchronicity and lack of verbal immediacy—email communication adds an extra degree of anonymity and control, allows for sharing of emotions without having a

direct witness, and gives both help seekers and counselors additional time to compose a message.

Anonymity and confidentiality are likely facilitators underlying improved engagement, yet they also are the very same factors that lead to challenges when considering how to support those in crisis when a provider is not in the same room as the patient, particularly given the built-in time delays in this form of communication (Krysinska & De Leo, 2007). Thus, with the growth of technology-based suicide prevention and intervention approaches, there will be a continued need to closely evaluate the balance between anonymity and liability, ensure proper risk protocols are embedded within clinical and research protocols, and refine risk algorithms as described earlier.

Another clinical implication that is necessary to note is the importance of provider technology education. Providers are inundated with many options for technology, with some providers reporting avoidance of technology-based methods due to preference for traditional methods of care (Haun et al., 2014). When providers are experiencing technology-based challenges within the realm of suicide-specific interventions, an area of practice notoriously characterized by lack of provider comfort and confidence, greater assistance and support will be necessary (Bush et al., 2019). This training could include support on how to evaluate the evidence base and clinical aspects of integration, in addition to guidance on navigating security, privacy, and ethical considerations.

Conclusions

Perhaps one of the most exciting aspects of the role of technology in suicide prevention is the numerous opportunities for future research. It is important to acknowledge up front that there is always an inherent challenge to translating research findings for the frontline clinician, and the field of suicidology is no different. The fast pace of technological advances is contributing to an even greater tension surrounding how best to systematically document empirical evidence while keeping up with societal demand and interest (Bush et al., 2019). Readers are encouraged to consider the recommendations provided by Bush et al. (2019) for quality of content and level of evidence strategies. Despite these invaluable suggestions, given the inherent challenges involved in studying suicidal behaviors (i.e., low base rate, transdiagnostic, complex outcome derived from multi-determined behavioral factors), researchers need to access and utilize multidisciplinary teams and designs, both of which necessitate adequate funding and regulatory support to meet the pace and demand for suicide-specific outcome measurement.

If utilizing a public health approach, several future research recommendations are appropriate. First, prospective research is necessary to determine whether universal approaches, including strategies like social media campaigns, improve critical targeted outcomes like improved education/

awareness and enhanced likelihood to seek and receive support. Second, continued research utilizing selected interventions targeting comorbid suicide risk factors could prove useful if these technological interventions demonstrate efficacy in reducing suicide risk indirectly via comorbid symptom mitigation and directly with suicidal ideation and self-directed violence behavior reduction. Continued research on indicated interventions also holds incredible promise. For example, researchers could employ quasi-experimental methods to investigate if safe spaces online for individuals with suicidal ideation facilitate or hamper access to care and whether certain technological or online cultural variables moderate outcomes.

Most importantly, as argued throughout this chapter, it is essential for technology-based researchers to consider ways to build a portfolio that utilizes a comprehensive population-based approach. For example, communication and social networking site (SNS) apps on smartphones have been found to improve social capital and reduce social isolation (Cho, 2015), but this association is complex, especially when considered within a suicide prevention framework and would require deliberate conceptualization to build a population-based approach. To build a comprehensive research program in just this domain would necessitate consideration of the following: (1) adequate study methods to allow for this association to be empirically examined in a range of populations (universal, selected, indicated), (2) studying an array of technology-based options (e.g., apps, social media, websites) to ensure findings hold regardless of the technology-based vehicle, and, most importantly for the focus of this chapter, (3) directly assessing suicide risk (e.g., suicidal ideation, burdensomeness, belongingness) as an outcome to ascertain mechanisms of risk.

For the clinician, because there are no evidence-based guidelines to inform when and how to use technology with those who are at risk for suicide, we recommend utilizing clinical judgment in synthesis with recommendations put forward in this chapter. These approaches, highlighted in our case examples, will allow you as a clinician to collaboratively develop treatment goals related to suicide risk while incorporating technology in a way that could enhance patient motivation, engagement, and/or ability to benefit from your intervention approach. For example, although there is insufficient evidence on the efficacy and effectiveness of adjunctive technology-based interventions (e.g., digital/mobile applications used in treatment), when working with an individual at risk for suicide, if shared decision making suggests that adding a technological approach to your intervention could mitigate risk, improve well-being, and would not add harm, then it would likely be worth pursuing. Exploring the privacy, safety, and other relevant concerns, as outlined throughout other chapters, is another important consideration prior to utilizing technology for suicide prevention efforts.

Although there is inherent complexity involved in the study of technology and its association with suicide risk, the opportunity for improved access to care and consumer autonomy along with decreased health care costs is incredibly promising. These opportunities are perhaps the most influential when thinking about suicide as a public health problem, as the solutions require strategies that are multifaceted, dynamic, and versatile—all characteristics that perfectly characterize the strengths of technology.

Note

This material is based upon work supported in part by the Department of Veterans Affairs (VA) and the Rocky Mountain MIRECC for Suicide Prevention. The views expressed are those of the authors and do not necessarily represent the views or policy of the VA or the United States Government.

References

Aboujaoude, E., Savage, M. W., Starcevic, V., & Salame, W. O. (2015). Cyberbullying: Review of an old problem gone viral. *Journal of Adolescent Health, 57*(1), 10–18. doi:10.1016/j.jadohealth.2015.04.011

Abramson, L. Y., Alloy, L. B., Hogan, M. E., Whitehouse, W. G., Gibb, B. E., Hankin, B. L., & Cornette, M. M. (2002). The hopelessness theory of suicidality. In T. Joiner & M. D. Rudd (Eds.), *Suicide science* (pp. 17–32). Boston, MA: Springer.

Allen, K., Ryan, T., Gray, D., McInerny, D., & Water, L. (2014). Social media use and social connectedness in adolescents: The positives and the potential pitfalls. *The Australian Educational and Developmental Psychologist, 31*(1), 18–31. doi:10.1017/edp.2014.2

American Association of Suicidology. (2019). Suicide and social media a tipsheet for parents and providers. Retrieved from https://suicidology.org/wp-content/uploads/2019/07/SUICIDE-SOCIAL-MEDIA.pdf

Anderson, K. N., Goldsmith, P., & Gardiner, A. (2014). Pilot evaluation of an online cognitive behavioral therapy for insomnia disorder—targeted screening and interactive Web design lead to improved sleep in a community population. *Nature and Science of Sleep, 6*, 43–49. https://doi.org/10.2147/NSS.S57852

Andreasson, K., Krogh, J., Bech, P., Frandsen, H., Buus, N., Stanley, B., . . . Erlangsen, A. (2017). MYPLAN -mobile phone application to manage crisis of persons at risk of suicide: Study protocol for a randomized controlled trial. *Trials, 18*(1), 171. https://doi.org/10.1186/s13063-017-1876-9

Arendt, F. (2019). Suicide on Instagram—content analysis of a German suicide-related hashtag. *Crisis: The Journal of Crisis Intervention and Suicide Prevention, 40*(1), 36–41. doi:10.1027/0277-5910/a000529

The Assessment and Management of Suicide Risk Work Group. (2019). *VA/DoD clinical practice guideline for the assessment and management of patients at risk for suicide.* Retrieved from www.healthquality.va.gov/guidelines/MH/srb/

Azarang, A., Pakyurek, M., Giroux, C., Nordahl, T. E., & Yellowlees, P. (2018). Information technologies: An augmentation to post-traumatic stress disorder treatment among trauma survivors. *Telemedicine and e-Health, 24*(4), 263–271. doi:10.1089/tmj.2018.0068

Beck, J. S. (2011). *Cognitive behavior therapy: Basics and beyond* (2nd ed.) New York, NY: Guilford Press.

Berridge, V., & Bourne, S. (2005). Illicit drugs, infectious disease and public health: A historical perspective. *Canadian Journal of Infectious Diseases and Medical Microbiology, 16*(3), 193–196. doi:10.1155/2005/530160

Berry, N., Lobban, F., Emsley, R., & Bucci, S. (2016). Acceptability of interventions delivered online and through mobile phones for people who experience severe mental health problems: A systematic review. *Journal of Medical Internet Research, 18*(5), e121. doi:10.2196/jmir.5250

Biddle, L., Donovan, J., Hawton, K., Kapur, N., & Gunnell, D. (2008). Suicide and the internet. *British Medical Journal, 336*(7648), 800–802. doi:10.1136/bmj.39525.442674.AD

Boudreaux, E. D., Brown, G. K., Stanley, B., Sadasivam, R. S., Camargo, C. A., Jr., & Miller, I. W. (2017). Computer administered safety planning for individuals at risk for suicide: Development and usability testing. *Journal of Medical Internet Research, 19*(5), e149. doi:10.2196/jmir.6816

Brown, E. A. (2019). Suicide memes might actually be therapeutic: Online meme-sharing communities have taken a morbid turn, but some mental-health experts believe this could benefit isolated young people. *The Atlantic.* Retrieved September 13, 2019, from www.theatlantic.com/health/archive/2019/02/suicide-memes/582832/

Brownson, R. C., Seiler, R., & Eyler, A. A. (2010). Measuring the impact of public health policy. *Preventing Chronic Disease, 7*(4), A77. Retrieved from www.cdc.gov/pcd/ issues/2010/jul/09_0249.htm

Burnap, P., & Williams, M. L. (2015). Cyber hate speech on twitter: An application of machine classification and statistical modeling for policy and decision making. *Policy & Internet, 7*(2), 223–242. doi:10.1002/poi3.85

Bush, N. E., Armstrong, C. M., & Hoyt, T. V. (2019). Smartphone apps for psychological health: A brief state of the science review. *Psychological Services, 16*(2), 188–195. doi:10.1037/ser0000286

Bush, N. E., Smolenski, D. J., Denneson, L. M., Williams, H. B., Thomas, E. K., & Dobscha, S. K. (2017). A virtual hope box: Randomized controlled trial of a smartphone app for emotional regulation and coping with distress. *Psychiatric Services, 68*(4), 330–336. doi:10.1176/appi.ps.201600283

Buus, N., Juel, A., Haskelberg, H., Frandsen, H., Larsen, J. L. S., River, J., . . . Erlangsen, A. (2019). User involvement in developing the MYPLAN mobile phone safety plan app for people in suicidal crisis: Case study. *JMIR Mental Health, 6*(4), e11965. doi:10.2196/11965

Caine, E. D. (2013). Forging an agenda for suicide prevention in the United States. *American Journal of Public Health, 103*(5), 822–829. doi:10.2105/AJPH.2012.301078

Cartreine, J. A., Ahern, D. K., & Locke, S. E. (2010). A roadmap to computer-based psychotherapy in the United States. *Harvard Review of Psychiatry, 18*(2), 80–95. doi:10.3109/10673221003707702

Cavanagh, K., Seccombe, N., & Lidbetter, N. (2011). The implementation of computerized cognitive behavioural therapies in a service user-led third sector self-help clinic. *Behaviouraland Cognitive Psychotherapy, 39*(4), 427–442. doi:10.1017/S1352465810000858

Coppersmith, G., Leary, R., Crutchley, P., & Fine, A. (2018). Natural language processing of social media as screening for suicide risk. *Biomedical Informatics Insights, 10*, 1–11. doi:10.1177/1178222618792860

Cheng, S. K., & Dizon, J. (2012). Computerized cognitive behavioral therapy for insomnia: A systematic review and meta-analysis. *Psychotherapy and Psychosomatics, 81*(4), 206–216. doi:10.1159/000335379

Christensen, H., Batterham, P. J., Gosling, J. A., Ritterband, L. M., Griffiths, K. M., Thorndike, F. P., . . . Mackinnon, A. J. (2016). Effectiveness of an online insomnia program (SHUTi) for prevention of depressive episodes (the GoodNight Study):

A randomized controlled trial. *Lancet Psychiatry*, *3*(4), 333–341. doi:10.1016/S2215-0366(15)00536-2.

Cho, J. (2015). Roles of smartphone app use in improving social capital and reducing social isolation. *Cyberpsychology, Behavior, and Social Networking*, *18*(6), 350–355. doi:10.1089/cyber.2014.0657

Entertainment Industries Council. (n.d.). *Social media guidelines for mental health promotion and suicide prevention* [PDF file]. Retrieved from www.eiconline.org/teamup/wp-content/files/teamup-mental-health-social-media-guidelines.pdf

Espie, C. A., Kyle, S. D., Williams, C., Ong, J. C., Douglas, N. J., Harmes, P., & Brown, J. S. (2012). A randomized, placebo-controlled trial of online cognitive behavioral therapy for chronic insomnia disorder delivered via an automated media-rich web application. *Sleep*, *35*(6), 769–781. doi:10.5665/sleep.1872

Ferrari, A. J., Charlson, F. J., Norman, R. E., Patten, S. B., Freedman, G., Murray, C. J., . . . Whiteford, H. A. (2013). Burden of depressive disorders by country, sex, age, and year: Findings from the global burden of disease study 2010. *Public Library of Science Medicine*, *10*(11), e1001547. doi:10.1371/journal.pmed.1001547

Haun, J. N., Lind, J. D., Shimada, S. L., Martin, T. L., Gosline, R. M., Antinori, N., . . . Simon, S. R. (2014). Evaluating user experiences of the secure messaging tool on the Veterans affairs' patient portal system. *Journal of Medical Internet Research*, *16*(3), e75. doi:10.2196/jmir.2976

Hawton, K., Casanas, I. C. C., Haw, C., & Saunders, K. (2013). Risk factors for suicide in individuals with depression: A systematic review. *Journal of Affective Disorders*, *147*(1–3), 17–28. doi:10.1016/j.jad.2013.01.004

Hedegaard, M. D., Curtin, S. C., & Warner, M. (2018). *Suicide rates in the United States continue to increase*. Hyattsville, MD: National Center for Health Statistics. Retrieved from www.cdc.gov/nchs/products/databriefs/db309.htm

Heron, M. (2018). *Deaths: Leading causes for 2016*. Hyattsville, MD: National Center for Health Statistics. Retrieved from www.cdc.gov/nchs/data/nvsr/nvsr67/nvsr67_06.pdf

Jiang, F. F., Xu, H. L., Liao, H. Y., & Zhang, T. (2017). Analysis of internet suicide pacts reported by the media in mainland china. *Crisis: The Journal of Crisis Intervention and Suicide Prevention*, *38*(1), 36–43. doi:10.1027/0227-59/a000402

Joiner, T. E. (2005). *Why people die by suicide*. Cambridge, MA: Harvard University Press.

Karamshuk, D., Shaw, F., Brownlie, J., & Sastry, N. (2017). Bridging big data and qualitative methods in the social sciences: A case study of twitter responses to high profile deaths by suicide. *Online Social Networks and Media*, *1*, 33–43. doi:10.1016/j.osnem.2017.01.002

Kleiman, E. M., Law, K. C., & Anestis, M. D. (2014). Do theories of suicide play well together? Integrating components of the hopelessness and interpersonal psychological theories of suicide. *Comprehensive Psychiatry*, *55*, 431–438.

Knox, K. L., Kemp, J., McKeon, R., & Katz, I. R. (2012). Implementation and early utilization of a suicide hotline for Veterans. *American Journal of Public Health*, *102*, S29–S32. doi:10.2105/AJPH.2011.300301

Ko, H., & Kuo, F. (2009). Can blogging enhance subjective well-being through self-disclosure? *CyberPsychology and Behavior*, *12*(1), 75–79. doi:10.1089/cpb.2008.0163

Kowalski, R. M., Giumetti, G. W., Schroeder, A. N., & Lattanner, M. R. (2014). Bullying in the digital age: A critical review and meta-analysis of cyberbullying research among youth. *Psychological Bulletin*, *140*(4), 1073–1137. doi:10.1037/a0035618

Kruse, C. S., Atkins, J. M., Baker, T. D., Gonzales, E. N., Paul, J. L., & Brooks, M. (2018). Factors influencing the adoption of telemedicine for treatment of military

Veterans with post-traumatic stress disorder. *Journal of Rehabilitation Medicine, 50,* 385–392. doi:10.2340/16501977-2302

Krysinska, K. E., & De Leo, D. (2007). Telecommunication and suicide prevention: Hopes and challenges for the new century. *OMEGA Journal of Death and Dying, 55*(3), 237–253. doi:10.2190/OM.55.3.e

Learmonth, D., Trosh, J., Rai, S., Sewell, J., & Cavanagh, K. (2008). The role of computer-aided psychotherapy within an NHS CBT specialist service. *Counseling and Psychotherapy Research, 8*(2), 117–123. doi:10.1080/14733140801976290

Lee, S. Y., & Kwon, Y. (2018). Twitter as a place where people meet to make suicide pacts. *Public Health, 159,* 21–26. doi:10.1013/j.puhe.2018.03.001

Linehan, M. M. (1993). *Cognitive-behavioral treatment of borderline personality disorder.* New York: Guilford Press.

Luxton, D. D., June, J. D., & Kinn, J. T. (2011). Technology-based suicide prevention: Current applications and future directions. *Telemedicine and e-Health, 17*(1), 50–54. doi:0.1089/tmj.2010.0091

Marchant, A., Hayton, K., Stewart, A., Montgomery, P., Singarvelu, V., Lloyd, K., . . . John, A. (2017). A systematic review of the relationship between internet use, self-harm and suicidal behavior in young people: The good, the bad and the unknown. *Public Library of Science, 12*(8), e0181722. doi:10.1371/journal.pone.0181722.

Matyus, A. (2019). On world suicide prevention day, Facebook announces it will ban self-harm images. Retrieved September 12, 2019, from www.digitaltrends.com/news/facebook-bans-images-of-self-harm-in-attempt-to-fight-suicide/

McCrone, P., Knapp, M., Proudfoot, J., Clash, R., Cavanagh, K., Shapiro, D. A., . . . Tylee, A. (2004). Cost-effectiveness of computerised cognitive—behavioural therapy for anxiety and depression in primary care: Randomised controlled trial. *British Journal of Psychiatry, 185,* 55–62. doi:10.1192/bjp.185.1.55

McMurchie, M., Macleod, F., Power, K., Laidlaw, K., & Prentice, N. (2013). Computerised cognitive behavioural therapy for depression and anxiety with older people: A pilot study. *International Journal of Geriatric Psychiatry, 28*(11), 1147–1156. doi:10.1002/gps.3935

Meurk, C., Leung, J., Hall, W., Head, B. W., & Whiteford, H. (2016). Establishing and governing e-mental health care in Australia: A systematic review of challenges and a call for policy-focused research. *Journal of Medical Internet Research, 18*(1), e10. doi:10.2196/jmir.4827

Murphy, L. J., & Mitchell, D. L. (1998). When writing helps to heal: Email as therapy. *British Journal of Guidance and Counselling, 26,* 21–33. doi:10.1080/03069889808 253835

National Suicide Prevention Lifeline. (n.d.). *Support for suicidal individuals on social and digital media* [PDF file]. Retrieved from https://suicidepreventionlifeline.org/wp-content/uploads/2018/09/lifeline_socialmedia_toolkit.pdf

NICE. (2006). Computerised cognitive behaviour therapy for depression and anxiety. *Technology Appraisal Guidance [TA97].* Retrieved from www.nice.org.uk/Guidance/TA97

Ormrod, J. A., Kennedy, L., Scott, J., & Cavanagh, K. (2010). Computerized cognitive behavioural therapy in an adult mental health service: A pilot study of outcomes and alliance. *Cognitive Behaviour Therapy, 39*(3), 188–192. doi:10.1080/16506071003675614

Patchin, J. W., & Hinduja, S. (2006). Bullies move beyond the schoolyard: A preliminary look at cyberbullying. *Youth Violence Juvenile Justice, 4*(2), 148–169. doi:10.1177/1541204006286288

Perlis, M. L., Grandner, M. A., Chakravorty, S., Bernert, R. A., Brown, G. K., & Thase, M. E. (2016). Suicide and sleep: Is it a bad thing to be awake when reason sleeps? *Sleep Medicine Reviews, 29*, 101–107. doi:10.1016/j.smrv.2015.10.003

Pham, T., & Adesman, A. (2015). Teen victimization: Prevalence and consequences of traditional and cyberbullying. *Current Opinion in Pediatrics, 27*(6), 748–756. doi:10.1097/MOP.0000000000000290

Pigeon, W. R., Pinquart, M., & Conner, K. (2012). Meta-analysis of sleep disturbance and suicidal thoughts and behaviors. *Journal of Clinical Psychiatry, 73*(9), e1160–e1167. doi:10.4088/JCP.11r07586

Pourmand, A., Roberson, J., Caggiula, A., Monsalve, N., Rahimi, M., & Torres-Llenza, V. (2018). Social media and suicide: A review of technology-based epidemiology and risk assessment. *Telemedecine and e-Health.* doi:10.1089/tmj.2018.0203

Predmore, Z., Ramchand, R., Ayer, L., Kotzias, V., Engel, C., Ebener, P., . . . Haas, G. (2017). Expanding suicide crisis services to text and chat: Responders perspective of the differences between communication modalities. *Crisis: The Journal of Crisis Intervention and Suicide Prevention, 38*(4), 255–260. doi:10.1027/0227-5910/a000460

Proudfoot, J., Goldberg, D., Mann, A., Everitt, B., Marks, I., & Gray, J. A. (2003). Computerized, interactive, multimedia cognitive-behavioural program for anxiety and depression in general practice. *Psychological Medicine, 33*(2), 217–227. doi:10.1017/s0033291702007225

Quinn, S., & Oldmeadow, J. A. (2013). Is the *i*Generation a 'we' generation? Social networking use among 9- to 13-year-olds and belonging. *British Journal of Developmental Psychology, 31*(1), 136–142. doi:10.1111/bjdp.12007

Reporting on Suicide. (2015). Retrieved from http://reportingonsuicide.org/onlinemedia/

Ritterband, L. M., Gonder-Frederick, L. A., Cox, D. J., Clifton, A. D., West, R. W., & Borowitz, S. M. (2003). Internet interventions: In review, in use, and into the future. *Professional Psychology: Research and Practice, 34*(5), 527–534. doi:10.1037/0735-7028.34.5.527

Ritterband, L. M., Thorndike, F. P., & Ingersoll, K. S. (2017). Effect of a web-based fognitive behavior therapy for insomnia intervention with 1-year follow-up. *JAMA Psychiatry, 74*(1), 68–75. doi:10.1001/jamapsychiatry.2016.3249

Robinson, J., Hill, N., Thorn, P., Teh, Z., Battersby, R., & Reavley, N. (2018). *#chatsafe: A young person's guide for communicating safely online about suicide.* Melbourne: Orygen, The National Centre of Excellence in Youth Mental Health. Retrieved from www.orygen.org.au/Education-Training/Resources-Training/Resources/Free/Guidelines/chatsafe-A-young-person-s-guide-for-communicatin/ChatsafeUS_guidelines_Orygen

Rudd, M. D. (2006). Fluid vulnerability theory: A cognitive approach to understanding the process of acute and chronic suicide risk. In T. E. Ellis (Ed.), *Cognition and suicide: Theory, research, and therapy* (pp. 355–368). Washington, DC: American Psychological Association.

Ryan, C., & Lewis, J. M. (2017). *Computer and internet use in the United States: 2015.* Retrieved from www.census.gov/content/dam/Census/library/publictions/2017/acs/acs-37.pdf.

The Samaritans. (n.d). *The Samaritans Radar Twitter plug-in was closed permanently in March 2015.* Retrieved June 3, 2019, from www.samaritans.org/about-samaritans/research-policy/internet-suicide/samaritans-radar/

Segal, Z. V., Williams, J. M. G., & Teasdale, J. D. (2002). *Mindfulness-based cognitive therapy for depression: A new approach to preventing relapse.* New York: Guilford Press.

Simblett, S., Greer, B., Matcham, F., Curtis, H., Polhemus, A., Ferrao, J., . . . Wykes, T. (2018). Barriers to and facilitators of engagement with remote measurement technology for managing health: Systematic review and content analysis of findings. *Journal of Medical Internet Research, 20*(7), e10480. doi:10.2196/10480

Stack, S. (2005). Suicide in the media: A quantitative review of studies based on nonfictional stories. *Suicide and Life-Threatening Behavior, 35*(2), 121–133.

Stanley, B., Brown, G. K., Brenner, L. A., Galfalvy, H. C., Currier, G. W., Knox, K. L., . . . Green, K. L. (2018). Comparison of the safety planning intervention with follow-ups vs usual care of suicidal patients treated in the emergency department. *JAMA Psychiatry, 75*(9), 894–900. doi:10.1001/jamapsychiatry.2018.1776

Townsend, E., Hawton, K., Altman, D. G., Arensman, E., Gunnell, D., Gunnell, D., . . . Van Heeringen, K. (2001). The efficacy of problem-solving treatments after deliberate self-harm: Meta-analysis of randomized controlled trials with respect to depression, hopelessness and improvement in problems. *Psychological Medicine, 31*(6), 979–988. doi:10.1017/s0033291701004238

Ueda, M., Mori, K., Matsubayashi, T., & Sawada, Y. (2017). Tweeting celebrity suicides: Users' reaction to prominent suicide deaths on Twitter and subsequent increases in actual suicides. *Social Science & Medicine, 189*, 158–166. doi:10.1016/j.socscimed.2017.06.032

U.S. Department of Health and Human Services (HSS) Substance Abuse and Mental Health Services Administration (SAMHSA). (2015). National Registry for evidence-based programs and practices. *Federal Register, 80*(129), 38716–38718. Retrieved from https://www.federalregister.gov/documents/2015/07/07/2015-16573/national-registry-of-evidence-based-programs-and-practices

U.S. Department of Health and Human Services (HSS) Office of the Surgeon General and National Action Alliance for Suicide Prevention. (2012). *National strategy for suicide prevention: Goals and objectives for action.* Washington, DC: HSS. Retrieved from www.ncbi.nlm.nih.gov/books/NBK109917/

U.S. Department of Veterans Affairs. (n.d.). *Social media safety toolkit* [PDF file]. Retrieved from www.mentalhealth.va.gov/suicide_prevention/docs/OMH-074-Suicide-Prevention-Social-Media-Toolkit-1-8_508.pdf

Van Den Berg, S., Shapiro, D. A., Bickerstaffe, D., & Cavanagh, K. (2004). Computerized cognitive-behaviour therapy for anxiety and depression: A practical solution to the shortage of trained therapists. *Journal of Psychiatric and Mental Health Nursing, 11*(5), 508–513. doi:10.1111/j.1365-2850.2004.00745.x

Van Geel, M., Vedder, P., & Tanilon, J. (2014). Relationship between peer victimization, cyberbullying, and suicide in children and adolescents: A meta-analysis. *JAMA Pediatrics, 168*(5), 435–442. doi:10.1001/jammapediatrics.2013.4143

Van Orden, K. A., Witte, T. K., Cukrowicz, K. C., Braithwaite, S. R., Selby, E. A., & Joiner, T. E. Jr. (2010). The interpersonal theory of suicide. *Psychological Review, 117*(2), 575–600.

Van Spijker, B. A., Van Straten, A., & Kerkhof, A. J. (2014). Effectiveness of online self-help for suicidal thoughts: Results of a randomized controlled trial. *Public Library of Science One, 9*(2), e90118. doi:10.1371/journal.pone.0090118

Wachs, S., Wright, M. F., & Vazsonyi, A. T. (2019). Understanding the overlap between cyberbullying and cyberhate perpetration: Moderating effects of toxic online disinhibition. *Criminal Behavior and Mental Health, 29*(3), 179–188. doi:10.1002/cbm.2116

Wenzel, A., Brown, G. K., & Beck, A. T. (2009). *Cognitive therapy for suicidal patients: Scientific and clinical applications*. Washington, DC: American Psychological Association.

Witt, K., Spittal, M. J., Carter, G., Pirkis, J., Hetrick, S., Currier, D., . . . Milner, A. (2017). Effectiveness of online and mobile telephone applications ('apps') for the self-management of suicidal ideation and self-harm: A systematic review and meta-analysis. *BMC Psychiatry, 17.* doi:10.1186/s12888-017-1458-0

13 Ethical and Legal Issues in the Clinical Use of Technology

Jeffrey E. Barnett

Mental health clinicians regularly use a wide range of technologies in their practices. These technologies may be used for administrative purposes such as for scheduling appointments, billing, filing insurance forms, and sending reports or letters and for clinical purposes, including assessment and treatment. These may include the use of a telephone, fax machine, photocopier, computer, one's website, email, text messaging, smartphone apps, videoconferencing, virtual or augmented reality software and equipment, and social media. As is highlighted in the chapters throughout this book, each of these technologies and their applications bring with them great potential benefits for mental health clinicians and clients alike that include increased practice efficiency and significant expansion of access to assessment and treatment services. But as will be explained and illustrated in this chapter, each of these technologies brings risks with them that must be effectively addressed in order to protect each client's rights and to ensure that all mental health services provided, regardless of the technology used, are consistent with the ideals of the mental health professions, that they effectively meet each client's treatment needs, and that they are provided ethically and legally. Issues to be addressed in this chapter include professional competence, legal issues relevant to practicing across state or national borders, informed consent, confidentiality, boundaries and multiple relationships, and managing crises and emergencies.

Competence

Prior to offering any professional services via the various technologies mentioned, it is essential to first ensure that one possesses the requisite level of competence to offer these services effectively. This competence comprises clinical, technological, and legal competence. Each are important for ensuring that each client's clinical needs are appropriately met. The following case example[1] will be used to illustrate how competence is relevant to telemental health practice.

Case Example

Dr. T.K. Savvy is a licensed mental health clinician who specializes in the treatment of depression and anxiety disorders. Having made the decision not to participate in managed care, she was looking for ways to more broadly market her outpatient psychotherapy practice. She decided to market her practice online and was contacted by numerous individuals who were seeking treatment for a wide range of mental health issues. A significant portion of these individuals lived in other areas of her state as well as in other states. After corresponding with them by email she agreed to provide treatment to them by email for some, and for those who preferred it, by videoconferencing. She presently uses Skype to communicate with family members in other states, so she feels comfortable using this technology. She also knows that many prospective clients are familiar with Skype, so this is easy for them to use. Dr. Savvy is especially excited about the fact that many of these new clients are from diverse cultural and linguistic backgrounds, which will help her to have a more diverse and interesting practice.

Clinical Competence

All the standards that apply to providing in-person professional services apply to providing them online. Thus, if one is not competent to treat a certain type of client or to provide a specific service in-person, the fact that the service is being offered online does not change applicable ethical standards. Regardless of the medium of delivery used, mental health clinicians must possess the necessary knowledge, skills, attitudes, and values as well as the ability to consistently apply them for the benefit of their clients (Haas & Malouf, 2005). Consistent with the other mental health professions' codes of ethics, the American Psychological Association's Ethical Principles of Psychologists and Code of Conduct (APA, 2017) makes it clear that all the ethics code's standards (including those pertaining to competence) apply to all professional services provided, regardless of the communication medium used, including "in person, postal, telephone, Internet, and other electronic transmissions" (p. 1).

To determine if one possesses the requisite competence to offer particular professional services, it is important to ensure familiarity with relevant ethics standards, laws, and practice guidelines. Access to a wide range of standards, guidelines, ethics codes, and resources for best practices in telemental health for all mental health professionals may be found at https://telehealth.org/ethical-statements/. These include important resources for mental health professionals practicing both in the United States and internationally. Clinicians should be familiar with their profession's applicable guidelines when planning to offer online services or to otherwise integrate the use of technology into their clinical practices. While ethics code standards, laws, and regulations set minimal enforceable standards that bring consequences if violated, guidelines are consensus statements developed by professional organizations that establish the profession's recommendations on best practices. These guidelines help set each profession's prevailing professional practice recommendations. While they are not enforceable, they do provide mental health clinicians with valuable information on the knowledge and skills each professional should have in this area of practice and on how they should be applied. For representative examples of practice guidelines for psychologists, including the Guidelines for the Practice of Telepsychology, see www.apa. org/practice/guidelines/index.aspx.

Familiarity with the ethics code of one's profession is also essential, and these standards are enforceable for members of that profession. Ethics standards relevant to the practice of telemental health are most fully developed in Standard H, Distance Counseling, Technology, and Social Media, of the American Counseling Association's Code of Ethics (ACA, 2014). This standard includes sections on knowledge and legal considerations, informed consent and security, client verification, distance counseling relationships, records and web maintenance, and social media. This very comprehensive standard serves as a model for all mental health professionals to follow. Of equal importance is familiarity with the laws in one's practice jurisdiction(s) relevant to professional practice in general and the practice of telemental health in particular.

We should not rely solely on our own determinations when considering if we possess the competence needed to offer particular services. This decision is a complex one and research shows that we tend not to be the best judges of our own level of functioning and performance (e.g., Dunning, Heath, & Suls, 2004: Dunning, Johnson, Ehrlinger, & Kruger, 2003). For example, Dunning and colleagues found that clinicians with the lowest level of clinical competence and the greatest amount of impaired functioning tended to be the ones who assessed their level of competence least accurately. They also found that the greater the impairment in one's functioning, the less effectively we are able to assess it accurately. Relatedly, Walfish, McAlister, O'Donnell, and Lambert (2012) found strong evidence that mental health clinicians frequently are inaccurate in their self-assessments of clinical competence, with 25% of clinicians rating their competence in the ninetieth percentile in comparison to their peers. Further, Eva and colleagues (2004) found that clinicians' self-ratings of competence showed no correlation with external expert ratings of their competence. This finding has also been found with trainees' self-assessments of their developing competence when learning new skills (Gordon, 1991).

In addition to ensuring familiarity with relevant professional guidelines and standards, it is essential that we consult with colleagues who are recognized experts in this new area of practice before providing these services to clients. These expert colleagues can provide us with a more objective assessment of our competence and offer suggestions for any additional education or training we may need (and that we may not be aware that we need) before we provide these services.

Our clinical competence also includes multicultural competence. This means that mental health clinicians must possess the cultural knowledge, skills, and awareness to be able to interact with, assess, and treat diverse clients effectively (Sue et al., 1998). This is in keeping with guidance provided in the codes of ethics of the mental health professions. For example, the Code of Ethics of the National Association of Social Workers (NASW, 2017) lists as one of the profession's core values dignity and worth of the person, including the need to be "mindful of individual differences and cultural and ethnic diversity" (p. 5). The Code of Ethics further specifies how respect for individual differences must be integrated into treatment, assessment, supervision, and training by social workers.

Mental health clinicians should understand how various individual differences may impact how we communicate with clients, with how they exhibit distress or difficulties, and how these individual differences may impact how treatment may most effectively be provided. Such individual differences include "age, culture, disability, ethnicity, race, religion/spirituality, gender, gender identity, sexual orientation, marital/partnership status, language preference, socioeconomic status, immigration status, or any basis proscribed by law" (ACA, 2014, p. 9). These points are of particular salience when considering that online mental health services expand each clinician's reach to possibly provide services to clients around the world. It is important to note that our having the ability to access potential clients online does not mean that we have the needed multicultural competence to do so ethically and effectively. Further, little is known at present about the effectiveness of telemental health for clients from diverse backgrounds internationally, since most studies of telemental health effectiveness to date have been conducted in Western settings in the context of Western health care systems (Varker, Brand, Ward, Terhaag, & Phelps, 2019). It is therefore recommended that clinicians "make a reasonable effort to understand the manner in which cultural, linguistic, socioeconomic and other individual characteristics . . . may impact effective use of telecommunication technologies in service delivery" (American Psychological Association, 2013, p. 794).

Technological Competence

Each mental health clinician should possess the competence necessary to effectively work with the various technologies being utilized to provide professional services (e.g., email, texting, videoconferencing). As Barnett and Kolmes (2016) explain, mental health clinicians need to possess "knowledge about various technology requirements for providing telemental health services to include hardware, software, type of internet connection, privacy safeguards, and security precautions needed to help ensure each client's privacy is protected" (p. 56). We then need to be able to explain each of these to clients and guide clients in their application (e.g., how to download and install needed software). Mental health clinicians also need to remain current with developments in technology and be able to make informed decisions about new products and applications.

Both software and hardware may present technologic challenges at times. Mental health clinicians need to be able to instruct or train clients in the effective use of these technologies and must be prepared to troubleshoot challenges that may arise while treating clients. Internet connections can be lost and interruptions of audio or video may occur. Additionally, clients may need assistance in determining the appropriate settings and making needed adjustments so they will have an optimal connection.

Thus, mental health clinicians should remain current on the recent technology developments relevant to the practice of telemental health through professional reading and attendance at continuing education workshops and other telemental health training programs. While many exist, one representative example is the training, certificate programs, and webinars offered by the Telebehavioral Health Institute (https://telehealth.org/). Several of the training modules focus on the specifics of technologic competence and the practical steps to take to set up and run a telemental health practice.

It also is essential that we possess the necessary competence to be able to determine the most appropriate and effective treatment and technological mode of treatment delivery for each client. Some clients' clinical needs may not effectively be treated across distances or via specific technologic modalities (i.e., email vs. videoconferencing). Mental health clinicians should possess an understanding of the strengths and limitations of each technology and be sure that their use is appropriate, based on each client's clinical presentation and needs (Manhal-Baugus, 2001).

Legal Competence

In addition to being familiar with applicable ethics standards and relevant practice guidelines, mental health professionals who practice telemental health should be knowledgeable about the laws relevant to their practice. While most mental health clinicians are familiar with the laws and regulations applicable to the practice of their profession in their state, those who are practicing across distances may be assessing and treating clients in other states and nations. Knowledge of the laws in these other jurisdictions is essential to ensure one is practicing legally.

Interestingly, Maheu and Gordon (2000) found that only 60% of the mental health clinicians they surveyed who practiced across state lines inquired about each client's state of residence, and 74% were uncertain or incorrect about their state's telehealth laws. Clinicians should inquire about the client's location where they will be receiving telemental health services, and when practicing across state lines, clinicians should be knowledgeable of and follow applicable laws in both jurisdictions (DeMers, Harris, & Baker, 2018). Failure to do so can result in harm to clients and can have adverse consequences for the mental health clinician (Koocher & Mooray, 2000). Consistent with guidance found in the other mental health professions' ethics codes, the Code of Ethics of the American Association for Marriage and Family Therapy (AAMFT, 2015) requires that prior to delivering services "through electronic means," clinicians should "ensure that they are compliant with all relevant laws for the delivery of such services" (Standard 6.1, Technology Assisted Services).

In addition to familiarity with one's licensure law, there are three laws that are essential to be knowledgeable of and to follow: mandatory reporting requirements for the suspicion of child abuse and neglect, mandatory reporting requirements for the suspicion of elder abuse and neglect, and dangerousness/duty to warn and protect requirements.

These laws may vary significantly between jurisdictions. Mental health clinicians should keep in mind that even though they are providing a professional service *from* one practice jurisdiction, for clients in other states, these mental health services are being received *in* another jurisdiction, necessitating that we must follow that state's laws as well. Differences may exist in specific reporting requirements, the age of majority may vary in different states, and just what must be reported can vary. For example, while some states have the legal requirement to report all suspicions of abuse (sexual and physical) of older adults (and how older adults are defined can vary by state), in some jurisdictions these laws are worded to apply to the abuse, neglect, self-neglect, and exploitation of vulnerable adults, with 'vulnerable' being defined in these laws. Knowledge of such details is essential to ensure the protection of clients' rights and the promotion of their welfare.

Similarly, with regard to when clients make a threat to harm an identifiable victim or group of victims, some states have "duty to warn" laws (notify the intended victim), some have "duty to report" laws (notify the police), some have "duty to warn and protect" laws, some allow treatment first and only require other steps if treatment is not effective or possible to prevent the threatened harm from occurring, and some states do not allow breaching confidentiality at all in these situations. Thus, knowledge of these laws for the states in which all clients are located is of great importance. Yet these can be very challenging situations, especially when conflicts exist between the laws in the mental health clinician's state and those in the client's state. Consultation is considered a core competency for mental health clinicians (Rodolfa et al., 2005), and this is one situation where the application of this competency is essential. Consultation with knowledgeable colleagues, including legal professionals, may be of great help in these situations to ensure that we engage in interjurisdictional practice legally and ethically.

The laws relevant to the practice of psychology in each state in the United States and in each province in Canada may be accessed at www.asppb.net/page/BdContactNewPG. Laws relevant to the practice of other mental health professions may be found on the websites of the applicable licensing boards. But while licensing laws vary by profession, the laws in each state on

mandatory reporting requirements and "duty to warn and protect" requirements apply to all licensed health professionals in those states.

Discussion

So, how did Dr. T.K. Savvy do? It is certainly appropriate for her to market
her practice, but she must be sure that she does so ethically and appropriately. For example, the APA Ethics Code (APA, 2017) makes it clear
in Standard 5, Advertising and Public Statements, that we must accurately
represent to the public the professional services we provide. And Standard
2.01, Boundaries of Competence, requires that psychologists only offer and
provide services "within the boundaries of their competence, based on their
education, training, supervised experience, consultation, study, or professional experience" (p. 4). Thus, she should represent her competence to the
public accurately and limit the clients she works with and the specific services she provides to those areas where she has demonstrated competence.

Assessing prospective clients' treatment needs by email is likely to be inadequate for evaluating these individuals and for determining if their needs are
amenable to telemental health interventions. As Barnett and Sheetz (2003)
point out, important auditory and visual cues are missed when communicating by email. We miss out on observations of affect, speech, eye contact,
dress, and grooming, among other important aspects of communication and
clinical presentation. Email can be a very effective means of communicating between sessions to schedule or reschedule appointments and to check
in with clients between in-person sessions, but it has not been found to
be effective as a sole means of providing assessment and treatment services
(Recupero & Rainey, 2005).

Videoconferencing is superior to email for providing clinical services to
clients, but even here, Dr. Savvy's competence is suspect. While Skype may
be convenient and familiar to her from her use of it in her personal life, it
is important to know that Skype is not compliant with the requirements of
the Health Insurance Portability and Accountability Act (HIPAA), and only
HIPAA-compliant videoconferencing platforms should be used. This helps
ensure that minimally acceptable protections are in place to limit threats to
clients' privacy and prevent unauthorized access to confidential communications with clients when using these technologies. The HIPAA Privacy Rule
(U.S. Department of Health and Human Services, 2002) mandates certain
actions on the mental health clinician's part to protect each client's privacy
when transmitting protected health information electronically. However,
when state laws are more protective of clients' privacy, they preempt HIPAA
(Knapp, VandeCreek, & Fingerhut, 2017). Actions to protect clients' privacy include the encryption of electronic communications and only using
electronic communication goods and services (e.g., videoconferencing software, billing software) that are certified as being HIPAA-compliant. This
is done by requesting and receiving a written business services agreement

from the vendor that verifies its compliance with HIPAA to protect each client's privacy from unauthorized breaches and releases. Our competence thus includes knowledge of legal and ethics requirements, including those relevant to protecting each client's privacy and developing the technological competence needed to effectively use appropriate technologies.

With regard to treating many new clients from diverse cultural and linguistic backgrounds as a means of helping her to have a more diverse and interesting practice, Dr. Savvy's motivations may be misguided. Her decisions should be motivated by her clients' best interests and she should only practice telemental health when she possesses the needed competence to do so (including multicultural competence) and when it is in these clients' best interests. Consistent with the other mental health professions' codes of ethics, the Code of Ethics of the National Association of Social Workers (NASW, 2017) states in Standard 1.05, Cultural Awareness and Social Diversity: "Social workers who provide electronic social work services should be aware of cultural and socioeconomic differences among clients and how they may use electronic technology" (p. 9).

It would be helpful for Dr. Savvy to conduct assessments of each prospective client's clinical needs before deciding to treat them, and this assessment should include a thoughtful consideration of individual differences. As the NASW Code of Ethics (NASW, 2017) further states in Standard 1.05, "Social workers should assess cultural, environmental, economic, mental or physical ability, linguistic, and other issues that may affect the delivery or use of these services" (p. 9).

When the results of this deliberative process are unclear, we should consult with knowledgeable colleagues to determine the appropriateness of treating specific clients from diverse backgrounds. We should also seek input on any additional education and training we might need in order to competently work with these diverse clients. It appears that Dr. Savvy overlooked this important step, and the risks to her and to her clients may be substantial.

Informed Consent

The process of informed consent involves sharing with each prospective client adequate information about the professional services being offered so they may make an informed decision about participation. In essence, it is important that clients have realistic expectations about what to expect from the clinician and from the professional services being offered. Any factors that might reasonably be expected to impact a client's decision to participate should be discussed with the client.

Case Example

Mr. Kahn Cent is a licensed mental health clinician who regularly integrates various technologies into his clinical practice. He uses a standard informed consent procedure with all his clients, regardless of the technologic medium used. When asked about his informed consent practices, he states that he doesn't want to intimidate clients or overload them with needless information, so he keeps the information shared to a minimum. He describes informed consent as a process of discovery in which he and his clients address his policies as issues arise during the course of treatment. Yet he is repeatedly surprised when clients are upset that he doesn't respond to their late-night emails, and he ignores their friend requests via social media.

Informed Consent Goals and Elements

It is recommended that mental health clinicians follow informed consent practices that are articulated in their "profession's" ethics code and in their licensure law and accompanying regulations. As Knapp et al. (2017) state, the issues addressed in the informed consent process should address what a reasonable person would want to know "to prevent future misunderstandings and disappointments" and to help ensure "a shared set of expectations for their professional relationship" (p. 84). This information should be shared at the outset of the professional relationship so that clients have the opportunity to make decisions about participation prior to the professional services being offered.

Ethics codes, licensing laws, and regulations specify minimal requirements for informed consent. Beyond these minimal expectations, Barnett (2015) recommends addressing the following issues in every client's informed consent agreement:

- The nature and anticipated course of the proposed evaluation or treatment.
- The psychotherapist's credentials and relevant professional experience.
- The client's right to refuse or withdraw without penalty, emphasizing the voluntary nature of participation.
- Reasonably available treatment options and alternatives, and their relative risks and benefits, including no treatment at all.
- Fees and financial arrangements, including billing, payment, and the role, if any, of insurance.
- Confidentiality and its limits, including all applicable mandatory reporting requirements.
- The involvement of any third parties. (para. 12)
- And emergency contact information and procedures.

Informed Consent and Telemental Health

In addition to the basics just described, several modifications to the informed consent procedure will need to be made when engaging in the practice of telemental health. When meetings with clients occur virtually and not in person, it can be much more difficult to ensure the client's understanding of the information being shared (Reamer, 2017). Special care should be taken to confirm each client's understanding and acceptance of the information presented. With regard to information shared with clients, careful attention should be given to confidentiality issues, including risks to confidentiality associated with each technology being used, actions to be taken to reduce these risks and the client's role in these actions (e.g., the use of encryption to protect email communications), and how client information will be stored and any risks associated with these methods (Adams, Larsen, & Juntunen, 2018). Information on the technology to be used, any hardware and software requirements, and any training needed should all be discussed as well (Barnett & Kolmes, 2016).

The specific technologies to be used in the provision of professional services should be reviewed, including information on how to effectively use them and procedures to follow if communications are interrupted at any time during treatment. Client expectations for communication outside of regularly scheduled treatment sessions should also be addressed. Clients may assume that it is acceptable to ask clinical questions via text messaging or email, often expecting an immediate or very timely response. Clinicians should clarify for clients their policies regarding such communications and ensure that clients understand the types of information that may be communicated online (e.g., administrative vs. clinical), that clients have realistic expectations about clinician responsiveness and about any fees charged for the time spent responding to these communications.

Consistent with the information shared in chapter 6, clinicians should anticipate that some clients will seek to engage with their mental health clinician via social media. Clients may send friend requests and seek to expand the professional relationship into a more personal one. It is strongly recommended that such issues be anticipated and that each mental health clinician develop an electronic communications and social media policy that is included in each client's informed consent process. Psychologist Keely Kolmes has a model policy available on her website that can be downloaded and modified for use by mental health clinicians (http://drkkolmes.com/social-media-policy).

Discussion

Clearly, Mr. Kahn Cent needs intensive training about the informed consent process in general and as it applies to telemental health in particular. Unfortunately, his situation appears not to be atypical. Maheu and Gordon (2000) found that only 48% of the mental health clinicians they surveyed utilized a formal informed consent process prior to providing telemental health services. For those who do use a formal informed consent process, using one's "standard" informed consent agreement with telemental health clients is risky and likely to result in difficulties that could have been prevented if the informed consent was modified to include discussion of, and agreement on, the additional issues relevant to telemental health practice. Providing clients with minimal information and then responding to the resulting difficulties as they arise violates the goals of informed consent and robs clients of the ability to make informed decisions about participating in treatment. In fact, there are issues that regularly arise during the course of telemental health practice that can easily be anticipated and discussed with clients in advance. These include how to manage technology interruptions, clinician availability and responsiveness for electronic communications in between regularly scheduled sessions, and the clinician's policy on social media interactions with clients. By sharing with clients one's electronic communications and social media policy, a number of difficulties can be avoided and potential violations of the client's trust and harm to the treatment alliance can be greatly minimized.

Confidentiality

As has been highlighted in the discussions of competence and informed consent, confidentiality is a central issue for mental health clinicians in their work with clients. Confidentiality is addressed in each of the mental health professions' ethics codes. For example, the ethics code for Psychiatrists states in Section 4 that psychiatrists "shall safeguard patient confidences and privacy within the constraints of the law (American Psychiatric Association, 2013, p. 2).

Case Example

Ms. Ima Pro is a licensed mental health clinician with an extensive online practice. She regularly communicates with clients via text messaging and email. She uses Skype for videoconferencing sessions and she never inquires about where clients are located when participating in these online treatment sessions. Ms. Pro regularly uses her cell phone to conduct these sessions so she can be available to her clients when out of her office. To ensure that she doesn't forget her passwords, she uses the same simple easy-to-remember password for all her devices.

Confidentiality and Telemental Health

Mental health clinicians should take all reasonably available precautions to ensure that each client's confidentiality is protected. As the ethics code for psychologists states, "Psychologists have a primary obligation and take reasonable precautions to protect confidential information obtained through or stored in any medium" (APA, 2017, p. 7). These precautions should include downloading and regularly updating virus, malware, and firewall protection on all devices. The hard drives of all devices can be encrypted, and remote disabling software can be downloaded so that if a device is lost or stolen, its contents can be wiped from the hard drive. It is essential that clinicians use strong passwords for each of their devices. Interestingly, the widely followed advice of the past 14 years to have passwords be of at least eight random characters that include upper case and lower case letters, numerals, and symbols has been changed by its originator, Bill Burr, in response to developments in hacking technology (McMillan, 2017). We are now advised to have passwords comprised of an easy to remember sequence that has meaning to you. As Burr states, the password of Tr0ub4bor&3 can now be cracked in about three days while the password correcthorsebatterystaple would take 550 years to crack using current hacking technology (McMillan, 2017).

In addition to the use of appropriate passwords, two-factor authentication is recommended (Rousmaniere & Kuhn, 2016). Such authentication involves downloading software to your device that will send you a text message each time you attempt to log in that includes a single use code that you will then input to access your device. This provides a second layer of security to ensure that all confidential information is protected. It is also important to log off all devices when they are not in use and even when taking a short break from using them. Doing this also will help prevent unauthorized access. These recommendations are consistent with the guidance provided in the codes of ethics of each of the mental health professions. For example, the code of ethics for Social Workers (NASW, 2017) states, "Social workers should take reasonable steps to protect the confidentiality of electronic communications, including information provided to clients or third parties. Social workers should use applicable safeguards (such as encryption, firewalls, and passwords)" with all electronic devices used to communicate with clients (p. 13).

Another important recommendation for mental health clinicians and their clients alike, is to only communicate confidential information using password-protected Wi-Fi networks. Free Wi-Fi such as typically found at libraries, coffee shops, and restaurants is not secure. All electronic communications on these networks can easily be intercepted by others. As highlighted by Higgs (2013), anyone using free Wi-Fi should assume that all information they share online, including credit card information and other personal data, will be intercepted and used by hackers and identity thieves. This guidance is especially important when considering that approximately 87% of the public uses free Wi-Fi and that of these individuals, up to 22% are accessing banking and other financial data, and 13% are sharing personal data and identifying information through these unsecured networks (Schlesinger, 2016). One may use a Virtual Private Network (VPN) which will encrypt electronic communications, but clients should understand that communicating with a mental health clinician in one of these public settings (even if they have a portable password-protected Wi-Fi connection or VPN) leaves them open to eavesdropping or the reading of written communications by others nearby. During the informed consent process, clients should be informed of these threats to their confidentiality, and clinicians should recommend that clients only communicate from a secure and private setting. This is consistent with the guidance that "[p]sychologists who offer services, products, or information via electronic transmission inform clients/patients of the risks to privacy and limits of confidentiality" (APA, 2017, p. 7).

Electronically stored records must be protected as well. In addition to the security precautions already addressed, such protection can include the use of an external storage device or storing records "in the cloud." This advice is consistent with the guidance provided to Marriage and Family Therapists (AAMFT, 2015), that they "store, safeguard, and dispose of client records in ways that maintain confidentiality and in accord with applicable laws and professional standards" (Standard 2: Confidentiality).

Discussion

Ms. Ima Pro is not practicing in ways that will ensure protection of her clients' confidentiality. She needs to only use HIPAA-compliant videoconferencing software and she should discuss with each client the potential impact of using unsecured Wi-Fi networks and participating in videoconferencing sessions in public settings. Communicating with clients via email and text messaging may be a great convenience for administrative communications, but these methods bring great risks to confidentiality. Text messaging should not be used for clinical communications, with the exception of encrypted text messaging systems developed for use by health care systems, and email should only be used for this purpose when encryption software is utilized by both clinician and client. The use of one's personal cell phone for telemental health services should only occur with appropriate password protection; updated virus, malware, and firewall protection; and remote disabling capabilities. Ms. Pro is needlessly placing her clients' privacy at risk She should address each of the issues mentioned before providing additional telemental health services.

Boundaries in Telemental Health

Boundaries are the ground rules of the professional relationship and help differentiate it from other types of relationships such as personal ones (Smith & Fitzpatrick, 1995). The maintenance of appropriate boundaries can be challenging at times, but is important for promoting a positive therapeutic experience for clients and for preventing harm to them.

Case Example

Ms. Fren Lee is a licensed mental health clinician who is new to the provision of online mental health services. She regularly sends and responds to text messages and emails between regularly scheduled appointments. Being one who regularly uses these online communication media in her personal life and having great facility with them, she frequently uses common abbreviations and emoticons to communicate with clients. She also drops the typical salutations or greetings typically used to be able to communicate more quickly and easily. Being a night owl, she often sends clients these messages late at night to check in with them.

Boundaries in the Online Environment

As is stated in the Code of Ethics for Psychiatrists (American Psychiatric Association, 2013), "The psychiatrist shall be ever vigilant about the impact that his or her conduct has upon the boundaries of the doctor-patient relationship, and thus upon the well-being of the patient" (p. 3). It is vital that mental health clinicians consider how their online presence might impact the clinician–client relationship. A distinction should be made between how one uses electronic forms of communication in one's personal life and how these are used professionally. Setting and maintaining a professional tone to these interactions is important. Further, the boundaries the clinician sets help establish reasonable expectations for the relationship on the client's part.

The establishment and maintenance of appropriate professional boundaries is a requirement stated in each of the mental health professions' codes of ethics. For example, the ACA Code of Ethics (ACA, 2014) states:

> Counselors understand the necessity of maintaining a professional relationship with their clients. Counselors discuss and establish professional boundaries with clients regarding the appropriate use and/or application of technology and the limitations of its use within the counseling relationship (e.g., lack of confidentiality, times when not appropriate to use).
>
> (p. 18)

Discussion

Ms. Lee appears to have applied the boundaries she uses in her personal life to her interactions with clients in her professional role. Mental health clinicians model appropriate boundaries for clients. A marked loosening of boundaries can result in the professional relationship being jeopardized with the possibility of harm to the treatment relationship and to the client. Clients may misinterpret the clinician's intentions and may feel encouraged to pursue a more personal relationship with the clinician. It is important that a professional tone be established and maintained in all communications and interactions with clients to ensure that each client's best interests are served.

Managing Crises and Emergencies

Mental health clinicians who provide clinical services across distances may be unfamiliar with resources in the client's local community. During times of crisis or emergency for a client, clinicians may be ill-equipped to quickly and appropriately respond to their client's emergent treatment needs.

Case Example

Dr. Shaq N. Awe is a licensed mental health clinician who treats clients in other states across the nation. When clients are doing well, the provision of telemental health services across great distances seems to go well. But when clients experience an emergency or crisis, Dr. Awe finds herself needing to do research about the resources in the client's local area. One client experiencing a significant substance abuse disorder needed inpatient treatment but experienced a significant delay while Dr. Awe did research to find a suitable treatment program in the client's local area. The client's condition worsened during this period of delay, and the client was very unhappy with Dr. Awe's inability to find an appropriate treatment placement within a reasonable time period. Dr. Awe is quite distressed over this but feels she did all she could do under the circumstances.

Preparing for Crises and Emergencies Across Distances

It is each telemental health clinician's responsibility to be knowledgeable of resources in each client's local community, regardless of where that community is located (Barnett & Kolmes, 2016). Such resources may include inpatient psychiatric facilities, substance abuse treatment programs, primary care physicians, and psychiatrists. The research one must do to learn about these resources should occur at the beginning of the treatment relationship, not when a crisis arises. When a client is in crisis, it may be a very emotionally charged experience for both client and clinician. Further, in emergency situations there may be great urgency for accessing needed services, and a failure to do so can have devastating consequences.

It is also important that mental health clinicians make clear to clients how they may contact them, or some other on-call colleague, should difficulties arise between regularly scheduled appointments. These arrangements should include a discussion of what types of issues and difficulties should trigger the client contacting the clinician, the means of contact to be used, and how the client can access local resources and support when issues fall outside of the clinician's ability to meet the client's emergency needs.

Clinicians also need to make advance arrangements for coverage during periods of absence or inaccessibility. Failure to do so can leave clinicians open to charges of client abandonment and may result in harm to clients. As stated in the ethics code for Psychologists (APA, 2017), "[P]sychologists make reasonable efforts to plan for facilitating services in the event that psychological services are interrupted by factors such as the psychologist's illness, death, unavailability." (p. 7).

Discussion

Dr. Shaq N. Awe should not have been shocked when a client's condition worsened while she took an extended amount of time looking for appropriate inpatient treatment resources in the client's local community. This should have been researched at the beginning of the treatment relationship so that she could have responded in a timely manner if the need for services in the client's local area arose. It is quite reasonable to assume that at times, mental health clients will experience crises and need more intensive treatment services. Thus, Dr. Awe did not do all she could, and she did not live up to her professional obligations to her client.

Summary and Recommendations

This chapter has reviewed a range of ethics and legal issues of importance for mental health clinicians who practice telemental health. The goal of this chapter is not to dissuade clinicians from telemental health practice but rather to help promote its ethical, legal, and clinically effective practice. It is recommended that all mental health clinicians who provide professional services via any electronic means give careful attention to clinical and technologic competence, informed consent, confidentiality, legal requirements associated with interjurisdictional practice, boundaries, and preparing for crises and emergency situations across distances. Careful attention to each of these issues should help mental health clinicians to provide much-needed telemental health services to clients in a manner that best meets their needs.

Note

1 The case examples provided in this chapter have been created by the author and do not reflect individuals known to him.

References

Adams Larsen, M., & Juntunen, C. (2018). Informed consent. In L. F. Campbell, F. Millán, & J. N. Martin (Eds.), *A telepsychology casebook: Using technology ethically, and effectively in your professional practice* (pp. 47–67). Washington, DC: American Psychological Association.

American Association for Marriage and Family Therapy. (2015). *AAMFT code of ethics.* Retrieved from www.aamft.org/Legal_Ethics/Code_of_Ethics.aspx

American Counseling Association. (2014). *2014 ACA code of ethics.* Retrieved from www.counseling.org/resources/aca-code-of-ethics.pdf

American Psychiatric Association. (2013). *The principles of medical ethics with annotations especially applicable to psychiatry.* Arlington, VA: American Psychiatric Association. Retrieved from www.psychiatry.org/psychiatrists/practice/ethics

American Psychological Association. (2013). Guidelines for the practice of telepsychology. *American Psychologist, 68*(9), 791–800. Retrieved from www.apa.org/practice/guidelines/telepsychology.aspx

American Psychological Association. (2017). *Ethical principles of psychologists and code of conduct.* Retrieved from www.apa.org/ethics

Barnett, J. E. (2015, March). *Informed consent in clinical practice: The basics and beyond.* [Web article]. Retrieved from www.societyforpsychotherapy.org/informed-consent-in-clinical-practice-the-basics-and-beyond

Barnett, J. E., & Kolmes, K. (2016). The practice of tele-mental health: Ethical, legal, and clinical issues. *Practice Innovations, 1*(1), 53–66.

Barnett, J. E., & Sheetz, K. (2003). Technological advances and telehealth: Ethics, law, and the practice of psychotherapy. *Psychotherapy: Theory, Research, Practice, Training, 40*(1/2), 86–93.

DeMers, S. T., Harris, E. A, & Baker, D. C. (2018). Interjurisdictional practice. In L. F. Campbell, F. Millán, & J. N. Martin (Eds.), *A telepsychology casebook: Using technology ethically, and effectively in your professional practice* (pp. 141–164). Washington, DC: American Psychological Association.

Dunning, D., Heath, C., & Suls, J. M. (2004). Flawed self-assessment: Implications for health, education, and the workplace. *Psychological Science in the Public Interest, 5,* 69–106.

Dunning, D., Johnson, K., Ehrlinger, J., & Kruger, J. (2003). Why people fail to recognize their own incompetence. *Current Directions in Psychological Science, 12,* 83–87.

Eva, K. W., Cunnington, J. P. W., Reiter, H. I., Keane, D. R., & Norman, G. R. (2004). How can I know what I don't know? Poor self assessment in a well-defined domain. *Advances in Health Sciences Education, 9,* 211–224.

Gordon, M. J. (1991). A review of the validity and accuracy of self-assessments in health professions training. *Academic Medicine, 66,* 762–769.

Haas, L. J., & Malouf, J. L. (2005). *Keeping up the good work: A practitioner's guide to mental health ethics* (4th ed.). Sarasota, FL: Professional Resource Press.

Higgs, L. (2013, July 1). *Free Wi-Fi? Beware of security risks.* Asbury (N.J.) Press. Retrieved from www.usatoday.com/story/tech/2013/07/01/free-wi-fi-risks/2480167/

Knapp, S. J., VandeCreek, L. D., & Fingerhut, R. (2017). *Practical ethics for psychologists: A positive approach* (3rd ed.). Washington, DC: American Psychological Association.

Koocher, G. P., & Mooray, E. (2000). Regulation of telepsychology: A survey of states attorney general. *Professional Psychology: Research and Practice, 31*(5), 503–508.

Maheu, M. M., & Gordon, B. L. (2000). Counseling and therapy on the Internet. *Professional Psychology: Research and Practice, 31,* 484–489.

Manhal-Baugus, M. (2001). E-therapy: Practical, ethical, and legal issues. *Cyberpsychology & Behavior, 4,* 551–563.

McMillan, R. (2017, August 7). The man who wrote those password rules has a new tip: N3v$r M1-d! *The Wall Street Journal.* Retrieved from www.wsj.com/articles/the-man-who-wrote-those-password-rules-has-a-new-tip-n3v-r-m1-d-1502124118

National Association of Social Workers. (2017). *Code of ethics of the national association of social workers.* Retrieved from www.socialworkers.org/About/Ethics/Code-of-Ethics/Code-of-Ethics-English

Reamer, F. G. (2017). Evolving ethical standard in the digital age. *Australian Social Work,* *70*(2), 148–159.

Recupero, P. R., & Rainey, S. E. (2005). Informed consent to e-therapy. *American Journal of Psychotherapy, 59*(4), 319–331.

Rodolfa, E., Bent, R., Eisman, E., Nelson, P., Rehm, L., & Ritchie, P. (2005). A cube model for competency development: Implications for psychology educators and regulators. *Professional Psychology: Research and Practice, 36,* 347–354.

Rousmaniere, T., & Kuhn, N. (2016). Internet security for clinical supervisors. In T. Rousmaniere & E. Renfro-Michel (Eds.), *Using technology to enhance clinical supervision* (pp. 103–113). Alexandria, VA: American Counseling Association.

Schlesinger, J. (2016, June 28). Most people unaware of the risks of using public Wi-Fi. *CNBC.* Retrieved from www.cnbc.com/2016/06/28/most-people-unaware-of-the-risks-of-using-public-wi-fi.html

Smith, D., & Fitzpatrick, M. (1995). Patient-therapist boundary issues: An integrative review of theory and research. *Professional Psychology: Research and Practice, 26*(5), 499–506.

Sue, D. W., Carter, R. T., Casas, J. M., Fouad, N. A., Ivey, A. E., Jensen, M., . . . Vazquez-Nutall, E. (1998). *Multicultural counseling competencies: Individual and organizational development.* Thousand Oaks, CA: Sage.

U.S. Department of Health and Human Services. (2002). *Health insurance portability and accountability act privacy rule.* Retrieved from www.hhs.gov/hipaa/for-professionals/privacy/index.html

Varker, T., Brand, R. M., Ward, J., Terhaag, S., & Phelps, A. (2019). Efficacy of synchronous telepsychology interventions for people with anxiety, depression, posttraumatic stress disorder, and adjustment disorder: A rapid evidence assessment. *Psychological Services, 16*(4), 621–635.

Walfish, S., McAlister, B., O'Donnell, P., & Lambert, M. J. (2012). An investigation of self-assessment bias in mental health providers. *Psychological Reports, 110*(2), 639–644.

14 Improving Mental Health Outcomes With Artificial Intelligence

David D. Luxton

Introduction

Artificial intelligence (AI) is the simulation of intelligent behavior in machines. AI and other technological advancements, such as in wireless technology, cloud computing, sensors, and microprocessors, are together transforming the ways that mental health care is provided. Intelligent mobile and wearable devices, for example, can collect and analyze health-related data in real time and also provide users with information to assess and monitor progress toward personalized treatment goals. Chatbots and virtual humans that interact with people are available to assist and coach care-seekers. Smart homes and robots are advancing rehabilitation psychology by assisting people with everyday functioning and rehabilitation goals. Furthermore, AI-supported clinical decision support tools provide clinicians with computerized alerts and diagnostic information to help them make decisions about diagnoses and treatments for their patients.

While AI and associated technologies are playing an important role in helping people to improve their mental and physical well-being, they also bring with them new requirements and considerations that health care professionals should know about. These considerations include emerging ethical and practical issues, such as ensuring patient safety when using automated systems, reducing bias in design and application of behavioral health technologies, and addressing liability concerns.

This chapter provides an overview of the application of AI in behavioral and mental health care and how AI can improve outcomes. First, the chapter presents an overview of AI applications and their benefits. Then it offers a look at the need-to-know ethics considerations associated with AI and related technologies. All of the technologies covered in this chapter presently exist and have been tested in practical situations to some extent. Many of these innovations are rapidly developing, however, and their novelty may limit use in some applications and settings. Thus, further review of the referenced literature is recommended.

AI Applications in Mental Health Care

AI-Assisted Clinical Decision-Making Tools

An *expert system* is a form of AI program that simulates the knowledge and analytical skills of human experts (Bennett & Doub, 2016). *Clinical Decision Support Systems* (CDSS) are a subtype of an expert system that is designed to aid in the process of clinical decision making (Finlay, 1994). While traditional CDSSs relied on preprogrammed data and rules to provide decision options, modern ones are making use of AI and machine learning to advance capabilities.

Machine learning (ML) is a subtype of AI that involves giving machines the ability to learn without being explicitly programmed (Samuel, 2000). Machine learning is used to learn knowledge from data and then apply this knowledge to provide predictions about future data (Luxton, 2015; Mitchell, 1997). Supervised ML is when the program is "trained" on a predefined set of "training examples" or "training sets." Unsupervised ML is when the program is provided with data but must discover patterns and relationships in that data.

Machine learning methods allow CDSSs to provide recommendations without preprogrammed *a priori* knowledge. For example, ML software can be used to detect patterns in large electronic health record datasets by identifying subsets of data records and characteristics that are abnormal or that reveal factors associated with patient outcomes (Neill, 2012; McFowland, Speakman, & Neill, 2013). For example, ML can be used to predict early-stage mental illness using clinical, neurophysiological, and MRI data (Koutsouleris et al., 2018) or predict treatment outcomes for persons with schizophrenia (Cao et al., 2018). *Neural networks*, a type of ML that simulates the learning function of neurons in the brain, is also used in modern CDSSs to improve clinical decision making, such as by predicting treatment outcomes for persons with obsessive compulsive disorder (Salomoni et al., 2009).

IBM's Watson is an example of a commercially available CDSS that employs AI. The purpose of Watson is to assist and improve the decision making of health care professionals by providing them with greater confidence in their diagnostic and treatment decisions for their patients (IBM, 2014). IBM's Watson is as example of *augmented intelligence*, whereby normal human intelligence is improved by machines (Luxton, 2019). IBM Watson Health™ presently offers commercialized applications of the Watson system for genomics, health care management, drug discovery, and oncology (IBM, 2018).

Watson makes use of several AI approaches, including natural language processing, information retrieval, semantic analysis, automated reasoning, and ML. Watson software uses what IBM calls *DeepQA* (*QA* stands for question and answering). First, enormous amounts of unstructured and semi-structured data from sources such as electronic health records, the clinical literature (i.e., journal articles), and test results (e.g., pathology reports) are entered into the Watson system's massive database. A health care provider then poses a query to the system that describes the symptoms of their patient and other pertinent characteristics. Watson analyzes the input to identify the most relevant parts of information and then mines a patient's data to find facts about the patient's clinical and genetic history. The system then inspects the available data in order to form hypotheses that it will output as a list of recommendations, such as a patient's suitability for particular treatments. The system uses several statistical scoring methods and algorithms to make its confidence-scored recommendations. The system can then describe the supporting evidence in text form for each of its ranked responses (Ferrucci, Brown, Chu-Carroll et al., 2010). Because the Watson system is constantly exposed to new inputted data, the system can learn over time to improve its recommendations.

By speeding up decision-making processes, AI-enabled clinical decision support systems, like Watson, can reduce demands on clinical staff time and thereby improve the overall efficiency of medical care. Computational modeling and simulation techniques can be used to help complex health care systems to become more efficient and focused on patient-centered care.

Intelligent Mobile and Wearable Devices

One of the most significant technological innovations in health care over the last decade is intelligent mobile health (mHealth) technology (Luxton, McCann, Bush, Mishkind, & Reger, 2011; Martínez-Pérez, de la Torre-Díez, & López-Coronado, 2013; Ventola, 2014). The most pervasive mHealth technologies are commercially available smartphones and tablet computers, as well as consumer wearable devices (e.g., smartwatches) from companies such as Apple, Fitbit, Jawbone, or Nike. *Mobile apps* refers to the software applications that run on mobile devices.

Mobile devices make an ideal platform for collecting health-relevant data. For example, they can be used to collect physiological information (e.g., heart rate), behavioral (body movement), environmental (e.g., such as time of day), biological, self-reported assessments, and contextual data, such as a person's physical location (Luxton, June, Sano, & Bickmore, 2015; Patel, Park, Bonato, Chan, & Rodgers, 2012; Piwek, Ellis, Andrews, & Joinson, 2016). Mobile devices can thus increase the amount of data that is made available to users, providing them with more individualized information to assess health and monitor progress (Luxton, June, Sano, et al., 2015). Wearable devices also provide the benefit of being in physical contact with users for extended periods of time, and they do not require the user to manually interact with a keyboard or touch screen while wearing them (Luxton, June, Sano, et al., 2015).

Examples of the use of mobile devices for passive sensing and predictive analytics include optimizing sleep (Ong & Gillespie, 2016) and for the monitoring of depression symptoms (Cornet & Holden, 2018). In the area of suicide prevention, the automated analysis of data, and in real time, can potentially detect worsening of symptoms or perhaps suicide risk, and the system could automatically alert health care providers and/or the user to use their safety plan and coping skills (Luxton, June, & Chalker, 2015). The Durkheim Project (Poulin, Thompson, & Bryan, 2016), for example, tested the collection of data from several sources, including smartphone and social media use to estimate suicide-risk among U.S. military veterans. Machine learning was used to analyze text data collected from these sources and monitor the content and behavioral patterns associated with suicidal behavior to identify persons at heightened risk.

Mobile devices also give health care providers point-of-care tools that can improve the efficiency of services. For example, a health care provider can access electronic health records at bedside or other information, such as from CDSSs, which assists them in making treatment decisions.

One of the ways that AI is advancing the capabilities of mobile and wearable devices is through how data is collected, processed, and analyzed. Machine learning allows mobile devices to learn the patterns of patients, adapt to their preferences, and customize information and content that's made available to them. AI also facilitates collecting and managing medical and other patient data and reduces the need for repetitive manual activities, such as data entry for patient's tests and reports. AI-assisted mobile devices also help patients to monitor their own progress toward health goals and also can provide more efficient scheduling of health care visits (Luxton, June, Sano, et al., 2015).

Chatbots and Intelligent Virtual Agents

A *chatbot* is a computer program that is designed to emulate conversation with human users, typically through a text dialogue. The first example of simulated therapist chatbot was the ELIZA program, which was created by Joseph Weizenbaum in the late 1960s (Weizenbaum, 1976). Eliza used a simple programming language and language syntax to convey responses based on a programmed model of script. The "DOCTOR" script imitated the empathic conversational style of psychologist Carl Rogers (Rogers, 1951). Users would type a question or answer to a question on a keyboard and the program would rephrase the statements into new, preprogrammed questions or statements in order to mimic conversation. Dozens of ELIZA simulations can presently be accessed on the internet.

Examples of modern, commercially available chatbots that provide mental health coaching are Woebot (https://woebot.io/) and Wysa (www.wysa.io/). Woebot, for example, is a chatbot app that's accessible on mobile devices. The app employs principles of cognitive-behavioral therapy (CBT) and Dialectical Behavioral Therapy (DBT) to coach users, through self-care and mindfulness techniques, to help improve symptoms of anxiety and depression. Woebot also tracks user's mood ratings over time and provides it as feedback to users so that they can monitor their progress.

An *intelligent virtual agent* (IVA) is a computer-generated, animated, artificial intelligent virtual character that's designed to take on the visual appearance of humans, animals, or any other form (Hudlicka, 2015; Prendinger & Ishizuka, 2004). Their design can range from cartoonlike characters to highly detailed and lifelike three-dimensional simulations. IVAs have been developed for use on personal computers and on mobile phones and tablet computers (Luxton, 2015). They can also be used on the displays of robots to make them interactive and personable (Luxton & Riek, 2019). Speech recognition and natural language processing can allow the IVA to converse with the user through basic text interface or through verbal conversation. *Natural language processing* (NLP) is the ability for computers to process human written or spoken language (Manning & Schütze, 1999). IVAs can also be built with stores of information, or a *knowledge-engine*, that it uses in conversation to allow it to recognize and reason with new information.

IVAs can be designed to make use of affective computing techniques to recognize and express human emotions through analysis of natural language and through sensors that detect nonverbal information such as eye gaze and facial expressions (Hudlicka et al., 2008; Hudlicka, 2015; Luxton, 2014a). IVAs can also be engineered to explicitly model emotions, thereby allowing them to respond to social cues and user goals. This capability gives these systems what is called emotional and social intelligence (Hudlicka, 2015). This facilitates the creation and maintenance of relationships with human users, as well as the ability to adapt to the changing states and needs of the user in real time. IVAs with this ability are sometimes called *relational agents*.

IVAs, such as virtual humans, provide many potential benefits, including the capability to provide clinical care and coaching tasks (Luxton, 2015). For example, Bickmore and colleagues (2010) developed and tested a virtual nurse for use in hospital discharge planning and found that patients preferred to receive the discharge planning from the simulations because they spent more time with the patient and never seemed to be rushed by other demands. Other studies have provided data suggesting that IVAs can make users feel more understood while also reducing social anxiety (Bailenson & Yee, 2005; Gratch, Wang, Gerten, Fast, & Duffy, 2007; Kandalaft, Didehbani, Krawczyk, Allen, & Chapman, 2013; Lucas, Gratch, King, & Morency, 2014). IVAs have the potential to provide a more interactive and engaging experience for providing patients with information than, for example, an informational website or video. IVAs also have the potential to extend the benefits of telehealth services by providing some types of services to care seekers in remote geographical areas and provide access to specialty care services that may not be available in the patient's locale (Luxton, 2014b).

IVAs have also been developed to emulate patients for training purposes (Talbot, Sagae, John, & Rizzo, 2012). They can be designed to simulate various psychiatric conditions or personal situations in order to allow trainees to practice their interview skills and to gain experience in a controlled environment. More than a decade ago, The Institute for Creative Technologies (ICT) at the University of Southern California pioneered this application by designing lifelike virtual military personnel with depression and suicidal thoughts to teach military clinicians and others how to recognize the risk for suicide (Kenny, Parsons, & Rizzo, 2009). Virtual patient simulations used for instruction have been shown to be associated with better learning outcomes when compared to conventional educational methods without the use of simulations (Hirumi et al., 2016).

One of the potential advantages of IVAs who "stand in" for human care providers, coaches, or trainers is that they will be insusceptible to fatigue, burnout, and cognitive errors, potentially making them more reliable than humans (Bindoff, Stafford, Peterson, Kang, & Tenni, 2012; McShane, Beale, Nirenburg, Jarrell, & Fantry, 2012; Luxton, 2014b). Such systems can be programmed with therapeutic approaches that are consistently applied while also adapting to the patient's individual needs and preferences (Luxton, 2014b). For example, if the IVA detects worsening of symptoms and frustration from the user, the IVA could respond with empathetic understanding, supportive encouragement, and adjustment of expectations regarding treatment goals. IVAs can also be designed to have modifiable physical appearance and mannerisms (e.g., eye contact), speech dialect, use of local colloquialisms, and other characteristics that facilitate alignment and sensitivity to specific aspects of a patient's background such as race/ethnicity or socioeconomic status. This could help the system to establish rapport with patients, potentially contributing to adherence to treatment and improved health outcomes (Luxton, 2014b). Also, IVAs may be perceived by users as being immune to personal biases that human therapists may have (Luxton, 2014b). Care seekers may thus experience less anxiety when discussing intimate, private issues with an IVA than they would with a human healthcare provider. This idea is supported by research indicating that some people may be more comfortable disclosing information to virtual humans during clinical interviews and prefer to interact with IVAs because they are able to spend more time with them and do not make them feel hurried or judged (Bickmore et al., 2010; Gratch et al., 2007; Lucas et al., 2014).

IVAs have the potential to help reduce economic burdens on health care seekers and health care systems (Luxton, 2014a). Stepped-care is a health care delivery process whereby the least resource-intensive care is provided to the most people first, with more intensive care provided to people who need it the most (Bower & Gilbody, 2005). Consistent with stepped-care, IVAs could help reduce overall health care costs by providing coaching and self-help services. By conducting triage assessments, these systems could identify patients to be transferred, if necessary, for additional services. The increased accessibility and lower costs of care-providing machines may provide opportunities for longer-term treatments that are currently restricted by managed-care costs (Luxton, 2014b). Patients could also receive more frequent checkups at reduced costs to health care providers and similar to telehealth capabilities, IVAs could help extend the reach of a limited pool of health care providers to underserved areas.

Ubiquitous Computing, Ambient Intelligence, and Persuasive Technology

Ubiquitous computing (also referred to as *pervasive computing*) entails embedding computational capabilities into everyday objects so they can collect and communicate information (Abowd & Mynatt, 2000; Fogg, 2002; Weiser, 1993). Thus, computing capability can occur using any device, at any location, at any time, and in any format. Ubiquitous computing systems can capture data *implicitly*, through passive sensing, or *explicitly* by periodically surveying people, such as via smart mobile device, a kiosk, or through speech detection and processing (Luxton, June, Sano, et al., 2015).

Ambient intelligence (AmI) is an example of ubiquitous computing involving intelligent electronic environments that are responsive and adaptive to the presence of people within them (Aarts & Wichert, 2009; Cook, Augusto, & Jakkula, 2009; Vasilakos & Pedrycz, 2006). Ubiquitous computing systems embedded within a person's home or a hospital room, for example, can monitor the needs, preferences, and functioning of occupants by analyzing data in real time, such as a person's physical location within the environment and the time of day. Machine learning is used to make sense of all the data that is collected from embedded sensor networks (e.g., motion sensors, ambient light sensors, microphones). How technologies determine the current activity state of the user (e.g., a person in a smart home) and the characteristics of the environment (e.g., time of day) is called *context awareness*. This is done to manage information content and the delivery of information, such as therapeutic feedback or behavioral prompts (Cook et al., 2009; O'Connor, & Riek, 2015).

Persuasive technology is technology that's designed to aid in behavior and attitude modification of users through persuasion and social influence (IJsselsteijn, De Kort, Midden, Eggen, & Van Den Hoven, 2006). Essentially, this involves incorporating concepts from psychology and behavioral science into the design of products such as mobile apps, wearables, and ambient intelligence. The intent of persuasive technology is not to coerce people into modifying behavior but to motivate them through reward and punishment, and positive reinforcements, such as indicators to remind the user how well they are progressing toward their personal goals (Luxton, June, Sano, et al., 2015). Persuasive technology can make use of *gamification*, whereby points or symbolic trophies or badges are awarded to users for the accomplishment of desired behaviors or goals that are met.

Smartphones and wearables are perhaps the most powerful platforms for modern persuasive technologies (Ananthanarayan & Siek, 2012; Fogg & Eckles, 2007). This is because of their pervasiveness and because users always have them in close contact. Mobile devices can be used to motivate users by increasing health awareness through feedback delivered at the appropriate time. Automated texting for behavioral reminders, such as a prompt to exercise or engage in social activity, is one example. Serious health games on mobile devices (discussed later in this chapter), is another example. The timely display of attractive visuals or points in a gaming system can be used to reward positive behavior and motivate behavioral change (Ananthanarayan & Siek, 2012).

Persuasive technologies can also be embedded within living spaces. For example, the Persuasive Mirror (del Valle, Mesnage, & Opalach, 2006; del Valle & Opalach, 2005; Mattheij, Postma-Nilsenova´, & Postma, 2015; Nakajima & Lehdonvirta, 2013; Nakajima, Lehdonvirta, Tokunaga, & Kimura, 2008) has the appearance of a standard bathroom mirror but has embedded technologies that allow users to see simulated reflections of themselves or other images in the mirror. This works by using augmented reality that reflects the user's image back to them in a way that appears similar to a mirror but that augments the image based on the user's goals and system collected data about their behavior. It works by using two cameras that are placed on the sides of a flat-panel display and video streams from both cameras are combined to simulate a realistic mirror reflection. Facial tracking technology is used and image processing software can alter the person's simulated reflection in the mirror. Sensors placed throughout a home or worn on a person can provide the system with data about the person's daily habits, such as whether they were physically active or used tobacco products (such as during tobacco cessation interventions). The mirror system can be configured to provide feedback of the user's recent behaviors, such as by showing a person aged and unattractive due to smoking tobacco products.

Therapeutic Virtual Reality and Gaming

Virtual and Augmented Reality

Virtual reality (VR) allows people to become immersed within and interact with three-dimensional computer-generated simulated environments (Rizzo, Buckwalter, & Neumann, 1997). *Augmented reality (AR)*, sometimes referred to as *mixed reality*, combines virtual reality with the physical world by superimposing computer-generated graphics with live video imagery (Caudell & Mizell, 1992; Craig, 2013). This technology allows information about the surrounding world to be digitally manipulated and interacted with by the user. The technology can also be paired with Global Positioning System (GPS) capabilities that can provide real-time location data to the user, such as descriptions of objects, places, or people that are seen in the real world.

Virtual and augmented reality systems have been used for various applications in health care, including innovative assessment and intervention, training, and health care education (Gorrindo & Groves, 2009; Reger, Parsons, Gahm, & Rizzo, 2011; Rizzoet al., 2009; Schultheis & Rizzo, 2001; Zhu, Hadadgar, Masiello, & Zary, 2014). Clinical uses of AR in behavioral and mental health care include reminding people to take medications on schedule, helping children with autism to learn facial emotions (Kandalaft et al., 2013), and creating virtual stimuli intended to provoke anxiety during prolonged exposure therapy (Powers & Emmelkamp, 2008; Chicchi Giglioli, Pallavicini, Pedroli, Serino, & Riva, 2015). Areas of therapeutic VR (or *clinical VR*) include treatment of body image disturbances in patients with eating disorders (Riva, 2005), fear reduction in persons with simple phobias (Parsons & Rizzo, 2008; Powers & Emmelkamp, 2008), and treatment for PTSD (Difede & Hoffman, 2002, 2007;Reger et al., 2016; Rizzo et al., 2009, 2010, 2011; Rothbaum, Hodges, Smith, Lee, & Price, 2000). The advantage of VR is that the environments and stimuli within them can be controlled and thus adjusted to the needs, such as level of exposure to a stressful stimuli. Olfactory and tactile stimuli can also be delivered into the simulation to further augment the user's experience of' the virtual environment. For example, during Prolonged Exposure Therapy for combat PTSD, sound and vibrations caused by a vehicle or explosion can be simulated, along with the odors of smoke, diesel fuel, and more (Rizzo et al., 2009).

Artificial intelligence is advancing the capabilities of VR and augmented reality in several ways. For example, intelligent virtual agents (IVAs), such as virtual humans or other simulated life forms, can be created inside of virtual environments, such as in computer games. AI can give these IVAs autonomy in how they interact with the user, the virtual environment, and other virtual agents within the environment. Machine learning can also allow virtual humans and environments to learn the patterns of users, emulate behaviors, and respond to them in a personal way (Cipresso & Riva, 2015; Luck & Aylett, 2010).

Serious Games

Serious games are computer games developed for training and learning purposes (rather than games designed exclusively for entertainment purposes; Hudlicka, 2015). Serious games make use of gamification, which can be defined as the use of game mechanics and experience design to digitally engage and motivate people to achieve their goals (Burke, 2014). In health care, serious games are used for training and education purposes for health care professionals (e.g., nursing care, surgery), as well as for therapeutic and educational purposes for patients and clients (e.g., education about diet and exercise, coaching to increase physical activity, pain management, social skills training for persons with autism; Horne-Moyer, Moyer, Messer, & Messer, 2014). The skills to be learned or practiced are embedded within the game tasks and can be customized to the user's specific learning needs or therapeutic goals.

One example of a serious game is SPARX (www.sparx.org.nz/). Made available by the University of Auckland, this online-based serious game is designed to help young people who are experiencing mild to moderate depression and anxiety by teaching Cognitive-Behavioral Therapy (CBT) skills. SPARX is based on adventure-style games, whereby the player, in the form of a customizable avatar, goes on a quest and solves puzzles and mini games that entail defeating negative thoughts. The game has been shown to be effective in a randomized controlled non-inferiority trial (Merry et al., 2012).

Serious games provide numerous benefits. The game aspects provide the advantage of motivating users (i.e., behavioral reinforcement) while also making the training or tasks more engaging. Serious games also provide a safe, risk-free environment to practice skills. Just as with other VR applications described previously, AI provides characters within serious games autonomy in how they interact with the user, other game characters, and the virtual game environment. Machine learning allows the game to learn the patterns of users by data mining past behavior of players, and player experience modeling allows the game to adjust to the user's needs (Yannakakis, 2012).

Robots and Robotics

Robots are machines that are capable of carrying out physical change in the world. *Robotics technology* refers to associated systems such as sensors and algorithms for processing data (Riek, 2015). Robots make use of effectors, which can move the robot in its physical environment or manipulate objects. Sensors provide robots with data to make decisions, such as how to appropriately navigate, identify objects, and receive commands. The design of robots can range from fully autonomous (the robot makes all decisions independently) to teleoperated (a person makes all decisions for the robot via remote control). Most systems, however, make use of some level of shared autonomy. Robots can be designed to be human-like (anthropomorphic), animal-like (zoomorphic), or machine-like (Riek, Rabinowitch, Chakrabarti, & Robinson, 2009).

At first thought, robots in behavioral and mental health care may seem like they belong in the realm of science fiction. Not so. Robots and robotics are being used in a variety of health-related applications today and have enormous potential to improve how care is provided. For example, robots can be used to provide physical and cognitive support to people (Luxton & Riek, 2019). These types of robots can be a companion, coach or instructor, or therapeutic play partner. *Robot therapy* replaces animals with robots in animal-assisted therapies and activities (Shibata & Wada, 2011). *Paro*, for example, is a robotic baby seal designed to provide therapy for patients with dementia (Shibata & Wada, 2011). Robots also provide services in hospitals. For example, the Food and Drug Administration (FDA) has approved robots for use in hospitals that can maneuver from room to room to connect health care providers to patients or to other health care providers via wireless video teleconferencing.

Ethics Considerations

Mental health care providers who are interested in using the technologies described in this chapter should also be familiar with the ethical issues associated with them. While the application of AI and associated technologies in health care entails many of the same ethics (and legal) requirements as traditional methods of providing care services, there are additional considerations, such as when using autonomous or semi-autonomous systems. This section covers some of the primacy issues. For additional reading on this topic, see Luxton, Anderson, and Anderson (2015).

Algorithmic Bias

It is possible that biases and deficiencies in data used by machine learning algorithms may contribute to socioeconomic disparities in health care (Gianfrancesco, Tamang, Yazdany, & Schmajuk, 2018). *Algorithmic bias* is when a computer system makes systematic and repeatable errors that create unfair outcomes, such as privileging one arbitrary group of users over others. The causes of algorithmic bias may include things such as missing data, small sample size and underestimation, patients not identified by algorithms, and misclassification and measurement error. Moreover, the implicit values of the programmers and organizations collecting, selecting, or using data to train the algorithm may also introduce bias (Gianfrancesco et al., 2018).

Programmers, machine learning engineers, and end users of systems should consider bias and limit it by taking human biases into account. Ensuring that the training data is diverse and includes different groups is essential. Moreover, keeping real humans "in the loop" is important. An autonomous or semi-autonomous system, through machine learning, can develop its own algorithms that may inherently results in biases. Thus, having humans watch for and compensate for biases in the algorithm or model can help to mitigate algorithmic bias.

Black-Box Problems in Deep-Learning

The *black box* refers to the inexplicability of sophisticated AI. Consider that machine learning methods are often based on complex neural networks and deep learning, which operate like a mysterious black box that processes data that is inputted and then the computer outputs data, but how it does it is not easily understood. This is an ethical issue because it challenges traditional ideas of accountability and thus responsibility for the decisions and actions a machine is making.

Take, for example, a scenario whereby a clinician seeks recommendations from a CDSS for a patient with cancer and symptoms of depression. The CDSS, which uses deep learning techniques, recommends a change in anti-depressant medications, as it predicts that this will have better outcomes for the patient. The clinician goes with the recommendations, but the change in medication results in worsening depression, and the patient unexpectedly takes their own life. The family sues the hospital. The clinician is perplexed, thinking that the system should have predicted the risk, but given the complexity of the computational models used by the CDSS, how the system made its recommendations are unknown. In this hypothetical situation, how could the decisions made about the patient's care be justified by the clinician, the hospital, or the developers of the CDSS system?

One of the solutions to the black box problem may be the use of an "audit trail" of the decision making of AI systems (Luxton, 2015). While the complexity of neural networks and deep learning may make it difficult to produce an audit trail, it should be possible to engineer methods for systems to describe decision making, similar to how a human health care provider would have to do in a court of law. This would entail what data was (or was not) used to derive decisions, how decisions were weighted against others, what standards of practice were followed, and what ethical principles were (or were not) applied. This way, it would be possible to understand and demonstrate the decision making of an autonomous AI system and thus help with monitoring and accountability associated with its recommendations.

Over Reliance on Autonomous Systems

The previous example whereby a clinician overrelies on the recommendations of a CDSS is also an example of automation-bias (Goddard, Roudsari, & Wyatt, 2012). Automation-induced complacency, or insufficient monitoring of automation output, could cause clinicians to overlook alternative and potentially better options or potential risks to patients. Thus, it is essential for users of these systems to understand the limitations of use and responsibilities regarding review of alternative options.

Also, with increased use of autonomous systems, we need to think about whether these systems will perform ethically in diverse situations, especially when facing complex ethical dilemmas. Pope and Vasquez (2011) note that formal ethical principles cannot be substituted for an active, deliberative, and creative approach to meeting ethical responsibilities. In the case of autonomous IVAs that provide care services, for example, requirements specified in ethics codes can't be applied in a routine manner because patient's situations are unique and may require different solutions (Luxton, 2014b). In other words, scripted decision paths may not be adequate in situations that require complex ethical decision making and value judgments. In order for IVAs to ever fully function unsupervised and in place of humans, these systems will need to follow established ethical codes of conduct just as human health care providers do, and they must also be capable of selecting the best course of action that would be considered to be reasonable based on existing standards.

Scope of Use and Patient Safety

Health care professionals are expected to be competent in their skills and have appropriate qualifications (i.e., education and professional licensure requirements). They also should not, as a matter of ethics and the law, practice outside of their scope of practice. There presently is not any established professional guideline or law, however, which addresses these requirements for AI systems that stand in for human care providers, such as chatbots and IVA systems. The potential for harm to the public exists if the quality of services provided by AI systems or the appropriateness of their use does not meet requirements that are inherent to mental and behavioral health care.

Relatedly, there is potential risk of harm to the public if an automated system does not adequately address situations when a patient expresses intent to harm themselves or others. Take for example a scenario whereby a person is seeking treatment for anxiety management from an online chatbot. During the course of conversation, the person discloses that they are experiencing suicidal thoughts and plan to die. What should the chatbot program do?

Designers of autonomous and semi-autonomous systems that interact with people should consider giving them the capability to detect risks and then take appropriate action. In some scenarios, the detection of threat can be automated, and some responses, such as immediate display of help resources (e.g., crisis lines or to call 911) are possible. Procedures for keeping a human in-the-loop, when feasible, is also a way to help address this issue. That is, when a threat is detected, a human can review the information and then, if appropriate, contact the user and directly intervene or make an appropriate referral for help. The concept of human-in-the-loop is also important for web-based tools and social media services when users may indicate heightened risk for self-directed violence or threat to harm others. The social media site Facebook, for example, leverages both machine learning to detect and flag risk content while also including human-moderated review (Gomes de Andrade, Pawson, Muriello, Donahue, & Guadagno, 2018).

Requirements to address these safety and protection issues will depend on the setting and intended scope of use of these systems. Presently, online chatbots are generally considered "coaches," and not stand-ins for human licensed health care professionals. Thus, many of the ethical and legal requirements that human health care providers are expected to follow, such as "duty to warn," may end up being, unfortunately, overlooked. It is therefore essential that developers and administrators of these systems provide adequate information to patients regarding scope of use, risks, and expectations.

Also, as noted by Luxton, Anderson, et al. (2015), it's essential to design care-providing IVAs (or robots) to perform in an ethically responsible way rather than putting the burden of determining the ethically correct use of the machine on the user. Because it is difficult to anticipate every situation where it is important that an IVA behave appropriately, it's better to have ethical principles built into them to ensure that they function correctly, no matter what situation they are in, rather than attempting to program them to do so in an ad hoc way.

Patient Autonomy and Choice

Concern has previously been raised by this author (Luxton, 2014a) about whether health care insurance companies or governments might one day require the use of virtual care providers without providing consumers with the option to seek services from people. The use of virtual care providers may primarily be driven by cost savings without full consideration of a person's preferences, beliefs, and values. I also noted that an overreliance on machines could cause us to lose the things that are inherent in human interaction in the therapeutic context. Physical presence and contact, such as shaking hands, placing a hand on the shoulder of a person who is experiencing grief, or handing a tissue to a patient in tears are all expressions of human-to-human empathy, care, and compassion that could be lost. Moreover, what if a virtual care provider makes decisions that a person does not agree with and has valid reasons for that disagreement? Joseph Weizenbaum brought up these types of concerns decades ago, stating that we should not be using machines in place of humans when it comes to making judgments that require empathy (Weizenbaum, 1976).

Intelligent Virtual Agents and robots are being constantly improved to better recognize, respond to, and express emotions, thus giving them the capability to interact with humans in an empathetic manner. We know from some existing research that simulated behaviors of caring kindness and empathy expressed by IVAs and robots can be experienced by humans in the same way as they would with other humans (Luxton, 2014b). Nonetheless, worries about whether the field of mental and behavioral health care is at risk of losing something essential are valid, and this is an area in need of more research and discussion.

Equitable Access to Health Technologies and Services

The majority of adults and children with behavioral health needs in the United States do not receive any services (Merikangas et al., 2011; SAMSHA, 2014). This is in part due to the fact that approximately 80 million

Americans reside in areas with scarcity of mental health care practitioners to meet the needs of those communities (U.S. Health and Human Services Health Resources and Services Administration, 2013). This shortage in health care services extends to the entire planet. According to the World Health Organization (WHO, 2017), in low-income nations, the rate of mental health workers is estimated to be as low as two per 100k population, compared with more than 70 per 100k in high-income countries. AI-assisted technologies, such as intelligent mHealth apps, web-based treatments, and care-providing IVAs are examples of how technology can help meet the need for mental health care services. Of course, this depends on whether these technologies are accessible to the populations that could benefit from them.

Equitable access to health care technologies is a topic that must be addressed with the shift to increased automation of services with AI-assisted technologies (Luxton, 2015, 2020). Technological infrastructure investment in underserved communities and countries is necessary. The issues that contribute to health disparities is complex, consisting of multiple factors in addition to the availability of health care services. Access to education, food, employment, housing, and other social determinants of health (Office of Disease Prevention and Health Promotion, 2019) are all essential to consider. It is also necessary to include persons from diverse communities that are impacted by health care disparities in the identification, design, implementation, and evaluation of new health care technologies.

A Call for Updated Ethical Guidelines

Some of the mental health care professional organizations have provisions pertaining to the use of technology as part of their ethical guidelines or as complementary information. The American Psychological Association (APA) includes a section regarding technology competence for psychologists and covers electronic data security, use of the internet for providing services, and the use of electronic communication (e.g., email, social media). The National Association of Social Workers (NASW), in collaboration with several other organizations, has also published standards and guidelines to reflect the use of technology in social work practice. Many professional organizations, such as the American Telemedicine Association (ATA) and the American Medical Association (AMA), have published separate guidelines for the practice of telehealth. Other examples of technology in health care ethics codes or guidelines include the International Society for Mental Health Online's Suggested Principles for the Online Provision of Mental Health Services (www.ismho.org/suggestions.asp) and the eHealth Code of Ethics (www.ihealthcoalition.org/ehealth-code/).

Current professional ethics codes and practice guidelines do not address the emerging ethical implications associated with AI systems that "stand in" for human care providers (Luxton, 2014b). There are, however, several organizations and individuals who have proposed guidelines regarding the ethical use and design of intelligent machines. In 2011, the Engineering and Physical Sciences Research Council (EPRSC) and the Arts and Humanities Research Council (AHRC) (Great Britain) published a list of ethical principles for designers and users of robots. Riek and Howard (2014) have put forth ethics guidelines specific to robots and robotics, and this author has provided recommendations specifically for the use and design of AI care-providing machines, particularly IVAs (Luxton, 2014b). Continued technological innovation and the practical application of these machines will likely increase the professional demand for ethics codes and best-practice guidelines in the near future.

Conclusion

This chapter considered some of the applications of AI and associated technologies in mental and behavioral health care. These technological advancements are providing many useful benefits to both care seekers and health care professionals by improving the capabilities, efficiency, and quality of services. While these technologies are becoming more commercially viable and pervasive in their use, they are also raising important ethical considerations that require immediate attention. It's therefore important for mental health care professionals to be involved in the development of systems by providing theoretical and practical expertise to guide their design to ensure that their application and function are consistent with health care best practices and ethics requirements (Luxton, 2014a). Also included must be an examination of demographic, social, and cultural differences regarding the preferences for using these technologies and consideration of whether access to them will be equitable.

The technologies discussed in this chapter are generally envisioned to augment the services of professionals and not to replace the need for human health care providers. However, concern about whether some advances in AI could eventually put jobs held by behavioral and mental health professionals at risk has been raised (Luxton, 2014a). We know from history that technology has displaced workforces across industries, and this trend is expected to continue. According to a 2013 report from the Oxford Martin School's Programme on the Impacts of Future Technology, 45% of jobs in the United States are at risk of being displaced by computers over the next two decades (Frey & Osborne, 2013). This risk extends to "knowledge jobs" held by skilled professionals, including jobs in the banking sector, semiconductor design, customer service, and the law professions (Brynjolfsson & McAfee, 2011; Markoff, 2011). Others have suggested, however, that the AI industry will create more jobs in the coming years than it will supplant (Reese, 2019). One example of this is the involvement of psychologists and other health care professionals in the development and provision of services via the Internet (eHealth) and mobile devices (mHealth). In other words, mental health care professionals can benefit from involvement in businesses that develop these technologies or through the expansion of their practices via use of these technologies (Luxton, 2014b).

A possible troubling thought for health care professionals, however, is whether continued technological advances will make it possible to build and deploy human-like intelligent machine systems that fully replace human care providers. This author has previously proposed the concept of the *super clinician* (Luxton, 2014a), an AI system that could replace human psychologists and counselors because of its superior capabilities. The system would interact with humans via a robot, a virtual human, or perhaps as a voice only, using ambient sensors embedded within an office or in the home. With advanced sensing capabilities, the system could determine the identity of patients and observe and analyze nonverbal behavior such as vocal characteristics, facial expressions, eye blinking, and other patterns of behavior. Computer-sensing technology could also analyze internal states that are not detectable by the human eye, such as by observing changes in body temperature with infrared cameras or blood flow in the face with existing high-resolution digital video processing techniques. With access to all digital health and behavioral data about a person, the system would know how and when to apply the best treatment or intervention, and could do so without ever making a mistake, suffering from burnout, or needing to sleep. All of the technologies and capabilities proposed in the super clinician concept already exist today.

Time will tell whether the super clinician comes to fruition, although continued technological advances are making what may seem like science fiction a viable reality. For example, improvements in microprocessing and efficiency of designs, which equates to less power consumption, are advancing ways to embed intelligent technologies into everyday objects. Upgrades to wireless networks, including 5G, are expected to revolutionize how devices are interconnected, creating new opportunities for AI-assisted health care. Companies such as Amazon, Apple, Google, and Microsoft are making powerful AI capabilities, such as natural language processing and deep-learning, commercially available to developers. Moreover, these technology giants have themselves entered the multi-trillion dollar health care market, providing services directly, through their subsidiaries, or through collaborative ventures. We are in the age of technology-driven health care, with exciting times ahead.

References

Aarts, E., & Wichert, R. (2009). Ambient intelligence. In H. J. Bullinger (Eds.), *Technology guide*. Springer, Berlin, Heidelberg. https://doi.org/10.1007/978-3-540-88546-7_47
Abowd, G. D., & Mynatt, E. D. (2000). Charting past, present, and future research in ubiquitous computing. *ACM Transactions on Computer-Human Interaction*, 7(1), 29–58.
Ananthanarayan, S., & Siek, K. A. (2012). Persuasive wearable technology design for

health and wellness. *6th Annual International Conference on Pervasive Computing Technologies for Healthcare (Pervasive Health) and Workshops.* doi:10.4108/icst. pervasivehealth.2012.248694

Bailenson, J. N., & Yee, N. (2005). Digital chameleons: Automatic assimilation of non-verbal gestures in immersive virtual environments. *Psychological Science, 16*(10), 814–819. https://doi.org/10.1111/j.1467-9280.2005.01619.x

Bennett, C. C., & Doub, T. W. (2016). Expert systems in mental health care: AI applications in decision-making and consultation. In D. D. Luxton (Ed.), *Artificial intelligence in behavioral and mental health care.* San Diego: Elsevier/Academic Press.

Bickmore, T. W., Mitchell, S. E., Jack, B. W., Paasche-Orlow, M. K., Pfeifer, L. M., & O'Donnell, J. (2010). Response to a relational agent by hospital patients with depressive symptoms. *Interacting with Computers, 22*(4), 289–298.

Bindoff, I., Stafford, A., Peterson, G., Kang, B. H., & Tenni, P. (2012). The potential for intelligent decision support systems to improve the quality and consistency of medication reviews. *The Journal of Clinical Pharmacy and Therapeutics* (4), 452–458. doi:10.1111/j.1365-2710.2011.01327.x

Bower, P., & Gilbody, S. (2005). Stepped care in psychological therapies: Access, effectiveness and efficiency: Narrative literature review. *The British Journal of Psychiatry, 186*, 11–17 doi:10.1192/bjp.186.1.11

Brynjolfsson, E., & McAfee, A. (2011). *Race against the machine: How the digital revolution is accelerating innovation, driving productivity, and irreversibly transforming employment and the economy.* Cambridge, MA: MIT Sloan School of Management. Retrieved from http://ebusiness.mit.edu/research/Briefs/Brynjolfsson_McAfee_Race_Against_the_Machine.pdf

Burke, B. (2014). *Gartner redefines gamification.* Retrieved from https://blogs.gartner.com/brian_burke/2014/04/04/gartner-redefines-gamification/

Cao, B., Cho, R. Y., Chen, D., Xiu, M., Wang, L., Soares, J. C., & Zhang, X. Y. (2018). Machine learning helps predict treatment outcomes for schizophrenia. *Molecular Psychiatry.* doi:10.1038/s41380-018-0106-5

Caudell, T. P., & Mizell, D. W. (1992). Augmented reality: An application of heads-up display technology to manual manufacturing processes. In *System Sciences, 1992: Proceedings of the twenty-fifth Hawaii International Conference on System Sciences* (Vol. 2, pp. 659–669). New York, NY: IEEE. doi:10.1109/HICSS.1992.183317

Chicchi Giglioli, I. A., Pallavicini, F., Pedroli, E., Serino, S., & Riva, G. (2015). Augmented reality: A brand new challenge for the assessment and treatment of psychological disorders. *Computational and Mathematical Methods in Medicine, 2015*, 1–13.

Cipresso, P., & Riva, G. (2015). Virtual reality for artificial intelligence: Human-centered simulation for social science. *Annual Review of CyberTherapy and Telemedicine* (13), 177–181. doi:10.3233/978-1-61499-595

Cook, D. J., Augusto, J. C., & Jakkula, V. R. (2009). Ambient intelligence: Technologies, applications, and opportunities. *Pervasive and Mobile Computing, 5*(4), 277–298. doi:10.1016/j.pmcj.2009.04.001

Cornet, V. P., & Holden, R. J. (2018). Systematic review of smartphone-based passive sensing for health and wellbeing. *Journal of biomedical informatics, 77*, 120–132. doi:10.1016/j.jbi.2017.12.008

Craig, A. B. (2013). *Understanding augmented reality: Concepts and applications.* Amsterdam: Morgan Kaufmann.

del Valle, A. C., Mesnage, A. C., & Opalach, A. (2006). Intelligent home services initiative. *Gerontechnology, 5*(2), 118–120.

del Valle, A. C., & Opalach, A. (2005). The persuasive mirror: Computerized persuasion for healthy living. In *Proceedings of the 11th international conference on human-computer interaction.*

Difede, J., Cukor, J., Jayasinghe, N., Patt, I., Jedel, S., Spielman, L., et al. (2007). Virtual reality exposure therapy for the treatment of posttraumatic stress disorder following September 11, 2001. *Journal of Clinical Psychiatry, 68,* 1639–1647.

Difede, J., & Hoffman, H. G. (2002). Virtual reality exposure therapy for World Trade Center post-traumatic stress disorder: A case report. *Cyberpsychology, Behavior, and Social Networking, 5*(6), 529–535.

Ferrucci, D., Brown, E., Chu-Carroll, J., et al. (2010). Building Watson: An overview of the DeepQA Project. *AI Magazine, 31*(3), 59–79.

Finlay, P. N. (1994). *Introducing decision support systems.* Cambridge, MA: Blackwell Publishers.

Fogg, B. (2002). *Interactive computing systems designed to change people's attitudes and behaviors.* Palo Alto, CA: Stanford University Press.

Fogg, B. J., & Eckles, D. (2007). *Mobile persuasion: 20 perspectives on the future of behavior change.* Stanford: Stanford Captology Media.

Frey, C. B., & Osborne, M. A. (2013). The future of employment: How susceptible are jobs to computerisation? *Technological Forecasting and Social Change, 114,* 254–280. doi: 10.1016/j.techfore.2016.08.019

Gianfrancesco, M. A., Tamang, S., Yazdany, J., & Schmajuk, G. (2018). Potential biases in machine learning algorithms using electronic health record data. *JAMA Internal Medicine, 178*(11):1544–1547. doi:10.1001/jamainternmed.2018.3763

Goddard, K., Roudsari, A., & Wyatt, J. C. (2012). Automation bias: A systematic review of frequency, effect mediators, and mitigators. *Journal of the American Medical Information Association, 19*(1), 121–127. doi:10.1136/amiajnl-2011-000089

Gomes de Andrade, N., Pawson, D., Muriello, D., Donahue, L., & Guadagno, J. (2018). Ethics and artificial intelligence: Suicide prevention on facebook. *Philosophy & Technology 31,* 669. https://doi.org/10.1007/s13347-018-0336-0

Gorrindo, T., & Groves, J. E. (2009). Computer simulation and virtual reality in the diagnosis and treatment of psychiatric disorders. *Academic Psychiatry, 33,* 413–417.

Gratch, J., Wang, N., Gerten, J., Fast, E., & Duffy, R. (2007). Creating rapport with virtual agents. In *Intelligent virtual agents* (pp. 125–138). Berlin, Heidelberg: Springer.

Hirumi, A., Kleinsmith, A., Johnsen, K., Kubovec, S., Eakins, M., Bogert, K., . . . Cendan, J. (2016). Advancing virtual patient simulations through design research and InterPLAY: Part I – Design and Development. *Educational Technology Research and Development, 64,* 763–785. doi: 10.1007/s11423-016-9429-6

Horne-Moyer, H. L., Moyer, B. H., Messer, D. C., & Messer, E. S. (2014). The use of electronic games in therapy: A review with clinical implications. *Current Psychiatry Reports, 16*(12), 520. doi: 10.1007/s11920-014-0520-6

Hudlicka, E. (2015). Virtual affective agents and therapeutic games. In Luxton (Ed.), *Artificial intelligence in behavioral and mental healthcare.* San Diego, CA: Elsevier/Academic Press.

Hudlicka, E., Lisetti, C., Hodge, D., Paiva, A., Rizzo, A., & Wagner, E. (2008). Artificial agents for psychotherapy. In *Proceedings of the AAAI spring symposium on emotion, personality and social behavior.* Menlo Park, CA: AAAI. TR SS-08-04, p. 6064.

IBM. (2014). *IBM Watson: Ushering in a new era of computing.* Retrieved from http://www-03.ibm.com/innovation/us/watson/index.shtml

IBM. (2018). *IBM Watson health: Empowering heroes, transforming health.* Retrieved November 20, 2018, from www.ibm.com/watson/health/

IJsselsteijn, W., De Kort, Y., Midden, C., Eggen, B., & Van Den Hoven, E. (2006). Persuasive technology for human well-being: Setting the scene. In W. IJsselsteijn, et al. (Eds.), *Persuasive 2006, LNCS 3962* (pp. 1–5). Berlin, Heidelberg: Springer-Verlag.

Kandalaft, M. R., Didehbani, N., Krawczyk, D. C., Allen, T., & Chapman, S. B. (2013). Virtual reality social skills training for young adults with high-functioning Autism. *Journal of Autism and Developmental Disorders, 43,* 34–44.

Kenny, P. G., Parsons, T. D., & Rizzo, A. A. (2009). Human computer interaction in virtual standardized patient systems. Human computer interaction in virtual standardized patient systems. In J. A. Jacko (Eds.), *Human-computer interaction. Interacting in various application domains. HCI 2009. Lecture notes in computer science, vol 5613.* Berlin, Heidelberg: Springer.

Koutsouleris, N., Kambeitz-Ilankovic, L., Ruhrmann, S., et al. (2018). Prediction models of functional outcomes for individuals in the clinical high-risk state for psychosis or with recent-onset depression: A multimodal, multisite machine learning analysis. *JAMA Psychiatry, 75*(11), 1156–1172. doi:10.1001/jamapsychiatry.2018.2165

Lucas, G. M., Gratch, J., King, A., & Morency, L. P. (2014). It's only a computer: Virtual humans increase willingness to disclose. *Computers in Human Behavior, 37,* 94–100.

Luck, M., & Aylett, R. (2010). Applying artificial intelligence to virtual reality: Intelligent virtual environments. *Applied Artificial Intelligence, 14*(1), 3–32. https://doi.org/10.1080/088395100117142

Luxton, D. D. (2014a). Artificial intelligence in psychological practice: Current and future applications and implications. *Professional Psychology: Research & Practice, 45*(5) 332–339. doi:10.1037/a0034559

Luxton, D. D. (2014b). Recommendations for the ethical use and design of artificial intelligent care providers. *Artificial Intelligence in Medicine, 62*(1), 1–10. doi:10.1016/j.artmed.2014.06.004

Luxton, D. D. (Ed.). (2015). *Artificial intelligence in behavioral and mental health care.* San Diego: Elsevier/Academic Press.

Luxton, D. D. (2019). Should Watson be consulted for a second opinion? *AMA Journal of Ethics, 21*(2), E131–E137. doi:10.1001/amajethics.2019.131

Luxton, D. D. (2020). Ethical challenges of conversational agents in global public health. *Bulletin of the World Health Organization, 98,* 285–287. doi: 10.2471/BLT.19.237636

Luxton, D. D., Anderson, S. L., & Anderson, M. (2015). Ethical issues and artificial intelligence technologies in behavioral and mental health care. In D. D. Luxton (Ed.), *Artificial intelligence in behavioral and mental health care.* San Diego: Elsevier Academic Press.

Luxton, D. D., June, J. D., & Chalker, S. (2015). Mobile health technologies for suicide prevention: Feature review and recommendations for use in clinical care. *Current Treatment Options in Psychiatry, 2*(4), 349–362. doi:10.1007/s40501-015-0057-2

Luxton, D. D., June, J. D., Sano, A., & Bickmore, T. (2015). Intelligent mobile, wearable, and ambient technologies in behavioral health care. In D. D. Luxton (Ed.), *Artificial intelligence in behavioral and mental health care.* San Diego: Elsevier Academic Press.

Luxton, D. D., McCann, R. A., Bush, N. E., Mishkind, M. C., & Reger, G. M. (2011). mHealth for mental health: Integrating smartphone technology in behavioral healthcare. *Professional Psychology: Research & Practice, 42,* 505–512. doi: 10.1037/a0024485

Luxton, D. D., & Riek, L. (2019). Handbook of rehabilitation psychology 3rd Edition. In L. Brenner, B. S. Reid-Arndt, Elliott, et al. (Eds.), *Artificial intelligence and robotics for rehabilitation.* Washington, DC: American Psychological Association Books.

Manning, C., & Schütze, H. (1999). *Foundations of statistical natural language processing.* Cambridge, MA: MIT Press.

Markoff, J. (2011). Armies of expensive lawyers, replaced by cheaper software. *The New York Times*. Retrieved from http://www.nytimes.com/2011/03/05/science/05legal.html

Martínez-Pérez, B., de la Torre-Díez, I., & López-Coronado, M. (2013, June 14). Mobile health applications for the most prevalent conditions by the world health organization: Review and analysis. *The Journal of Medical Internet Research*, 15(6), e120. doi:10.2196/jmir.2600

Mattheij, R., Postma-Nilsenova´, M., & Postma, E. (2015). Mirror mirror on the wall: Is there mimicry in you all? *Journal of Ambient Intelligence and Smart Environments*, 7(2), 121–132.

McFowland III, E., Speakman, S., & Neill, D. B. (2013). Fast generalized subset scan for anomalous pattern detection. *Journal of Machine Learning Research*, 14, 1533–1561.

McShane, M., Beale, S., Nirenburg, S., Jarrell, B., & Fantry, G. (2012). Inconsistency as a diagnostic tool in a society of intelligent agents. *Artificial Intelligence in Medicine*, 55, 137–148. doi:10.1016/j.artmed .2012.04.005

Merikangas, K. R., He, J. P., Burstein, M., Swendsen, J., Avenevoli, S., Case, B., & Olfson, M. (2011). Service utilization for lifetime mental disorders in U.S. adolescents: Results of the National Comorbidity SurveyAdolescent Supplement (NCS-A). *Journal of the American Academy of Child & Adolescent Psychiatry*, 50(1), 32.

Merry, S. N., Stasiak, K., Shepherd, M., Frampton, C., Fleming, T, Lucassen, M. F. G., et al. (2012). The effectiveness of SPARX, a computerised self help intervention for adolescents seeking help for depression: Randomised controlled non-inferiority trial. *BMJ*, 344, e2598. https://doi.org/10.1136/bmj.e2598

Mitchell, T. M. (1997). *Machine learning*. Burr Ridge, IL: McGraw Hill.

Nakajima, T., & Lehdonvirta, V. (2013). Designing motivation using persuasive ambient mirrors. *Personal and Ubiquitous Computing*, 17(1), 107–126.

Nakajima, T., Lehdonvirta, V., Tokunaga, E., & Kimura, H. (2008). Reflecting human behavior to motivate desirable lifestyle. In *Proceedings of the 7th ACM conference on designing interactive systems* (pp. 405–414). ACM.

Neill, D. B. (2012). *New directions in AI for public health surveillance*. Retrieved from http://lifesciences.ieee.org/articles/120-new-directions-in-ai-for-public-health-surveillance

O'Connor, M. F., & Riek, L. D. (2015). *Detecting social context: A method for social event classification using naturalistic multimodal data*. Retrieved from https://cseweb.ucsd.edu/~lriek/papers/ fg2015-oconnor-riek.pdf

Office of Disease Prevention and Health Promotion. (2019). *Social determinants of health*. Retrieved from www.healthypeople.gov/2020/topics-objectives/topic/social-determinants-of-health

Ong, A. A., & Gillespie, M. B. (2016). Overview of smartphone applications for sleep analysis. *World Journal of Otorhinolaryngology—Head and Neck Surgery*, 2(1), 45–49. doi:10.1016/j.wjorl.2016.02.001

Parsons, T. D. & Rizzo, A. A. (2008). Affective outcomes of virtual reality exposure therapy for anxiety and specific phobias: A meta-analysis. *Journal of Behavior Therapy and Experimental Psychiatry*, 39, 250–261.

Patel, S., Park, H., Bonato, P., Chan, L., & Rodgers, M. (2012). A review of wearable sensors and systems with application in rehabilitation. *Journal of NeuroEngineering and Rehabilitation*, 9, 21. doi:10.1186/1743-0003-9-21

Piwek, L., Ellis, D. A., Andrews, S., & Joinson, A. (2016, February 2). The rise of consumer health wearables: Promises and barriers. *PLoS Medicine*, 13(2), e1001953. doi:10.1371/journal.pmed.1001953

Pope, K. S., & Vasquez, M. J. T. (2011). *Ethics in psychotherapy and counseling: A practical guide* (4th ed.). Hoboken, NJ: John Wiley & Sons Inc.

Poulin, C., Thompson, P., &b Bryan, C. (2016). Public health surveillance: Predictive analytics and Big data. In D. D. Luxton (Ed.), *Artificial intelligence in behavioral and mental health care.* New York: Elsevier/Academic Press.

Powers, M. B., & Emmelkamp, P. M. (2008). Virtual reality exposure therapy for anxiety disorders: A meta-analysis. *Journal of Anxiety Disorders, 22*(3), 561–569.

Prendinger, H., & Ishizuka, M. (Eds.). (2004). *Life-like characters: Tools, affective functions, and applications (cognitive technologies).* Berlin, Heidelberg, Germany: Springer-Verlag.

Reese, B. (2019). *AI will create millions more jobs than it will destroy. Here's how.* Retrieved from https://singularityhub.com/2019/01/01/ai-will-create-millions-more-jobs-than-it-will-destroy-heres-how/#sm.000018ncwpxzyevkqlu151n09txfl

Reger, G. M., Koenen-Woods, P., Zetocha, K., Smolenski, D. J., Holloway, K. M., Rothbaum, B. O., . . . Gahm, G. A. (2016). Randomized controlled trial of prolonged exposure using imaginal exposure vs. virtual reality exposure in active duty soldiers with deployment-related posttraumatic stress disorder (PTSD). *Journal of Consulting and Clinical Psychology, 84*(11), 946–959. doi:10.1037/ccp0000134

Reger, G. M., Parsons, T. D, Gahm, G., & Rizzo, A. (2011). Virtual reality assessment of cognitive functions: A promising tool to improve ecological validity. *Brain Injury Professional, 7,* 24–26.

Riek, L., & Howard, D. (2014). A code of ethics for the human-robot interaction profession. *We Robot.* Retrieved from https://www.researchgate.net/ publication/286220724_A_Code_of_Ethics_for_ the_Human-Robot_Interaction_Profession

Riek, L. D. (2015). Robotics technology in mental healthcare. In D. Luxton (Ed.), *Artificial intelligence in behavioral health and mental health care* (pp. 185–203). San Diego, CA: Elsevier. http://dx.doi.org/10.1016/ B978-0-12-420248-1.00008-8

Riek, L. D., Rabinowitch, T., Chakrabarti, B., & Robinson, P. (2009). *How anthropomorphism affects empathy toward robots, HRI'09.* Retrieved from https://dl.acm.org/doi/pdf/10.1145/1514095.1514158

Riva, G. (2005). Virtual reality in psychotherapy: Review. *CyberPsychology & Behavior, 8*(3), 220–230.

Rizzo, A. A., Buckwalter, J. G., & Neumann, U. (1997). Virtual reality and cognitive rehabilitation: A brief review of the future. *The Journal of Head Trauma Rehabilitation, 12*(6), 1–15.

Rizzo, A. A., Difede, J., Rothbaum, B. O., Johnston, S., Mclay, R. N., Reger, G., . . . Pair, J. (2009). VR PTSD exposure therapy results with active duty iraq war combatants. In J.D. Westwood, et al. (Eds.), *Studies in Health Technology and Informatics* (Vol. 142, pp. 277–282). Amsterdam, NL: IOS Press.

Rizzo, A. S, Difede, J., Rothbaum, B. O., Reger, G., Spitalnick, J., Cukor, J., & McLay, R. (2010). Development and early evaluation of the virtual Iraq/Afghanistan exposure therapy system for combat-related PTSD. *Annals of the New York Academy of Sciences, 1208,* 114–125.

Rizzo, A. A., Lange, B., Buckwalter, J. G., Forbell, E., Kim, J., Sagae, K., et al. (2011). An intelligent virtual human system for providing healthcare information and support. *Studies in Health Technology and Informatics, 163,* 503–509.

Rogers, C. (1951). A theory of therapy, personality and interpersonal relationships as developed in the client-centered framework. In S. Koch (Ed.), *Psychology: A study of a science. Vol. 3: Formulations of the person and the social context* (pp. 184–256). New York: McGraw Hill.

Rothbaum, B. O., Hodges, L. F., Smith, S., Lee, J. H., & Price, L. (2000). A controlled study of virtual reality exposure therapy for the fear of flying. *Journal of Consulting and Clinical Psychology, 68,* 1020–1026.

Salomoni, G., Grassi, M., Mosini, P., Riva, P., Cavedini, P., & Bellodi, L. (2009). Artificial neural network model for the prediction of obsessive-compulsive disorder treatment response. *Journal of Clinical Psychopharmacology, 29*(4), 343–349.

SAMSHA, (2014). *Receipt of services for behavioral health problems: Results from the 2014 National Survey on Drug Use and Health.* Retrieved from https://www.samhsa.gov/data/sites/default/files/NSDUH-DR-FRR3-2014/NSDUH-DR-FRR3-2014/NSDUH-DR-FRR3-2014.pdf

Samuel, A. (2000). Some studies in machine learning using the game of checkers. *IBM Journal of Research and Development, 1*(44), 2. doi:10.1147/rd.441.0206

Schultheis, M. T., & Rizzo, A. A. (2001). The application of virtual reality technology in rehabilitation. *Rehabilitation Psychology, 46*(3), 296.

Shibata, T., & Wada, K. (2011). Robot therapy: A new approach for mental healthcare of the elderly—a mini-review. *Gerontology, 57*(4), 378–386. doi:10.1159/000319015

Talbot, Sagae, John, & Rizzo. (2012). Designing useful virtual standardized patient encounters.

U.S. Health and Human Services Health Resources and Services Administration. (2013). *National projections of supply and demand for selected behavioral health practitioners: 2013–2025.* Rockville, MD: HRSA.

Vasilakos, A., & Pedrycz, W. (2006). *Ambient intelligence, wireless networking, and ubiquitous computing.* Norwood, MA: Artech House, Inc.

Ventola, C. L. (2014). Mobile devices and apps for health care professionals: Uses and benefits. *Pharmacy and Therapeutics, 39*(5), 356–364.

Weiser, M. (1993). Some computer science issues in ubiquitous computing. *Commun. ACM, 36*(7), 75–84.

Weizenbaum, J. (1976). *Computer power and human reason: From judgment to calculation.* San Francisco, CA: W. H. Freeman.

WHO. (2017). *WHO's Mental Health Atlas 2017 highlights global shortage of health workers trained in mental health* [Internet]. Geneva: World Health Organization. Retrieved from https://www.who.int/hrh/news/2018/WHO-MentalHealthAtlas2017-highlights-HW-shortage/en/

Yannakakis, G. N. (2012). Game AI revisited. *Proceedings of the 9th conference on Computing Frontiers,* 285–292.

Zhu, E., Hadadgar, A., Masiello, I., & Zary, N. (2014). Augmented reality in healthcare education: An integrative review. *PeerJ, 2,* e469. doi:10.7717/peerj.469

15 Shared Immersive Environments and Virtual Worlds and Their Application in Behavioral Health

Kevin M. Holloway, Jenna Ermold,
and Kelly R. Chrestman

Science fiction and Hollywood have helped imagine a future that includes regular interactions in shared, alternative virtual environments. Many early science fiction stories, such as Laurence Manning's 1933 series *The Man Who Awoke* (Manning, 1975), Stanley G. Weinbaum's short story "Pygmalion's Spectacles" (Weinbaum, 2012), and Ray Bradbury's short story "The Veldt" (Bradbury, 1951), predicted a future where users could enter into shared computer-generated environments perceived as a substitute for the physical world around them and in which users interact with the environment and with each other. In these stories, users inhabited these alternative realities by means of direct electrical neural impulses, a type of virtual reality "glasses," or a virtual reality room or "cave."

Similarly, more recent, and perhaps familiar, examples in cinema include *The Matrix* (Silver, Wachowski, & Wachowski, 1999), in which humans receive direct neural stimulation/substitution to create the perception of a shared alternative reality; *Ready Player One* (Farah, De Line, Krieger, & Spielberg, 2018), in which users utilize sophisticated head-mounted displays to access the shared virtual environment, and *Star Trek's* (Roddenberry & Berman, 1987–1994) "holodeck," demonstrating a virtual reality room or cave setup.

Perhaps in true life-imitating-art fashion, technology that once seemed only to be a convenient storytelling device for science fiction and fantasy is a reality today. Shared virtual environments are already popular and widespread in massive, multiplayer, online games (MMOGs). The utility of virtual worlds goes well beyond entertainment and escape. Currently, virtual worlds are being employed in a variety of real-world settings to enhance training and skill acquisition exercises for professionals from computer programmers (Sajjanhar & Faulkner, 2019) to border crossing agents (Hudson & Degast-Kennedy, 2009) to medical personnel (Kidd, Knisley, & Morgan, 2012), including dental school students (Maha, Tantawi, El Kashlan, & Saeed, 2013) and mental health providers (Mallonee, Phillips, Holloway, & Riggs, 2018).

This chapter will discuss recent psychological applications of shared online virtual worlds for professional training in evidence-based practices, patient psychoeducation, and behavioral health treatment. The potential of these technologies to support behavioral health will also be discussed, including the development of serious game experiences, the possibilities of practicing skills in advance of new intervention implementation, and the opportunity for patients to rehearse new skills in a virtual world prior to using them in the real world.

Professional Training

The traditional gold standard for disseminating empirically based psychotherapies (Hepner, Holliday, Sousa, & Tanielian, 2019) is a live, instructor-led classroom-style training workshop composed of didactics, skills practice, and expert observation and feedback that is followed by expert consultation. Despite their effectiveness vis-à-vis increased clinical competency and improved clinical outcomes (Karlin & Cross, 2014), dissemination models that rely primarily on in-person workshops are unsustainable over the long term. In-person workshops require significant cost in travel and accommodations as well as time away from patient care and other primary responsibilities. Training venue logistics add additional cost and burden. Because of these limitations, access to high-quality provider training is constrained, inevitably excluding a significant proportion of behavioral health providers who are distant from or cannot afford to travel to training locations.

At the other end of the spectrum, on-demand online learning has attempted to fill the gap by offering training in a much less costly and more easily accessible format. Sometimes called "click-through" courses, on-demand online courses allow learners to access pre-developed content within courses or modules that learners access through the internet. Such content typically includes various forms of didactic lecture and skills demonstration, and is often offered in "voice over PowerPoint" or pre-recorded video styles. These courses can be accessed at any time and are therefore considered more convenient because they can accommodate practitioners' busy schedules. They can be stopped and started as needed and consumed in smaller "chunks" rather than all at once as multi-day, instructor-led training events demand. On-demand courses do not require the expense or time of travel, nor the resulting disruption to clinical care.

However, these courses come with their own barriers and limitations. For example, learners cannot interact in real time with an instructor or other learners. While some click-through courses make use of occasional pre-populated questions or prompts that require interaction (clicks) from the learner, click-through courses are generally passive activities that require little input from the learner beyond clicking from screen to screen. Teaching techniques such as group discussion, roleplay with expert feedback, and Socratic questioning cannot be employed, and information is generally less engaging. Unsurprisingly, studies investigating training efforts that rely solely on on-demand online courses have concluded that these platforms are typically inadequate for effective professional training in evidence-based psychotherapies (EBPs; Hepner et al., 2019).

Between the two extremes of cost and accessibility, live in-person training vs. click-through prerecorded material, there are a variety of blended models that have been offered to expand the availability of high-quality-training. Many of these models make use of computerized technology to extend the reach of a live trainer. Using platforms such as Zoom, Adobe Connect, Skype and others, trainers can provide live online training that is almost identical to that provided in similar in-person training events. In other models, trainers may spend less time with learners either in person or online, supplementing in-person contact with prerecorded video, readings, and other forms of communication. For example, communication tools that are asynchronous (e.g., email, discussion boards) and synchronous (e.g., chat rooms, desktop audio/video technology platforms) respectively allow trainers to interact with learners at their convenience or offer scheduled interaction with the instructor and other learners. Well-designed, blended models have demonstrated similar results to traditional in-person trainings in some cases and offer a more hopeful alternative for increasing the availability of well-trained providers (Smith et al., 2017).

Given the range of interactivity and potential learner engagement inherent in these various online training modalities, it is imperative to evaluate conclusions of some studies suggesting that "online training" is less effective or ineffective compared to in-person learning with caution, as such studies almost always refer to online on-demand click-through courses. In particular, these conclusions should not be inappropriately extended to virtual worlds simulations (to be further defined in the next section), for which there is very little data regarding the efficacy of training outcomes.

One possible reason for misapplied conclusions regarding online training and virtual learning is that these terms are broad descriptors that are often applied to any number of training models that utilize a computer device to access learning material, whether through the internet or using stand-alone storage materials (e.g., USB drive, DVD). These may include online, on-demand click-through courses, viewing prerecorded webcast videos, reading text-based material on a website, or even virtual simulation environments used in a synchronous or asynchronous manner. Therefore, an important step before we discuss virtual worlds and learning is to clarify the conversation by offering a standardized language. In the next section we provide definitions of commonly used terms.

Important Definitions and Terms

"Digital learning" or **"computer-based learning"** refers to any learning that requires a computer device for access to and display of learning material. Only if that material is available from a website or other internet resource can the platform be described as **"online learning."** Online learning is a general term that would include online click-through courses, especially those administered by a **learning management system** (LMS) such as Blackboard or Sakai, but would also include live, synchronous learning in a virtual world simulated environment. A **"webcast"** is a prerecorded event that is broadcast on the internet at a specific, scheduled time, and participants watch the playback of the recorded event simultaneously. Similarly, a **"webinar"** refers to an online training event in which the instructor presents live content, and learning materials are available using web conferencing software and/or hardware (e.g., Zoom, Adobe Connect). Often in webinars the instructor or instructors is visible to participant learners through a live webcam, and instructor or instructors and learners can interact through instant messaging or even voice-over IP protocols.

Training instances may be described as **"synchronous"** or **"asynchronous."** Synchronous learning refers to any training event that occurs live and where the presentation of the learning material by an instructor or instructors occurs at the same time as the reception of the learning material by attendees. Synchronous learning includes in-person training, webinars as defined earlier, and other live, online, instructor-led training. Asynchronous learning, alternatively, refers to on-demand access to learning material at any time and can include reading books or other printed learning materials, watching videos, accessing on-demand click-through courses, watching webcasts, or even engaging in game-play experiences for serious purposes (known as **"serious play"**).

Finally, for the purposes of this chapter, **"virtual learning"** refers only to learning via simulation, whether or not it is mediated by a computer, and can include physical mannequins (e.g., CPR training mannequins or surgery simulation mannequins), shared virtual environments (i.e., virtual worlds), or virtual reality in a three-dimensional environment that employs multiple sensory modalities. Virtual learning can be a special case of "online learning" if the virtual learning environment is accessed through the internet or can be a special case of digital learning if the virtual environment is accessed on a stand-alone computer system. In the next section we will further define and explore virtual worlds, including their attributes and limitations.

Virtual Worlds and Their Application

Virtual worlds are computer-generated three-dimensional simulated environments accessed via a computer on a high-speed internet connection. Users are represented in the environment as an avatar, or computer character, that can interact with the environment and with other users who access the same space. Virtual worlds environments can be persistent, meaning that they may be accessed any time of day, and changes to the environment remain after users depart and return, rather than non-persistent, meaning the environment reverts to an initial or default state each time it is accessed.

There are a number of key attributes of virtual worlds training and education that have the potential to enhance learning and distinguish it from other types of online learning. Two such attributes often discussed in the literature as features that distinguish virtual environments from other types of online experiences include the constructs of **immersion** and **presence** (McLellan, 2004; Mikropoulos, 2006; Mikropoulos & Strouboulis, 2004). Immersion can be understood as the perception of being encompassed by the environment, while presence is defined as the subjective experience of being in one place or environment (e.g., sitting in a virtual auditorium), even when one is physically situated in another (e.g., at their office desk). To put it differently, immersion represents the more objective properties of the virtual environment that lead to the subjective experience of presence in that environment. The more "real" the environment, the more "present" one is, which allows for more engaged and focused learning opportunities. Optimal levels of presence and immersion can enhance both asynchronous and synchronous learning activities.

Virtual worlds offer unique affordances that can result in improved dissemination of evidence-based practice and better implementation of these skills, due to increased knowledge gain, improved application of skills, improved access to consultation and support, and opportunities to practice and hone these skills in a low-stakes context via simulated and/or automated patients. While the use of shared virtual environments in the behavioral health professions is admittedly limited at this time, we will present some "case" examples of how virtual environments have been used and the potential learning benefits that continue to be explored. In the next section we will share some important examples that illustrate the exciting potential to be realized in the exploitation of these technologies, with a focus on the mental health field.

Virtual Education Center: A Synchronous Learning Experience

The Center for Deployment Psychology (CDP) at the Uniformed Services University (USU) has developed and utilized several example applications of shared virtual environments in its mission to train highly skilled and culturally competent behavioral health providers who treat US military Service members, both within and without the U.S. Department of Defense.

Built in the virtual world platform Second Life, CDP's Virtual Education Center (VEC) is a three-dimensional simulated training venue intended to support multiple-day professional development workshops in a shared virtual environment. This venue includes a main auditorium with seating for up to 45 attendees for didactic instruction, group discussion, and video demonstrations; 24 breakout rooms for roleplay and practice exercises by groups of two to six participants; a registration and reception desk at which attendees initially "sign in" for events and collect workshop materials and handouts; a virtual library for storing and distributing materials from previous workshops; and meeting space for informal group discussions following workshops.

Instructors and attendees are represented as avatars and interact through a variety of communications channels, including voice over IP (VOIP), text chatting, and nonverbal communication, such as avatar gestures and animations. Workshop instruction includes didactic lectures, slides, demonstration videos, downloadable workshop handouts, group discussion, and breakout skills practice with expert observation and feedback.

Tools developed in the VEC to support training workshops include audience polling, automatic attendance taking, attendee identification, question and answer facilitation, automatic breakout group assignment, automatic breakout room "teleportation" and retrieval, push-button access to technical assistance, count-down clocks and note-taking tools in breakout rooms, an attendee tracking map, and links to external resources supporting the workshop content.

Instructors present the same curriculum and materials as that offered in CDP's in-person workshops, modified only slightly for the virtual environment. For example, the same PowerPoint-style slides, handouts, resources, and demonstration videos utilized during in-person training events are utilized "in world" for virtual workshops. Roleplay exercises, essential for learning new EBP skills, are the same in virtual workshops as in-person workshops, with instructors able to observe learner skills practice and offer feedback and correction as needed.

Benefits of Live Virtual Worlds Training Workshops

Learners at CDP's virtual training workshops report a sense of presence in the virtual venue similar to, and at times greater than, the presence that attendees to CDP's in-person training events report (Mallonee et al., 2018). The high level of interaction and (faculty-observed) experiential learning demonstrates student engagement arguably higher than an in-person classroom experience. Unlike in-person workshops, the learner's ability to interact with the presenters or other participants is not limited to discrete, predetermined times, such as during question and answer segments, direct roleplay, or during breaks. Instead, synchronous text-based interactions with peers and instructors facilitate participant contributions to the learning and timely clarifications of questions. The average number of interactions with faculty or other participants during workshops in Second Life far exceeds that typically experienced in an in-person classroom, as anecdotally reported by instructors.

Role plays, which are a key mechanism used to enhance active learning for students in both in-person and virtual workshops, have inherent limitations in in-person workshops that are addressed in a virtual setting. During in-person workshop roleplays, participants often group up with friends or colleagues, and instructors typically move from breakout group to breakout group, listening in on the exercise, confirming that they are on task, and offering observations and corrections as needed. However, it is a common experience among CDP instructors to find breakout groups engaged in off-task behavior or conversations. Instead of engaging in the prescribed exercise, conversations about current clients, office politics, social engagements, or even plans for lunch are not uncommon. It appears easier for colleagues or friends to collude in avoidance of sometimes awkward roleplay exercises. However, in CDP's virtual worlds workshops, breakout groups are randomly and automatically assigned, almost always resulting in participants being paired with strangers. Participants are automatically teleported to breakout rooms, and at the conclusion of the exercise automatically teleported back to the virtual classroom, avoiding the significant amount of time spent forming groups, finding a workspace, and moving to and from the exercise. The resulting exercise participation appears to be much more focused and on task for many possible reasons, resulting in exercises that are more efficient and effective than those in in-person workshops. It may be that being paired with a stranger results in a feeling of responsibility to not interfere with the learning of another professional. It may be that without a pre-workshop relationship, there is little common experience to chat about. Participants may also be more motivated to stay on topic because they are aware that instructors can and do teleport into breakout rooms unannounced and could catch them off topic, rather than being able to see an instructor physically approaching the group as a signal to get back on topic.

Similarly, participation during didactic presentations can be better managed in a virtual workshop as compared to an in-person event. During in-person workshops, questions from audience members unavoidably interrupt the presentation, usually appropriately so. However, the quality of questions can range from insightful requests for clarification or elaboration to redundant, unhelpful, or off-topic comments or questions. At in-person events, the quality of the question is unknown until the presentation is already interrupted, potentially with considerable time required to adequately address the question, regardless of quality. On the other hand, legitimate questions by some audience members may go unasked perhaps due to concerns of being judged by other participants, worries that their question will appear uninformed, hesitation to interrupt the flow of presentation, or even concerns that the question is poorly timed.

However, in a virtual workshop, audience members are encouraged to utilize parallel text-based group messaging, which all participants can see, throughout the workshop at any time to ask any questions, challenge assertions, react to information, interact with other learners, and reflect on course content. A co-presenter monitors the chat, answers questions, encourages more participation and interaction, and facilitates discussion. When appropriate, the co-presenter interrupts the primary presenter to elevate only the most relevant and pressing questions to facilitate a larger verbal discussion, preventing less-relevant discussion from derailing the presentation while still encouraging and acknowledging all contributions from the audience. An additional benefit with this co-presenter model is that instructors report a higher level of attention and engagement when not presenting as they are "in charge" of tracking chat and providing additional examples during discussion which enhances the quality of the training and reduces redundancy sometimes seen in in-person co-presented training workshops.

One of the most notable benefits of virtual training workshops as compared to in-person workshops is a phenomenon we've termed "synergistic learning." With in-person workshops, the expectation is that learners will sit quietly and passively throughout the presentation, absorbing knowledge and interacting almost exclusively with the instructor through direct questions. Attendees talking to each other, outside of planned activities or role-play exercises, is generally discouraged and considered inconsiderate at best and disruptive to others' learning at worst. However, in the virtual learning environment, participant interaction is expected and encouraged. Utilizing the text-based chat feature, attendees can ask each other questions, and even better, answer questions from fellow learners. They can fact check what is being presented and even challenge information, assertions, or interpretations offered by presenters or fellow learners. They can share resources with each other that broaden the discussion and enhance the learning experience. Instead of multiple one-to-one communication streams (instructor to each learner), the learning environment becomes a learning network with all (or at least most) contributing and benefiting beyond the sum of all of these individual learning pieces. It does not take long, in our experience, for a cultural expectation of participation in this shared discussion to be established, and the lack of participation is quickly viewed as divergent rather than the norm.

Certainly, some of the benefits described here are not unique to virtual worlds training and are shared with video teleconference-based training events, including no need for instructors or participants to travel, interactivity between instructors and participants, and interactivity between learners. However, the sense of presence in a virtual environment contributes to a sense of community, of being co-present together in this learning experience. Additionally, simulation can be readily incorporated into the training curriculum, and pedagogical tools can be expanded to include things such as guided tours, scavenger hunts, co-building/developing, and prototyping, which are not available in video teleconferencing platforms.

Instructors find that there are opportunities to illustrate certain concepts in novel ways that are not available in the physical world. For example, instructors can demonstrate the mechanisms of serotonin reuptake inhibitors in an oversized, three-dimensional simulation of a neural synapse, or lead a tour through a re-creation of an index trauma in a combat zone to discuss the development of PTSD, or demonstrate patient flow through an optimized clinical layout. The possibilities for simulation, demonstration, or creating learning context are virtually endless in a shared virtual environment.

Limitations of Virtual Worlds Training Workshops and Mitigation

Virtual worlds training workshops are not a good fit for all learners. Some are not comfortable enough with the technology to benefit from these workshops. The environment may be foreign to them, especially if they are not gamers or may not seem intuitive. This results in high time and energy investment at start-up and a steep learning curve to become proficient in the environment such that they can benefit from the workshop. We do not advocate virtual training replacing all live, instructor-led training when virtual training is not a good fit for some people who would have no alternatives. Traditional in-person training workshops are still considered the gold standard.

However, many learners may benefit from tech-support through which their technology issues can be identified and resolved prior to a virtual workshop, allowing them to focus on the training material without the stressful distraction of technology issues. CDP provides a number of tech-support options to its learners to help lower the start-up time requirements for most learners and help them have a positive experience. For example, all virtual attendees are strongly encouraged at registration to attend one of several scheduled open house meetings in the VEC, at which some very basic functions are tested, including whether they can successfully login, hear VOIP audio, turn on their microphone and be heard, learn basic avatar navigation, and whether they can see streamed videos in the virtual environment. Any difficulties are addressed and resolved prior to the workshop. Then, at the beginning of every workshop, a short "tech orientation" presentation reminds users of basic functions, how to use the attendee tools (such as the heads-up display (HUD) tool), and how to ask for tech assistance throughout the workshop. Tech-support specialists are present throughout each of our workshops and provide help in real time as any tech issues arise so that they are quickly resolved and the attendee returns to learning quickly. Additionally, CDP has developed several media tools, including a helpful website with quick-start directions, a frequently asked questions (FAQ) section, short training videos, and downloadable reference sheets.

Just as virtual worlds training workshops are not a good fit for every learner, they may not be a good fit for some instructors. While the parallel communication modalities of VOIP and text chat can facilitate more interactive learning, it can also be distracting to both learners and instructors. Some instructors find the ongoing text chat too distracting, often derailing their presentation while trying to track and respond to questions in real time. To address this issue, we recommend using a two-presenter model wherein one actively presents the course material while the other tracks and responds to text chat. The two presenters can switch roles throughout the workshop.

Some presenters may not be comfortable enough with the technology to manage all of the tech features of the virtual training venue. Just as we recommend having tech-support specialists attend the entire workshop to quickly respond to any technology issues attendees may face, we also recommend that these tech-support specialists be assigned to manage some of the technology features in the venue, such as setting up and starting demonstration videos, managing the breakout group assignment and teleport tools, and starting and managing breakout room countdown clocks, in addition to providing tech support for attendees.

Teaching in a virtual world can be challenging. Because all participants are represented by an avatar, instructors cannot see attendees physically, making it difficult to gauge attention and engagement. This requires the use of additional instructor skills such as increasing check-ins with attendees, asking frequent questions, utilizing audience polling, encouraging and rewarding chat comments and responses, encouraging the use of audience avatar animations for nonverbal feedback, and seeking additional opportunities for interactions, more than would be typical of an in-person workshop. Instructors need to be especially charismatic to prevent attendees from becoming bored with a less-energetic presentation. Additionally, without being able to see the audience physically, it can be difficult to assess when concepts have been explained adequately, which often leads instructors to overexplain. Instructors therefore need to practice presenting tersely and checking in with the audience for comprehension. And finally, the audience cannot see the instructor physically, either, which can present challenges when presenters would normally use their own natural gestures to illustrate points (e.g., drawing a habituation curve in the air, or showing workshop handouts). Our instructors have developed alternative means of conveying this information, such as including images of handouts in their presentation slides, illustrating concepts using videos, images, drawings, or 3D objects, and at times creating avatar animations for concepts that cannot be illustrated adequately any other way.

Accessing virtual world platforms such as Second Life requires a high-speed internet connection, such as cable or fiber optics-based networks. Cellular data hotspot connections can be minimally adequate for low-resource environments but can be easily overwhelmed with data lag at points of high data utilization. Not all potential attendees have access to adequate high-speed internet. However, with high-speed internet access almost ubiquitous and growth of access continuing to expand, this is a limitation experienced by only a few potential learners.

The most reliable thing about technology is that it does not always work as planned. Technology sometimes breaks down, and therefore it is always a good idea to have contingency plans in place for such breakdowns. For example, in case of power outages and network outages, it is advisable to have more than one instructor available who can present workshop content and who can take over instruction in the case of the sudden disappearance of the other instructor from the virtual venue. Additionally, CDP instructors have cell-based internet hotspots as a backup network connection. In

Second Life, a region restart (essentially a reboot of the specific server running the simulated environment) may cause all participants to be logged out temporarily, and while this is a rare occurrence, especially for unscheduled maintenance, we have found that explaining to the audience what to do in such an event during the workshop introduction can mitigate distress and confusion. Participants also sometimes experience media difficulties, such as not being able to view demonstration videos "in world," sometimes due to driver issues on their personal computer. To combat this, whenever a video is shown in the virtual workshop venue, a URL (uniform resource locator, or "web address") for the video stream is posted in the chat window to allow participants to view it in a separate web browser if needed. And while we have never experienced this to date, sometimes complete platform failure can occur. For such a situation, we always have available a backup conference call line for audio, and even alternative conferencing platforms, such as Zoom or Adobe Connect, available and ready in case there is a need to switch over. Overall, we have found it invaluable to have tech-support specialists at the ready that can problem solve on the fly.

Virtual worlds platforms may not be allowed on some government or institutional computers or networks. This can be due to a number of factors, including high resource utilization by virtual worlds platforms, concerns about network security, viewer applications not having been reviewed and approved by network control boards, or perhaps because the virtual world platform is seen as merely "gaming" and therefore inconsistent with productivity or professionalism. Many attendees have found that they cannot attend a CDP Second Life workshop from their work/office computer. Additionally, attending a training workshop from their clinic or office may result in frequent interruptions from colleagues or clinic managers who may see the attendee as "not doing anything productive" and therefore available to accommodate a walk-in client or an emergent situation. Some may be tempted to multitask during the training workshop, such as writing case notes or even meeting with clients.

For all of these reasons, we strongly recommend that attendees attend from a location away from their primary work location, preferably from their own home, on a personally owned device, and on a network they control. The attendee is out of the office for the workshop, much like they would have been for an in-person event. By being away from their primary work location, attendees can focus on the training event as though they were physically present, without the additional distractions and interruptions of being in the office. They can also avoid the technological issues posed by trying to attend from a controlled network and hardware. Most clinic managers recognize the benefit of access to high-quality training with no travel, resulting in fewer days out of the clinic and reduced costs. CDP has at times made a template memo available that potential attendees can provide to clinic managers to outline the benefits of attending a virtual workshop to support their request to work from home.

Outcomes

Since May 2014, CDP has conducted 54 two-day training workshops in Second Life across five different evidence-based psychotherapies with over 1,600 mental health provider attendees. Approximately 20% of these participants have attended more than one training workshop.

A recent comparison of CDP's Second Life-based workshops to in-person workshops suggested the two modalities are comparable in terms of both knowledge gained by attendees and overall satisfaction with the training experience (Mallonee et al., 2018). Knowledge scores increased significantly from pre-workshop to post-workshop for all subjects and in both modalities. Some topics, such as Cognitive-Behavioral Therapy for Suicide Prevention (CBT-SP) and Cognitive-Behavioral Therapy for Depression (CBT-D) demonstrated significantly greater knowledge gain in virtual workshops than in-person workshops (Birman, French, & Holloway, 2018; Paxton, Phillips, Weinstock, Sacks, & Birman, 2019). Additionally, self-reported readiness to use the EBP were higher for attendees in virtual workshops vs. in-person workshops. Attendee satisfaction was similar between modalities. While not established by these studies, possible explanations include increased attendee engagement, greater interaction between instructors and attendees, greater participation in roleplay exercises, synergistic learning, and self-selection bias (meaning that attendees who would otherwise not thrive in a virtual environment choose not to register for virtual training events).

User feedback has been almost universally positive, with a vast majority of attendees reporting positive experiences and intent to attend future Second Life-based workshops. Some examples of user feedback include the following statements on post-workshop surveys: "I just love this training, extremely interactive. Great opportunities to ask questions. I feel like I participated more in this format than I might in face-to-face workshops." "Really great training. Second life makes the training accessible to providers anywhere and still allows for an interactive training experience. Very helpful!" "Easily one of the best trainings I have ever been in—and I am a trainer :-/" "At first I was reluctant but found it a very positive experience," and "Keeping up with the chats and the speaker was difficult. I stopped attending to the chats so I could better focus—but I worry then I wasn't as active as I could have been."

Consultation in Virtual Worlds

Consultation is considered an essential part of best-practices in training in EBPs, providing support and correction as providers new to a skill implement these protocols. In-person consultation may be ideal because it allows for a wealth of information about consultation cases to be reviewed by the consultant and the consultees. However, in-person consultation may be limited by the availability and proximity of an EBP consultant or by a lack of sufficient number of consultees nearby to form a consultation group. Remote access to a consultation group removes many of these barriers by allowing consultees in almost any location to reach expert consultants and other consultees at similar experience levels. Telephone consultation groups have existed for many years and have resulted in improved utilization and protocol fidelity. However, telephone conference calls have significant limitations in that documents, session recordings, and demonstration videos are simply not available for review. Consultation in virtual worlds can be a much richer experience than telephone conference calls and more closely resembles in-person consultation groups but with all of the benefits of telecommunication.

CDP has explored conducting consultation groups in Second Life in specially designed consultation rooms connected to the virtual training environment. Consultation groups meet at weekly meetings during the normal workday schedule. Attendees are represented by an avatar, just as they are in virtual workshops. Consultees benefit from discussion with a consultation group, both through VOIP (to facilitate natural communication and discussion) and text chatting. This chatting includes discussing their ongoing cases and challenges they may be encountering but also includes hearing other providers' questions or implementation challenges, the consultant's responses and direction, and descriptions of situations that they perhaps have not yet encountered. Consultees also contribute their own experience and expertise, responding to colleague questions or offering thoughts and perspectives of the challenges posed by their fellow consultees. To support these discussions and ongoing learning, media screens in the consultation room allow for sharing relevant case documents, such as de-identified assessment data and session work product (e.g., an in vivo hierarchy for Prolonged Exposure cases). Even session video recordings (with client permission) can be viewed by all group members and discussed. Demonstration videos can be viewed and discussed as a group to reinforce relevant discussion points and reinforce prior training.

Not all communication platforms are HIPAA compliant, and virtual worlds platforms are no different. Confidentiality must be considered and carefully protected. This is not an issue unique to virtual worlds. Telephone lines are not encrypted or secured to make eavesdropping impossible or even difficult, and yet few providers are uncomfortable with using telephones to discuss highly sensitive confidential information with clients, supervisors, or colleagues. Even so, it is incumbent on all consultation participants to be aware of the security limitations of virtual worlds communications technology and protect their clients' information accordingly. For example, Second Life VOIP technology is not HIPAA compliant in that voice streams from all sources are uploaded to VOIP servers, mixed, and re-streamed down to each user without encryption or heightened security measures. While it is not likely to happen, it is possible for the VOIP stream to be intercepted. Video or audio recordings meant to be shared in consultation can be streamed from media streaming services into the virtual environment without running through Linden Labs (the developer of Second Life) servers, but the streaming service and transmission connection used may have confidentiality limitations of their own. Therefore, all CDP consultees are cautioned to discuss cases without names, limit personally identifying information as much as possible, and secure client informed consent to share information in group consultation as needed, including for case documents and any recordings.

While consultation in virtual worlds presents an exciting and rich consultation possibility, it may not always be the right fit for all consultation needs. Again, all technology fails at some time or another. And because Second Life and other virtual worlds were not designed primarily to support behavioral health applications such as training and consultation, the technology was not designed to be continuously reliable and available. Connections sometimes go down. Hardware may fail. Accounts may be compromised and/or disabled. Any number of technology issues may come up. Technology may thus seem sometimes to cause more problems than it solves when it comes to using virtual worlds for consultation—telephone conference calls have been successfully and more easily utilized for decades. In many circumstances, therefore, telephone conference lines may be the right platform for the greatest success. Virtual worlds consultation should not be considered the *only* solution—it's but one solution to enhance EBP consultation following workshop training, and one that may provide a future solution with technology maturation over time.

One particularly challenging barrier CDP has encountered is the ability of consultees to access the virtual environment during the regular workday. As discussed earlier, accessing virtual worlds may be especially difficult on managed networks. Consultation sessions typically are relatively short compared to two-day training workshops. While it is generally easy to justify telework to attend a two-day virtual training workshop, it is much more difficult to justify requesting or granting telework all day for a clinician to attend a one-hour consultation session, taking them out of the clinic and therefore away from patient care. Acceptance of virtual worlds as a professional tool is in its early stages and limited, and so this issue of time away from the clinic may continue to be a significant challenge until virtual worlds applications are adopted more widely and access is considered a common and important tool in many aspects of life—much like access to the internet is common and expected in professional life now.

PTSD Learning Center and Snoozeum: Asynchronous Learning Experiences

Simulating live in-person training workshops in a virtual world is only one, and perhaps the most limited, use of virtual worlds for training and education. Beyond simply gathering avatars in a room and speaking to them, shared virtual environments also can be used to create *experiences* for learning. Based on Experiential Learning Theory (Kolb, 1984), or the idea that learning through experience is more efficient and leads to better retention than rote or didactic learning, the use of shared virtual environments to create learning experiences promises an exciting opportunity for deep, meaningful learning that goes beyond a simulated classroom experience. This theory is supported by a plethora of studies. A meta-analysis of almost 6,500 studies comparing computer-based simulation games against other traditional teaching methods found that post-training self-efficacy was 20% higher, declarative knowledge was 11% higher, procedural knowledge was 14% higher, and retention was 9% higher for trainees taught with simulation games, relative to a comparison group (Sitzman, 2011). Similarly, Kokcharov (2015) concluded that learning by doing, including simulation gaming, results in significantly higher retention of learning material (>75%) vs. more passive learning activities, such as reading, lecture, or reviewing audiovisual materials (<20%). Shared virtual environments are perfectly tailored for learning simulation games, immersing the student in an experience created for learning by doing.

These experiences need not be bound by the limitations of the physical world. The setting, circumstances, physics, reactions, etc. can range from the familiar to the fanciful. Shared virtual environments have been used as training tools in a number of health disciplines, including training in communication and assessment skills for undergraduate mental health nursing students (Kidd et al., 2012), nurse anesthesia training in a virtual operating room (Gerald & Antonacci, 2009), and training in weight management for obese patients (Johnston, Massey, & De Vaneaux, 2013).

While the use of shared virtual environments to train mental health providers is still in its infancy, one early example of this is the Virtual Hallucination by Peter Yellowlees in Second Life (Yellowlees & Cook, 2006). Yellowlees developed the Virtual Hallucination experience as a teaching tool to help psychiatry students understand the experience of psychotic patients. In this scenario, visitors see unsettling representations of various psychotic symptoms, such as visual distortion hallucinations, delusions of reference, and auditory command hallucinations, all from a first-person perspective as though the user had schizophrenia. Yellowlees based the development of this tool on his extensive experience treating schizophrenia as a psychiatrist, further validating the experience with volunteer psychotic patients who could vouch for the validity of these representations and even recommend adjustments that would better communicate the terrifying experiences they had to others who had never had a hallucination. Of the 579 Second Life users who toured the simulation and completed the related survey, 440 (76%) stated that the environment improved their understanding of auditory hallucinations, 69% said it improved their understanding of visual hallucinations, and 82% reported they would recommend the environment to a friend. This early example demonstrated the vast potential for simulating the experience of mental health symptomatology as a tool to train mental health providers and the general public.

Inspired by Yellowlees work, The National Center for Telehealth and Technology (T2) developed the T2 Virtual PTSD Experience in Second Life as an experiential patient education tool (Holloway & Reger, 2013). Visitors experienced, in a first-person scenario, a U.S. Military Service Member's combat-related index trauma as well as simulations of the resulting symptoms of post-traumatic stress disorder (PTSD) in a Service member's life. As players encountered each symptom simulation, they were also shown how the symptom was connected to the original index trauma and other ways symptoms could be manifest. The intended audience was primarily United States Military Service members and veterans who may be experiencing post-trauma reactions, with a secondary audience of family members and friends. The purposes of the T2 Virtual PTSD Experience were to: (1) increase understanding of common post-trauma reactions; (2) increase family or friends' recognition of possible PTSD symptoms in others (or the users' own experience); (3) increase compassion and empathy for these experiences, and; (4) motivate appropriate care-seeking by offering information about available treatment services in the U.S. Department of Defense health systems and the Veterans Health Administration system.

At its height, the T2 Virtual PTSD Experience saw visitor volumes of approximately 500 users per month, with little to no marketing other than word of mouth. Several voluntary "in-world" visitor surveys indicate successful outcomes. For example, in one survey 65% of respondents strongly agreed or agreed that their experience helped them to better understand how PTSD may be acquired (n = 345). In another, 73% of respondents said they strongly agreed or agreed that they were more likely to seek care for themselves or recommend care for someone close to them following their visit to the Virtual PTSD Experience (n = 132; Holloway & Reger, 2013). While no longer available in Second Life, it represented an important example of utilizing virtual worlds for education and training beyond what is available in traditional learning models.

Following these examples, CDP developed two virtual worlds-based learning environments intended to extend experiential learning to behavioral health provider training in EBPs, especially in underlying theory behind the interventions. Specifically, CDP developed the PTSD Learning Center and the Snoozeum.

The PTSD Learning Center utilizes a "big game, small museum" format, meaning that introductory and supportive information regarding diagnostic criteria for PTSD, assessment tools, evidence-based therapies, and underlying theory is provided in a museum-like format with displays and small interactive elements. The bulk of learning occurs in a large role-play game called Operation AVATAR (A Virtual Allegory of Trauma And Recovery). In this game, learners take on the role of "John Smith," a simulated PTSD patient, and experience three significant days in John's history, including experiencing a representation of a combat-related trauma, experiencing simulations and representations of common PTSD symptoms, and experiencing representations of recovery from PTSD. Along the way, learners review and apply theoretical concepts regarding the development of PTSD, assessment of PTSD symptoms, and elements of evidence-based psychotherapies that successfully treat PTSD.

The Snoozeum, on the other hand, utilizes a "big museum, small game" format while teaching about normal sleep regulation, sleep stages, sleep disruptions, the development of sleep problems, clinical assessment of sleep problems, and treatment interventions, all in a series of interactive museum displays and mini-games. The culmination of this experience is in the "virtual sleep clinic" feature where participants apply all of the knowledge they've gained throughout the museum in a simulated treatment interview game. A more detailed description of the Snoozeum's features is available elsewhere (Lefkowitz, Dolan, Rogers, & Holloway, 2019).

While the Virtual PTSD Learning Center and the Snoozeum are available for public access for free on the Second Life platform, both of these environments were developed to augment live, instructor-led training. For example, in CDP's standard two-day training workshop in Prolonged Exposure therapy for PTSD (PE), the virtual character John Smith is used as a case example woven throughout the workshop, including discussions on the patient's history, assessment and diagnosis, appropriateness for PE therapy, and the course of his treatment. Students are invited to visit the virtual PTSD Learning Center and play Operation AVATAR as homework between the two days of instruction. Additionally, some workshops (particularly those offered in Second Life) have included a guided tour of the PTSD Learning Center as part of the workshop. Tours and homework assignments to visit the PTSD Learning Center have also been incorporated into CDP's Cognitive Processing Therapy for PTSD (CPT) workshop. Similarly, attendees to CDP's two-day Cognitive-Behavioral Therapy for Insomnia (CBT-I) workshops have been introduced to the Snoozeum, as assigned homework or through guided tours for workshops conducted in Second Life.

The development of these environments was informed by the essential work of Reeves and Read (2009) in their book *Total Engagement*, in which they describe ten key gaming elements that facilitate engagement and learning in a gaming environment. Elements can be applied to serious gaming situations to improve learning engagement, retention, and persistence. They are: (1) self-representation by an avatar, (2) 3D immersive environments, (3) narrative context, (4) instant feedback, (5) reputations, ranks, and level, (6) marketplace and economies, (7) competition with rules that are explicit and enforced, (8) teams, (9) parallel communication systems, and 10) time parameters. Each of these elements enhances learning and engagement in both environments, including the large role-playing game Operation AVATAR and multiple mini-games.

As far as we are aware, the PTSD Learning Center and the Snoozeum are the only virtual world environments focused on training behavioral health providers in the underlying theory, assessment, and treatment of PTSD and Insomnia. The use of such immersive, interactive experiences is in itself innovative. Given that these environments are relatively new, having launched in November 2018, little quantitative data exists regarding impact on student attainment of course objectives. However, anecdotal data strongly suggests that the virtual environments significantly increase learner engagement, promote reengagement when interrupted, and increase learning that is personally meaningful and more easily remembered. Additionally, the number of repeat visits by learners indicates the enhancement of learning through repetition.

Patient Psychoeducation

The promise of shared virtual environments goes beyond professional training for mental health providers. The potential for effective patient psychoeducation possibilities is endless. Consider the possibility to educate potential clients about what they may expect in therapy. For many who have never been in therapy before, much of what they "know" about mental health treatment comes from the media. Robison (2013) described the following:

> Concern about the impact of fictional psychotherapy portrayals is warranted, as they are rife with ridiculous, unethical, and even malicious depictions of treatment (Gabbard & Gabbard, 1999; Hyler, 1988; Kadushin, 1969). Indeed, the picture of therapy painted by popular media is rarely flattering; often showing therapists as incompetent, ineffective, and manipulative figures who typically cause more harm than good to befall their clients (Grinfeld, 1998; Lehmann, 2002; Von Sydow & Reimer, 1998). Misconceived expectations of psychotherapy could certainly result from such inaccuracies. Some have even argued these media depictions directly reflect society's beliefs about psychotherapy and that individuals form their image of treatment from these portrayals, making it irresponsible not to address them (Gabbard, 2001; Hyler, 1988). The APA has heeded such warnings and issued press releases on television therapy's lack of ethics (American Psychological Association, 2008). The Media Watch Committee was also formed, tasked with commenting on, counteracting, and rewarding portrayals of psychotherapy in film and television.
>
> (Schultz, as cited in Robison, 2013, pp. 11–12)

But consider an immersive simulation that accurately demonstrates high-quality, ethical care, demystifying it in the process. Perhaps fewer potential clients would find psychotherapy to be so foreign. Motivation to seek care and expectations for positive outcomes from psychotherapy may increase.

Patients could also benefit from an accurate walkthrough of treatment facilities, with the aim of helping them feel as though they have visited the clinic or office before, developing a familiarity with the layout and programs. For example, when the National Intrepid Center of Excellence (NICoE) first opened at the Walter Reed National Military Medical Center (WRN-MMC) in Bethesda, MD, a virtual simulation of the facility was developed in Second Life where incoming patients could visit, become familiar with the layout of the building, learn about the various programs available to them, find out about what assessment activities they would be involved in when they arrived, and even meet some of the staff that would greet them in the physical world when they arrived. Anecdotally, several patients who visited the virtual simulation before arriving reported feeling less anticipatory anxiety about arriving at check-in.

Other examples may include immersive simulations of the incorporation of technology into therapy, such as utilizing virtual reality exposure therapy and the equipment involved, biofeedback equipment and procedures, psychophysiological measurement equipment, or even electroconvulsive shock therapy equipment and procedures.

Patient psychoeducation does not need to merely simulate locations or interactions they may encounter in the physical world. The T2 Virtual PTSD Experience, mentioned previously, is an example of patient education about post-traumatic stress disorder (PTSD), how it develops, and how it is effectively treated. But consider a number of other possibilities, including a three-dimensional simulation of a synapse showing how various psychoactive medications are thought to act on neurotransmitters and receptors. For example, patients could explore the mechanisms of selective serotonin reuptake inhibitors at the synapse level or see how various medications and substances may interact in the body to potentiate or inhibit the main effect of each substance. The possibilities are limited only by the imagination and technical ability of those developing such educational experiences.

Mental Health Treatment

Shared virtual environments may someday be a common tool for dispensing and managing psychotherapy interventions. At a basic level, shared virtual environments could potentially be used as a form of telemental health wherein the therapist and patient occupy the same virtual environment and interact in ways very similar to in-person therapy. In an unpublished pilot study that was reviewed and approved by the local Institutional Review Board, researchers at the National Center for Telehealth and Technology (T2) provided Prolonged Exposure therapy to patients with PTSD, all within a virtual clinic in Second Life. For this proof-of-concept pilot, therapists and patients never saw one another in the physical world, even though they were physically located at the same clinic but in separate offices. Minor adjustments to the treatment protocol were made to accommodate the treatment in a virtual environment, such as using encrypted email transmission to exchange treatment forms and worksheets vs. hardcopy versions, having the patient complete assessment instruments in an online format, and acknowledging the fact that the therapist was unable to physically see the client. For the latter consideration, the therapist would engage more in inquiry about what the patient was thinking, feeling, and what the patient's reactions were to what was discussed in the session. All subjects in the pilot study experienced clinically significant improvement in their PTSD symptoms, as measured by the Clinician Administered PTSD Scale (CAPS) and the PTSD Checklist (PCL). One subject reported that he felt as though the treatment was more effective for him than traditional in-person treatment would have been because he believed it would have been much more difficult to talk about his trauma experiences with a physical person sitting in the same room. On the one hand, this pilot highlights opportunities for maladaptive avoidance via virtual worlds. On the other, this platform may mediate therapy and progressively difficult exposure for those with prominent avoidance symptoms. It is noteworthy that the patient just mentioned elaborated that despite meeting his therapist in the virtual environment and not being in the same physical space, he still felt as though his therapist was "there" and could easily work with him.

Beyond mere telemental health applications, however, shared virtual environments may someday offer possibilities unavailable in the physical world. Some of these possibilities are similar to those currently being developed in stand-alone virtual reality systems, such as virtual reality exposure therapy for PTSD and other anxiety disorders. However, the shared nature of the environments opens up additional possibilities for interventions that involve more than one person, such as scenario-based couples or family therapies where a therapist could observe and intervene in situation-based family dynamics. Patients with social phobia could try out various methods of interacting with other real people in an anonymous virtual environment in which missteps, mistakes, or unexpected outcomes have no lasting impact on the patient's reputation or important relationships. Substance abuse therapies could, for example, simulate environments or situations that present cued cravings for the patient, populated with confederates to enhance the exercise, or even populated with other therapy group members for a highly impactful experience.

Perhaps shared virtual environments could even be used to assist a client in communicating the experience of trauma to their therapist, significant other, or social support through assisted creation of a virtual simulation of their trauma. Similar procedures could be used in nightmare rescripting and imagery rehearsal-based therapies for trauma-related nightmares where the patient constructs a simulation of the nightmare, and with the assistance of their therapist, modifies important elements of the nightmare which they can replay repeatedly for rehearsal of the altered script. Again the possibilities are endless. Obviously, all such future innovations would require empirical testing and evaluation, but the potential is intriguing.

Other Future Possibilities

Other applications of virtual worlds can also be imagined. Shared virtual environments may be a useful tool in the development of ecologically valid assessment protocols. Following blast exposure downrange, military personnel may be returned to duty following assessment of their physical and cognitive abilities. Unfortunately, most testing protocols for cognitive abilities indirectly measure these abilities with tasks or skills that are not directly relevant to the military job to which they will be returned. For example, a Service member working a traffic checkpoint who must make frequent, rapid decisions about the individual level of risk of several vehicles must consider various and changing intelligence information, evolving rules of engagement, and their direct observations. While memory, attention and ability to accommodate changing requirements might be assessed with memorizing word lists, card sorting tests, or tests of attention and inhibition, consider the power of testing the Service member in a checkpoint simulation in which they could be evaluated more directly employing the kinds of cognitive skills required of their job. Such a simulation can be created, managed, and manipulated in a shared virtual environment.

As artificial intelligence continues to improve, it is not difficult to imagine applications in shared virtual environments that present automated simulated patients with which therapists may practice newly learned therapies or assessment skills in a safe environment. Therapists could rehearse treatment protocols to maintain effectiveness and protocol compliance during periods where they may not be seeing a large clinical caseload. New therapies could be developed where shared experiences in responsive environments change according to the interactions and choices of the participants, better approximating the complex variable dependencies in day-to-day living.

While the idea and promise of shared virtual environments is not new, technology may finally be catching up with that potential to the point that these and other as yet unimagined possibilities may become a normal part of mental health training, assessment, and treatment in the years to come.

The opinions and assertions expressed herein are those of the authors and do not necessarily reflect the official policy or position of the Uniformed Services University or the Department of Defense.

References

American Psychological Association. (2008). *Media psychologists: Educating the public; demystifying psychotherapy and modeling professional ethics.* Public and Member Communications, Arlington, VA: Public Affairs Office.

Birman, S., French, L., & Holloway, K. (2018, April). *Disseminating evidence based practice in suicide prevention and treatment for military communities.* Speaker presentation at the 2018 American Association of Suicidology Conference in Washington, DC.

Bradbury, R. (1951) *"The Veldt" The Illustrated Man.* Garden City, NY: Doubleday.

Farah, D. (Producer), De Line, D. (Producer), Krieger, K. (Producer), & Spielberg, S. (Director). (2018). *Ready player one* [Motion Picture]. United States: Warner Brothers.

Gabbard, G. (2001). Psychotherapy in Hollywood cinema. *Australian Psychiatry, 9*(4) 365–369.

Gabbard, G., & Gabbard, K. (1999). *Psychiatry and the cinema.* Washington, DC: American Psychiatric Press.

Gerald, S., & Antonacci, D. (2009). *Virtual world learning spaces: Developing a second life operating room simulation.* Retrieved from https://er.educause.edu/articles/2009/3/virtual-world-learning-spaces-developing-a-second-life-operating-room-simulation

Grinfeld, M. J. (1998). Psychiatry and mental illness: Are they mass media targets. *Psychiatric Times, 15*(3), 9–27.

Hepner, K. A., Holliday, S. B., Sousa, J., & Tanielian, T. (2019). *Training clinicians to deliver evidence-based psychotherapy: Development of the training in psychotherapy (TIP) Tool.* Santa Monica, CA: RAND Corporation, TL-306-BWF.

Holloway, K., & Reger, G. (2013). T2 virtual PTSD experience: A virtual worlds environment to educate service members and veterans about combat-related posttraumatic stress disorder. *International Journal of Human Computer Interaction, 29*(9), 594–603.

Hudson, K., & Degast-Kennedy, K. (2009). Canadian border simulation at Loyalist College. *Journal of Virtual Worlds Research, 2*(1), 3–11.

Hyler, S. E. (1988). DSM-III at the cinema: Madness in the movies. *Comprehensive Psychiatry, 29*(2) (Mar/Apr), 195–206.

Johnston, J., Massey, A., & De Vaneaux, C. (2013). Innovation in weight loss intervention programs: An examination of a 3D virtual world approach. *Journal of Medical Internet Research, 14*(5), e120.

Kadushin, C. (1969). *Why people go to psychiatrists.* New York: Atherton.

Karlin, B., & Cross, G. (2014). From the laboratory to the therapy room: National dissemination and implementation of evidence-based psychotherapies in the US Department of Veterans affairs health care system. *American Psychologist, 69*(1), 19–33.

Kidd, L., Knisley, S., & Morgan, K. (2012). Effectiveness of a second life simulation as a teaching strategy for undergraduate mental health nursing students. *Journal of Psychosocial Nursing, 50*(7), 28–37.

Kokcharov, I. (2015). *Heirarchy of skills, retention of learning* [PowerPoint slides]. Retrieved from www.slideshare.net/igorkokcharov/kokcharov-skillpyramid2015

Kolb, D. (1984). *Experiential learning: Experience as the source of learning and development.* Englewood Cliffs: Prentice Hall.

Lefkowitz, C., Dolan, D., Rogers, T., & Holloway, K. (2019). Using technology to promote sleep competencies for behavioral healthcare providers: Welcome to the Snoozeum. *Journal of Technology in Behavioral Science, 4*, 62–65.

Lehmann, C. (2002). Positive psychiatry portrayals a rarity in Hollywood. *Psychiatric News, 37*(15), 10–11.

Maha, M., Tantawi, E., El Kashlan, M., & Saeed, Y. (2013). Assessment of the efficacy of second life, a virtual learning environment, in dental education. *Journal of Dental Education, 77*(12), 1639–1652.

Mallonee, S., Phillips, J., Holloway, K., & Riggs, D. (2018). Training providers in the use of evidence-based treatments: A comparison of in-person and online delivery modes. *Psychology Learning & Teaching, 17*(1), 61–72.

Manning, L. (1975). *The man who awoke*. New York, NY: Ballantine Books, Inc.

McLellan, H. (2004). Virtual realities. In D. H. Jonassen (Ed.), *Handbook of research for education communications and technology* (2nd ed., pp. 461–497). Mahwah, NJ: Lawrence Erlbaum.

Mikropoulos, T. (2006). Presence: A unique characteristic in education virtual environments. *Virtual Reality, 10*(3/4), 197–206.

Mikropoulos, T., & Strouboulis, V. (2004). Factors that influence presence in educational virtual environments. *CyberPsychology & Behavior, 7*(5), 582–591.

Paxton, M. M., Phillips, J. P., Weinstock, M., Sacks, M., & Birman, S. (2019, May). *Online training for CBT-depression results in greater increases in knowledge and perceived readiness compared to in-person trainings.* Poster presentation at the annual meeting of the Association for Psychological Sciences, Washington, DC.

Reeves, B., & Read, J. L. (2009). *Total engagement. Using games and virtual worlds to change the way people work and businesses compete.* Boston, MA: Harvard Business Press.

Robison, T. (2013). *The impact of fictional television portrayals of psychotherapy on viewers' expectations of therapy, attitudes toward seeking treatment, and induction into dramatic narratives.* (Doctoral dissertation). Retrieved from https://etd.ohiolink.edu/!etd.send_file?accession=ohiou1375780084&disposition=inline

Roddenberry, G. (Producer), & Berman, R. (Producer). (1987–1994). *Star trek: The next generation* [Television series]. Los Angeles, CA: Paramount.

Sajjanhar, A., & Faulkner, J. (2019). Second life as a learning environment for computer programming. *Education and Information Technologies, 24*, 2403.

Silver, J. (Producer), Wachowski, L. (Director), & Wachowski, L. (Director). (1999). *The matrix* [Motion Picture]. United States: Warner Brothers.

Sitzman, T. (2011). A meta-analytic examination of the instructional effectiveness of computer-based simulation games. *Personnel Psychology, 64*(2), 489–528.

Smith, T., Landes, S., Lester-Williams, K., Day, K., Batdorf, W., Brown, G., Trockel, B., Smith, B., Chard, K., Healy, E., & Weingardt, K. (2017). Developing alternative training delivery methods to improve psychotherapy implementation in the U.S. department of veterans affairs. *Training and Education in Professional Psychology, 11*(4), 266–275.

Von Sydow, K., & Reimer, C. (1998). Attitudes toward psychotherapists, psychologists, psychiatrists, and psychoanalysis: A meta analysis of 60 studies published between 1948 and 1995. *American Journal of Psychotherapy, 52*(4), 463–488.

Weinbaum, S. (2012). *Pygmalion's spectacles.* Auckland, New Zealand: The Floating Press.

Yellowlees, P., & Cook, J. (2006). Education about hallucinations using an internet virtual reality system: A qualitative survey. *Academic Psychiatry, 30*(6), 534–539.

Index

For Product Safety Concerns and Information please contact our EU
representative GPSR@taylorandfrancis.com
Taylor & Francis Verlag GmbH, Kaufingerstraße 24, 80331 München, Germany

www.ingramcontent.com/pod-product-compliance
Lightning Source LLC
Chambersburg PA
CBHW070601270326
41926CB00013B/2382

9 781138 353947